MW01519081

EMPTY PROMISES

Empty Promises

*Why Workplace Pension Law
Doesn't Deliver Pensions*

ELIZABETH J. SHILTON

McGill-Queen's University Press
Montreal & Kingston • London • Chicago

© McGill-Queen's University Press 2016

ISBN 978-0-7735-4787-2 (cloth)
ISBN 978-0-7735-9959-8 (ePDF)
ISBN 978-0-7735-9960-4 (ePUB)

Legal deposit second quarter 2016
Bibliothèque nationale du Québec

Printed in Canada on acid-free paper that is 100% ancient forest free
(100% post-consumer recycled), processed chlorine free

This book has been published with the help of a grant from the Canadian
Federation for the Humanities and Social Sciences, through the Awards
to Scholarly Publications Program, using funds provided by the Social
Sciences and Humanities Research Council of Canada.

McGill-Queen's University Press acknowledges the support of the Canada
Council for the Arts for our publishing program. We also acknowledge the
financial support of the Government of Canada through the Canada Book
Fund for our publishing activities.

Library and Archives Canada Cataloguing in Publication

Shilton, Elizabeth, 1948–, author
    Empty promises: why workplace pension law doesn't deliver
pensions/Elizabeth J. Shilton.

    Includes bibliographical references and index.
    Issued in print and electronic formats.
    ISBN 978-0-7735-4787-2 (cloth). – ISBN 978-0-7735-9959-8 (ePDF). –
ISBN 978-0-7735-9960-4 (ePUB)

    1. Pensions – Law and legislation – Canada. I. Title.

KE3432.S55 2016   344.7101'252   C2016-902132-7
KF3649.S55 2016   C2016-902133-5

This book was typeset by Interscript in 10.5/13 Sabon.

Contents

Acknowledgments

I began the research for this book after a lengthy career in private practice as a labour and employment lawyer with the firm now known as Cavalluzzo Shilton McIntyre Cornish LLP. My interest in workplace pensions has deep roots in that practice, where my exceptional professional colleagues and clients gave me a very concrete perspective on the value of good jobs and the benefits that go with them, including income security in retirement.

I am immensely grateful to Kerry Rittich for her generosity in sharing her time and her wisdom with me in the formative stages of this book, and for her skillful and patient guidance in working through earlier drafts. Thanks also to Brian Langille and Morley Gunderson, whose expertise broadened and deepened my understanding of the intricate connections between workplace pensions and the employment relationship. Harry Arthurs provided a detailed and insightful critique of an earlier draft, which has greatly improved the final version. While Bernie Adell did not live to read the final manuscript, I learned much from his review of an earlier version, about both workplace law and good academic writing.

I would like to thank the Centre for Law in the Contemporary Workplace at Queen's University and its director, Kevin Banks, for providing me with an intellectual home for my continuing research. I am also grateful to several talented and hard-working law students at Queen's University who assisted with research on various aspects of the book over several summers: in particular, Giovanna Di Sauro, Jenna-Dawn Shervill, Jason Paquette, and Dayna Lubelski. All were intelligent and dogged researchers, with a highly developed capacity for digging out obscure references and documents. They learned more than they ever wanted to know about workplace pensions, but now have a stock of arcane knowledge they can put to good use in their future law practice – just as I promised!

The book has also been enriched by my exposure to the knowledge and experience of colleagues at the Ontario Financial Services Tribunal, where I sat as a member and vice-chair throughout the time I worked on this project. I learned much there about pension law and the practical context within which workplace pension plans function. In particular, I owe thanks to Jennifer Brown and Heather Gavin, who read and commented on earlier versions of Chapter 8, and to David Short, who very generously commented on an earlier version of the entire manuscript from the vantage point of his long and distinguished career as an actuary. Needless to say, the views reflected in the book are entirely my own and not those of the Financial Services Tribunal or the Financial Services Commission of Ontario (FSCO), where I also served as vice-chair.

My most important debt of gratitude is to my family. First to my siblings, who made better career choices than I did and will be able to retire with good pensions. Second, to my well-loved and long-suffering children, Graeme Lennon and Christina Mackenzie, who have lived with this project long enough to know the value of a workplace pension, but who belong to a generation that will probably never enjoy one. And last but never least, my husband, David Mackenzie, whose unflagging support for this project in large ways and small over the years has made an inestimable contribution to its completion. Against the backdrop of his own deep knowledge of labour history and public policy, he patiently endured innumerable conversations in which I worked through ideas and attempted to make sense of the many contradictions in the workplace pension system. He also brought his remarkable editorial skills to bear on endless drafts of this work. His love and encouragement throughout has made me a better scholar and a better person. Thank you, David, with all my heart.

EMPTY PROMISES

1

What's Wrong with Workplace Pension Plans?

INTRODUCTION

A good pension system delivers adequate, predictable, and secure income to retired workers. By that benchmark, Canada's workplace pension plans are not doing well. Most Canadian workers do not belong to workplace plans. Those who do frequently find after they retire that their plan does not deliver the pension they expected, and that pension does not fill the gap between public benefits and retirement expenses.

These outcomes are disappointing, but they should not be surprising. Canada's workplace pension system was not designed to produce adequate, predictable, and secure pensions for workers. It was designed to meet the business needs of employers. For much of the twentieth century, pension plans functioned as valuable human-resource management tools for employers whose business model demanded a stable workforce of loyal, well-trained employees. They assisted enterprises to attract career-minded employees, to retain them throughout their productive working lives, to influence their workplace behaviour, and to ease them out the door when they became too old to be productive. Employers with such managerial needs found pension plans a convenient and cost-effective part of employee compensation packages. But even in the heyday of the workplace pension system, many employers did not find pension plans compatible with their business objectives. Now, more and more Canadian employers find that the cost of pensions outweighs the benefits, while fewer and fewer find that providing a pension plan is good business.

The system began as a voluntary system, and it remains a voluntary system. Decisions about whether there will be a pension plan, what kind of benefits that plan will provide, and how long the plan will stay in place all lie in the hands of the employer. Employers are not altruists, and it is predictable that they will consult their own business interests in making those decisions. Those interests frequently clash with those of workers. But in a system that rests on the legal platform of the employment relationship, workers can do little to influence or alter the employer calculus. The employment relationship is defined by contract, and, in theory, employees can negotiate for good pensions as part of their compensation. In practice, the legal rules governing the employment relationship give employees little leverage in this "negotiation." Employment contracts are generally "take it or leave it" propositions, and workplace pension plans are even less negotiable than other terms and conditions of employment, for reasons that will be discussed in this book.

State efforts through statutory pension regulation and collective bargaining laws to make the system more responsive to workers' retirement income needs have been only modestly effective at improving benefit adequacy, predictability, and security, and demonstrably ineffective at expanding coverage. Indeed, some of those regulatory efforts have almost certainly had paradoxical effects. They have increased the costs of pensions at the same time as they have reduced their value to employers, undermining incentives to establish and maintain plans. The result is a system that produces uneven and unsatisfactory results, and is gradually worsening. For most Canadian workers, the promise of a pension is an empty promise.

In this book, I explore the evolution of workplace pension plans in Canada, with a focus on the role played by law and lawmakers in structuring a system that has produced such poor results. I trace the legal metamorphosis of workplace pensions from discretionary gifts to enforceable rights, showing the impact of both common law and statute law on the shaping of pension rights and responsibilities. I examine the short-sighted decision of Canadian lawmakers to leave workplace pension provision within the discretion of employers, intervening through regulation to improve pension quality but doing nothing to maintain or improve pension quantity. I investigate the failure of collective bargaining laws to come to grips with the market mechanisms that drive voluntary workplace pension provision. I evaluate judicial efforts to pigeon-hole employee pension rights into conventional common-law categories which do not correct for the imbalance of power in the workplace relationship and leave employers with carte blanche to shape the workplace pension system in their own interests. Ultimately, I argue that, in light of the inequality of bargaining power which characterizes the employment relationship within the Canadian legal system, a voluntary system will inevitably fail to produce good pensions for a significant majority of retired Canadians. If we want good pensions, we must look for a different platform from which to deliver them.

A SNAPSHOT OF CANADA'S WORKPLACE PENSION SYSTEM

Before embarking on an examination of the legal evolution of the workplace pension system, it is useful to drill down on how well that system has done to date at delivering retirement income. Its most obvious shortcoming is that it does not include most Canadian workers. At its finest flowering in the late 1970s, the system covered no more than 46 per cent of Canadian employees.[1] Coverage has been in slow but steady decline since then; by 2013, only about 38 per cent of employees belonged to plans. That percentage shrinks to 32 per cent when we look at the labour force as a whole, which includes the self-employed.[2] Of the working-age adult population as a whole – all of whom will one day need retirement income – only one in four is covered by a workplace pension plan.[3]

That lucky one-in-four is very likely among those Canadians who are already winners in the income-distribution sweepstakes. Pension wealth is highly concentrated in Canada.[4] Government researchers examining the distribution of pension coverage in the mid-1990s concluded that "[t]he most financially insecure workers today (the non-permanent, part-time, non-unionized, short-tenured, low-wage earners working in small firms) are *much* less likely to have [workplace pension] coverage than those who have been working in a permanent, full-time, unionized, high-wage position in a large firm for many years."[5] Available data on aboriginal status, disability, and racialization suggest that Canadians with characteristics typically associated with economic disadvantage are less likely to belong to and benefit from pension plans.[6] In a significant departure from historical patterns, Canadian women are now *more* likely than men to belong to pension plans.[7] Despite this increase in coverage, however, women continue to receive only 60 per cent of the benefits received by male plan members, *down* from highs of 65 to 69 per cent in the early 1980s.[8]

This coverage data is discouraging enough, but when we delve down further into the plans that do exist, the picture becomes even bleaker. Not all pension promises are of equal value, and mere coverage offers no guarantee that plans will deliver good pensions. Plans vary greatly in both the level and type of benefits they pay. Both these factors affect the adequacy, reliability, and security of the retirement income stream they can generate. For many years, the norm for Canadian pension plans was – and still is – the defined benefit (DB) plan, which calculates individual retirement benefits in accordance with a pre-determined formula and pays out a specific and consistent income stream to employees after retirement. In recent years, however, there has been a distinct trend away from plans that pay guaranteed benefits, towards capital accumulation (CAP) plans, such as defined contribution (DC) plans, group registered retirement savings plans (RRSPS), and more recently pooled retirement pension plans (PRPPS). In CAP plans, retirement income is neither guaranteed nor predictable, because it depends on the overall capital amount an individual worker is able to accumulate over a working life, and on conditions in the financial markets when that worker retires.[9] To complicate the picture, benefit formulae have now evolved beyond the simple binaries of DB and CAP/DC, into hybrid categories that improve on DC plans, but are nevertheless not as secure and predictable for retirees as DB plans. Forms of "target benefit" plans – plans that aspire to pay a particular level of benefit but do not promise to do so if the pension fund shrinks below expectations – are now rapidly taking over, even in public sector pension plans, still the gold standard for pension security.[10]

And finally, despite a stable and relatively efficient regulatory system, even plans that promise high quality, guaranteed benefits do not always keep that promise if they become underfunded and the companies that sponsor them become insolvent. Recent years have seen several high-profile fund failures and near-failures in Canada.[11] Struggling companies with poor pension track records are frequently given increased time to meet their statutory obligation to fund deficits, a policy strategy that postpones the day of reckoning for these plans but may not resolve their underlying problems.[12]

SYSTEM FAILURE MATTERS FOR CANADIANS

Three-quarters of Canadian adults are not covered by workplace pension plans, and the quarter who are covered may find that their plans do not deliver the pensions they expect. This is a significant problem for Canadians, because Canada is unusually dependent, by international standards, on the workplace pension system as a mechanism for delivering retirement income.[13] This dependence has its roots in a series of policy decisions made in the early 1960s. At that time, Canadian governments agreed that Canada, like most other developed countries of that era, should build a "three-pillar" (or "three-tier") retirement income system.[14] The first pillar – Old Age Security (OAS) – would be a basic universal poverty-relief benefit. This basic benefit would be supplemented by a second pillar, consisting of a public contributory pension plan: the Canada Pension Plan (CPP).[15] In designing this second pillar, Canadian governments chose to peg the benefit at a level yielding a significantly lower pension than many of their international models.[16] It is conventionally estimated that, to maintain pre-retirement standards of living, retirees must replace about 70 per cent of pre-retirement income.[17] It is not uncommon for European states to meet this target for a large proportion of their citizenry entirely from public (or mandatory) pension sources.[18] Canada set much lower targets for public provision – closer to 40 per cent for average-income earners, and considerably less for higher-income earners. The reasoning behind this decision was that income from public sources would be supplemented by voluntary private third-pillar instruments. Workplace pension plans were expected to be the key component of this third pillar, filling the gap between public pension provision and individual retirement income needs.

This expectation was never a reasonable one. As far back as 1938, a study by researchers at Queen's University judged workplace pension plans to be a seriously flawed model for retirement income delivery. The *Queen's Study* estimated that perhaps 30 per cent of the labour force at that time was employed in enterprises that offered workplace pension plans. The study emphasized, however, that only half these workers were likely to be members of those plans, and many who were members would never collect pensions, because they would not remain in their jobs until they reached retirement age.[19] The authors found significant problems in the adequacy and distribution of benefits paid by the plans, and were pessimistic about the potential for workplace pension expansion outside of narrow primary labour markets.[20] Workplace pensions could be useful as a supplement to public pensions, the authors argued, but they could not be regarded as a serious alternative to a comprehensive public plan.[21]

Studies in the 1960s came to similar conclusions. Ontario's Committee on Portable Pensions, appointed to examine the state of the workplace pension system in the lead-up to the establishment of the CPP, was at least as pessimistic as the *Queen's Study* about the prospects that a voluntary employment pension system could meet future retirement income needs. The committee did not favour a state pension system, but also saw no real future for a voluntary employment-based system.[22] Its unanimous conclusion was that to be effective, workplace pension plans must be made mandatory, a recommendation that did not come to fruition.[23]

A rich array of detailed research reports produced in the 1970s and 1980s bore out the pessimism of these earlier studies. Numerous federal and provincial task forces and royal commissions appointed throughout what became known as the Great Pension Debate were united in condemning the outcomes and prospects of the workplace pension system for most Canadians.[24] They concluded that a voluntary workplace-based system would never provide pension coverage and acceptable benefits for the majority of working Canadians. As a remedy, they called for either "a massive expansion of the CPP, along with a major overhaul of the private pension system,"[25] or for mandatory private pension coverage.[26]

Despite these ample and consistent warnings that the model was fundamentally flawed, Canadian policy-makers embraced a voluntary, workplace-based system in the 1960s, and refused to abandon it in the 1980s. They hoped that regulatory "fixes" could turn the system around.[27] The looked-for improvement did not happen; instead, the situation has worsened. The system now faces new challenges from significant increases in longevity since the 1960s, falling birthrates, and the aging of the massive demographic "blip" that is the baby-boom generation, which will inevitably produce fewer workers to make pension contributions and more pensioners whose needs these plans must meet. The pressures imposed by these developments on pension-plan assets have been aggravated by macroeconomic factors – uneven and uncertain economic growth since the late 1970s, recurrent and widespread national, regional, and global fiscal crises, and low interest rates on fixed-income investments – that have desta-bilized pension-plan funding. Significant changes in labour markets are eliminating jobs in the types of workplaces where employers favoured pension provision as a component of compensation – large, stable, unionized workplaces, offering permanent high-wage employ-ment – and increasing the number of jobs where pension plans deliver few advantages for employers. Despite these challenges, there is little evidence as yet that Canadian policy-makers are prepared to change direction on pension reform.

THE ARGUMENT OF THIS BOOK

This book lays the basis for the argument that a change in direction is essential, because the problems currently experienced by the sys-tem are symptoms of a fundamental problem that cannot be fixed. The defining characteristics of the workplace pension system – the fact that it is voluntary and employment-based – are also its fatal flaws. When the Canadian state made the policy choice to assign a significant share of retirement income provision to workplace pen-sion plans, it left employee pension rights exposed to legal rules that permit employers to make the foundational decision about whether or not a workplace pension plan will be provided. These rules also permit employers to make key subsidiary decisions about what ben-efits that plan will deliver and for how long. Most employees do not have the bargaining power to influence those decisions. This leaves employers free to make pension choices for reasons entirely unre-lated to the essential objectives of a good pension system. A system in which the welfare of retired workers depends for its success on the economic imperatives of employers cannot defend itself against shifts and changes in those imperatives in response to economic conditions or regulatory laws that affect the cost and complexity of providing workplace benefits. Such a system will flourish for only as long as it meets the needs of employers. Now, in the twenty-first century, most employers have determined that they are better off without work-place pension plans in their workplaces. The existing legal frame-work gives employees – the beneficiaries of workplace pension plans – few tools to push back.

This book fills a gap in the Canadian pension literature on the historical evolution of workplace pension plans, and on the role of law and legal decision-makers in that evolution. To date, most examinations of the development of pension policy in Canada have focused on the evolution of public pensions.[28] With respect to private pensions – workplace pensions – Richard Deaton's *The Political Economy of Pensions: Power, Politics and Social Change in Canada, Britain, and the United States* provides a useful, if now somewhat dated, comparative perspective on political and social factors shaping the evolution of both public and private plans. Ari Kaplan and Mitch Frazer's *Pension Law*, now in its second edition, offers a meticulous and thoughtful practitioners' perspective on the current state of pension law. But there is currently no comprehensive scholarly history of private workplace pension plans which can play the role for Canada that Steven Sass's *The Promise of Private Pensions: The First Hundred Years* plays for the US or Leslie Hannah's *Inventing Retirement: The Development of Occupational Pensions in Britain* plays for the UK. This book will cover much of that ground.

The book's argument is developed as follows. Chapter 2 explores the roots of workplace pension plans, tracing their transformation under Canadian law from discretionary rewards for long and faithful service to structured tools for assisting employers to control employee career mobility and job tenure. This chapter examines prototypical pension plans in the railway and public-utilities sectors, two sites of early pension development in Canada, linking the human resource management objectives of these businesses to the structural features of their pension plans, and to early funding models ranging from pay-as-you-go systems to insurance contracts and self-managed trusts. It lays out the contours of the conflict that has beset the workplace pension system from its outset, between the employer interest in minimizing pension liabilities and maximizing pension flexibility and the employee interest in pensions that meet the need for retirement income security.

Chapter 3 examines the emerging tendrils of what we now call "pension law," the set of legal rules "determining the pension rights and obligations of employees and employers."[29] It focuses on how courts dealt with employee claims for pension rights prior to the introduction of regulatory statutes and collective bargaining. Drawing on case law from Canada and the very similar US system, it explores the struggles of common-law courts to understand the complex role played by pension plans within overall employment-compensation structures, and to analyze employee pension claims using the conventional common-law categories of contract, property, and trust law. The chapter identifies the roots of a contract theory of pension rights that was to blossom in the second half of the twentieth century. It concludes, however, that although Canadian judges were prepared to give plan members a modest degree of procedural protection against egregiously unfair employer exercises of discretion in making pension decisions, they still clung as late as the 1950s to the notion that workplace pension promises were not legally enforceable.

Chapter 4 considers the dilemma faced by provincial and federal governments determined to leave room within Canada's developing retirement income system for private pension plans, but faced with an existing system that gave employees no effective legal recourse against employers who deliberately constructed their plans to produce little or nothing in the way of pension payouts. The chapter discusses the debate over the respective roles of public and private pensions that informed government decision-making, and explains the policy compromise – a minimalist public pension system that would not crowd out private plans, supplemented by regulatory measures designed to improve the quality of those plans. It analyzes the rights-conferring provisions of first- and second-generation regulatory statutes, which provided employees fortunate enough to be plan members with enforceable contract-based pension rights, but did not make pension provision mandatory. It also shows how the new regulatory standards significantly increased the cost of pension provision, a factor that has contributed to the decline in coverage and quality reflected in the current Canadian pension landscape.

Chapter 5 addresses the impact of collective bargaining frameworks on workplace pension provision. It argues that, despite labour board decisions as early as the late 1940s establishing the principle that pension issues fell within the scope of collective bargaining, pension plans have remained largely under employer control even in unionized workplaces. A number of factors have contributed to this outcome, including employer bargaining priorities and decisions of labour arbitrators that located many workplace pension plans within the realm of management rights. The chapter examines some of the structural features of collective bargaining in Canada that undermine its effectiveness as a mechanism for confronting employer power over pension plans. It concludes that, despite the significant correlation between unionized workplaces and workplace pension plans, collective bargaining has been able to play a relatively limited role in the establishment, shaping, and enforcement of workplace pension plans and pension rights.

Chapter 6 is the first of two chapters examining how Canadian adjudicators applied the common law – "private law" – in the new world of regulated and collectively bargained pension plans. It addresses the intersection between formal trust law and the contract theory of pension rights, showing how courts initially supplemented contract law with trust principles in order to exert some control over employer abuses of discretion, but then retreated from that high ground out of concern that, within a voluntary system, a too-orthodox application of trust law would deter employers from providing pensions. The chapter argues that courts now reject an "equitable" version of trust law, in which trust obligations are grounded in normative principle, in favour of a more "contractarian" version, in which employers are bound only by the trust obligations they assume voluntarily. This more "contractarian" approach gives employers continuing power to write the legal rules that govern the pension relationship, subject only to the minimum standards contained in regulatory legislation.

Chapter 7 moves beyond formal trust law to explore efforts to find principles within the broader and more flexible category of fiduciary law to control employer discretion in relation to workplace pension plans. It examines initial efforts by adjudicators to reconcile the contradictions between employer self-interest and fiduciary principles by constructing a "two hats" doctrine, which imposes fiduciary duties on employers when they are carrying out responsibilities as plan administrators, but relieves them of those duties when acting as "employers." When this schizophrenic distinction ultimately proved unworkable, courts reframed fiduciary standards along the same "contractarianism" lines they now apply to formal trust law, imposing fiduciary obligations only on employers who have agreed to assume them, and allowing them to shape the nature and scope of those obligations.

Chapter 8 shifts the focus to the public sector, where pension density is much higher than in the private sector and DB-type benefits continue to be the norm. It explores both public-service plans, where government is the direct employer, and plans in other key publicly funded enterprises, such as public schools, municipalities, and health care institutions, where government is not the direct employer, but where employee compensation is largely paid from public funds. The chapter explains how government created purpose-built pension structures designed to address both the specialized needs of public enterprises and the needs of their employees. It examines the mechanisms by which governments historically retained stringent unilateral control over workplace pension plans, and the more recent reversal in government policy, in which many public sector employers have now embraced jointly governed and jointly sponsored plans. It concludes that the public sector pension model is the exception that proves the rule; its success depends not on the ordinary mechanisms of employment law, but on the use of state power to create pension structures which have a large and diversified mandatory membership base, economies of administrative scale, and portability of benefits – essential features in the delivery of adequate, predictable, and secure pensions.

Chapter 9 concludes that an employer-driven system designed to meet employer objectives and embedded in a legal framework within which employees have little leverage will not deliver adequate, predictable, and secure pensions to most retired Canadians. Workplace pensions have become significantly more costly to provide, at the same time as they have become significantly less useful to employers because of changes in both the economic and the legal environment. Within a voluntary system, employers applying basic cost-benefit analysis to their pension decisions will inevitably become dropouts, and an already enfeebled system will get worse. Despite the long-standing Canadian aversion to state action in pension provision, state action is necessary to create pension instruments that will deliver the retirement income Canadians need.

SOME NOTES ON THE SCOPE OF THE BOOK

This book addresses what I call "workplace pension plans." That term is not found in most Canadian pension statutes, and it is important to define its boundaries at the outset. As I use this term, workplace plans are those provided by employers for their employees. Plans like these may also be called "private pension plans," "employment pension plans," "occupational pension plans," or "registered pension plans." As will be clear already, workplace pension plans are *not* plans established by the government for citizens and workers in general; plans of that type are called public pension plans.

Within the universe of workplace pension plans, this book focuses primarily on a model in which the plan is "sponsored" by a single employer – the model which is the historical foundation of the Canadian system. The term "sponsored," like the term "workplace pension plan," does not appear in pension regulatory statutes, and requires some explanation. One influential Canadian pension-law text defines "plan sponsor" as "one or more entities that, or persons who, establish the pension plan and to whom is reserved in the pension contract the ultimate power to amend or terminate the plan."[30] The term is also widely used in pension vernacular to refer to the "party or parties responsible for the ultimate funding of a [defined benefit] pension plan."[31] Although patterns are now changing, employers in Canada have historically played the dominant role as plan sponsors in both these senses. The book touches only lightly on multi-employer plans, which evolved out of unique collective bargaining relationships in industries such as construction, where employees have closer links to their trade unions than to any single employer. In these industries, pension plans are often described as "union sponsored," and have typically been governed in Canada either jointly by unions and employers, or solely by unions. The union-sponsored plan has always had a relatively small market share,[32] and raises unique policy and legal issues outside the scope of this book. In Chapter 8, however, the book addresses the emergence of multi-employer and newer "jointly sponsored" plans in the public sector, since those phenomena are closely linked to the theme of employer control that lies at the heart of this book's argument.

2

Shaping Private Sector Workplace Pension Plans: The Early Years

INTRODUCTION

The first workplace pension plan in a business enterprise in Canada – indeed in North America – was the Grand Trunk Railway Superannuation and Provident Fund, established in 1874.[1] Early studies document the slow spread of these plans from the railways to public utilities, and then to white-collar bureaucracies such as banks and insurance companies. Plans took hold more slowly in industry, but by the early 1930s they were visible in manufacturing enterprises in Canada, primarily among large subsidiaries of US corporations with pension plans already in place for their US employees.[2] In 1900, there were only seven private sector workplace pension plans in Canada outside the railway sector.[3] By 1937, that number may have been well over seven hundred.[4]

To understand why workplace pension plans took root and spread in these types of enterprises, it is important to start with the foundational fact that these plans were conceived and established to meet the needs of employers.[5] They were shaped by employers to respond to specific managerial objectives in the enterprises that emerged from the Industrial Revolution and ultimately took shape as the modern bureaucracies and mass-production establishments of twentieth-century capitalist economies. While early plans often came cloaked in the benevolent rhetoric of noblesse oblige and welfare capitalism,[6] not far beneath that rhetoric lurked very hard-headed calculations about their business benefits. Emory Johnson, a noted railway expert of the day, spoke for employers in general when he observed in an 1895 article on the spread of pensions and insured benefits in the railways that the motives of management were "partly philanthropic," but that "[i]t is not to be denied ... that the chief impelling force ... has been the conviction that the money thus expended by the corporation would prove to be a good financial investment."[7]

Some of the expected returns on that investment were reflected in the preamble to the 1903 pension plan of the Canadian Pacific Railway, where the company's president set out the corporate aspirations for the plan in language carefully calibrated to appeal to employees, shareholders, and the general public alike: "The Company hopes, by thus voluntarily establishing a system under which a continued income will be assured to those who after years of continuous service are by age or infirmity no longer fitted to perform their duties and without which they might be left entirely without means of support, to build up amongst them a feeling of permanency in their workplace, an enlarged interest in the company's welfare, and a desire to remain in and to devote their best interests to the company's service."[8] While the emphasis here is on fostering employee loyalty, loyalty was only one of a longer list of advantages employers hoped to derive from their plans. In his 1932 study, *Industrial Pension Plans in the United States and Canada*, economist Murray Latimer noted that employers looked to their pension plans both to attract and retain good employees, and to get rid of those same employees when old age (or disability) rendered them less efficient. Employers were motivated both by "the desirability of developing a stable personnel of competent employees" and "the advisability of removing from service elderly persons and others no longer able to perform their tasks efficiently."[9] They had learned by experience that pensioning off aging employees, instead of simply discharging them with no means of subsistence, improved both employee morale and public relations. In addition, employers looked to pensions as a means of maintaining employee discipline, including discouraging trade union membership and deterring strikes.[10] A 1938 study of Canadian plans, conducted by the newly established Industrial Relations Section of the School of Commerce and Administration at Queen's University, identified a similar list of benefits anticipated by employers from establishing workplace pension plans.[11]

These benefits were not expected to flow simply from the offer of a pension on retirement. It was soon understood that pension plans had to be carefully crafted to achieve the objectives sought by their employer sponsors. These objectives varied with the labour market position, work organization, and management structure of the particular enterprise.[12] Plans geared to white-collar enterprises like banks and insurance companies might be framed to attract and retain employees interested in job security and advancement up the salary hierarchy. Plans geared to industries that relied on unique employee skills and fostered internal labour markets placed high value on design features that discouraged employee turnover.[13] Plans in industries with high accident rates might combine retirement pensions with disability and death benefits. Plans in blue-collar enterprises concerned with curtailing the spread of trade unionism might deny pension credits to employees who went on strike, or confiscate pension contributions from employees discharged for misconduct. Plans geared to mass production enterprises might provide flatter benefit structures than white-collar plans, but reward long service with equal generosity. Most employers drafted their plans to build some structure into retirement decision-making, and most sought to pay benefits high enough to facilitate mandatory retirement.

SOME EARLY PENSION PLANS

A useful approach to exploring the relationship between plan design and employer human-resource objectives is to examine the provisions of some early Canadian plans and analyze their evolution over the first part of the twentieth century. A focus on specific plans reveals both commonalities and differences in design features from industry to industry, and helps us to understand how plans changed over time with changing labour markets, patterns of work organization, and management objectives. Plans selected for close study are those of the Grand Trunk Railway, Canada's first private sector pension plan, and the Bell Telephone Company, another Canadian pension pioneer. While other examples might have been chosen, the textual history of these two plans is readily available from public sources. The sample is small, but nevertheless valuable, because it includes both railways and public utilities, two important sites of early pension development in Canada,[14] and the provisions of these plans, while tailored to the enterprise, are reasonably typical of their eras.

Railway Pension Plans: The Grand Trunk Railway

Workplace pension plans have been a feature of railway human-resource management policy from the birth of that industry, first in the UK, and later in the US and Canada.[15] The Grand Trunk Railway plan led the way in North America.[16] By the first decade of the twentieth century, almost 75 per cent of Canadian railroad employees belonged to pension plans, a pension density dramatically higher than in other Canadian industries. By 1927, that figure had climbed to 90 per cent.[17]

The 1874 Grand Trunk plan, officially titled *Rules of the Grand Trunk Railway of Canada Superannuation and Provident Fund Association*, was legally constituted pursuant to a special federal statute.[18] The railway was British-owned and directed from London, and its pension plan followed the pattern of nineteenth-century British railway plans, which covered only salaried employees, from company officers down the hierarchy as far as locomotive foremen.[19] The statute explicitly directed the establishment of a "superannuation and provident fund" to be deployed in accordance with rules prepared by the company.[20] The plan was governed by trustees and managed by a committee consisting of company officers, other company appointees, and a minority of representatives elected by the more highly paid plan members. Any disputes about claims under the plan were referred to the company president, "whose decision shall be final and conclusive" (s.24). Membership was optional for existing employees, but compulsory for new employees under the age of thirty-seven (s.2).

The plan was contributory; while the company paid part of the cost, employees were required to contribute at the rate of 2 ½ per cent of salary.[21] It paid a defined benefit retirement pension: one-sixtieth of the employee's retirement salary for every year of plan membership, capped at two-thirds of career-average annual earnings. Benefits were payable to plan members who retired at age fifty-five or older. Employees who left the company with a minimum of five years' service were entitled to a return of half their contributions (presumably without interest, although the plan did not specify), provided they had not been terminated for "fraud, misconduct, or dishonesty" (in which case, they forfeited all benefits). The pension management committee had the discretion to return up to half the contributions of those with less than five years' membership, if their departure was due to illness. In addition to retirement benefits, the plan paid a discretionary disability benefit to any member who had belonged to the plan for at least ten years, and was forced to leave his workplace due to "severe bodily injury occasioned in the proper discharge of his duty, or by reason of infirmity of body or mind, not the result of his own misconduct, and whose permanent disability to discharge the duties of his situation, shall be certified by two duly-registered medical men" (s.8). There was also a death benefit, equal to the member's contributions (without interest), payable to the widow or other dependents of a member who died prior to retirement (s.7).

For that era, the plan's features were surprisingly favourable to employees. It provided pensions *as of right* to plan members who retired once they had reached retirement age, calculated according to a fixed formula based on salary and years of service. There was no minimum service requirement. By providing a meaningful (if limited) right to a return of contributions to employees who left the company prior to retirement, the plan acknowledged employee contributions as an investment in the plan. Pension value was further preserved both for employees and their dependents by the payment of disability and death benefits for employees who "died in harness" or lost their employment due to illness or injury. The plan did not impose mandatory retirement as a quid pro quo for the promise of a pension. From the perspective of the Grand Trunk's white-collar employees, these features were strengths of the plan. From the perspective of the employer, however, they came to be perceived as weaknesses – features suitable for a sedentary workforce aspiring to establish and protect a middle-class lifestyle, but unsuitable for an enterprise largely dependent on a workforce of skilled but relatively low-paid blue-collar employees engaged in dangerous physical labour.

A key weakness of the 1874 plan was that it did not cover blue-collar workers, the segment of the Grand Trunk workforce most vulnerable to on-the-job accident or injury, and therefore most likely to expose the company to liability in the days prior to workers' compensation legislation. In an effort to contain this liability, the Grand Trunk again followed British precedent, obtaining legislative authority to supplement its pension plan for white-collar workers with another fund that provided a form of disability insurance to blue-collar employees, as well as a life insurance benefit for their families.[22] This second fund was established as an Insurance and Provident Society (IPS). Membership was mandatory for all permanent employees under the age of forty who were not covered by the 1874 plan.[23] An important feature of the IPS *Rules* and *By-Laws*, unilaterally drafted by the company, was that members waived any right to compensation from the company if they were injured or killed on the job.[24] While membership and benefits in the IPS were generally restricted to permanent employees, this waiver provision was extended to temporary employees as well.[25] This audacious exercise of management rights ultimately backfired when the Grand Trunk's successful reliance on the waiver to defeat a lawsuit brought by an injured railway employee attracted unfavourable legislative attention.[26] The *Railway Act* was ultimately amended in 1904 to prohibit compulsory employee waivers of liability.[27] A timid federal government much under the influence of the powerful railway lobby did not put the amendment into effect until after it had been ruled constitutional by the Privy Council following a judicial reference.[28]

The unfavourable publicity over this "waiver of liability" litigation and the subsequent statutory amendments were no doubt part of the impetus for the Grand Trunk's 1907 decision to replace its 1874 plan with one better adapted to the human-resource-management needs of the modern railway.[29] These included a need for management tools that would assist in attracting and retaining a large labour force, of whom many had unique skills acquired by on-the-job training. As the industry matured and the workforce aged, the company also needed a mechanism to rid itself of older, less-productive workers in both white- and blue-collar jobs, with a minimum of damage to its reputation and its bottom line. The new 1907 Grand Trunk plan now made membership compulsory for *all* full-time employees (s.6). The plan was no longer contributory; all costs were paid by the employer. Like the 1874 plan, the 1907 plan was administered by a group of high-level managers, with power to enforce the terms of the plan, to amend them if necessary, and to determine individual employee eligibility for pensions, including the amount of any pension and any conditions attached to its receipt (s.5). The new plan set a retirement age of sixty-five, rather than fifty-five. In a significant change from the older plan, retirement was now mandatory, subject to managerial discretion to waive the requirement for up to five years, or to impose earlier retirement (ss.7–8). Retirement could be initiated at the request either of the employer or the employee, but the employer retained effective control, since an employee request could be refused.

Another significant departure from the 1874 plan was that employees no longer had any *right* to a retirement pension (ss.8,10). While an employee retiring at age sixty-five could expect to receive a pension, provided that he had at least fifteen years of service with the company (s.11), that pension was no longer guaranteed. Benefits were discretionary even for those who fully met eligibility conditions when they retired. Section 23 of the plan explicitly adjured any binding pension commitment on the part of the company:

> It is expressly provided that neither by establishing out of its revenues a system of Pensions by the Company, nor by any other action now or hereafter taken by them or by the Pension Committee, shall it be construed as giving to any Official, Agent or Employee of the Company a right to be retained in the service or any legal right or claim to have any pension whatsoever, and the Company expressly reserves its right and privilege to discharge at any time such Official, Agent or Employee when the interests of the Company in its judgment may so require, without liability for any claim for pension or other allowance than salary or wages due or unpaid.

Even employees who had already been granted a pension could forfeit that pension for misconduct, for "any action ... inimical to the interests of the company" (s.19), or for engaging in other business after retirement without the consent of the pension committee (s.21). Each pensioner was required to provide annually to the committee "satisfactory evidence that he still comes within the [Plan] Rules and Regulations" (s.20).

The plan was now exclusively a retirement plan; it no longer provided disability benefits, which were now dealt with elsewhere. If a pension was granted, it was paid at the rate of 1 per cent of average earnings over an employee's best ten years, multiplied by years of continuous service, a benefit roughly comparable to the prior plan (s.11). However, the new plan offered no death or survivor benefits for dependents. In addition, it provided that any employee who sued the company for damages for "personal injuries sustained by him in the course of his service" would have no claim under the plan (s.14).

A discretionary plan of this nature functioned as a more powerful deterrent to misconduct (i.e., conduct displeasing to the company) than the old 1874 plan, in which employees who reached the age of fifty-five while still in the company's employ were absolutely entitled to a pension. In a workplace already heavily unionized, misconduct clearly included strikes, which occurred with some frequency on the railways.[30] Railway employers, the Grand Trunk among them, had a history of using pension sanctions as an anti-strike weapon. Striking employees might be denied pensions altogether, or receive reduced pensions, because the company refused to credit pre-strike service towards their pensions.[31] Even retired employees actually receiving pensions might find their pensions affected if they failed to support the company during a strike.[32]

Public Utilities: The Bell Telephone Company

Like the railways, public utilities such as telephone companies also saw the wisdom of moving early from informal to more-structured pension arrangements. The Bell Telephone Company, founded in 1880 and still one of Canada's telecommunications giants, adopted its first formal pension plan in 1917.[33] The plan was administered by a pension committee, consisting of senior officers of the company, with the authority to "determine for all parties all questions arising in the interpretation and administration of the Plan and the Fund," subject only to the "superior authority of the Board" (s.4§1). It was a non-contributory plan, covering all regular full-time salaried employees, which blended features of both the earlier and the more mature Grand Trunk plans.

The plan established three different categories of retirement pension, with varying conditions of eligibility for each class. The Class A pension was payable to employees with twenty years of service who had reached the qualifying age of sixty for men and fifty-five for women; such sex differences were not seen in the railway plans, but were commonplace in other plans of the day. Class B and Class C pensions were available at younger ages but required more years of service (s.5§5). While the Class A pension was superficially non-discretionary, it could, like all pensions payable under the plan, be suspended indefinitely if "any retired employee shall engage in anything which in the judgement of the Committee is prejudicial to the interests of the Company" (s.5§6).[34] Class B and C pensions were payable "only at the discretion of the Committee and with the approval of the President." The benefit formula was the same for all three classes: 1 per cent of annual salary, averaged over the last (or at the discretion of the company, the best) ten years of service, multiplied by years of service (s.5§2). The plan established a mandatory retirement age of seventy, a requirement that could be waived by the company (s.10). Mandatory retirement could also be imposed earlier; the plan provided that employees forced to retire would be given "[s]ix months' previous notice, or such shorter notice as the Committee may for special reasons decide" (s.5).

The 1917 Bell plan also had a number of features more characteristic of modern disability and sickness benefit plans than of pension plans. (Disability pensions had appeared in the 1874 Grand Trunk plan, but had been dropped by 1907.) A discretionary Class D pension was available to employees with at least fifteen years' service who were totally disabled "by reason of sickness" (s.5). The plan also provided a type of workers' compensation benefit: a discretionary full and partial accident disability benefit for those injured on the job (s.6). In addition, the Bell plan offered a weekly indemnity payment for short-term illness, with some similarities to the Grand Trunk IPS benefit program (s.7). A discretionary death benefit was payable to spouses or dependents of employees who died while still employed, in the form of salary continuation for a period of time that varied depending on the employee's length of service, and was significantly longer if death was due to industrial accident [s.8(a) and (b)].[35] While these ancillary benefits could be denied to anyone who sued the company for damages for injury or death, this condition was less onerous than the Grand Trunk's "waiver of liability" approach, since it did not prevent employees from suing, although it penalized them for doing so [s.12§2(b)]. Overall, the plan had a more paternalistic and moralistic tone than the railway plans. Pensions were clearly dependent on good behaviour both before and after retirement. Disability, sickness, accident, and death benefits could be withheld if these misfortunes were linked to the use of drugs or alcohol, "unlawful acts or immoralities," or fighting in saloons or gambling houses "or other disreputable resort" (s.12§1).

The Bell plan was more explicitly cost-conscious than the Grand Trunk plans. The plan provided that, if the company were required to make payments under any statute in relation to injury, sickness, or death, those payments would be deducted from benefits provided under the plan (s.12§1). This language reflected the company's apprehension that new social legislation would impose compensation costs on the company, a distinct possibility in a wartime climate that saw Ontario passing its first workers' compensation legislation in 1914, and other Canadian provinces following close behind.[36] Cost-consciousness also motivated a provision that veterans returning to the company after the Great War would only be admitted as members of the plan on a case-by-case basis, with the approval of the board of directors (s.13).[37] The company bylaw authorizing the plan explicitly provided that the plan was "tentative only."[38] Underpinning the fundamentally contingent nature of the benefits was a general disclaimer in the bylaw to the effect that "[n]othing in this By-law contained, and nothing which may be done in pursuance thereof shall create expressly or by implication or by inference any contract or contractual relation or obligation between the Company and any employee or the legal representatives or dependents of any employee" (s. 1). The company reserved the right to repeal, amend, or alter the plan as it saw fit.

Bell's discretionary approach to pensions continued for more than two decades. By 1939, however, the company had decided that more certainty was desirable. Its new 1939 plan retained the basic benefit structure of the old plan, with eligibility criteria only slightly modified, and a benefit formula that remained essentially unchanged. The major break with the 1917 plan was in the approach to employee entitlement to retirement benefits. Under the heading "Undertaking," the plan commenced with a new declaration: "The Bell Telephone Company of Canada undertakes, in accordance with this Plan, to provide for the payment of definite amounts to its employees when they are disabled by accident or sickness or when they are retired from service, or, in the event of death, to their dependent relatives" (s.1).[39] The disclaimers of contractual liability in the 1917 plan were removed, as was the language which permitted the company to suspend or withhold pensions for conduct inimical to the company. Once employees qualified and were granted retirement pensions, they were entitled to keep them.[40] While the company continued to retain the right to amend or terminate the plan, that right was clearly more limited than it had been under the 1917 plan; the 1939 plan expressly provided that amendments or termination "shall not affect the rights of any employee, without his consent, to any benefit or pension to which he may have previously become entitled thereunder" (s.10), and acknowledged that employees might "accrue" the right to a pension prior to terminating their employment (s.8§1).

As an additional guarantee that pension promises would be honoured, the new plan spelled out that retirement pensions would be paid out of a pension trust fund, which the company expressly undertook to maintain at a level sufficient to fund existing pensions and fulfill the pension promises made by the plan (s.4§8).[41] In the event of plan termination, the trust fund would be used first to fund retirement pensions. The elaborate distribution scheme that followed acknowledged claims for a "deferred pension," which would be honoured if funds were available, regardless of whether or not the employee was still in the service of the company when he reached retirement age (s.4§9). While the plan does not clearly spell this out, this provision acknowledges a concept of pre-retirement vesting not seen in the earlier plans, and still uncommon in Canadian plans of this era.

COMMON FEATURES OF WORKPLACE PENSION PLANS

Discretionary Benefits and Pension Promises

The evolution of these plans reflects shifts in the conceptualization of pension benefits that provide important clues as to how employers sought to use these plans. The 1874 Grand Trunk plan was ahead of its time in offering a right to a pension for employees who met the eligibility requirements on reaching retirement age. It demanded employee contributions, but also promised some return on those contributions, even for employees who failed to stay with the employer long enough to earn a pension. By the early twentieth century, however, such guarantees were very rare. Plans did their work by keeping employees in a state of uncertainty about whether there would be a pension at the end of their working lives. Much more typical of this era were the 1907 Grand Trunk plan and the 1917 Bell plan, which expressly disclaimed contractual liability, even for the continued payment of pensions which had already been granted. Murray Latimer's 1932 survey found that no pension plans "contain[ed] any promise for its indefinite future maintenance" (707).[42] Most did the opposite, expressly reserving the employer's right to amend or terminate the plan at any time. Latimer's data showed that only about one-third of plans offered "some protective guarantee to the persons who actually are placed on the pension roll" (742). Fewer than 20 per cent of plans guaranteed any form of pension, even to employees who qualified on reaching retirement age, and only one plan out of the nearly four hundred Latimer examined reflected the concept we now call early vesting – the gradual accrual of pension rights throughout employment (743).

By 1939, however, the Bell Telephone Company was prepared to make a commitment to stand by its pension promises. The company still reserved the right to change or terminate the plan, but that right was qualified by a commitment to pay pensions already granted and respect benefits already earned. That very significant shift was not accounted for by any change in the legal climate. While there had been ample criticism of discretionary pension models in the intervening years from pension scholars, organized labour, and other employee advocates,[43] the law had not evolved far in the direction of protecting employee benefits. The shift clearly reflects a change in Bell's own business calculus, in response to changing labour-market exigencies. By 1939, the company believed that its pension objectives would be better served by offering its employees credible guarantees that long service and good behaviour would actually produce a pension.

The Bell Telephone Company was not alone in coming to the realization that its business interests were best served by providing pension benefits that were both more structured and less discretionary. Its move typified a shift in managerial practice in both the US and Canada often labelled "Fordism," although that term does not capture its many variations outside manufacturing industries. Scholars identify this as a shift from older authoritarian and discretionary management methods to newer, more "scientific" and rule-bound systems. They locate versions of this shift within both the mass-production industries, such as steel and auto, and the modern bureaucracies that were evolving over the first half of the twentieth century.[44] In these new types of business enterprises, both management philosophy and organizational imperatives demanded consistency in operational and personnel practices, and rendered old-style paternalism obsolete. By the mid-1930s, new-style managerial practice had taken firm hold in the larger North American enterprises that were the primary growth area for pension plans, and was spreading into medium and smaller enterprises. Companies like Bell Telephone now promulgated clear work rules and routinized day-to-day administration practices, which limited discretion in the hands of front-line supervisors. In the working environment created by this new-style management, treating pensions as old-fashioned corporate handouts to management favourites was ineffective and counterproductive.

Labour-market pressures to offer more structured benefits only went so far, however, and there remained serious limits on the pension guarantees employers felt compelled to offer. In general, binding commitments extended only to those employees who made their careers with the company and were still with the company when they reached retirement age. Employers saw little or no business advantage in our modern concept of pension benefits which are earned and vested throughout a career, and banked in the plan as a deferred pension or taken out of the plan as a "portable" benefit by an employee who departs for another job. In an era in which employer autonomy over plan design was unconstrained by law, very few plans offered benefits of that kind.

The Structure of Retirement Benefits

All the plans we have examined adhered to the defined benefit (DB) structure pioneered by the Grand Trunk in 1874, paying a fixed monthly sum calculated according to a formula known in advance, and based on earnings and years of eligible service. DB plans have been a durable preference in Canada, consistently chosen over their principal competitor, the defined contribution (DC, or "money purchase") plan. While DB plans have slipped somewhat in popularity, they continue to dominate the market in Canadian workplaces where pension plans are still to be found. It is not surprising that DB-type plans were attractive to *employees*, since they produced a predictable and reliable (although not always adequate) retirement income stream, as compared to DC plans, in which the pension payout was contingent. However, employees did not control plan design. From our twenty-first-century perspective, in which employers are rapidly abandoning defined benefits in favour of other benefit designs, it is easy to lose sight of the fact that the DB design gained its dominance because of its attractions to *employers*.

There were two key reasons why employers preferred DB plans. First, prior to the introduction of statutory funding rules, DB plans had very important cost advantages, with significantly less cash outlay. DC plans required employers to contribute money into the plan on an annual basis. By contrast, DB plans allowed employers to postpone pension costs far into the future, since payments did not come due until an employee retired. In young industries, costs could be deferred for years. In many cases, they could be avoided altogether, since under most DB plans employees were not eligible for a pension unless they stayed with the employer until retirement; for an employee who left prior to retirement, the employer's pension cost was zero. While there is little reliable data from this era on how many plan members actually received pensions, the available evidence suggests that most did not. A 1927 study on job turnover in the

US reported in the *Labour Gazette* found that "only 3.4 per cent of male workers and 2.4 per cent of female employees remain with the same concern for twenty years or more."[45] Turnover rates like these would preclude most employees from qualifying for a pension. Mary MacKinnon's study of the Canadian Pacific Railroad pension plan – a plan very similar in structure to the 1907 Grand Trunk plan – concluded that only about 7 per cent of CPR employees retired on pension.[46] One US scholar, citing a variety of contemporary sources, suggests a general figure closer to 2 per cent; based on her research, she concluded that the chance of a plan member receiving a pension was "exceedingly slim."[47]

In addition to direct cost, employers also preferred DB plans over DC plans because the structure of the DB benefit gave them more control over the workforce. In typical DC plans of the day, the employer's annual contribution for each employee was credited to that employee's account. These contributions were frequently used to purchase deferred annuities for employees on an annual basis; such annuities tended not to be "retractable," since the insurance companies that sold them regarded them as the property of the employee. DC plans thus gave employees more freedom to make their own cost-benefit analyses about whether to stay with one employer until the end of a career, or to leave to pursue better opportunities in the labour market. In typical DB plans, however, employees got no benefit from their plan unless they stayed with the employer until retirement, creating very severe pension penalties for premature departure from employment. DB plans operated by design as "golden handcuffs" for reducing labour mobility, making them more useful to employers for discouraging employee turnover and disciplining employee behaviour. By increasing employer control of employee tenure, DB plans gave employers maximum control at minimum cost.

Contributory or Non-contributory Plans?

One issue on which employers did not have a uniform view throughout this period was whether employers should pay the entire cost of the pension plan, or whether employees should contribute to their own pensions. As we have seen, the 1874 Grand Trunk plan followed British-style models, which required employee contributions, and early civil-service plans were also predominantly of the contributory type.[48] Outside the civil service, however, late-nineteenth-century plans in Canada tended to follow American models, which did not require employee contributions. By the early twentieth century, there was a clear trend in the private sector towards non-contributory plans, and by the 1920s, the non-contributory plan was the Canadian private sector norm.[49]

At first blush, this trend appears difficult to understand. Tax laws favoured non-contributory plans in the US, since employer contributions were tax-deductible in that country, but employee contributions were not. This was not true in Canada, however, where both employer and employee contributions were deductible almost from the inception of income taxes.[50] Some cautious legal advisers warned that employment standards legislation in some jurisdictions, which prohibited employers from making unauthorized deductions from employee wages, might impede compulsory pension contributions, a problem that would not arise if the employer was paying the entire cost of the plan.[51] This hypothesis was never tested in Canada, however. For employers preoccupied with costs, requiring employees to pick up part of the pension tab seems an obvious way to limit their own exposure to pension liabilities.

Cost considerations did not initially carry the day, however. Employers were aware that the cost savings generated by employee pension contributions might be short-term or even illusory, since employees required to contribute to their pensions might demand off-setting wage increases.[52] More compelling in the early decades of the twentieth century was a set of employer concerns about the impact employee contributions might have on the labour-market dynamics of the plan. As we have seen, the Grand Trunk Railway switched from a contributory to a non-contributory plan when it extended its plan to its less-well-paid blue-collar workforce, almost certainly because of the widespread perception that blue-collar employees would experience mandatory pension contributions as a cut in pay, and a significant hardship. Even for better-paid white-collar workers, employers had reasonable concerns that contribution requirements might send the wrong management message about the nature and purpose of the pension plan, and undermine unilateral employer control. Employees who contributed to their own pensions were more likely to develop a sense of entitlement to those pensions; they would see their contributions as a form of savings, and expect to get a return on those savings, even if they did not stay with the employer long enough to retire on pension.[53] By contrast, plans entirely funded by the employer reinforced the message to employees that their pensions were gifts in the discretion of the employer. Commenting on the fact that contributory plans had fallen out of favour by the early 1930s, Murray Latimer observed that the "policy [of establishing plans paid for solely by the employer] has the advantage, at least in the opinion of the management, of not complicating relations with trade unions, retaining full control of retirements and final judgment on the fulfillment of qualifications, discouraging strikes, and permitting retirement for the good of the services and the public safety."[54] For these reasons, employers who were determined to keep benefits discretionary favoured non-contributory plans.

Despite the perceived advantage of non-contributory plans, however, the Great Depression forced many employers to reconsider the relative costs and benefits of taking on full responsibility for pension funding. New plans established or amended during and after the Depression were typically contributory, and the shift back to contributory plans coincided with employer willingness to provide some guarantees in their plans. Not all employers made the switch; Bell Telephone's 1939 plan continued to be entirely employer-funded, despite its benefit guarantees. By 1965, however, approximately 85 per cent of Canadian plans were contributory, a proportion that has held relatively constant since then.[55]

Mandatory Retirement

Across all types of enterprises that found value in pension plans, a key objective was to discourage turnover; employers wanted competent, well-behaved employees to remain with them as long as they were useful and productive. However, they did not want those employees to stay on past that point. The departure of "worn-out" employees was critical to the safety records of enterprises like the railways. It was equally critical to the labour-intensive bureaucratic/Fordist enterprises, whose salary structures depended on internal labour markets and whose business models depended for profitability on the employer's ability to replace older workers with younger, cheaper workers on a predictable timetable. Encouraging retirement was an important component of the pension package. Indeed, for some analysts, the role played by pension plans in facilitating the orderly exit from the workforce of older, more-senior employees was their most important function.[56] The ideal pension plan was therefore crafted not only to attract and retain employees who would stay with the firm throughout their careers, but also to facilitate their departure when they became older and less productive.

The precise role played by retirement policy within pension plans is an issue on which there was some change over time. Early plans like the 1874 Grand Trunk plan sought simply to encourage retirement by offering long-service employees pensions that were pegged at a level high enough to maintain pre-retirement standards of living. Later plans were not content simply to provide incentives and leave the retirement decision in the hands of the employees. Instead, they established mandatory retirement ages, and explicitly made receipt of a pension conditional on the employee's willingness to retire when required to do so. Purely as a matter of law, employers were under no obligation to provide a pension as a quid pro quo for mandatory retirement; they could have terminated employees by complying with any applicable common-law notice requirements, an approach that would in most cases have been less costly than a pension.[57] However, pensions played an important role in maintaining employee morale and alleviating the reputational costs that would flow from simply discarding older workers. As American historian William Graebner put it in his 1980 *History of Retirement*, pension plans assisted corporations in "sloughing off traditional obligations to older workers" without significant damage to their public image.[58]

PAYING FOR PENSIONS

Although employers with DB plans could defer pension costs for a significant period, when employees eventually retired and were granted pension, those pensions had to be paid. Pension pioneers took a variety of approaches to managing these costs. Many early employers saw pensions simply as an ordinary cost of doing business, and paid pension benefits, like salaries and wages, directly out of operating revenues, an approach now known as pay-as-you-go (or paygo) funding. The pay-as-you-go approach posed potential problems, however, since pension costs, unlike wage costs, come due at a time when the pensioner has ceased to contribute to ongoing revenue generation. When businesses were growing, profits earned from the labour of current employees could cover those costs, but if the business was stagnant or shrinking, there might be not be sufficient profits from which to pay pensions. Furthermore, future pension costs were difficult to project, since they depended on such contingencies as how many individual employees would remain in the workforce long enough to qualify for a pension, what salaries they would be earning at the time of retirement, and how long they would live after retirement. For young businesses with few pensioners, pay-as-you-go pensions were inexpensive in their initial stages. As the pension rolls grew longer, however, annual pension costs increased exponentially. Even in a system in which only a small percentage of employees would ultimately receive pensions, these potential future liabilities could not be ignored by employers interested in the credibility of their pension promises. They sought methods of pre-funding which provided more cost predictability for them and more pension security for employees.

Nineteenth and early-twentieth-century legislation offered some statutory vehicles for pre-funding pensions. The 1887 federal *Pension Fund Societies Act*[59] permitted federally incorporated companies to establish "societies" for the provision of pensions for officers and employees "incapacitated by age or infirmity," as well as survivor benefits (s.6). Formally structured as employee membership organizations, these societies were actually adjuncts of corporations, since they could be established only by the senior officers of a corporation, who then controlled the drafting of the bylaws that governed the terms of the plan (s.5). The Act contemplated that pensions would be funded by contributions from members. It also specifically empowered corporations to make such contributions (s.7), a feature which may explain in part why Canada avoided litigation over one issue with which US courts grappled in the early part of the twentieth century: whether corporations had the legal capacity to use corporate funds to make "gifts" to employees in the form of discretionary pensions.[60]

Provincially incorporated companies did not have access to this federal statute. Up to late in the nineteenth century, they could offer pensions through loosely regulated "friendly societies."[61] However, in 1892 Ontario passed its new *Insurance Corporations Act*,[62] which consolidated several insurance-related statutes and introduced the province's first comprehensive regime of insurance regulation. This statute treated friendly societies as non-profit insurance providers,[63] imposing a stringent regulatory framework which conceptualized pension plans as contracts of insurance. The Act required a considerable degree of transparency about the terms on which benefits were offered,[64] and put severe limits on any "forfeiture clauses" that would take away existing benefits (s.40). This new approach to regulation made friendly societies impractical for employer pension purposes, and there is little evidence of their use.

By the early twentieth century, employers seeking cost control had simpler alternatives than pension societies and friendly societies: they could purchase annuities for their employees. The federal government began to sell annuities in 1908, both to individuals and to employers on behalf of their employees.[65] Private insurance companies also competed vigorously for a share of the annuity market. By the early 1920s, private insurers were aggressively promoting a variety of group annuity products as funding vehicles for workplace pension plans.[66] In exchange for an annual premium, these products transferred the liability for paying pensions to the annuity vendor. This was a significant advantage from the employer's perspective, but these products also had a major disadvantage; even when they were purchased as part of group plans, annuities frequently took the form of individually issued annuity certificates, giving employees irrevocable rights that accumulated on an ongoing basis. This arrangement seriously limited employer flexibility to withhold or withdraw pensions at will. Government annuities came with even more strings attached; they were generally irrevocable with respect to the portion purchased by employee contributions, and, by 1938, they also required employer contributions to become irrevocable (i.e., "vested") after twenty years of service.[67] Despite this additional drawback, government annuities continued to be a thorn in the side of the private insurance industry, maintaining a significant share of the annuity market until 1975, when the program was finally shut down, a victim of allegations that it had never been properly funded.[68]

While statutory pension society models and insured annuities gave employers predictable costs, neither provided the flexibility they needed to administer DB plans such as those of the Grand Trunk and Bell Telephone, under which employees forfeited pension rights if they left their workplace or were terminated prior to reaching retirement. These funding arrangements were also incompatible with plan provisions permitting employers to suspend pensions that were already being paid out, as a penalty for conduct inimical to the interests of the company. Employers large enough to afford the risk of "self-insurance" soon found a more attractive alternative – the self-administered plan, in which pensions were paid out of a dedicated pension fund. Both the Grand Trunk Railway and Bell Telephone espoused this model. The Grand Trunk's pension trust fund was contemplated by the legislation enabling its plan, and the company was expressly authorized to make annual contributions to the fund.[69] Bell established its own trust fund in 1917, in conjunction with the establishment of its first plan. The company's initial contribution to the fund was $400,000, an amount well short of modern regulatory requirements but sufficient to make initial pension payments.[70]

Like insurance contracts, pension trust funds relieved employers of the uncertainties of pay-as-you-go funding, and allowed them to set aside predictable amounts of money on an annual basis to fund future pension liabilities. They were both cheaper and more flexible to administer than annuity contracts, and they left employers free to write their own rules regarding employee rights and the conditions under which pensions would be paid. Early funds were sometimes administered by employers themselves, although many companies placed their funds in the custody of financial institutions in the form of pension trusts. Contemporary commercial trust arrangements typically required that contributions be dedicated to trust purposes, but they did not otherwise place awkward fetters on employer pension discretion, since they were structured to require trustees to take direction from the employer. Through their power to nominate the trustees, pension trust arrangements also allowed employers to retain effective control over the investment of trust capital.[71]

Insurance contracts and pension trusts fought for ascendancy as preferred pension funding vehicles throughout much of the twentieth century.[72] Their relative advantages and disadvantages varied with the shifting specifics of tax laws and pension regulatory laws.[73] They also varied with the size of the employer and with its pension objectives.[74] Small employers saw a cost advantage in the security and cost-predictability of insurance plans, despite the limits they placed on employer discretion. For larger employers, the cost advantage usually lay with the trust model, particularly if they opted to self-administer and could eliminate trust-company profits on top of the cost of pensions. Employers who opted for trust funding had broader scope for discretion in the administration of pension benefits and the deployment of the fund. Insured plans held a steady market share in Canada, but the trust model ultimately became the mid-century model of choice.[75]

As we have seen in this chapter, the pension plans of this era attempted to achieve two somewhat contradictory objectives: to keep power over pension decisions in the hands of the employer, and at the same time to make credible pension promises to employees. The tensions between these two objectives created both ambiguities in plan drafting and unfulfilled expectations on the part of employees, two factors which led almost inevitably to litigation. In the next chapter, we look at how the common-law courts dealt with the issues raised by the legal claims beginning to emerge even in the latter part of the nineteenth century, and increasing in the first half of the twentieth century – claims that workplace pension plans created concrete, enforceable legal rights for employees.

3

Pension Rights as Contract Rights: The Early Common Law

PENSION RIGHTS AND ORTHODOX CONTRACT THEORY

As we have seen in Chapter 2, early employers took pains to structure pension plans to maximize their control over benefits. At the same time, however, pension plans could play their intended role as human-resource-management tools only if employees believed they would get the pensions promised by the plans if they fulfilled the conditions laid out in the plans. Accordingly, although plans came hedged with disclaimers, they were intended to create real employee expectations, and they did so. When those expectations were not realized, employees sought the assistance of the courts from time to time. Their claims forced courts to grapple with the legal nature of the pension promise in the context of the employment relationship.

To twenty-first-century lawyers it is obvious that pensions are part of employee compensation and workplace pension plans are terms of the contract of employment. Those propositions were not nearly so obvious to lawyers and courts of the late nineteenth and early twentieth century. The English treatise writers who were still a strong influence on common-law thought in Canada had no clear category within which to slot workplace pensions. Even the terminology was not settled. While the title of Murray Latimer's 1932 text refers to "industrial pension systems," Latimer observes that historically the term "pension" was associated with gifts; payments to which the recipient had a contractual right were more commonly called "annuities."[1] In his *Commentaries*, Blackstone slotted "annuities" (which he understood to be "rights to sustenance") in a category of property he labelled "incorporeal hereditaments."[2] Blackstone's conception is highly abstract: "An annuity is ... an incorporeal hereditament: for though the money, which is the fruit or product of this annuity, is doubtless of a corporeal nature, yet the annuity itself, which produces that money, is a thing invisible, has only a mental existence, and cannot be delivered over hand to hand."[3]

Early Canadian courts operating in this abstract mode located pensions in the world of noblesse oblige, and dealt with pension claims by applying British precedents shaped by the law of gifts and charitable trusts.[4] This approach is clearly reflected in the 1898 decision of the Supreme Court of Canada in *Balderson v The Queen*, in which a senior civil servant who had been dismissed "to promote economy" claimed that the pension he had been awarded under the *Civil Service Superannuation Act* should have been calculated on the basis of twenty-five rather than fifteen years of service.[5] Although Balderson's argument had a plausible statutory basis, the Act made pensions discretionary and provided that pension determinations would be made by executive decision. The court refused to address Balderson's claim, holding that it was not the role of the judiciary "to review the exercise of the discretion vested by the statute in the Governor-General-in-Council."[6] The court gave short shrift to the plaintiff's argument that he had a contractual right to a pension: "There is no room whatever for the appellant's contention that it was a condition of his contract of employment that in the event of being superannuated in order to promote economy in the civil service he was to have a legal right to any allowance whatever. The superannuation allowance that the Governor-General-in-Council may grant in such a case to any person is a gratuity."[7]

In its 1921 decision in *Bacon v The Queen*, the Exchequer Court was even more peremptory in dismissing the claims of a former military officer who was suing for a pension payable pursuant to orders-in-council. Those orders had explicitly referred to the pension as a "gratuity." The court commented acerbically, "Does not the word 'gratuity' contain in itself its very meaning and definition and primarily denote a grant of money *ex gratia*? It implies an act of generosity, beneficence, munificence, a gift out of kindness, free from any valuable or legal consideration. It is a voluntary gift or *beneficium* – the donation of it being absolutely unilateral and depending entirely upon the inclination of will of the giver. It would seem of the very essence and character of a gratuity not to be bilateral; otherwise, it

would cease to be a gratuity."[8] The court cited consistent UK authority to the effect that a military pension "is in its very nature a bounty
or gift ... depending entirely upon the grace and benevolence of the
Crown for its recovery" (para. 9), and concluded that the same rule
applied in Canada (para. 22).[9] Accordingly, there was no right of
action for recovery, notwithstanding that the orders-in-council
referred to the pension as an "entitlement" (para. 6).

While concepts deriving from state patronage and noblesse oblige
were adaptable to government service, they were not so obviously
adaptable to pension arrangements embedded solely in private
employment relationships. Courts faced with pension claims in the
private sector were forced to search for an alternative framework
that could reconcile Blackstonian arcana with emerging concepts of
employment law. The law of contract was the prime candidate. Canadian courts of the late nineteenth and early twentieth centuries had
already begun to conceptualize the employment relationship as contractual; by the 1890s they were using the language of contract with
some consistency to explain the legal rights and responsibilities of
employers and employees.[10] But plaintiffs seeking to apply contract
law to workplace pension arrangements faced some serious challenges. Although pension plans were normally in writing, they rarely
took any form that resembled a bilateral contract. They did not emerge
out of the negotiation scenarios that courts recognized as establishing
contracts in the commercial context. To common-law courts, pension
promises looked like the "bare promises" (*nudum pactum*), to which
courts typically refused to lend the force of law. There was no "offer"
or "acceptance"; pensions were not visibly bargained and paid for
through relationships of reciprocal exchange. In addition, courts had
trouble identifying "consideration" for the employer's promise to pay
a pension. Unlike standard wage agreements, in which employees
laboured in exchange for the payment of immediate wages, pension
promises did not come due until employees had ceased to render valuable service. Courts typically took the view that what they called "past
consideration" (i.e., value already exchanged) would not support a
promise to pay continuing benefits.[11]

The failure of pension arrangements to conform to the technical
requirements of contract created obstacles when employees sought to
establish pension claims in the courts. Theoretical problems of contract formation, including the problem of consideration, were discussed in court decisions and journal articles dealing with employment

pensions until well into the twentieth century.[12] But pension cases rarely foundered directly on theoretical problems. Typically, employees lost their claims – and they almost invariably did lose them – because of a more mundane reality: the fact that the plan texts under which the claims were brought expressly disclaimed contractual liability. Orthodox contract theory demanded that, before an agreement or document would be characterized as a contract with enforceable obligations, it must reflect not only the technical requirements of a contract – offer, acceptance, and consideration – but must also show an "intention to create legal relations."[13] In the normal commercial context, courts inferred such an intention from agreements which contained the technical elements of a contract. But outside the commercial context, they were not nearly so quick to assume that, simply because parties had made clear and concrete promises, they intended those promises to be legally enforceable. Where employers specifically disclaimed an intention to be bound in contract by their pension promises, they could count on courts to give effect to those disclaimers.

EVOLVING CONCEPTS
OF VESTED PENSION RIGHTS

The early Canadian case law reflects considerable judicial ambivalence about the proper legal framework within which to assess pension claims against non-governmental employers. The earliest workplace pension lawsuit on record in Canada, a case which ultimately reached the Supreme Court of Canada in 1885, is *The Rev. Joel Tombleson Wright v The Incorporated Synod of the Diocese of Huron*.[14] The Reverend Mr Wright's claim, framed as an early species of "class action," concerned an ecclesiastical dispute about the disposition of the "Commutation Fund," a trust fund consisting of sums paid to the church by the government in compensation for the so-called "secularization" of Upper Canada's "clergy reserves."[15] The fund was primarily dedicated to the payment of stipends for individual clergymen who had previously been paid out of revenues from the clergy reserves. However, the church's governing council had drafted the trust deed to provide that, if there were surplus funds, they could be used to supplement the stipends of other clergy working in the diocese who met certain specified conditions with respect to qualifications, service, and good standing. These supplements took the form of annuities.

Wright was among the clergy who had been awarded an annuity out of surplus funds. After paying this group for a three-year period, the governing council decided to terminate their annuities and use the funds for other purposes. Wright contended that once the governing council had made the decision to pay a specific annuity, it could not rescind that decision. At first instance, Vice-Chancellor William Proudfoot of the Chancery Court analyzed the dispute as a hybrid problem in property, contract, and trust law. He accepted the church's argument that its governing council had discretion to deploy the Commutation Fund. But he took the view that, once a formal decision had been made to award specific annuities, the council, as trustees, had "executed" that part of the trust fund and could not revoke that execution. As he saw it, once Wright was awarded his annuity, it became a "vested" property right that could not thereafter be divested (paras. 36–9). Faced with a considerable body of UK authority establishing that discretionary annuities could lawfully be withdrawn or reduced, the vice-chancellor reverted to a form of contract analysis, noting that Wright and his colleagues were entitled to keep their annuities because they were still performing services for them; presumably the legal relevance of this fact, although the vice-chancellor does not spell this out, is that they were providing continuing "consideration" for their annuity payments (paras. 42–3). He gave judgment in Wright's favour.

The Court of Appeal took a different view. Justice Patterson interpreted the Chancery Court's decision as a finding that there was a "sort of contract" between the clergymen and the diocese to pay the annuities, "from which contract the Synod could not lawfully recede" (para. 46).[16] He disagreed with that characterization, although "not without some fluctuation of opinion" (para. 49). In his view, the bylaw which conferred the annuities was not contractual; it was merely an "expression of intent," which the clergy would have known to be "revocable" (para. 51). He reasoned: "The weakness of the plaintiff's case arises from his inability to shew that his service was rendered in consideration of a promise to pay him this money. There was no bargain. There was no mutuality. He was not bound to serve, but was at liberty to cease his ministrations at his pleasure; and he was not, by reason of anything connected with these arrangements, relieved from liability to any proceeding which might interfere either with the continuance of his active service or with his good standing, on which two requisites the right to participate always depended" (para. 56).

A divided Supreme Court of Canada ultimately agreed with the appeal court that the church's governors were free to revoke annuities already granted, and dismissed Wright's claim.[17] The basis for that decision is probably best summed up in Chief Justice William J. Ritchie's very brief judgment, in which he concluded that Wright had no "valid or binding contract or vested rights" to the annuity. The various Supreme Court judgments analyze the problem by applying a somewhat incoherent mélange of contract, property, and trust law concepts. The court was unanimous, however, that Wright had acquired no contractual right to his annuity. Even the dissenting judges, who concurred with the result in the Chancery Court, were careful to distance themselves from any inference that they accepted Vice-Chancellor Proudfoot's contractual analysis (if indeed it was a contractual analysis), grounding their judgments solely on highly technical constructions of the trust deed.

It is important to note that the *Wright* case did not deal with a *retirement* pension; although it dealt with an annuity in the workplace context, that annuity was payable only to working clergy. A decade later, the Supreme Court was faced with its first retirement pension claim in *Dionne v Québec*.[18] *Dionne* addressed the legal status of the civil service pension of Charles John Burroughs, a clerk employed by the Quebec government who had taken early retirement because of ill health. Under the Quebec statute in effect at that time, Burroughs was eligible for and had been granted a monthly pension on his retirement. Shortly after retiring, "without the knowledge of his said wife and in a moment of despondency"(456), Burroughs negotiated an agreement with the government to commute his pension into a single lump-sum payment equivalent to the return of his contributions, a sum considerably smaller than its value as a pension. For reasons not disclosed in the court's decision, he had second thoughts about the prudence of this arrangement and sued the government to restore the pension, arguing that the agreement to commute was void. Joining him in the lawsuit was his wife, Edmée Dionne, who argued that she was entitled to independent standing because of her interest in the spousal survivor benefit attached to her husband's pension. Both their claims were dismissed by the Quebec courts.

As it had in *Wright*, the Supreme Court divided. The dissenters took the view that, since Burroughs was of full legal capacity when he made his decision to commute his pension, he was now bound by that decision. A majority allowed Burroughs's claim, holding that under the statute establishing the civil service plan, once a civil servant retires and has been granted a pension, his right to that pension becomes "inalienable" even by his own action (473). Since the decision was grounded in the statute, however, there was no common-law analysis of the nature of employee pension rights.

Mme Dionne's spousal claim had almost certainly been joined to Burroughs's claim out of concern that he might be barred from pursuing the claim because of his own conduct. Since Burroughs had succeeded, it was not necessary to deal with her rights, and not all judges did so. Those who did, however, approached the problem as a matter of common law as well as statute law. The two dissenters dismissed her claim along with her husband's, forcefully expressing the view that, where a man has a legal right to dispose of his pension, his wife has no business standing in his way (453). Two of the three judges who made up the majority, however, accepted Mme Dionne's argument that she had an independent interest in her husband's pension. Justice John Gwynne, who wrote most fully on the Dionne claim, saw her legal interest as twofold: she had an interest in the spousal pension she would receive if she survived her husband, and also an interest "jointly with him during his life in the monthly instalments which are made payable in that manner for supplying maintenance and support not only to the husband himself alone, but for his wife and children also" (470). He saw those interests as the foundation of rights that "vested" when her husband retired, and sufficient to give her standing to challenge the commutation of his pension. As applied to her claim, his decision reflects an emerging recognition that certain pension rights might "vest," even though those rights did not yet translate into an immediate pension.

Both the *Wright* and *Dionne* courts used the language of "vesting," a concept borrowed from property law that would become commonplace in subsequent judicial discussions of pension rights. In *Wright*, the core issue was whether someone who has been granted the right to receive a pension can have that right taken away, or whether that right has become "vested," in the sense that it is irrevocable. In *Dionne*, Justice Gwynne's analysis of the claim of Burroughs's wife pushed the notion of vesting a step further; he was prepared to allow Mme Dionne a vested right, even though her personal spousal claim was a contingent claim that would materialize only if her husband predeceased her. These are both promising lines of analysis, but neither case ultimately turned on them, and neither case is cited in subsequent Canadian case law considering whether pension plans created irrevocable rights either before or after the actual awarding of a pension.[19]

This issue of vesting was considered anew in the 1902 decision in *Armstrong v Toronto Police Benefit Fund*,[20] in which the Ontario Court of Appeal addressed a retired officer's claim to a pension from the Toronto Police Benefit Fund. That claim had been denied, because the officer did not have enough service to qualify under the eligibility rules in place at the time of his retirement. He would have qualified under the rules in place when he joined the fund, but those rules had been changed in the interim to increase the service requirement. In a very brief judgment, the court dismissed Armstrong's claim. The decision is interesting, however, because it contains the tantalizing hint that, if Armstrong *had* accumulated enough service to be eligible for the pension he sought *before* the rule had changed, his right to a pension might have vested, even if he had not actually retired and claimed the pension before the change. On the facts, however, the court found "no question of vested interests involved. The plaintiff had acquired no absolute right to a pension at the time of the amendment in 1894. His rights continued to be the same as those of all other members until he acquired a vested right under the rules in force at the time" (para. 5).

The question of whether pension plans could create rights that vested, even though they would not crystallize into a pension until some future date, resurfaced in 1925 before the Supreme Court of Canada in *Pension Fund Society of La Banque Nationale, Trudel v Lemoine et al.*, this time in the context of competing claims to the fund held by a pension society established to provide pensions for certain bank employees.[21] All employees of the bank were members of the society.[22] The bank ceased to operate, triggering a distribution of the fund's assets. The question of how individual member shares should be calculated ultimately made its way through the Supreme Court of Canada and up to the Privy Council, the final Canadian appeal court at that time.

The society's bylaws, drafted in French, drew a sharp line between the entitlements of members with and without *droits acquis* ("acquired rights"); on a liquidation and distribution of the fund, the former could claim a pro rata share in the capitalized value of their pensions, while the latter got only a return of their own contributions with interest. At issue was whether the class of members with *droits acquis* consisted only of those who were already pensioners, or also included members who met the qualifications for pension, but had not yet retired. The Supreme Court's decision considered definitions of the term "*droits acquis*" offered by civil law treatises, which effectively equated *droits acquis* to "vested rights."[23] It ultimately concluded, however, that in the context of the society's bylaw, the term did not have this highly specialized meaning. The court emphasized that, under civil law, a *droit acquis* was essentially a property right; it could be bought, sold, or bequeathed, even if it remained conditional. As the court saw it, the rights created by the bylaw were "temporary" and "personal" rights, not property rights. Accordingly, under the bylaw, *droits acquis* must have been intended to have a broader and less technical meaning. In the result, the court decided that those with *droits acquis* included not just pensioners, but also those who met the qualifications for pension at the time of the liquidation, even though they had not yet retired;[24] both these groups were therefore entitled to claim for the capitalized value of their pensions.[25]

The Privy Council agreed only in part. It accepted that the term "*droits acquis*" should not be equated with "vested rights"; in context, the term meant "present rights," or "matured rights." It disagreed, however, that a society member who had not yet retired had a "present right" to a pension simply because he met the qualifications to claim that pension; he would have a "present right" only once he had actually retired and been awarded a pension. Accordingly, the Privy Council concluded that only actual pensioners were entitled to a capitalized share of the fund. It was prepared to expand this category marginally to include employees who had retired and had not yet begun to collect their pension, but not those who qualified for pension but were still in the employ of the bank at the time of dissolution.

Both the Supreme Court and the Privy Council in *Trudel* emphasized that their decisions turned on the interpretation of the particular pension society's bylaw, and had no broader application. The decisions are nevertheless instructive for the clues they provide as to how those courts viewed claims that workplace pension plans created rights prior to retirement. Although the Supreme Court's discussion about whether "acquired rights" and "vested rights" are equivalent is not helpful in the abstract, it tells us that, at least at the time *Trudel* was decided, the court viewed "vested rights" through the narrow lens of property law and would be unlikely to apply that term to accumulated pension credits, especially in plans where pension decisions were ultimately discretionary. The Privy Council's view was even less generous; if the term "*droits acquis*" applied only to actual pensioners, the term "vested rights" might have even narrower application.

This review of the Canadian case law in the late nineteenth century and the first quarter of the twentieth century reveals a judiciary that had not yet developed a comprehensive legal framework for addressing pension claims. The courts' analytical approach hovered somewhere between property law and contract law, occasionally drawing on trust concepts when trust funds were involved. The courts of this era had made no firm decisions on whether it was possible for employees to acquire enforceable pension rights, either before or after retirement, where employers were not prepared to acknowledge those rights. However, the auguries were not favourable for the evolution of a rights-based understanding of pensions. Although the legal picture became more complex in the second quarter of the twentieth century, it did not become a great deal clearer.

THE COMMON LAW OF PENSIONS IN THE 1930S

In his 1932 study of industrial pension plans, Murray Latimer provided a comprehensive survey of the legal status of workplace pension plans and employee pension rights up to the early 1930s.[26] US courts were confronted with pension claims much more frequently than Canadian courts, and although Latimer's treatise generally covered both the US and Canada, his discussion of the jurisprudence focuses on US court decisions. His analysis is nevertheless useful for Canadian pension scholars, since both the plans themselves and the legal context within which they evolved were substantially similar in both countries.

The results of Latimer's survey were discouraging for proponents of employee pension rights. While not entirely consistent in their theoretical approaches, US courts rarely interpreted the language of plans in favour of employee claims. Typical was *McNevin v Solvay Process Company*, an 1898 decision of the New York Court of Appeals and the earliest pension case identified by Latimer.[27] The Solvay plan was a species of defined contribution plan, with individual accounts set aside for each employee. It expressly provided that employees who left the company under certain conditions would receive the money standing to their credit. However, it also expressly provided that the monies were gifts, and that the fund's trustees would decide whether or not they would be paid out to any employee. When McNevin left the company, the trustees refused his pension claim. The Court of Appeal dismissed his action to recover the monies standing to his credit. It emphasized that pensions were gifts, and took the conventional common-law view that the promise of a gift was not enforceable; no matter how unconditional the promise, a donor who did not voluntarily fulfill that promise would not be compelled by the courts to do so.[28] Based on *McNevin* and a series of similar decisions, Latimer concluded that "[t]he trend of the law so far has been to say to industry that it may make its own law of pensions. The court will take the pension plan as the statute in each case and decide in accordance with it."[29] Even where employees had contributed to their plans, courts were unwilling to find enforceable employee rights unless the plan spelled out such rights. Latimer summed up his survey with this comment: "It seems clear ... that it is possible for a company to frame a pension plan which will constitute no legal liability and which may be completely abolished at any time."[30]

Shortly after Latimer's treatise was published, arguments that pension plans could impose liability on employers began to find more favour with US judges, as they gradually abandoned gift theory and embraced the law of contract as the appropriate legal framework within which to analyze workplace pension claims.[31] By the mid-1930s, some US courts were prepared to agree that the promise of a pension was a contractual commitment to make future payment for services currently rendered: in other words, a pension was a form of "deferred compensation."[32] The deferred-compensation approach was grounded in the theory that workplace pension arrangements were "unilateral contracts," a type of contractual agreement in which acceptance of an offer to form a contract could be implied from conduct without the need for express bilateral agreement or written communication. As applied in the pension context, "unilateral contract" theory typically constructed the pension plan itself as the employer's "offer," which employees then "accepted" by providing their labour and fulfilling the conditions for eligibility established by the plan text. Under this theory, if a plan offered pensions for employees with twenty years of service at a retirement age of sixty-five, an employee who reached the age of sixty-five with at least twenty years' service become absolutely entitled to claim a pension on retirement. A variant on the theory went further and argued that an employer became bound by its pension offer as soon as the employee accepted pensionable employment, establishing ongoing liability as pension credits were earned by work on a day-to-day basis.[33]

But although the application of contract theory was a promising start for employees pressing pension claims, it did not resolve the question of liability. The *terms* of the contract remained an obstacle. Even if pension plans were contracts, orthodox contract theory held that a party claiming the benefit of a contract must take its burdens as well. Despite conceptual breakthroughs based on theories of unilateral contract and deferred compensation, courts continued in the first half of the twentieth century to reject concrete claims that employers were required to honour their pension promises, based largely on the language of the plans themselves. One 1925 report on the state of pension plans and pension law in the US in the first quarter of the twentieth century describes the resulting paradox in these cynical terms: "The discretionary principle is carried to its logical limit when the employer requires the employee to subscribe to a contract by which all possible contractual rights and obligations under the pension are expressly waived."[34]

MONITORING PROCEDURAL FAIRNESS IN PLAN ADMINISTRATION

Canadian courts took longer to adopt contract theory, but when they did so, they took a similar approach. Judicial focus on the plan language, evident in both the US and Canadian cases, meant that, where pension plans contained explicit disclaimers, those disclaimers would be given effect. In addition, where pension plans gave employers (or their delegated trustees or pension committees) discretionary power to grant or deny pensions, or to suspend or withdraw them after they had been granted, courts rarely interfered to second-guess their decisions.[35] Where pension plans purported to make employers or their delegates final arbiters on disputes over the interpretation or application of the plan, courts generally enforced these terms literally.[36]

From time to time, however, courts did intervene in particularly compelling circumstances, where employees had fulfilled all the qualifications for a pension but were denied it for arbitrary reasons.[37] In early cases that take this approach, courts applied what have come to be called the "rules of natural justice," then developing in the context of administrative law and statutory tribunals. In a 1906 decision in

Lapointe v Montreal Police Benefit Society,[38] the Privy Council applied the *audi alteram partem* principle to a decision of the Montreal Police Benevolent and Pension Society denying a pension to Louis Lapointe, a police officer and society member who had been forced to resign his employment.[39] The society's rules provided that "[a]ny member entitled by length of service to a gratuity or pension who is dismissed from the force, or is obliged to resign, shall have his case considered by the board of directors, and his right to such gratuity or pension determined by a majority of the board" (383). Lapointe brought court action to challenge the refusal of his pension. In response, the society argued that, since Lapointe was a member of the society, he was bound in contract by its bylaws, which "constituted the board of directors a board of arbitration between him and the society" (382); accordingly, he was precluded from challenging the board's decisions in court.

Clearly offended by the high-handed manner in which Lapointe's claim had been processed, the Privy Council characterized the board's conduct as "most extraordinary" (384). It made no direct comment on the society's argument that Lapointe was bound in contract by the bylaws; indeed, it characterized the problem as one involving the proper administration of a trust.[40] However, it took the view that the board had acted improperly by not following its own decision-making rules, since it had not given Lapointe's claim the "consideration" to which it was entitled under the society's bylaws. The Privy Council recited a litany of deviations from acceptable procedure,[41] culminating in a conclusion that the board's decision to reject Lapointe's claim was "irregular, contrary to the rules of the society, and above all contrary to elementary principles of justice" (384). These flaws rendered the decision null and void, a conclusion so obvious in the Privy Council's view that "[i]t is hardly necessary to cite any authority on a point so plain" (385).[42] By way of remedy, it remitted the case to a differently constituted board for a decision, retaining supervisory jurisdiction over the proceedings.[43]

Canadian courts also had recourse to estoppel principles to rectify egregious procedural unfairness in pension plan administration and decision-making. *Tawny v City of Winnipeg*,[44] a 1936 decision of the Manitoba King's Bench, involved a pension plan established in 1921 under a Winnipeg city bylaw for permanent city employees. Plan members with a minimum of fifteen years of service were eligible for a pension if they became unfit for further employment with the city.

Tawny, a manual labourer paid hourly, had been enrolled in the plan by the city when it was first established, and plan contributions had been deducted from his pay. Some eighteen years later, in failing health, he applied for a pension, believing on the basis of information supplied by city officials that he had accumulated sufficient service to qualify. His application was initially refused on the ground that he was seventy-two days short of the required service. At that time, he was offered and accepted sufficient light work to make up those days. He then reapplied for a pension, but his claim was again denied, this time on three separate grounds: first, that he was not a "permanent employee"; second, that even with the additional seventy-two days, he was *still* short the requisite fifteen years of service; and third, that he did not meet the plan's medical requirement, because although he had been certified by the medical examiners as "unfit for manual labour," he had not been expressly certified as unfit for any position with the city (para. 4). On this second occasion, his employer was not willing to offer him any further employment to allow him to qualify.

The court was not prepared to see Tawny denied his pension. It accorded him permanent employee status, largely on the basis that the employer had treated him as a member of the plan. On the issue of whether or not he had enough service, Tawny argued estoppel, submitting that he had reasonably relied on the employer's calculation that he had sufficient service to qualify for a pension, and he was no longer in a position to render more service (para. 9). The court accepted this argument, holding that, since the employer was responsible for keeping reliable records, it would be inequitable to allow it to rely on Tawny's inability to prove his length of service. It would be equally inequitable, as the court saw it, to allow the employer to rely on the absence of an explicit medical finding that Tawny was unfit for any work with the City: "The plaintiff has done only one kind of work, and that is manual labour in the water works department. He is now old and ill and cannot turn to other occupations. He has not applied to the city for other work, and it seems to be useless for him to do so ... it would be unfair now to assume that the city declines to re-engage the plaintiff for any reason other than that he is unfit for further service" (paras. 11 to 12). Under these highly sympathetic circumstances, the court made a declaration in Tawny's favour.

A similarly sympathetic pension claim reached the Supreme Court of Canada in 1939 in *Mantha v Montreal (City)*.[45] Montreal's pension plan, also established by city bylaw, provided disability pensions for firefighters unable to perform their duties "by reason of a chronic or incurable disease or of permanent infirmity." Under the bylaws, the executive committee had the responsibility for determining eligibility in individual cases. Philias Mantha, a firefighter employed by the city, submitted an application to retire on the ground of ill health, together with an application for a disability pension. When he was examined by medical officers, they determined that he was still fit for continuing duty. He was nevertheless permitted to retire, without being advised of the medical findings. Many months later, after what the court described as "repeated inquiries," he was given the bad news that he had not been ruled incapacitated and was therefore not eligible for a pension. In an action against the city to claim his pension, he was successful at trial, but that verdict was quashed by the provincial appeal court on the ground that Mantha had no right to sue, since the plan required pension decisions to be made by the city's executive committee.

In the Supreme Court of Canada, Chief Justice Sir Lyman Duff, speaking for the majority, took care to emphasize his agreement with the appeal court "that primarily the appellant's right to superannuation and a pension must rest upon the decision of the [executive committee]" (461); that committee, and not a court, had jurisdiction to make decisions about pension entitlement. Chief Justice Duff emphasized his disagreement with the basis of the trial court's decision that "a decision by the Committee favourable or unfavourable to an applicant in the execution of their duties, after a proper consideration of the applicant's claim, is susceptible of review upon the merits by any court" (461). However, he added an important qualification. In his view, "it was the duty of the executive committee, upon application by the appellant for superannuation on the ground of ill health, to entertain his application and, after due consideration, to decide whether eligibility was established." Accordingly, "[i]f the Executive Committee refuses to entertain the application, or if they give a decision without having afforded the applicant a fair opportunity of supporting his claim, then, since the Corporation is responsible for the acts of its administrative organ, it may by the fault of that body be precluded from setting up this condition and the court may be in a position to enter upon an examination of the merits of the claim" (461–2). Chief Justice Duff concluded that the committee had failed to provide Mantha with a fair and bona fide opportunity to respond to the facts in the medical report (467). Like the Privy Council in *Lapointe* (although without citing that decision), he took the view that elementary principles of law required administrative bodies to give both sides a fair hearing when making decisions which involve "the civil rights of parties" (467). Since its executive committee had not provided Mantha with a fair hearing on the evidence against his claim, the city could not now set up the committee's decision as a bar to Mantha's action. The court accepted the trial judge's finding on the merits that Mantha was medically unfit for duty, and held that he was entitled to his pension.[46]

AN EMERGING CONTRACT THEORY OF PENSIONS

These cases show Canadian courts still searching for a coherent legal framework for understanding the legal nature of the pension relationship and the legal status of workplace pension plans. The courts had not entirely abandoned gift theory, and were careful to draw a distinction between procedural and substantive review of employer decisions about pension eligibility. But they were edging ever closer to a contract theory of pensions. As early as *Lapointe*, contract theory was explicitly argued, although ironically it was the Pension Society rather than the claimants who relied on contract principles to support its argument that Lapointe was bound by the term of the pension plan that left decision-making to the society's internal bodies. Ultimately, as we have seen, the Privy Council did not decide the case based on contract law; it characterized *Lapointe* as a trust case, and drew on principles of administrative law to conclude that the board of directors, as trustees, were required to conform to the rules of natural justice in deciding questions of pension entitlement. In *Mantha*, by contrast, contract theory essentially grounded the court's analysis. Without acknowledging the novelty of his conclusion, Chief Justice Duff held that the provisions of the pension plan constituted a binding agreement between the city and its employees "as terms of the engagements between the respondent corporation and its employees" (461). Later in the decision, he was even more explicit in emphasizing the contractual nature of the plan. He expressed his complete agreement that Mantha was bound by the provisions of the plan: "Where parties have agreed that their rights shall rest upon the condition that a given individual or body shall be satisfied that a certain state of facts exists, [the Code of Civil Procedures] does not enable the Superior Court to make a new contract between the parties and to declare their rights without regard to the contract and by reference solely to the court's own view of the facts"(465). He emphasized

52   Empty Promises

that, if the executive committee had followed fair procedure in making its decision, Mantha could not have come to court to challenge
that decision. But he saw the city as equally bound to fulfill its contractual obligation under the bylaw to give Mantha's claim appropriate consideration (466–8).

JUDICIAL RESISTANCE TO CONTRACT THEORY: THE SUCCESSION DUTY CASES

The Supreme Court's embrace of contract theory in *Mantha* was
unambiguous but understated, and contract law did not take over
immediately as the legal framework of choice for analyzing workplace pension claims. Canadian courts remained reluctant to abandon the old gift theory. Their stubborn commitment to the proposition
that workplace pensions were gratuitous and not contractual is
reflected in a series of cases decided in the 1940s and early 1950s.
These cases dealt with succession duties assessed by governments on
death benefits paid to survivors of employees who had been members
of workplace pension plans. Two of the most prominent addressed
the 1939 Bell Telephone plan. As we saw in Chapter 2, the 1939 Bell
plan represented a distinct change in approach from its progenitor,
the 1917 Bell plan, with the company now prepared to embrace,
albeit cautiously, a meaningful degree of liability to its employees.
Ironically, Bell's fundamental change in approach remained invisible
to the courts in these cases.

The first Bell case, *Williamson v Ontario (Treasurer)*,[47] reached the
courts in 1941. It involved the legal status of a death benefit paid
under the terms of Bell's 1939 pension plan to the widow of Robert
James Williamson, who had died in Bell's employ. The government of
Ontario sought to tax that benefit as part of Williamson's estate
under the terms of the *Succession Duty Act*, which included in the
estate "any annuity, income or other interest ... purchased, or in any
manner provided by the deceased either by himself alone or in con-
cert or by arrangement with any other person to the extent of the
beneficial interest accruing or arising by survivorship or otherwise,
on the death of the deceased."[48] The government argued that the
death benefit was a contractual benefit which was "part of the consideration for [Williamson's] services" (para. 12), and therefore fell
within the scope of the statute. Williamson's family resisted, arguing
that, under the terms of the plan, payment of the death benefit was
purely voluntary on Bell's part.

The government produced evidence of the 1939 changes to the Bell plan, which clearly bolstered the contract argument (para. 9). Despite the new language, which made explicit reference to "undertakings" on the part of the company, the court was not prepared to find that the plan established any contractual obligation to pay the benefits. The court conceded that, on its face, the company's undertaking "seems to amount to an offer or promise to the employees of the company to pay the benefits provided by the plan." As such, "if communicated to the employees and accepted by them expressly or impliedly, the prospective benefit might be looked upon as part of the consideration for their services, and, being a provision made by them, would come within section [10(b)] of the *Succession Duty Act*" (para. 12). The court insisted, however, that before an offer could become a contract, that offer had to be accepted. Since the government failed to produce evidence that Williamson was personally aware of the terms of the plan, the court concluded that it had failed to prove acceptance on his part. There was therefore no contract.

The absence of proof that the employer's offer had been accepted was not the only flaw the court identified in the government's case. In addition, it found language in the plan which it held to be incompatible with contractual commitment. It focused on the standard clause providing that plan administrators "may from time to time make changes in the Plan, and the Company may terminate the Plan, but such changes shall not affect the rights of any employee, without his consent, to any benefit or pension to which he may previously have become entitled thereunder" (para. 15).[49] In the court's view, the language of entitlement protected only pensions actually being paid out. With respect to active employees (and their surviving dependents), it found that the employer could retract its pension promises at any time. It found such a unilateral right to retract a promise "repugnant to the idea that the award and payment of the benefit are anything else but voluntary" (para. 15). Accordingly, the death benefit was held to be "a voluntary payment, a gift, or a compassionate allowance" (para. 15), and therefore not taxable as part of the Williamson estate.

Williamson was a decision of the Ontario Supreme Court applying the provincial *Succession Duties Act. McDougall v MNR*,[50] the second case involving the Bell plan, was a decision of the Exchequer Court of Canada some eight years later, this time applying the federal *Succession Duty Act*.[51] The question before the court was fundamentally the same as it had been in *Williamson*: was a death benefit paid to an employee's dependents taxable under the statute as part of the employee's estate? The taxing authorities had learned some lessons from the *Williamson* litigation, however, and were careful to place in evidence an admission that McDougall was aware of the terms of the plan. This meant that the government's claim could not be rejected, as it had been in *Williamson*, on the basis that McDougall had not "accepted" the employer's "offer" of a pension. To bolster the contractual nexus, the government produced evidence that, in 1939, when the company altered its pension plan to eliminate the gratuity clause, it had distributed a pamphlet to employees spelling out in clear non-legalistic language its intention to be bound by its pension and benefit promises (322–3).[52] The government's case was further strengthened by language in the federal statute that was broader than the Ontario statute applied in *Williamson*; the federal language swept in not only "an annuity purchased ... by the deceased," but also any "superannuation or pension benefits or allowances payable ... under any ... superannuation or pension fund."[53]

Despite these differences, the *McDougall* court, like the *Williamson* court, rejected the government's claim. The court held that a death benefit was not a "superannuation or pension benefit or allowance," and therefore was not caught by the express language of the statute. In addition, it followed the *Williamson* analysis in concluding that the death benefit was not "purchased" by the employee, because the employer had no contractual obligation to pay it. The court highlighted the unilateral nature of the plan: "The employees as such have had no part in its initiation or administration, nor were they consulted at any time in regard thereto, and there is no evidence that its terms were at any time the subject of collective bargaining between the Company and its employees" (317).[54] It also emphasized the company's unilateral right to terminate or amend the plan. In language virtually identical to that in *Williamson*, it held that a right of amendment or termination was incompatible with a contractual undertaking; such language "negative[d] the suggestion that the Company's undertaking in section 1 of the plan is part of the consideration for an employee's services" (320).[55]

Even if it had found contractual language in the plan, however, the court made it clear that it would have refused to find entitlement, based on a host of technical quibbles more characteristic of nineteenth- than of twentieth-century jurisprudence. It refused to consider the explanation of the plan provisions found in the employee pamphlet explaining the new plan, on the ground that there was no evidence that the pamphlet had been authorized by the Bell board of directors (323). In addition, it held that any attempt to enter into contractual arrangements about benefits would have been ultra vires in any event, because the company bylaws did not authorize the board to make binding benefit agreements with employees.[56] And, as a final nail in the coffin of the government's case, the court held that if the pension plan did create contractual obligations, those obligations would flow only between the company and McDougall; he was now dead, and his surviving spouse and other dependents would have been mere third-party beneficiaries with no right to enforce the contract (324). Accordingly, the court found that the death benefit was an entirely voluntary payment from Bell to McDougall's widow, and therefore non-taxable. Like the Ontario Supreme Court in *Williamson*, the Exchequer Court clearly saw little legal distinction between the old style of pension drafting, heavily laden with disclaimers of contractual liability, and the new style, in which employers took on obligations.[57]

THE COMMON LAW AT MID-CENTURY

The doggedly doctrinaire insistence in these mid-century cases that the benefits provided under pension plans are gifts and not rights may be accounted for in part by the fact that the cases were taxation cases, which invite a "strict constructionist" approach to governmental claims.[58] None involved a direct claim for a pension under the plans; in all cases, the employer had already paid up. It was the government that asserted contractual liability, with widows and orphans resisting the liability theory in order to avoid significant estate tax bills. The employers who drafted the plans played no role in the litigation. Had the context been different – had they had been faced with a sympathetic retiree or widow arrayed against a hard-nosed employer attempting to deny liability – the courts might well have been more willing to see the shifts in plan language as relevant to the issue of whether or not employees had enforceable rights.

Even accounting for the taxation context, however, these decisions reflect remarkable judicial resistance to the idea that employers might actually be required to pay promised benefits to their employees. While there is some evidence that courts were gradually warming to the notion that pension plans could be understood within a contractual framework, their instinctive hostility to pension claims made the contractual framework a double-edged sword for employees. The substitution of contract theory for gift theory held out the hope that employees might be able to assert enforceable claims to promised pensions, but the realities of power in the workplace meant that employers still wrote the terms on which those promises were made. Employers therefore enjoyed almost as much autonomy under contract theory as under gift theory to limit or completely abnegate any legal obligations their plans might appear to impose.

Some common-law judges, borrowing concepts from property law and trust law, were prepared to consider the possibility that claims to pensions might become "vested" as the absolute property of the employee even before retirement, depending on the context in which those claims arose and the language of the plans on which they were based. Others drew on both contract law and administrative law to impose procedural safeguards on pension decision-making. These approaches had the potential to correct obvious abuses. By the late 1930s, when the Supreme Court of Canada decided *Mantha*, that court was comfortable in locating procedural rights to fair pension decision-making within the framework of the contract of employment. However, as the succession duty cases illustrate, courts remained reluctant to confer substantive pension rights on employees unless they were thoroughly persuaded that employers intended to make enforceable commitments. The legal burden on those who sought to assert employer pension liability was a heavy one.

Up to the middle of the twentieth century, the courts dealt with employee pension claims by drawing on a grab bag of property, trust, administrative, and contract-law concepts which had left employers largely at liberty to shape workplace pension plans and employee pension rights in their own interests. If left to their own devices, they might have found a firmer foundation for employee pension rights in the common law. We will never know, however, because two important legislative developments in the second half of the twentieth century intervened to exert major influence on the legal construction of pension rights. These developments – the statutory regime for regulating workplace pension plans and the statutory framework for collective bargaining – had important potential to strengthen employee rights within the voluntary system. In the next two chapters, we set the common law aside and examine the extent to which these pieces of legislation were able to achieve that result.

4

Workplace Pensions and Statutory Regulation

INTRODUCTION

The labour-market forces that operated in Canada in the first half of the twentieth century produced workplace pension plans calibrated to meet the needs of employers, not employees. Plans were designed to pay benefits only to long-service employees, and normal turnover ensured that most employees did not qualify. Employer discretion over benefits meant that even long-service employees could not count on receiving a pension. As new methods of organizing work produced new managerial imperatives, employers began to design their plans to provide enhanced coverage and better benefit security. Employers began to make firmer pension promises, and courts began, very slowly, to develop legal theories of pension rights that would make employers accountable for those promises. But these legal theories did not disrupt the power of employers to frame their promises as they saw fit, hedged with qualifiers and conditions that most employees could never meet. Accordingly, they did not correct for the serious deficiencies of an employer-driven platform for the delivery of retirement income.

The 1960s marked a critical turning point in the legal history of workplace pension plans, with the emergence in Canada of pension standards legislation. The story of the many different pressures that produced that legislation is part of the larger story of the construction of Canada's three-pillar retirement income system, in which old-age security benefits, the Canada Pension Plan (CPP), and workplace pension plans all play a role. That story has been well and thoroughly told elsewhere.[1] My focus in this chapter is on the survival of workplace pension plans within that larger system, and on the role of statutory regulation as part of the compromise that ensured their survival. Statutory regulation improved pension adequacy, predictability, and security for those who belonged to pension plans, but at the same time impaired employer incentives to establish and maintain such plans in two ways: by limiting employer autonomy to design plans to meet their objectives, and by significantly increasing the cost of providing workplace pensions.

A REPORT CARD FROM THE MID-TWENTIETH CENTURY

Before embarking on an examination of pension standards regulation, it is helpful to take a close look at the strengths and weaknesses of mid-century workplace pension plans. In 1947, Canada's Dominion Bureau of Statistics conducted its first official survey of these plans.[2] That survey laid the groundwork for a series of more detailed government studies, subsequently published over the next few years in the Labour Gazette, examining coverage, types of benefits, vesting rights, and retirement policies imposed by employers as a quid pro quo for pensions.[3] While the data reported in these studies must be approached with some caution, particularly when used for comparative purposes,[4] the studies provide a useful snapshot of the system at mid-century, and help to explain why governments were persuaded that statutory regulation was necessary.

The mid-century studies reveal a workplace pension landscape considerably changed from the 1930s. The 1947 survey, which focused on industrial workplaces with fifteen or more employees, showed that, after stalling in the Depression, coverage rates were on the rise. Over 32 per cent of employees now belonged to pension plans,[5] compared to closer to 15 per cent in the 1930s at the time of the Queen's Study. Much of that growth had occurred during and immediately after the Second World War; some 70 per cent of the plans identified had been established since the late 1930s.[6] There continued to be an obvious correlation between workplace pensions and what we now call the "primary labour market"; the survey found that workers in stable industries and larger workplaces were much more likely to have coverage.[7] As in the 1930s, however, many employees in covered workplaces were not members of their employers' plans; the 1947 survey found that plans covered only about

60 per cent of employees on payroll.[8] This gap was largely attributable to exclusionary membership rules; most plans did not cover part-time, temporary or casual workers, many had lengthy waiting periods and/or age restrictions on membership, and some did not admit women employees.[9]

The studies also reveal that the old discretionary approach to benefits was giving way to models that permitted employees to accrue an entitlement to benefits through continued service – in other words, models that provided for some form of vesting. By the late 1940s, it was no longer rare for plans to acknowledge that employees who had accumulated sufficient service acquired a right to a pension that could not be taken away, even if they left the workplace prior to the normal date of retirement. A government survey conducted in the mid-1950s, which looked at pension plans in larger workplaces, found that 82 per cent of plans now acknowledged some vested rights – typically full vesting by age fifty for employees with twenty years of service.[10] A "substantial proportion" provided more-favourable vesting standards. While this was a significant advance on earlier approaches, which had at best permitted employees leaving prior to retirement to take their own contributions out of the plan, it still left many employees without pensions when they reached retirement age because their employment had terminated before their rights vested.

In mid-century Canada, pension plans were much more likely to be contributory than non-contributory, unlike the US, where non-contributory plans were still holding their own,[11] and some of the improvement in vesting practices may be accounted for simply by the increased incidence of contributory plans. In the early 1930s, Murray Latimer had found contributory plans more likely to provide some financial guarantee to employees, typically in the form of a right to withdraw employee contributions, but occasionally in the form of some version of vesting.[12] By mid-century, the trend to guarantees in contributory plans had accelerated. Almost invariably, they allowed a return of employee contributions (often with interest) for those who left the plan prior to retirement.[13] Over 90 per cent offered some form of vesting, compared with only one-third of non-contributory plans, although departing employees sacrificed vested rights if they elected to take a refund of contributions, as they frequently did.[14]

The dominant postwar benefit type remained the defined benefit.[15] Typically, plans used a "unit-benefit" formula, in which pensions were calculated by multiplying years of service (or years of plan membership) by a percentage of earnings. While some unit-benefit formulae averaged earnings over an entire career, more frequently the average was calculated over the last ten years of service.[16] An alternative to the unit-benefit formula was the flat-rate benefit, in which a fixed dollar amount was multiplied by years of credited service; the studies found flat-rate benefits more commonly associated with what they described as "negotiated plans."[17] It was not uncommon for newly established plans to provide credit for past service, usually at the employer's expense. Past-service credit could be expensive, but was convenient for employers who wanted their plans to pay immediate benefits high enough to be attractive to employees already nearing mandatory retirement age.[18]

Mandatory retirement continued to be central to employer pension objectives. Indeed, the *Labour Gazette* described provision "for the orderly retirement of the older worker" as "the basic purpose of a pension plan, from the employer's point of view."[19] On this issue, plan drafting styles had changed considerably since the 1930s. While earlier plans provided for a "normal" age of retirement, they often left retirement decisions to the discretion of the employer, without establishing a specific mandatory retirement age. By mid-century, more structured approaches to mandatory retirement had become the norm, and almost all plans imposed some form of mandatory retirement, although many expressly acknowledged employer discretion to permit employees to stay longer.[20] The typical age of mandatory retirement for men was now sixty-five, with women often forced to leave at age sixty.[21] Since both vesting rights and overall monthly benefits were almost always pegged to years of service, women forced to retire earlier were less likely to qualify for a pension; if they did qualify, their pensions would be smaller, because of shorter service.

These mid-century studies do not tell us how many Canadian employees actually got pensions when they retired, or what kind of pensions they got. However, they clearly reveal the many obstacles to achieving an adequate, predictable, and secure pension from a workplace plan. While coverage was expanding, many workers continued to be employed in workplaces without plans, and where there were plans, many workers did not have access to them. Rules on delayed vesting resulted in loss of pension credits for employees who changed jobs or left the workforce prior to reaching the normal retirement age. These results were not design flaws; they were clearly intended. The government study on "Vesting Provisions in Canadian Industrial

Pension Plans" emphasized that employers deliberately shaped their plans to impede employee turnover; indeed, this objective was ranked second only to mandatory retirement as a motivation for employers to establish pension plans. The study concluded that "[s]ecurity under industrial pensions ... is not readily available to the mobile worker."[22]

PENSIONS AND PUBLIC POLICY: THE WAR YEARS AND POSTWAR TAX POLICY

The considerable growth in workplace pension coverage revealed in the mid-century government studies can be accounted for in large part by changes in workplace organization. The wartime economic boom had nurtured the type of large manufacturing enterprise in which pension plans were most useful and attractive to employers.[23] An additional short-term factor was state intervention in the form of the wartime Excess Profits Tax. Imposed in the early 1940s by a federal government concerned about war profiteering, this tax was targeted at corporate profits that exceeded a pre-war base. Since the tax rate was a confiscatory 100 per cent, it provided a compelling incentive for employers to keep profits below that base. At the same time, military deployment created severe national labour shortages. Employers making war profits were both able and willing to pay more for labour, but by 1942 wage stabilization legislation prevented direct wage adjustments. To recruit and retain labour, employers turned to indirect compensation in the form of employee benefit plans. Workplace pension plans acquired new momentum.[24]

The studies also reveal significant improvement in the quality of pension benefits. This too can be accounted for by the combined impact of market forces and state intervention that altered the legal rules within which pension plans functioned. Changes in work organization to accommodate mass production – "Fordism" – impelled employers to provide more structured benefits and more guarantees to employees. Employer discretion nevertheless continued to be an important design feature of pension plans. The increasing numbers of these plans ultimately drew the attention of federal authorities. They were concerned about the potential for tax abuse lurking in a discretionary model in which employers could shelter contributions, as well as the investment income from those contributions, without any commitment that the funds would ultimately go towards employee pensions. In 1942, the minister of national revenue introduced an administrative requirement that plans must have ministerial approval before employers and plan members could take advantage of the deductions and exemptions provided under the *Income Tax Act*. In 1946 this requirement was formalized in legislation, and the ministry published its rules for obtaining approval in the first of two thin volumes between blue covers which became known as the *Blue Books*.[25] From 1942 to 1957, the *Blue Books* governed Canadian pension plans that were seeking tax relief.[26]

The *1946 Blue Book* established a number of rules aimed at ensuring that plans were bona fide retirement arrangements and not simply tax shelters for business owners, shareholders, and high-paid executives. To qualify for approval, plans were required to cover "employees" (as opposed to partners, officers, or shareholders: s.3).[27] They had to be "definite, continuing undertakings" (s.1), as opposed to ad hoc arrangements. Plans could be partly funded by employee contributions, but they could not be wholly employee-funded; employers must contribute as well (ss.6–7).[28] If plans were funded by trusts, those trusts must be actuarially sound, and investments within pension trusts were restricted to those available under the *Canadian and British Insurance Companies Act* (s.15).

One important target of the *Blue Books* was restrictive plan membership rules. While plans could establish entry requirements, the minimum age for membership could not be more than thirty-five years, and the maximum service requirement was ten years (s.3). Plan membership could be restricted to a particular "class" of employees (a term that was not defined), but the rules specified that "classes of employees could not be established on the basis of pay levels," nor could they "favour those receiving higher remuneration" (ss.3–4). Once a class was established, all employees within that class must be permitted to join. In a further effort to control favouritism, benefit formulae were required to be "equitable" and "not excessive" (s.4).[29] Some membership discrimination was expressly permitted; a plan that limited eligibility to full-time employees would be acceptable, and "[d]ifferent terms of eligibility will be permitted as between male and female employees" (s.4).[30]

The *Blue Books* also took aim at plan provisions that enabled employers to confiscate the pension credits and contributions of employees who left their employment prior to retirement age. Delayed vesting was a particular target. As a minimum standard, the *1946 Blue Book* required benefits to vest upon retirement (s.8), which meant that employees who met plan eligibility requirements at the time they retired could not be denied a pension. A higher standard was encouraged; if benefits under the plan did not meet a "50 and 20 rule" – vesting by fifty years of age with twenty years of service – the more onerous standard "must be substantiated by adequate reasons" before the plan would be approved (s.8). If plans were contributory, they were required to permit employees who departed prior to retirement to remove their own contributions from the plan, unless the plan provided for immediate vesting (ss.8, 12). The 1950 revision of the *Blue Book* tightened vesting requirements further by making the "50 and 20 rule" mandatory [s.10(a)].[31] If a plan was discontinued, all contributions from both employee and employer must vest immediately. In addition, "any surplus not apportioned must be distributed by an equitable formula to provide increased benefits for those employees then covered" (s.19). Interestingly, where plans were collectively bargained, the ministry did not enforce the minimum vesting standard. While no official rationale for this exception was offered, contemporary commentators speculated that a government seeking to promote plan coverage may have been reluctant to insist that negotiated plans be re-opened, and may have seen the involvement of a union as evidence that plan terms were satisfactory to employees, even if they did not meet government standards.[32]

STATE V MARKET, PART I: THE PLACE OF WORKPLACE PENSION PLANS IN A NATIONAL RETIREMENT INCOME SYSTEM

The rules reflected in the *Blue Books* were short-lived. By 1957, the *Blue Books* had vanished as a consequence of nagging doubts about the validity of using federal income-tax rules to establish pension standards within a constitutional system in which both social policy and employment are areas of jurisdiction claimed by the provinces.[33] Even under *Blue Book* standards, there continued to be significant problems with the quality and quantity of the pensions generated by workplace plans. Without those standards, there was serious concern that workplace plans would become even less effective. These concerns came sharply to the fore throughout the 1950s and early 1960s, as Canadian policy-makers took up the challenge of addressing the broad social problem of retirement income security.

At mid-century, that challenge was creating significant political pressures. Canada had been slower than many other developed countries to establish a comprehensive old-age income policy. The federal government's first tentative step in that direction, the voluntary government annuity program launched in 1908, had enjoyed only modest take-up among a Canadian working class with a very limited capacity for savings.[34] The federal *Old Age Pensions Act*,[35] introduced in 1927, filtered pension applications through a punitive means test, which was administered inconsistently by the provinces and left many worthy claimants without redress.[36] In the mid-1930s, the United States enacted its *Social Security Act of 1935* as an important weapon in its New Deal arsenal of economic measures to combat the Great Depression.[37] Canada had considered its own Depression-generated "New Deal," a federal social insurance package that would have included a contributory earnings-related supplementary pension plan.[38] However, its first legislative foray in this direction, an *Unemployment Insurance Act*, was ruled unconstitutional, on the basis that it regulated the employment contract and therefore belonged within provincial jurisdiction.[39] In consequence, the government abandoned plans for an earnings-based pension plan that would almost certainly suffer the same constitutional fate.

In the immediate postwar period, Canadian governments therefore found themselves with both a social and a political problem. Canada had no comprehensive retirement income policy, and no effective public pension instruments. At the same time, there was a considerable public appetite for economic security, and an expectation that the state would play a key role in providing social insurance.[40] There were some improvements in old-age benefits in the early 1950s,[41] but these did little to relieve the pressure for a contributory, earnings-based public pension plan on the US model, a plan that would generate benefits high enough to secure not just relief from poverty, but a comfortable and dignified retirement.[42] These pressures ultimately culminated in the mid-1960s in the emergence of Canada's three-pillar retirement income system. Most accounts of the evolution of this system focus on the social and political forces that generated its first two public pillars, the Old Age Security pension and the earnings-based contributory CPP. For our purposes, the more interesting question is how the workplace pension system survived as the core of the third pillar of private, tax-assisted retirement income instruments.

The answer lies at least in part in the intricacies of Canada's federal political system. By the late 1950s, a federal-provincial consensus had emerged that Canada needed a contributory earnings-based pension plan to supplement old-age security, and that state action would be required to establish such a plan. Within Canadian federalism, however, it was far from clear at which level of government the problem of designing and implementing such a plan should be tackled. While old-age security issues had been addressed primarily at the federal level over the years, federal assertion of jurisdiction was controversial. The 1908 federal annuity program had escaped contemporary constitutional challenge.[43] By the 1920s, however, the federal government was careful to involve the provinces in its means-tested old-age pension.[44] Before enacting new old-age security legislation in the 1950s, it showed even more caution, negotiating a narrowly worded constitutional amendment with the provinces that clarified federal authority to enact "laws in relation to old age pensions in Canada," but also acknowledged provincial paramountcy (i.e., priority) in the field.[45] Jurisdictional antennae were high in the discussions of the 1950s and 1960s, and there was consensus that, before a national contributory earnings-based pension plan could be implemented, another constitutional amendment would be required.[46] This constitutional uncertainty gave the provinces leverage they might not otherwise have had in shaping the national plan. Quebec used its leverage to establish its own provincial version of the Canada Pension Plan, the Quebec Pension Plan, which allowed that province to use plan contributions for provincial investment purposes.[47] Ontario used its leverage quite differently.

Ontario's key concern was to preserve a continuing and significant role for workplace pension plans. The province had carefully positioned itself for this struggle. In 1960, the Ontario government had appointed a Committee on Portable Pensions to examine problems in the workplace pension system. The committee's report confirmed the findings of the earlier federal studies that there was a significant pension coverage problem.[48] It also confirmed the presence within plans of a "high proportion of workers whose pension accumulations do not come to fruition."[49] The committee concluded that most contemporary pension plans left many workers without benefits because of delayed vesting rules, which forced them to abandon their pension credits if they did not stay in their jobs until they reached retirement age. This critical problem was labelled "lack of portability."[50] In its report, the committee characterized delayed vesting as "the principal obstacle to portability of pensions" (51).

Despite the numerous problems generated by existing employment-based plans, however, the committee did not recommend public pensions. It saw public pensions as depriving employers of an important human-resource management tool (4–5). In addition, and even more importantly, it feared the economic consequences of allowing pension funds to leave private control and fall under the aegis of a state agency with "monopoly power" over investment capital (10–13, 67–8). The committee's report frankly acknowledged that the system was in trouble, and that state intervention would be necessary to make workplace plans more responsive to the retirement-income needs of employees. It accepted minimum-standards regulation as inevitable. But it pointed to the negative effects that minimum-standards legislation could have within a voluntary pension system. It was impractical, the committee observed, to expect that, within a competitive marketplace, employers who offered pensions would take on the higher costs of improved pension standards, while other employers did not offer pensions at all (65–9). Its recommendation was that workplace pension plans should be made mandatory. The Ontario government responded positively to this recommendation. In a chapter in Canadian pension history that has now been almost forgotten, it enacted *The Pension Benefits Act, 1962–63*, which required employers in every workplace employing more than fifteen people to provide a pension plan.

Although this statute was passed in 1963, it was designed not to come into force until 1 January 1965.[51] This time lag allowed Ontario to go into the key phase of the federal-provincial negotiations for a Canada-wide public pension plan armed with a compulsory private solution as a backup if negotiations for a public plan failed. In those negotiations, Ontario's Premier John Robarts assumed the role of standard-bearer for private enterprise, taking up the mantra that private employment-based plans would bridge the gap between retirement income needs and public retirement benefits.[52] Speaking to the Canadian Pension Conference in 1963, Robarts argued that "[p]ublic plans provide a basic floor for everyone, but except in a socialist state no government pension system even attempts to provide for all the pension needs of all the people." He lauded the role of private pension funds as "a most important source of savings essential to our developing and capital-hungry country," and emphasized his government's commitment to an approach to retirement income policy in which "capital formation through pension funds [w]ould not be stunted."[53]

Ontario was not successful in blocking a public earnings-based pension plan altogether, if that had indeed been its goal. It was successful, however, in ensuring that benefits from the public plan were kept low. When the constitutional dust settled, the maximum CPP benefit was pegged at a level that replaced only 25 per cent of an average salary,[54] inadequate to maintain pre-retirement living standards for the average worker, even if he or she had a continuous full-time employment record throughout a working life. This compromise left ample room for private employment-based plans, a fact which both federal and provincial governments took care to highlight. Almost one-quarter of the federal *White Paper* that introduced the new CPP in 1964 was devoted to reassuring business that the public plan would have no negative impact on capital markets.[55] The paper emphasized that, above the benefit level provided by the CPP, "[income p]rotection ... will remain a matter of individual choice. That is to say, the individual – in association in many cases with his employer – will remain responsible for the saving by which, as incomes rise, more and more people can afford to make further provision for themselves if they so desire."[56] Content that the overall framework was one in which workplace plans would thrive, Ontario repealed its *Pension Benefits Act, 1962–63,* and Canada's experiment with mandatory workplace pension plans never got off the ground.

"FIRST GENERATION" REGULATORY STATUTES

While the accommodation reached between provincial and federal governments assured the survival of workplace pension plans, employers paid a price for that survival. The policy-making process had shone a harsh light on problems within the employment-based system, and it was widely acknowledged that government action in the form of pension standards legislation was an essential adjunct to the new three-pillar system. Although there was no binding agreement to regulate, it was understood that both levels of government would do so, and that efforts would be made to ensure a reasonable degree of uniformity across the country.[57] Ontario was poised to lead the way. Its 1965 statute *Pension Benefits Act, 1965 (PBA 1965)*[58] became the national model for first-generation regulatory statutes.[59]

The *PBA 1965* signalled a significant shift in the legal construction of workplace pensions. The statute unequivocally acknowledged employee entitlements, and placed some significant limits on the hitherto unrestricted power of employers to shape workplace plans to meet their business objectives. Its principal targets were the problems of "portability" (i.e., delayed vesting) and fund solvency in defined benefit plans, perceived as the two most serious obstacles to ensuring that employees got meaningful pensions from their plans.[60] The approach taken to defining employee entitlements was radical, in view of the common law's continued ambivalence on the question of whether contract law applied to pensions. The *PBA 1965* embedded minimum standards directly within the contract of employment, requiring that pension plans "contractually provide" for statutory minimum standards (ss.21–2). Although the *PBA 1965* established a Pension Commission of Ontario (PCO) to provide some degree of oversight over the new regulated system,[61] it set up no administrative apparatus for the enforcement of statutory entitlements. As contractual rights, the new standards were presumably intended to be enforced by civil action, an assumption reinforced by statutory provisions explicitly acknowledging a right of action for third-party beneficiaries with respect to death benefits provided by plans [s.17(2)].[62]

The first and most important standard for the protection of portability was a minimum vesting rule. The government chose a somewhat higher standard than the one reflected in the *Blue Books* – a "45 and 10 rule" instead of a "50 and 20 rule." To implement this standard, plans were required to "contractually provide" that a plan member who had reached the age of forty-five and had accumulated at least ten years of continuous service (or plan membership) was "entitled, upon termination of his employment prior to his attaining retirement age ... to a deferred life annuity commencing at his normal retirement age equal to the pension benefits ... provided in respect of service as an employee ... under the terms of the plan" [s.21(1)(a)]. To ensure that vested credits would ultimately be paid out as pensions, plans were required to "lock" them in; once credits had vested, plan members could enjoy their value only in the form of a deferred pension, to be claimed when they reached the normal age of retirement [s.21(1)(c)].[63] As further protection, plans were required to provide that benefits and annuities under the plan could not be "alienated or assigned" [s.21(1)(b)].[64]

With respect to the solvency and security of pension funds, first-generation statutes again took a stricter approach than the *Blue Books*, which had encouraged prefunding of pension promises, but had not made prefunding a requirement. Like the minimum standards for benefits, statutory solvency rules and investment standards were explicitly required to be "contractually provided" [s. 22(1)(a) and (c)]. Pension funds were now seen not simply as reserve funds to control cash flow and take the pressure off operating funds, but as guarantees that pension promises would and could be fulfilled. To that end, the PBA 1965 required employers to fund their plans through either trusts or insurance, in accordance with solvency levels prescribed by the regulations [s.22(1)(a)].[65] A very significant incentive to maintain solvent funds was the statutory requirement that, if plans terminated with insufficient funds, employers must "top up" the fund to the regulatory standard [s. 22(2)].[66] While no overriding fiduciary obligation was imposed, the Act placed restrictions on the investment and use of pension funds; administrators must invest in accordance with the federal prudential rules applicable to insurance companies.[67] Conflict-of-interest rules were imposed to ensure that employers did not misuse pension funds.[68] In addition, plans were required to provide that each plan member would be given basic plan information, in the form of "a written explanation ... of the terms and conditions of the plan and amendments thereto applicable to him, together with an explanation of the rights and duties of the employer with reference to the benefits available to him under the terms of the plan" [s.22(1)(b)].

CONTINUING PROBLEMS:
THE GREAT PENSION DEBATE

The compromise that had produced the CPP and the first generation of regulatory statutes plugged some of the holes in Canada's retirement income system. Nevertheless, serious deficiencies remained. With CPP benefits pegged at very modest levels, the continuing gap between pension income and the retirement income needs of most Canadians made a second round of pension reform almost inevitable. In the first reform round, federal-provincial conflicts had diverted much of the public attention from underlying differences in political philosophy about the legitimate objectives of national retirement income policy and the role of the state in implementing that policy (although those differences had important influence on the shape of the ultimate compromise). Between the mid-1970s and the mid-1980s, those differences erupted, and fuelled a national policy debate that engaged business, labour, and civil society, in addition to governments at the federal and provincial level. This protracted discussion and the many reports and studies that it generated became known as the Great Pension Debate.

The labour movement has been universally credited with initiating the Great Pension Debate by launching a national campaign in 1975 for a major expansion of the CPP.[69] By that point in the evolution of the workplace pension system, Canada's trade unions had been engaged in collective bargaining over pensions for almost a quarter-century.[70] However, their experience at the bargaining table had taught them some hard lessons about the utility of collective bargaining as a mechanism for generating adequate, predictable, and secure retirement income. To borrow the words of sociologists John Myles and Les Teichroew, unions had learned "that, dollar for dollar, the public system and especially the CPP provided a superior product to private sector alternatives."[71] Unconvinced that either more bargaining or more pension standards regulation could solve the problems inherent in a workplace-based system, labour sought a collective public solution. In their support for public pension expansion, unions were joined by feminists, church groups, and other anti-poverty activists. Equally keen participants on the other side of the debate included the business community and a vociferous private pension industry, with important territory to defend in keeping the CPP small and private pensions free from increased regulation.[72]

A 1982 federal *Green Paper*, entitled *Better Pensions for Canadians*, laid out a number of the key issues for a new round of pension reform.[73] Most prominent was the continuing problem of coverage. Coverage had improved since the 1960s, although first-round reform had not addressed it. By 1970, workplace pension plans covered 42 per cent of employed workers, and by 1978 that figure had risen to almost 48 per cent, according to the *Green Paper*. However, growth had stalled, and by 1980 it had dropped marginally (19).[74] Exclusionary membership rules continued to leave employees without plan membership, even where there was a pension plan in their workplace (31). Where coverage did exist, the *Green Paper* identified key quality shortcomings which reduced the value of that coverage: "Point-in-time coverage does not take into account whether the pensions being accrued will be forfeited due to inadequate vesting rules, or if vested, whether they will retain a reasonable value in the face of inflation. They make no distinction between generous pension plans and those with poor benefits ... They also do not indicate the

extent of adequacy of survivor pensions" (19). The *Green Paper* estimated that "over half of middle-income couples and individuals will,
over their working careers, be unable to build up employer-sponsored
pensions, with adequate inflation protection and survivor benefits, to
replace more than 10% of pre-retirement earnings" (19).

In addition, a variety of operational and structural features of
workplace pension plans had serious implications for gender equality.
In the first round of pension reform, scant attention had been paid
to how workplace plans affected women as workers; the focus had
been on women as dependent homemakers.[75] As women surged into
the workforce in the late 1960s and early 1970s,[76] policy-makers
could no longer ignore gender issues. But Canada's retirement income
system had not been designed with women in mind; its basis was
the assumption that workers inhabited male-breadwinner families
in which women were either dependent unpaid caregivers or secondary wage-earners. A search for remedies for gender pension equality
within a system based on rewards for market work forced policy-
makers to grapple with fundamental labour-market and social
inequalities, since, as one federal parliamentary committee succinctly
put it, "women's work and the patterns of their working lives are not
the same as those of men."[77]

Task forces and commissions debating the gender issue did not agree
on whether women's pension inequality could best be addressed by
conceptualizing the family as an economic partnership in which
"marriage would be explicitly recognized in plan design" and provision for survivor benefits and division of pension credits on marriage breakdown would be strengthened,[78] or whether the "family
approach" and survivors' benefits were outmoded relics of an obsolete male-breadwinner world.[79] The *Green Paper* enumerated a range
of gendered concerns within both public and private plans: workers
who left the labour force to raise children lost opportunities to accrue
retirement benefits (14); homemakers were treated as dependents
within pension plans and did not have the opportunity to accrue
their own pensions (14–15); life annuities were more expensive for
women because sex-based annuity pricing took account of the greater
longevity of women (14); and women were more seriously affected
by the impact of inflation on their benefits because they lived longer
(42). The paper singled out workplace plans as particularly ineffective at delivering benefits to women; women constituted only about
30 per cent of workplace pension-plan members (6), and the general

frailties of the system hit women harder than men, because of their work patterns, their higher turnover rates, and the failure of plans to provide adequate survivor benefits or division of pension credits on marriage breakdown (13).

STATE V MARKET, PART II:
THE MARKET WINS AGAIN

The location of the boundary between state and market in the provision of retirement income had been only the subtext of the debate in the first round of pension reform. It was now expressly identified by the *Green Paper* as a core issue for the Great Pension Debate. The *Green Paper* candidly acknowledged that maintaining space for private pension instruments was an important design feature of the original three-pillar system of the 1960s (17–23, 34–9). A change in this foundational choice was never seriously on the table. Although an increase in CPP benefits was listed as one option for consideration, the *Green Paper* admonished that "any increase should still leave room for employer-sponsored plans and private savings" (59). The paper highlighted the difficult economic context within which the debate was taking place, and identified as its "first priority" the need "to restore the health of the Canadian economy to its full vigour" (iii). It stressed that whatever decisions were made on pension policy, "the private sector must continue to be the primary engine of growth" (59). It emphasized the government's commitment to "an appropriate balance," an unspecified but nevertheless crucial equilibrium between "public pensions and employer-sponsored plans, between universal mandatory pensions and the personal responsibility of Canadians to provide for their individual retirement goals" (2–3), and "between mandatory programs and voluntary arrangements" (59).

Influential voices from the business community urged a continuing role for the employment-based pension system. While the business lobby continued to value pension plans as a human-resource management tool, by the 1980s this concern now came a distant second to its more central preoccupation – the role of the private sector in the accumulation and control of pension funds. Between the 1960s and the 1980s, both pension funds and their importance in the Canadian economy had increased in magnitude, in part as a result of the stringent plan-funding standards imposed by the first round of pension reform. By the time the Great Pension Debate moved into high gear, pension funds were dominant sources of investment capital.[80] Business groups saw any expanded role for public pensions as a threat both to the continued accumulation of this capital pool, and its continued control by the private sector. A *sine qua non* of any pension reform was that pension funds should not be shifted into the hands of government.[81]

The government clearly took these business concerns seriously. In weighing the pros and cons of expanding public pensions, the *Green Paper* reported that "the main criticism leveled at a public sector approach relates to its impact on investments and capital markets" (38). Weighed against that criticism were the reports and recommendations of the many task forces and commissions studying the workplace pension system over the span of the Great Pension Debate, which had been virtually unanimous in declaring that the current workplace-based system would not and could not provide adequate, predictable, and secure retirement income.[82] In the teeth of this expert consensus, the 1984 federal *White Paper, Action Plan for Pension Reform: Building Better Pensions for Canadians*,[83] nevertheless declared the market side of the debate the winner. The *White Paper* made some concrete commitments to gender equality in private plans, including mandatory survivor benefits, mandatory credit splitting on marriage breakdown, and a prohibition against sex-discriminatory benefits (7–8). However, it rejected an expansion of the CPP. It characterized its status quo approach to the division of labour between public and private pensions as "a balanced package designed to improve public pension plans while ensuring that employer-sponsored plans and voluntary savings continue to be a vital part of the Canadian retirement income system" (18).

"SECOND GENERATION" REGULATORY STATUTES

The *White Paper* committed the federal government to improvements in its own pension standards for federally regulated workplace plans, and expressed the hope that the provinces too would apply a similar supplementary dose of regulatory "fixes." Most jurisdictions responded with second-generation regulatory statutes. While the federal government moved first to enact its *Pension Benefits Standards Act, 1985*,[84] as with first-generation statutes it was the Ontario statute, the *Pension Benefits Act, 1987* (*PBA 1987*), that once again became the model for most other provinces.[85]

Unlike its predecessor, which had embedded statutory rights in the employment contract, the PBA 1987 took a more "public law" approach to constructing pension rights; minimum standards now took their force directly from the statute. The Act set out a closed list of persons or entities permitted to assume the role of plan administrator [s.8(1)].[86] It imposed detailed statutory duties on administrators, including the duty to "ensure that the pension plan and the pension fund are administered in accordance with [the] Act and the regulations" (ss.20–3). While administrators were given front-line responsibility for delivering statutory rights to plan members, the Act established a complex regulatory apparatus for the enforcement of statutory rights. The Superintendent of Pensions was now assigned a more active role in supervising plan administrators, with the Pension Commission of Ontario now constituted as both a "court of appeal" from the superintendent's decisions (ss.88–93),[87] and a "trial court" on issues like surplus extraction from pension funds (ss.79–80). Second-generation statutes left employers with a unilateral right to amend their plans, but spelled out an important limitation on that right that had been at best only implicit in first-generation statutes: plan amendments could not take away already-accrued benefits (s.14).[88] The new statutes also enhanced disclosure requirements, requiring employers to share more information about plans and benefits with plan members.

On the critical issue of plan coverage, first-generation statutes had said nothing. Second-generation statutes were equally silent where employers did not choose to establish a pension plan at all. Where plans existed, however, second-generation statutes made serious efforts to broaden coverage by enacting mandatory membership-eligibility rules. The PBA 1987 prohibited waiting periods for plan membership of longer than two years [s.32(2)]. Hearkening back to the old *Blue Books*, it required that, where employers established a plan for a "class of employees," all members of that class must be eligible for membership [s.32(1)]. In addition, it required employers to provide coverage for part-time employees that mirrored coverage for full-time employees of the same "class" [s.32(3)].[89] The Act provided little guidance, however, on what constituted a "class," leaving the door open for restrictive interpretations that permitted the exclusion of employees with less than permanent attachment to the workforce.[90]

As signalled by the *White Paper*, the PBA 1987 addressed a variety of issues with impact on gender equality. The new statute contained a general prohibition against sex discrimination in contributions, benefits, and conditions of eligibility for plan membership [s.53(1)].[91] The Act also mandated that plans provide "joint and survivor" benefits, with a minimum 60 per cent survivor benefit that continued even if the spouse remarried [ss.45(1), 48(1)],[92] a significant departure from the older gendered concept of survivor pensions as "dependency insurance." The *PBA 1987* deviated from the *White Paper*'s approach of mandatory pension credit-splitting between spouses by leaving the value of a pension to be dealt with as part of the overall division of matrimonial property on separation or divorce. If parties had agreed to divide pension credits, the *PBA 1987* required plan administrators to give effect to such "domestic contracts," subject to the statutory limitation that a non-member spouse could not receive more than half the value of the pension, and could begin to receive a payout only on the member's actual or normal date of retirement (s.52). Spousal rights were acknowledged for both married and common-law partners (provided they were of the opposite sex).[93] The *PBA 1987* ducked the controversial and potentially expensive issue of inflation protection through the peculiar expedient of mandating indexation in accordance with a "prescribed" formula, but providing that the formula would only come into effect by statutory amendment. No formula was ever prescribed, and mandatory indexation never became operative (s.54).[94]

To enhance pension security, the *PBA 1987* imposed general standards of care on administrators and other fiduciaries with respect to both fund and plan administration (s.23). The Act strengthened funding standards by requiring plans to provide funding sufficient to pay all benefits. Accompanying regulations now required plans to meet not one, but two, funding benchmarks: a "going concern" standard and a "solvency" standard.[95] Employers were required to "top up" the funding for plans that were being wound up to a level sufficient to pay all vested benefits [s.76 (1)(b)];[96] the former rules had required a top-up only to statutory funding standards, which did not always meet the need. The Act also created "deemed trusts" for unremitted pension contributions, and mandated a Pension Benefits Guarantee Fund, which would ensure payment of the first $1,000 per month of pension benefits if a pension plan became insolvent and was unable to meet claims for benefits (s.58, ss.83–7). For the first time, the *PBA 1987* directly addressed pension-fund surpluses. Employers were now prohibited from removing surplus funds from a plan without the consent of the regulator, and the statute placed stringent restrictions on the circumstances under which regulatory consent would be granted (ss.79–80).[97]

The PBA 1987 also enhanced employee entitlements in a variety of ways. It went much farther than its predecessor in increasing the basic vesting standard, replacing the old "45 and 10 rule" with a "0 and 2 rule": benefits vested after a maximum of two years of plan membership, with no age restriction (s.38).[98] The new statute required employers to return all contributions, with interest, to plan members who left employment before their pension rights vested [s.64(4)], an issue on which the prior statute had been silent. With respect to vested pension credits, plans were required to offer departing members three "transfer" options: a deferred annuity on reaching retirement age, a right to transfer the commuted value of the credits to another employer's plan (provided that the new plan agreed to the transfer), or the right to deposit the commuted value in an individual locked-in account held by a financial institution (s.43).[99] Plan members who left their employment could also take their pensions early in the form of a reduced early retirement benefit any time within ten years of the normal retirement age provided by their plan [ss.42(2)–(5)]. Since most plans established a normal retirement age of sixty-five, this meant that employees could retire on pension any time after reaching age fifty-five (s.42).

In addition to enhanced vesting rights, the PBA 1987 created three brand-new rights for employees. The first was a relatively straightforward, but potentially expensive, death benefit, payable to the surviving spouses or beneficiaries of an employee who died prior to retirement; its value was equal to the commuted value of the employee's pension [s.49(6)].[100] The second was more complex. Known as the "50-per-cent rule," it required that employer contributions account for at least 50 per cent of the commuted value of the pension at the time a member left the plan. The new rule had a significant impact on contributory defined benefit plans which did not fix the employer's contribution, but simply required the employer to maintain the fund at a level sufficient to pay promised benefits. Under standard actuarial practice, the annual cost of funding such benefits was significantly lower for younger employees than for older employees; employees in contributory plans essentially paid for their own pensions in the early years of plan membership, since their own contributions covered all or most of the total cost of the benefit. If employees left the plan early, the value of their vested credits sometimes amounted to less than their own contributions.[101] Under the "50-per-cent rule," if the employee's contribution exceeded half the commuted value of vested benefits, the employee was entitled to a lump-sum refund equal to the excess [ss.40(3)–(6)].[102] An additional, complex new benefit, required by the Ontario statute but not replicated in most other provinces, was a "grow-in" right, which enhanced the benefit entitlements of older employees in situations where they were affected by plan windups. "Grow in" operated by accelerating the employee's right to receive unreduced early retirement benefits if her individual age and service at the time of the windup equalled at least fifty-five, even if she was not entitled to early retirement benefits under the terms of the plan (s. 75).[103] This new right had the potential to be expensive for employers who terminated their plans or restructured their operations in ways that triggered partial windups affecting older employees. It also increased costs in ongoing plans, since the potential liability for grow-in benefits had to be taken into account in solvency valuations.

THE COSTS AND BENEFITS OF REGULATION

The new regulatory statutes created valuable rights for employees and provided an important measure of security for those rights. In creating value for employees, however, the statutes imposed significant new costs on employers at the same time as they imposed limitations on the ability of employers to shape their pension plans to their business needs. They unquestionably altered the cost-benefit calculus that had previously driven employer pension decision-making. A foreseeable – indeed inevitable – consequence was that employers would reconsider decisions about the value of continued pension provision. If left to their own devices, it was entirely predictable that employers would seek cost savings within their plans. They would reduce the value of benefit formulae for future benefit accumulations within defined benefit plans. They would switch from defined benefit plans to defined contribution plans. They would eliminate ancillary benefits like early-retirement incentives. If and when they determined that the ratio of costs to benefits no longer made pension provision a good business decision, they would shut down their plans altogether.

Governments could have chosen to intervene by statute and prohibit employers from taking such steps. That could not be done, however, without interfering with the foundational principle of the system: that workplace pension provision was voluntary. Canadian governments were not prepared to do that. They could also, within the context of voluntarism, have chosen to regulate to give employees more power within the pension relationship, perhaps by requiring employers to negotiate before making material changes, or legislating forms of joint governance. They were not prepared to do that either; like voluntarism, employer control was sacrosanct. While first-generation statutes constructed pension rights as contract rights, they essentially recognized only one contracting party, the employer. Second-generation statutes did little better at giving plan members meaningful leverage as parties to the pension contract. The *PBA 1987* acknowledged the right of plan members and former members to establish pension "advisory committees," but imposed no obligation on the employer to consult them or to take their "advice" (s.25).[104] Despite recognizing the potential for conflict of interest when employers became plan administrators [s.23(4)], the *PBA 1987* left employers free to assume that role [s.8(1)(a)]. As we shall see in subsequent chapters, employers used the freedom accorded by the legislation to pursue aggressive strategies to gain access to surplus pension funds, to draw on pension funds to cut administrative costs, to convert plans from defined benefit to less costly (and less valuable) defined contribution plans, and to shut down plans altogether.

In Chapters 6 and 7, we will examine how courts and tribunals responded to efforts by employees to use the legal tools available both at common law and in regulatory statutes to combat employer initiatives that undermined pension value for employees. Before doing so, however, let us turn to an important topic on which both generations of regulatory statutes were curiously silent: the role of unions and collective bargaining in shaping workplace pension plans and employee pension rights.

5

Pensions in the Unionized Workplace

UNIONIZATION AND PENSIONS IN CANADA

Unions in the US were initially suspicious of workplace pension plans.[1] In the struggle between capital and labour for power and control in the workplace, unions saw pension plans as weapons in capital's arsenal. Writing early in the twentieth century, lawyer Louis Brandeis called pensionable employment the "new peonage,"[2] and later critics coined the term "industrial feudalism" to describe workplace practices like pension plans that were designed to bind workers to their employers and impede their mobility in the labour market.[3] While early union attitudes to workplace pension plans have not been studied as closely in Canada as in the US, given the parallels in the labour histories of the two countries, it is likely that Canadian unions shared the suspicion of their US union brethren. Unions nevertheless saw few alternatives to workplace plans for addressing the urgent social problem of income in old age for workers and their families. Experiments with union-sponsored welfare plans funded by member contributions proved uneconomic, and few such plans survived the Great Depression.[4] Public pensions were an attractive option, but existing public benefits were inadequate to provide a comfortable and dignified retirement. In a political climate in which public pensions were unlikely to be expanded, collective bargaining for workplace-based pensions was the logical next step.

Early pension bargaining in the US was fractious, and strikes over pension and benefit issues accounted for more than one-quarter of all US strikes in 1949.[5] By the early 1950s, however, pension bargaining in that country had fallen into a pattern in which unions focused their bargaining efforts on benefit increases rather than power-sharing in pension governance, and plans in unionized work-places did not differ greatly in their general contours from plans already in place prior to collective bargaining.[6] As labour economist Teresa Ghilarducci put it, "the bones of the pension plans in each industry were ... drawn from skeletons of preexisting employer plans."[7] Collective bargaining put some meat on those bones, but in general, employers remained in firm control of key pension decision-making, untrammelled by collectively bargained obligations.

Collective bargaining came somewhat later to Canada than to the US; while the US formalized collective bargaining in its 1935 *National Labor Relations Act* (*NLRA*, often called the *Wagner Act*), Canada did not get its first modern collective bargaining statute until 1948.[8] There is little evidence that unions were involved in obtaining pension coverage to any significant degree in Canada before that time.[9] Once statute-sanctioned collective bargaining was in place, however, Canadian unions became almost immediately engaged with pension issues. In 1949, the *Labour Gazette* reported that "[s]everal CIO unions, both in Canada and the United States, notably the United Automobile Workers, have publicly announced their intention of seeking pension plans through collective bargaining."[10] By 1950, Canada had on record its first plan to result from collective bargaining. That plan arose out of negotiations between the United Automobile Workers of America and the Ford Motor Company of Canada, and was modelled roughly on plans Ford had already implemented for unionized workers in the US.[11] By the mid-1950s, the *Labour Gazette*, which had previously reported on unilateral employer pension initiatives, had begun to report regularly on pension bargaining.[12] Pensions were high on the agenda of the newly formed Canadian Labour Congress (CLC). Reporting to the second CLC Constitutional Convention in 1958, the Congress's Social Security Committee urged pension standards that included full and immediate vesting, adequate and guaranteed benefits, transferability of pension credits, stable and regulated funding, transparency of plan information, and "adequate union representation in the administra-tion and review of such plans."[13]

THE IMPACT OF COLLECTIVE BARGAINING ON PENSION QUANTITY AND QUALITY

It is not easy to assess the direct impact of collective bargaining on Canadian pension plans. There is a long and close correlation between union density and pension coverage;[14] unionized employees are much more likely to belong to pension plans than non-unionized employees.[15] Correlation is not causation, however, and although unionization and workplace pension plans enjoyed parallel growth in Canada, evidence of the direct impact of unionization on workplace pensions is far from clear. Pension plans were well established in many sectors of the economy prior to the introduction of formal collective bargaining. This is most obvious in the public sector, an important seedbed for pensions. While the public sector is now heavily unionized, unions did not obtain bargaining rights in many public sector workplaces until the 1970s, by which time pension plans had been long entrenched.[16] In other unionized workplaces, pension plans coexisted with collective bargaining, but the plans themselves did not always come to the bargaining table and often remained independent of collective agreements. The densely pensioned railway sector is an important example. It was a site of vigorous union activity for decades before the introduction of formal collective bargaining legislation,[17] but its pension plans were clearly employer-instigated, and as late as the 1960s, railway unions complained that their employers steadfastly refused to engage in pension bargaining.[18]

There was considerable growth in pension coverage in the third quarter of the twentieth century, at the same time that union density was increasing.[19] Canadian surveys conducted in the 1960s found that pension coverage had risen from 32 per cent in 1947 to 38 per cent in 1965.[20] The extent to which collective bargaining accounts for that growth is difficult to verify. Writing in 1964, Gordon Milling, a former research director for the Ontario Federation of Labour, acknowledged that, while "the labour movement [cannot] take credit for inventing pensions in the first place ... it is probably fair to say that bargaining pressure is responsible for a major share of the recent expansion of industrial pension plans – from one and a quarter million members to about two million in the past ten years."[21] The conclusions of Ontario's Royal Commission on the Status of Pensions suggest that this claim should not be accepted uncritically; examining growth in plan membership between 1960 and the late 1970s, the commission found much of that growth accounted for by increased employment in public sector workplaces,[22] where the effect of unions would be weaker, because of legal rules that limited collective bargaining over pension rights.

If it is difficult to measure the impact of unionization on pension quantity, it is even more difficult to assess its impact on pension quality, since collective bargaining and pension standards legislation operated largely in tandem. Government surveys of the 1960s give us a snapshot of workplace pension plans in the period immediately predating the introduction of first-generation regulatory statutes.[23] The studies reported modest progress in vesting standards. In the early 1950s, 82 per cent of plans offered at least some level of vesting;[24] by 1965, that number was over 96 per cent, although most plans still required ten to twenty years of service prior to vesting.[25] Since the survey data of the 1960s does not distinguish between union and non-union plans, however, it is not possible to assess the relationship between improved vesting standards and collective bargaining. Earlier survey data had suggested that vesting standards might be *worse* in plans in unionized workplaces,[26] a difference possibly accounted for in part by the fact that the minimum vesting standards of the *Blue Books* had not been applied to collectively bargained plans.

With respect to adequacy of benefits, the 1965 survey found defined benefit plans growing in popularity. By 1965, over 75 per cent of plan members belonged to such plans, while "money purchase plans [defined contribution plans] continued to lose ground."[27] The survey also reported, however, that when it came time to collect benefits, "less than one third of retired plan members received pensions in excess of 50 per cent of their annual earnings at retirement, with pensions for most of this group ranging between 50 per cent and 70 per cent of such earnings; and for over half, the pensions ranged between 20 per cent and 50 per cent of final earnings."[28] In the absence of earlier Canadian data, we cannot assess whether collective bargaining had a positive impact on these benefit levels. A 1960 US study speculated that collective bargaining had probably not significantly improved benefit levels. It found that pensions replacing 50 per cent of pre-retirement income were the norm both before and after the introduction of collective bargaining in that country.[29]

Despite the CLC's call for "more adequate union representation in the administration and review" of workplace pension plans, this feature was conspicuously absent from plan changes negotiated by unions over this period. There is little evidence of union attempts to bargain for joint governance or power-sharing arrangements over fundamental plan decisions. With few exceptions, employers continued to maintain control over both the establishment and the administration of their plans.

COLLECTIVE BARGAINING AND THE REGULATORY FRAMEWORK FOR PENSIONS

The legal framework within which unions function and the way that framework was interpreted and applied to workplace pensions is undoubtedly a factor in the failure of collective bargaining to transform the Canadian pension landscape. Before moving directly to an examination of that framework, however, it is useful to consider how the role of unions and collective bargaining was addressed in pension statutes. Although first-generation statutes erected their conception of employee pension rights on the platform of the employment contract, they were almost completely silent on the possibility that there could be more than one contracting party directly involved in establishing and administering a pension plan. The premise of Ontario's *PBA 1965* was that employers made all key decisions; it imposed obligations in connection with registration and administration only on employers. Most other jurisdictions followed Ontario in assuming exclusive employer control. The Quebec *Supplemental Pensions Act* stood alone in imposing a joint obligation on "the parties to a collective labour agreement containing provisions relating to a supplemental [workplace] plan existing at the time of the coming into force of this act" to file information and a copy of the plan with the regulator.[30]

In the consultations and discussions of the Great Pension Debate, the labour movement lobbied for change. In its 1982 manifesto, *The CLC Proposal for Pension Reform*, the Canadian Labour Congress sought increased statutory recognition for collective bargaining as a legitimate mechanism for establishing and amending pension plans, as well as status for unions in the administration of plans and funds. It pointed out that "a central element in the reality of employer-employee relations at many places of employment where workers are covered by private pensions is that workers are represented by a trade union and their relationship with their employer is defined by collective bargaining."[31] However, "both the law and the practice of employer-employee relations has tended to deal with private pension plans as if they belonged to employers" (148–50). To patch the hole in the regulatory framework, the CLC called for statutes to spell out clearly that pensions fell within the scope of bargaining, and to ensure that, where there was a bargaining agent, collective bargaining would be the mechanism for the introduction or amendment of a plan. The CLC insisted that workers had a right to participate in the

administration of pension plans and pension trusts, and in all disputes about whether plans conform to regulatory requirements. It
also sought broader information rights for employees and their bargaining agents, and an explicit role for unions in negotiating benefit
improvements on behalf of retirees (150).

This CLC manifesto had little impact on reform outcomes. Second-
generation statutes were almost as silent as the first on the role of
unions.[32] The PBA 1987 indirectly acknowledged the representative
role of trade unions by permitting plans established by collective
agreements (or trust agreements) to contract out of certain minimum
standards established by the Act, including the general requirement
that plan amendments could not reduce already-accrued benefits,
and the more specific requirement that employers top up the funds
in such plans when they fell below specified funding standards
[ss.14(2)–(3)]. In general, however, where plan members had rights,
they were expected to exercise those rights as individuals,[33] and
unions got no assistance from these statutes in establishing their
authority to represent employees in bargaining over the terms of the
pension contract.

The source of union authority to bargain over pensions was the
collective bargaining statutes that became ubiquitous in Canadian
jurisdictions after 1948. As we shall see, collective-bargaining statutes brought both good news and bad news for unions. While they
acknowledged the right of unions to place pensions and pension
issues on the bargaining table, they provided few effective tools that
unions could use to force employers to cede any part of their unilateral control over key pension decisions.

PENSIONS AND THE SCOPE OF BARGAINING

The foundation for the relationship between collective bargaining
and pension rights in Canada was first laid in the US, where pension
bargaining got an earlier start. By the mid-1940s, US unions had
commenced in earnest to use the NLRA to engage employers in bargaining about pension plans.[34] When they brought pension issues to
the table, however, they met forceful resistance from employers, who
sought amendments to the NLRA to exclude all benefit plans from
the scope of the Act. When these lobbying efforts failed,[35] employers
continued the battle for control in the labour tribunals and the courts,
claiming that all aspects of the establishment and administration of

workplace pension plans were integral to the management function, and therefore did not fall within the scope of mandatory bargaining under the NLRA. In 1948, that issue came before the National Labor Relations Board (NLRB) in the celebrated case of *Inland Steel*.[36]

The *Inland Steel* dispute crystallized over the fact that the employer had made unilateral amendments to the pension plan without bargaining with the union, and had subsequently refused to submit to arbitration over a grievance challenging the mandatory retirement of a number of employees under the plan.[37] The company defended its conduct by arguing that a workplace pension plan, including the establishment of a retirement age, was inherently a matter of management prerogative.[38] In addition, it argued that because pension plans were complex, technical, long-term arrangements, which cut across bargaining-unit boundaries, they could not realistically be addressed through short-term agreements negotiated for single bargaining units.[39] Finally, the company insisted that pensions, like bonuses, were gifts, not rights; they were voluntary payments and therefore not matters for bargaining.[40]

The NLRA required employers to bargain over "wages" and "other conditions of employment." The legal question was whether pension issues were encompassed by these terms. The NLRB held that pension benefits were "wages," and the age of mandatory retirement was a "condition of employment," bringing pension plans well within the scope of mandatory bargaining. As the board put it, a workplace pension "provides a desirable form of insurance annuity which employees could otherwise obtain only by creating a reserve out of their current money wages or by purchasing similar protection on the open market." Therefore "the [employer's] monetary contribution to the pension plan constitutes an economic enhancement of the employee's money wages." It found "an inseparable nexus between an employee's current compensation and his future pension benefits."[41] The Court of Appeal upheld this decision without definitively resolving the question of whether pension benefits were "wages." It concurred that pensions were a mandatory subject of bargaining, but grounded that concurrence on the less controversial ground that pension plans were "conditions of employment."[42] The employer's argument that pensions were gifts was peremptorily dismissed as "far-fetched."[43] The appeal court took more seriously than the NLRB the employer's argument that pensions were not bargainable, because the pension plan spanned multiple bargaining units. Ultimately it concluded, however, that the scope of mandatory bargaining could not depend on bargaining-unit structures in individual workplaces. While multiple bargaining units might raise practical complications for bargaining, these complications were not material to the fundamental issue of whether pensions were "conditions of employment."[44]

The early trajectory of pension bargaining in Canada largely tracked that in the US, since many of the same corporations and unions were involved. Canadian labour statutes were modelled on the NLRA, and, after *Inland Steel*, the legal right of Canadian unions to bargain over pensions went largely unchallenged.[45] However, the right to place pension issues on the bargaining table did not guarantee that meaningful negotiations would take place. Canadian labour law takes a generous view of the scope of collective bargaining.[46] But it takes an equally generous view of the right of bargaining parties to maintain hard-nosed – even intransigent – positions on particular bargaining issues. The limitations of this approach for pension outcomes are clearly illustrated by a 1978 decision of the British Columbia Labour Relations Board, in which the board dismissed a union complaint that the employer's refusal to discuss improvements to retirees' pension benefits constituted bargaining in bad faith.[47] The board accepted the union's argument that pension benefits for retirees fell within the scope of bargaining,[48] but rejected the companion submission that the employer's refusal to discuss the subject was unlawful. As the board saw it, "[e]ither a union or an employer is entitled to insist, as a matter of principle, that certain of its affairs will not be subject to the restraints of the contract,"[49] always provided that the party is bargaining in good faith towards a collective agreement as a whole. This means that unions could insist on placing pension issues on the table and could strike over the employer's refusal to agree to the union's proposals. However, if the union was not willing to strike, employers could remain obdurate about incorporating a pension plan within the collective agreement or limiting its authority over pension matters in any way.[50] In most cases, unions do not take pension issues to impasse, and pension strikes in Canada have been rare.

The result was that, in many unionized workplaces, employers were successful in keeping their workplace pension plans off the bargaining table. Even where collective bargaining over pensions took place, it focused mainly on benefit increases; the pension plans themselves remained outside the collective agreement. There were exceptions, of course; pension plans could be expressly linked to collective agreements in various ways, including full incorporation by reference into the agreement. In a significant number of cases, however, collective agreements remained altogether silent about the fact that there was a pension plan covering bargaining-unit employees.

EMPLOYER CONTROL: THE "RECOGNITION RULE" V "RESERVED RIGHTS"[51]

The silence of collective agreements about workplace pensions raised important conceptual and practical questions about the extent to which the legal designation of a union as exclusive bargaining agent restricted an employer's power to unilaterally establish, amend, and terminate a pension plan. Answers to these questions were intimately linked to a foundational debate within labour law about the impact of unionization on pre-existing management powers and prerogatives. It was understood that, where there was a lawful bargaining agent, labour statutes placed the employer under an obligation to "recognize" the authority of that agent to bargain about all terms and conditions of employment. (I call this the "recognition rule.") It was also understood that the recognition rule prohibited direct negotiations between the employer and individual employees. But controversy remained about the extent to which the employer could act unilaterally on matters that the collective agreement did not address. Some theorists argued that the certification of a union as bargaining agent swept away existing terms and conditions of employment, leaving a tabula rasa upon which unions and employers would jointly craft new workplace rules as equal partners. Others argued for a "reserved" or "residual rights" approach, in which employers retained all their pre-collective bargaining powers and prerogatives *except* those that they had "given away" in the collective agreement. Under this theory, the governing terms and conditions of employment in a unionized workplace were a combination of collectively bargained terms and terms imposed by employers outside collective bargaining.[52] Labour statutes did not unequivocally resolve this controversy, and it was left largely to labour arbitrators to resolve it on a case-by-case basis in the context of specific disputes.

In view of the importance employers ascribed to management control of pension plans, it was predictable that many disputes over management rights would involve pension issues. Two early arbitration decisions illustrate very different approaches to the problem. *International Chemical Workers Union, Local 279 v Rexall Drug Co. Ltd*[53] was a decision of a board of arbitration chaired by Bora Laskin, then law professor and arbitrator, and subsequently Chief Justice of the Supreme Court of Canada. *Rexall* involved a challenge to the termination of four employees over the age of sixty-five pursuant to the employer's mandatory retirement policy, which was part of its pension plan. The collective agreement contained what the arbitrators described as the "traditional protective clauses respecting security of workplace" (i.e., seniority and just cause) and "the usual provisions respecting Management rights."[54] It was silent, however, on the pension plan, which predated collective bargaining in the plant by some six years. The arbitration board took note that, although the union had attempted to "draw [the pension plan] into the orbit of collective relations through suggested improvements in benefits,"[55] the company had successfully resisted that attempt. Membership in the pension plan was a condition of employment for all eligible employees, although age and service requirements meant that not all employees were eligible. Two of the terminated employees had qualified for pensions, and two had not, because they were not permitted to join the plan. The grievance alleged that all four had been unjustly discharged.

Because the retirement policy was integral to the pension plan, the arbitration board was obliged to sort out the legal relationship between the plan and the collective agreement. This task required it to address both the broad question of whether work rules that predated collective bargaining continued to apply in unionized workplaces, and the narrower question of whether collective bargaining provisions, such as seniority and just cause clauses, protected older employees against forced retirement. The board took what we would now call a contextual approach.[56] Since the pension plan was "known to the employees and to the Union prior to the execution of the first Collective Agreement between the Union and the Company" (1468), the board was prepared to presume that the agreement was intended to allow for its terms, as long as those terms were consistent with the terms of the agreement (1468–9). The board made it clear, however, that in the event of conflict between the plan and the agreement, the agreement would prevail. It also emphasized that a compulsory retirement policy in a unilateral pension plan could have effect *only* if the plan *predated* collective bargaining: "[i]f the company had sought to introduce a compulsory retirement policy unilaterally after the advent of the Union, then clearly no force could be given to it" (1470). Although the arbitration board does not spell out its reasons for this conclusion, it presumably took the view that it followed as a straightforward application of the recognition rule; terms and conditions of employment must be negotiated with the union. In the result, the board found the retirement policy consistent with the collective agreement for those employees eligible for pension, and allowed their terminations to stand (1469). For those *not* eligible for pension, however, mandatory retirement was inconsistent with the job-security rights in the agreement; those employees were reinstated with full compensation.

A few years later, in a decision that was to become a *locus classicus* for reserved-rights theory, a different board of arbitration reached a very different conclusion about the right of an employer to impose changes to a pension plan in a unionized workplace. *Re Canadian Union of Public Employees, Local 1000, and Hydro-Electric Power Commission of Ontario*[57] dealt with a challenge to an employer's unilateral decision to integrate its existing pension plan with the newly created public plan, the CPP.[58] The Hydro pension plan had not been established through collective bargaining; indeed, it was a statutory plan, although the decision treats it in the same way as any other plan established outside the collective agreement. As in *Rexall*, the plan was not incorporated into the agreement, although it was certainly acknowledged, and there was considerable evidence of ongoing discussions between employer and union about pension issues. The employer made a preliminary objection to the board of arbitration hearing the grievance (i.e., an objection to "arbitrability"). The board allowed the objection and refused to address the case on its merits, holding that "where a pension plan is entirely separate from a collective agreement and the union has no connection with it, a board of arbitration, which derives its authority from the collective bargaining agreement and which can deal only with disputes under that agreement, lacks jurisdiction, unless the agreement draws the plan into it in some way" (245). It concluded that "[h]ad the parties intended the plan to be incorporated into the collective agreement they would have *expressly* stated this to be the case" (246).[59]

As reserved-rights theory became more deeply entrenched in Canadian labour law, the *Hydro-Electric* approach, requiring that plans be expressly incorporated by reference before pension issues could be arbitrated, took firm hold among labour arbitrators. They got considerable encouragement from decisions of the Supreme Court of Canada upholding the right of employers to impose mandatory retirement notwithstanding seniority rights and "just cause" clauses in collective agreements.[60] Absent clear intent within the collective agreement to "give away" what would otherwise have been the employer's unilateral right to control plan design and plan administration, arbitrators refused to review employer pension decisions on their merits. In the first few decades after the introduction of statutory collective bargaining frameworks, arbitrators made routine use of jurisdictional filters to dismiss grievances, not only on mandatory retirement, but also on a wide range of other pension issues. These included the unilateral imposition of a compulsory contributory pension plan,[61] a shortfall in employer pension contributions,[62] and denial of pension benefits to individual retired employees.[63]

The application of reserved-rights theory to pension and other benefit plans contained in "ancillary" documents became so routine that it eventually crystallized into what has become known as the "four-category test." This "test" takes its name from a classification matrix identified by Donald Brown and David Beatty in their influential labour-law treatise, *Canadian Labour Arbitration*.[64] For our purposes, two categories are critical: Category 1, where the collective agreement is completely silent about an ancillary document such as a pension plan, and Category 4, where the collective agreement clearly incorporates the ancillary document by reference. (Categories 2 and 3 encompass the broad range of intermediate cases, in which the agreement makes some reference to the plan, but does not clearly incorporate it.) In Category 1 cases, Brown and Beatty concluded that arbitrators invariably dismiss grievances as inarbitrable. In Category 4 cases, arbitrators take plenary jurisdiction to enforce the plan. The authors emphasize the obstacles to securing a Category 4 categorization: "[C]lear language will be required to effect such an incorporation. For example, where an agreement merely provided that 'there will be no reduction in the benefits of the Company Pension or Death Benefit Plans ... during the life of the current agreement,' it was held to be insufficient to incorporate the insurance policies by reference. Indeed, where the agreement only stated that the application of the plans continued, but provided for grievances over their application, it was held to be insufficient to incorporate the plans themselves into the agreement."[65] By the 1990s, the four-category test had solidified into an almost impenetrable barrier to the arbitration of pension grievances, except in exceptional cases in which the plan was expressly incorporated into the collective agreement.

Where plans were incorporated by reference, arbitrators did take jurisdiction to deal with pension grievances on their merits. Even in these cases, however, arbitrators were reluctant to limit the employer's unilateral control over the plan. As we have seen in previous chapters, typical workplace pension plans included clauses permitting employers to amend or terminate them, and plans incorporated into collective agreements were likely to contain similar clauses. Most arbitrators held that since such clauses came into the collective agreement along with the rest of the pension plan, they gave employers much the same scope for unilateral amendment and termination as they would have had prior to collective bargaining.[66]

But what about the recognition rule? The application of reserved-rights theory and the four-category test to workplace pension rights is not easily reconciled with the obligation to negotiate all terms and conditions of employment with the union. If pension rights are contract rights – and courts and legislatures have now made it clear that they are – it follows inexorably from the recognition rule that employers cannot negotiate those rights directly with individual employees. It follows equally that, once a union is in place, pension plans cannot be unilaterally amended or discontinued or new plans unilaterally established without violating the recognition rule, since those actions involve creating or amending contractual relations with individual employees. This is the subtext of Laskin's conclusion in *Rexall* that "[i]f the company had sought to introduce a compulsory retirement policy unilaterally after the advent of the Union, then clearly no force could be given to it."[67] Some arbitrators agreed with this logic, and allowed grievances challenging the post-certification imposition of unilateral changes to a workplace pension regime.[68] More simply ignored the recognition rule, leaving pension plans in a contractual penumbra, in which employers exercised their management rights unmolested by collective bargaining obligations.

ENFORCING PENSION RIGHTS: JURISDICTIONAL BOUNDARIES BETWEEN COURTS AND ARBITRATORS

The tension between reserved-rights theory and the recognition rule posed serious conceptual problems for the enforcement of individual pension rights in unionized workplaces. The recognition rule draws much of its force from the fundamental principle that, in a unionized workplace, the collective agreement replaces the common-law individual contract of employment, making direct negotiation between employer and employee irrelevant. This principle has been undisputed law in Canada since the mid-1970s, when the Supreme Court of Canada, in a decision penned by then-Chief Justice Laskin, made its oft-quoted pronouncement that "[t]he common law as it applies to individual employment contracts is no longer relevant to employer-employee relations governed by a collective agreement."[69] More recently, the Supreme Court has shown some ambivalence on the question of whether the individual employment contract vanishes altogether while the union holds bargaining rights, or whether it simply becomes dormant.[70] It has been unequivocal, however, that individual contracts cannot be enforced while a collective agreement exists.

In its most recent pronouncement on this issue, *Isidore Garon Ltée v Tremblay*, Justice Marie Deschamps emphasized that the individual contract "cannot be relied on as a source of rights" as long as a union continues to hold bargaining rights.[71] She linked that proposition directly to the recognition rule: "If the right claimed can be characterized as a condition of employment, it cannot be negotiated individually by the employer and the employee. The union alone performs this task, and it must do so for the employees collectively."[72] Under the recognition rule, the collective agreement occupies all of the legal space for unionized employees that would otherwise be occupied by individual contractual terms.

If this is so, what is the legal status of employee pension rights that are not acknowledged as part of the collective agreement? Up until the mid-1990s, this question did not appear to present practical enforcement problems in pension cases. If arbitrators were reluctant to deal with pension disputes, the courts were content to do so, and unionized employees took their pension disputes to the regular courts along with non-unionized employees.[73] In a very few cases, employers objected to court jurisdiction; when they did so, they usually succeeded.[74] But in general, employers who had fought to maintain a strict separation between pension plans and collective bargaining did not see their longer-term interests advanced by raising jurisdictional challenges to the judicial forum for resolving pension disputes. Courts dealt with the pension claims of unionized workers in the same way that they dealt with those of non-unionized workers, applying the same common-law and statutory principles.

The Supreme Court's 1995 decision in *Weber v Ontario Hydro*[75] threatened to disturb this convenient equilibrium by redrawing jurisdictional boundaries between labour arbitrators and courts. *Weber* involved a lawsuit filed by a unionized employee against his employer which raised tort and constitutional claims. The employer brought a jurisdictional challenge, arguing that the matter was an employment dispute that belonged within the exclusive jurisdiction of an arbitrator. Arbitrators derive their basic jurisdiction from labour statutes, which confer a mandate to resolve "differences involving the interpretation, application, administration or alleged violation of collective agreements."[76] Over many years, the Supreme Court has insisted that this jurisdiction is *exclusive*; even if employment disputes overlap with matters over which the common-law courts would otherwise have jurisdiction (such as wrongful dismissal), courts cannot get involved if the dispute concerns matters addressed in the collective agreement. This rule was well understood. It was equally well understood, however, that arbitrators do not have jurisdiction to deal with matters not addressed in the collective agreement. Indeed, this was the essence of reserved-rights theory. Tort and constitutional claims prima facie fall into the category of claims that do not involve the collective agreement and, under pre-*Weber* rules, the employer's challenge to the court's jurisdiction might well have been dismissed. Instead, it succeeded.

Weber did not purport to change the basic rules, but the decision nevertheless almost certainly broadened the scope of arbitral jurisdiction. Justice Beverley McLachlin defined the test for identifying that jurisdiction as follows: "The question in each case is whether the dispute, in its essential character, arises from the interpretation, application, administration, or violation of the collective agreement" (para. 52).[77] To answer that question, adjudicators must first determine the "nature of the dispute," and then the "ambit of the collective agreement" (paras. 51–3). Importantly, the court emphasized that the dispute need not arise directly from the agreement; it was sufficient if it arose inferentially. The language used to describe the new test was not necessarily inconsistent with decisions that required a dispute to have a solid anchor in the collective agreement before it could be found to fall within the exclusive jurisdiction of an arbitrator. In applying the new test, however, Justice McLachlin made it clear that it was both more capacious and more flexible than prior articulations of the test. Based on only the most tenuous of links between the dispute and the language of the agreement, she held that the tort and constitutional claims in *Weber* fell within the "ambit" of the collective agreement, and hence within the exclusive jurisdiction of an arbitrator.[78] She took the same approach in *Weber's* companion case, *New Brunswick v O'Leary*, holding that an employer's negligence claim against an individual employee belonged before an arbitrator and not a court.[79]

This broader approach to arbitral jurisdiction provided fuel for the argument that collective agreements that had previously been regarded as "silent" on pension issues might now be found to address those issues at least "inferentially." For several years, however, arbitrators hearing pension grievances largely ignored the implications of *Weber*, refusing to depart from four-category orthodoxy, and continuing to dismiss on jurisdictional grounds a variety of grievances dealing with improper crediting of pensionable service,[80] improper calculation of CPP offsets of pension benefits,[81] improper calculation of pension benefits,[82] unilateral implementation of an early-retirement incentive plan,[83] denial of same-sex benefits,[84] denial of the opportunity to buy pension credits for past service,[85] and refusal to deduct employee pension contributions.[86] In 2006, however, the Supreme Court of Canada issued a decision in *Bisaillon v Concordia University*[87] that directly addressed the scope of an arbitrator's jurisdiction to deal with pension issues, and sent an unambiguous message that arbitrators, and *not* courts, should adjudicate these issues in unionized workplaces.

Bisaillon involved a defined benefit plan established for all employees of Concordia University. Although 80 per cent of plan members were unionized, collective bargaining had played no role in the genesis of the plan. Sometime in the 1980s, the plan began to accumulate significant surplus. The university used approximately $71 million of that surplus to take contribution holidays, pay plan expenses, and fund early-retirement packages, unilaterally amending the plan to authorize its use of the funds, and to spell out that any surplus would revert to the university on plan termination (para. 8). Plan members, backed by most of Concordia's unions, challenged the amendments through a civil class action. The Concordia University Faculty Association (CUFA), which had settled its pension differences with the university prior to the commencement of the case, refused to support the challenge. Backed by the university, CUFA moved to have the action dismissed, on the ground that the matters it raised properly belonged within the exclusive jurisdiction of grievance arbitrators under Concordia's various collective agreements.

The Supreme Court of Canada agreed, dismissing the class action on the ground that civil litigation was "incompatible with the exclusive jurisdiction of grievance arbitrators and the representative function of certified unions" (para. 8). The majority decision, written by Justice Louis LeBel, drew clear links between the recognition rule (paras. 23–8, described as the union's "monopoly of representation") and the scope of the exclusive jurisdiction of an arbitrator. Justice LeBel characterized the collective agreement as "the regulatory framework governing relations between the union and the employer, as well as the individual relationships between the employer and employees" (para 25). The union's exclusive bargaining authority, he stressed, is "not limited to the context of the collective agreement; it extends to all aspects of the employee-employer relationship." Accordingly, "any negotiations regarding conditions of employment that are not mentioned in the current collective agreement must be conducted by the certified union" (para. 28).

Consistent with this perspective, Justice LeBel took a broad view of the scope of the arbitrator's exclusive jurisdiction. He acknowledged that jurisdiction must be determined by applying the *Weber* test, which requires an assessment both of the facts and of the collective agreement. He emphasized, however, that in applying that test, the court took a "liberal position according to which grievance arbitrators have broad exclusive jurisdiction over issues relating to conditions of employment, provided that those conditions can be shown to have an express or implicit connection to the collective agreement" (para. 33). He considered the possibility that the exclusive jurisdiction of arbitrators might be co-extensive with the scope of collective bargaining, which would give arbitrators exclusive jurisdiction over pension claims simply on the basis that pension plans were part of the "employee's remuneration and conditions of employment," irrespective of the language of particular agreements (para. 38). Ultimately, he did not find it necessary to go that far, since he found himself able to resolve the issue before him on the ground that the collective agreement referred to the pension plan, and "[i]n effect, the parties decided to incorporate the conditions for applying the Pension Plan into the collective agreement" (paras. 50–1).

While Justice LeBel made no reference to the four-category test, his conclusion can be formally aligned with that test, since "incorporation" would make *Bisaillon* a Category 4 case, giving the arbitrator jurisdiction to enforce the plan. In fact, it is clear from an examination of the language in the Concordia collective agreements that Justice LeBel was working from a very different conception of incorporation. In the decision, he summarized the language of the agreements before him as follows:

> Each of these collective agreements refers in one way or another to the Pension Plan. Seven of them specifically provide that the employees they cover are entitled to participate in Concordia's pension plan in accordance with the terms set out in the plan. In the collective agreement between Concordia and one union, CUPFA, Concordia agrees to maintain the existing Pension Plan for employees in its bargaining unit. Finally, the collective agreement applicable to another union, CULEU-Vanier, refers indirectly to the Pension Plan by specifying the ages at which employees become eligible for full retirement benefits or for early retirement. (para. 5)

None of this language comes at all close to the "clear" expression of intent to incorporate required to fit within Category 4 as conventionally applied. At best, it might qualify as "maintenance of benefits" language, sufficient to ground limited forms of Category 3 review, but insufficient to ground jurisdiction to enforce the plan or deal with the surplus ownership issues raised in the *Bisaillon* case.

Justice LeBel's substantive conclusion that arbitrators would have exclusive jurisdiction over the dispute in *Bisaillon* cannot be reconciled with existing jurisprudence. *Bisaillon* was therefore a clear signal that the court intended both to open arbitral channels to pension claims, and to keep courts out of the enforcement process. Arbitrators have been remarkably resistant to this signal, with many continuing to insist that *Bisaillon* left the four-category test intact. In a 2008 decision, *Atlas Copco Exploration Products v International Association of Machinists and Aerospace Workers*, arbitrator Richard Brown canvassed the post-*Bisaillon* arbitration case law and identified an emerging consensus that *Bisaillon* "does nothing to change the settled law."[88] In the same year, in *Telus Communications Inc. v Telecommunications Union (Kellie Grievance)*, arbitrator Andrew Sims characterized the four-category test as "part of the climate against which parties negotiate their collective agreements."[89] Indeed, he pressed the status quo position a step further by claiming that *Bisaillon* actually "reinforces the analysis" embedded in the four-category test.[90] In another case, arbitrator Kevin Burkett acknowledged that *Bisaillon* had moved the goal posts with respect to the arbitrability of claims under ancillary documents: "an incorporation by reference under Category 4 may now be inferred if the benefit plan is provided under the collective agreement and the employer commits not to alter the plan and maintains effective control over its administration."[91] He nevertheless dismissed the claim before him as inarbitrable on the ground that the agreement reflected the parties' joint understanding that they were bound by prior decisions that had dismissed grievances under the older test. The Divisional Court found this conclusion reasonable.[92]

Not all arbitrators have clung so stubbornly to the status quo. In *National Automobile, Aerospace and Agricultural Implements Workers Union of Canada, Local 1015 v Scotsburn Dairy Group (Pension Funds Grievance)*,[93] arbitrator Innis Christie accepted jurisdiction over a complex grievance challenging employer contribution levels and ownership of surplus. The employer argued that "matters of the proper interpretation and administration of the Pension Plan, contract, trust law and the effect of the Nova Scotia pension legislation are for the courts, not an arbitrator under a Collective Agreement" (para. 27). Christie correctly interpreted *Bisaillon* as directing a "liberal" approach to arbitral jurisdiction on pension issues (para. 58).[94] He concluded that a commitment in the agreement that employees would be "covered by a suitable pension plan on the contributory basis of wages from the employee and a likeable [*sic*] amount from the employer" and a "maintenance of existing privileges" clause gave him jurisdiction to determine the issues placed before him (paras. 59–61). Importantly, he also invoked the Nova Scotia *Pension Benefits Act*, which, like most Canadian pension statutes, mandated compliance with the plan itself, as well as with the regulatory rules governing the plan. In his view, this statute was a "statute of the Province governing relations between the parties to the collective agreement," which he was instructed by s.43(1)(e) of Nova Scotia's *Trade Union Act* to treat as part of the collective agreement (para. 71). Christie allowed important aspects of the grievance.[95]

The Christie decision remains exceptional, however, and *Bisaillon* has not dislodged the four-category test; arbitrators continue to require incorporation by reference before they will enforce pension plans.[96] The decision has had some measurable impact in deterring arbitrators from refusing altogether to deal with the merits of pension-related claims. After *Bisaillon*, they are more likely to find arbitrable issues of the Category 2 or 3 type, which do not require direct enforcement of the pension plan, but do permit some limited testing of unilateral employer conduct against substantive rights in the collective agreement. While maintaining formal adherence to the four-category test, arbitrators agreed that they had the power to determine whether an employer's approach to integrating a workplace pension plan with the CPP was barred by estoppel,[97] whether an employer was accountable for failing to enrol a particular employee in the pension plan,[98] and whether particular provisions of a pension plan complied with obligations under the human rights code.[99] In doing so, however, they took care to emphasize the restricted scope of their jurisdiction over pension issues.

In treading this narrow path, arbitrators have left significant problems in their wake. As already noted, the courts had two objectives in *Bisaillon* – to widen channels for arbitrating workplace pension claims, and to restrict access to civil actions for pursuing such claims – which were clearly a "package deal." Unfortunately, although *Bisaillon* has had very limited success in achieving the first goal, it has been far more successful at achieving the second – keeping courts out of the enforcement process. Where arbitrators have narrowly defined their jurisdiction and refused to address issues raised by ancillary documents, courts have typically upheld their decisions under the "reasonableness" standard of review.[100] But where employees or unions bring similar challenges directly to court, courts have taken a more generous view of arbitral jurisdiction, applying liberal readings of *Weber* and *Bisaillon* to find that specific claims arise "in their essential nature" from collective agreements in circumstances where it is by no means self-evident that arbitrators would take the same view and accept jurisdiction on the merits.[101] Whether these jurisdictional decisions are right or wrong, they pose a practical dilemma for unionized employees seeking to locate the proper forum within which to enforce their pension claims.

THE CONSTRAINTS OF THE COLLECTIVE BARGAINING FRAMEWORK

The problems reflected in these decisions, rooted in continuing debates about the relationship between reserved management rights and the recognition rule, may be difficult to resolve at a conceptual level. But at a practical level, they could be managed by bargaining provisions in collective agreements that set clear limits on employer control and expressly establish that all disputes connected with the workplace pension plan must be submitted to arbitration. As labour-law scholar Brian Langille has pointed out, reserved-rights theory raises the cost of bargaining for unions, because it "weighs the scales in favour of employers ... grant[ing them] a head start in negotiations by guaranteeing that employers [are] given certain rights for free."[102] However, it does not remove issues that involve management pre-rogatives from the bargaining table; they continue to fall within the scope of bargaining, and unions can use their lawful strike weapon, if necessary, to demand that employers make the necessary conces-sions. Unions that walk away from the bargaining table without achieving joint governance and unambiguous incorporation of pen-sion plans into collective agreements have made a choice not to exer-cise the strike weapon in support of those goals. Most unions in Canada made that choice.

There are no doubt many reasons for this. Institutional economists have charged that unions do not really want to change the pension status quo – they have no serious quarrel with a pension model in which they bargain over only such matters as benefit levels and early-retirement incentives, and employers bear the administrative, regula-tory, and financial burdens of the plan.[103] These arguments have merit. But it is also important to acknowledge that bargaining to alter pension power relations at the bargaining table within the Canadian legal framework for collective bargaining would be no easy task. There are jurisdictions outside Canada in which collective bargaining has been an effective tool for spreading pension coverage and improving pension quality. A frequently cited example is the Netherlands, where 91 per cent of the working population belongs to workplace pension plans, largely as a result of collective bargain-ing.[104] In the Netherlands, however, collective bargaining operates on a centralized model, in which the fruits of bargaining are applied broadly to employees regardless of their relationship to trade unions or particular workplaces. By contrast, the Canadian model, like the US model, allocates bargaining rights on an enterprise-by-enterprise basis.[105] Unions bargain for specific and well-defined groups of employees within the bargaining units for which they hold bargain-ing rights. In workplaces where there is no union, collective agree-ments have no application. Even in workplaces in which unions do hold bargaining rights, the direct impact of bargaining is confined within the boundaries of the bargaining unit. Historically, Canadian labour boards excluded part-time, short-term, and casual employees from standard employee bargaining units, a practice that replicated and reinforced existing patterns of exclusion in pension coverage and benefit design. While labour boards now construct more inclusive bargaining units,[106] the effect of this change on pensions has been limited, since it postdates the most fertile period of workplace pension expansion.

Another core problem that undermines union bargaining power on pension issues is the general lack of alignment between the boundaries of bargaining units and those of pension plans. There may be many bargaining units within a single unionized workplace, including blue-collar units, white-collar units, professional units, and skilled-trades units.[107] By contrast, the typical pension plan in Canada covers all employees, both unionized and non-unionized.[108] As labour boards and courts have pointed out as early as *Inland Steel*, the fact that pension plans straddle different bargaining units is not a legal impediment to pension bargaining; unions can and do place pension issues on the bargaining table in these circumstances. However, it operates as a practical limitation on what can be achieved in bargaining. Where a union represents only a relatively small percentage of the employees covered by the pension plan, its bargaining clout is necessarily limited, and the motivation of bargaining-unit members to make sacrifices for pension improvements is undermined by the reality that resources expended on pension bargaining are likely to benefit "free riders," who have not made such sacrifices. Multiple unions can, of course, bargain together by agreement with the employer, but different bargaining units may well have different bargaining objectives for the plan, and different strategies for achieving those objectives. Such differences erode collective bargaining power, a problem that was clearly operative in *Bisaillon*.

Furthermore, workplace pension plans affect the rights and interests not only of active employees, but also of groups such as retirees, deferred plan members, and spouses. Canadian collective bargaining frameworks confer bargaining rights on unions only for units of *employees*; unions cannot look directly to labour statutes for authority to represent interest groups who do not fall into that category.[109] It is now well established that unions may bargain improvements to retiree benefits because the active employees represented by the union have a legitimate interest in improving their deferred as well as their current compensation.[110] But it is much more doubtful whether unions can negotiate cuts to those benefits.[111] And even if unions have authority to bargain for classes of plan members who are not active employees, it is unclear whether that authority is exclusive, or whether an employer could act unilaterally on issues relating to the rights and benefits of plan members and beneficiaries who are not active employees.

In addition, there is uncertainty about the role of unions in disputes about enforcing the pension rights of non-members of the bargaining unit. In *Dayco (Canada) Ltd v National Automobile, Aerospace, and Agricultural Implement Workers Union of Canada (CAW-Canada)*,[112] the Supreme Court of Canada made it clear that, where retiree rights arise under a collective agreement, unions can enforce those rights through the grievance and arbitration procedure, even though the retirees are no longer represented by the union. They are not required to do so, however, and as the court pointed out in *Dayco*, Canadian labour law gives retirees no statutory recourse against a union which refuses to pursue a grievance on their behalf (paras. 48, 86). The court suggested that retirees might need direct access to the courts, contrary to the usual rule with respect to the enforcement of rights arising under collective agreements (paras. 86–7). Subsequent courts have taken up this suggestion and allowed retirees to sue to enforce post-retirement benefits.[113] Where such claims involve matters which have been clearly negotiated with the union, however, they may well be dismissed in any event. In a class action brought by retirees involving Hydro-Québec's pension plan, the Quebec Court of Appeal dismissed the argument that retirees were individual parties to the pension contract,[114] and therefore that contract could not be amended without their consent. The court held that retiree pension rights continue to be embedded in the collective agreement, even after retirement. Since the union and the employer were the sole parties to that agreement, they alone had the right to amend it, and the retirees could not block such amendments as long as their vested pension rights were respected.[115]

As a tool for spreading workplace pension coverage to Canadian workplaces, collective bargaining has had disappointing results. While there are unquestionably workplace pension plans in place that would not be there without collective bargaining, bargaining for expanded pension coverage has been hampered by features built into the Canadian collective bargaining framework that limit the impact of bargaining to discrete bargaining units where the union holds bargaining rights. Collective bargaining has also had limited success as a tool for combatting the consequences of unilateral employer control. With few exceptions, arbitrators and courts have shown no inclination to limit that control simply because there is a union in place; they have insisted that unions must bargain for any such limitations. Unions have not had great success in doing so, and even where such limitations do exist in collective agreements, arbitrators have frequently read them narrowly, leaving employers with unilateral power to amend and terminate, even where plans have been incorporated by reference into collective agreements.

Collective bargaining has not been effective as a solution to the policy problem of leaving workplace pensions in the hands of employers. There remains a strong correlation between unionization and pension coverage, however, and if arbitrators had been quicker to take jurisdiction over pension issues, the hard work of attempting to reconcile statutory pension rights with common-law rights and collective agreements would likely have taken place at arbitration. However, the propensity of arbitrators to cede jurisdiction to the courts has meant that most of that work has been done by the courts. In the next two chapters, we pick up where we left off at the end of Chapter 3 and return to the courts to explore how employee pension rights have developed there since the mid-twentieth century.

6

Trust Law v Contract Law

INTRODUCTION

In Chapter 3, we left the common law of workplace pensions in an important transitional phase. Courts acknowledged that pension plans might confer rights on employees, but were still struggling with the legal nature of those rights. Gift theory still influenced such decisions as *Williamson* and *McDougall*, but *Mantha*, a decision of higher authority, saw pension promises as "terms of the engagement" between employers and employees (i.e, terms of the employment contract). Courts placed procedural constraints on pension decision-making in something closely resembling a contractual framework. Contract law, however, was only one of the bodies of law courts mined for concepts and doctrines that would assist in understanding pension plans and pension rights. The concept of "vested rights," which entered legal pension discourse much earlier than the concept of "deferred wages," was borrowed from property and trust law. The principle of fairness applied to pension administration was a hybrid of trust and administrative law. Hybrids are unstable, however, and the search continued throughout the latter half of the twentieth century for a primary legal framework within which to locate and construct workplace pension rights. The major contenders for that role were contract law and trust law.

Contract law got a helping hand when regulatory statutes cemented the emerging link between pension rights and the contract of employment. That link was cemented even more firmly by collective bargaining law, which located pensions within the broad category of terms and conditions of employment. For an important few years, however, it appeared that trust law might gain ascendency. In the landmark decision in *Schmidt v Air Products Canada Ltd*,[1] the Supreme Court of Canada held that, where trust law applied, it trumped contract law, and could prevent employers from promoting their own pension interests at the expense of their employees' interests. In a pioneering law review article in the mid-1990s, pre-eminent Canadian pension expert Eileen Gillese argued that, within the emerging field of pension law, trust law and equity "contain the principles and approaches which can lead to a sensible and successful development of this new area of the law."[2]

As we shall see in this chapter, however, trust law dominated pension law for only a short time. Courts ultimately concluded that placing trust fetters on employer power within the pension relationship was too radical a disruption of the market forces that sustain the system, and trust law has now been decisively demoted below contract law in the hierarchy of legal rules governing pension rights and obligations. Even where trust law continues to have application, its normative power has been largely neutralized, since judges have moved away from an "ethical" conception of trust law towards a "contractarian" conception that leaves control over the nature and scope of trust obligations in the hands of employers, rather than in the hands of courts.

SOME DISTINCTIONS BETWEEN CONTRACT LAW AND TRUST LAW

To understand why trust law had attractions for courts within the evolving common law of pensions, it is helpful to review some of the basic concepts structuring contract law and trust law. By the time workplace pension plans came seriously to the attention of the courts, contract law had become the basic legal framework governing the employment relationship. It was therefore logical to slot pension rights into the same category. There is no moment of epiphany in Canadian courts in which gift theory gave way to a clear understanding that pensions were part of the wage package, but once that notion took hold, it became self-evident. Decisions like *Williamson* and *McDougall* gradually disappeared from view. By 1960, it was obvious to the Ontario High Court judge who decided *Bardal v Globe & Mail* that damages for wrongful dismissal should include the value of membership in a workplace pension plan, since pension rights had a contractual basis.[3] By the 1970s, the language of "deferred wages" was making its way into the decisions of courts and tribunals dealing with pensions.[4] By the 1980s, courts across Canada referred expressly to pension plans as contracts.[5] By 1991, Justice Marie Corbett could state with confidence in *Otis Canada Inc. v Ontario (Superintendent of Pensions)* that "[c]learly the promise of ... pension benefits is a contractual matter."[6] The idea that pension promises are contractual is now a commonplace in Supreme Court of Canada jurisprudence.[7]

For employees, contract law had one very obvious advantage over gift theory: it converted pension promises into enforceable rights. But it also has a serious downside. Under classic liberal contract theory, courts see contracts as agreements – exchange relationships – which reflect the intention of the parties to that agreement. They do not concern themselves with the inequalities of bargaining power that generate these agreements. Parties are assumed to know their own best interests, and to reject contracts which do not meet their needs. In many circumstances, this assumption is a fiction, but except in a narrow range of cases in which they find duress or unconscionability, it is a fiction with which courts are content to live.[8] Although workplace pension plans have been judicially recognized as "contracts of adhesion," which give employees no meaningful room to negotiate,[9] courts generally treat the content of workplace pension plans as arrangements to which employees are bound by their own consent. Liberal contract law thus permits employers to frame pension plans in much the same way they did when the operating premise was that pensions were gifts, not rights. It permits employers to draft plans that give themselves unbounded discretion in the administration of benefits, and the power to withdraw or change the fundamental nature of the pension promises made by their plans. As one Ontario judge observed in the 1990s, "[a]bsent union negotiation, an employer ha[s] the legal right to determine the terms of a pension plan."[10]

The one-sided nature of such contractual bargains does not trouble liberal contract theory. But the abuses it has produced within pension plans have troubled Canadian courts from time to time, particularly in light of the fact, however belatedly acknowledged, that pensions are earned benefits with an important social role as a source of retirement income. Courts have looked outside the law of contract for legal rules that might fetter employer power to undermine the legitimate pension expectations of their employees. One potential source of such fetters is the law of trusts.

Trust law is a body of legal rules that evolved in the English Court of Chancery to regulate the transfer and management of property within landed families.[11] At root, trust law is a subset of property law; a trust is a species of property ownership in which the original owner of the property (the "settlor")[12] transfers title to one party (the "trustee") to be managed for the benefit of another party (the "beneficiary"). While the trustee is the legal owner, the beneficiary is the beneficial, or "true," owner. The terms of the trust are typically set out in an agreement between the settlor and the trustee called the "trust deed" or "declaration of trust."[13] Trust law operates to ensure that the trustee keeps faith with the settlor by managing the property in the interests of the beneficiaries. It holds trustees to the terms of the trust deed, and regulates the manner in which they carry out their duties, binding them to a very high duty of loyalty to the beneficiaries which obligates them to avoid conflicts of interest and to subordinate their own interests to those of the beneficiaries.[14]

The trust law template was designed for relationships which typically involve one-time gratuitous transfers of property from the settlor to the trustee. The archetypal example is the marriage settlement within the landed gentry, in which certain assets are placed in trust at the time of the marriage in order to protect the financial security of the wife and prospective children. In such relationships, settlors (typically family members) turned the management of the trust assets over to a trustee and ceased to have an ongoing relationship with those assets. This template is by no means ideal for the management of workplace pension arrangements for a wide variety of reasons, including the fact that there is a continuing transfer of assets into the trust, and some measure of continuing control of trust assets by the employer/settlor. But some aspects of the pension relationship do invite trust analogy. As we saw in Chapter 3, early judges who struggled with the legal nature of the pension promise were drawn to the idea that pension plans might create "vested rights," which impose an obligation on the employer to convert those rights into an annuity. Once dedicated pension funds entered the picture, formal trust arrangements were frequently linked to pension plans as funding vehicles. Impelled in part by early forms of tax regulation, these pension trusts followed conventional trust models by creating a formal separation between ownership and control of assets and designating plan members as fund beneficiaries. Regulatory statutes acknowledged the trust nature of pension funds by imposing trustee-like obligations upon those who managed them.[15]

It was therefore inevitable that trust law would enter the pension picture in some way. But its primary attraction for common-law judges was a dimension in trust law that distinguished it from contract law. While trust law is fraught with arcane rules, it is fundamentally based on relationships of "trust" in the lay sense, and has historically been shaped by principles and standards of behaviour that operate as a counterpoint to the self-interest animating contract law. This ethical dimension draws at least some of its sustenance from the roots of trust law in the courts of equity, which enforced conscientious norms not recognized by common-law courts. An important purpose of trust law has always been the protection of the powerless (the beneficiaries) from the powerful (those who control the trust property).

But there is a deep tension within trust law itself. Like contract law, trust law governs relationships created through private arrangements. The rights and obligations of the parties to these relationships are constituted primarily by documents drawn up by private parties. In interpreting and enforcing these documents, courts are essentially enforcing the intentions of those who established the trust, in much the same sense as they enforce the "intention of the parties" to contracts. This reality undermines the notion that trust law has an ethical foundation different from contract law, and many legal scholars reject the view that it contains an ethical bedrock which cannot be defeated by the intention of the settlor or the terms of the trust document. Instead, they promote a "contractarian" perspective in which trust law is simply a species of private law like contract law, in which private parties make their own arrangements, and in which the only role for the courts is to determine what those arrangements are and enforce them as written.[16] The tension between ethical and contractarian views of trust law is very evident in the case law discussed in this chapter.[17]

THE PENSION SURPLUS WARS

The practical problem that brought trust law to the fore in modern pension litigation concerns the ownership of so-called pension "surpluses" – pension assets in excess of the level required to fund promised pension benefits.[18] As we have seen, the regulatory statutes of the 1960s and the 1980s required employers with defined benefit plans either to insure their pension promises or to set aside trust funds to guarantee payment of the promised pensions. Many large employers took the second option. However, determining proper funding levels was not an exact science. Defined benefit plans create future obligations, and the amounts required to make good on those obligations cannot be definitively ascertained at any given moment. For planning purposes, appropriate funding levels are estimated by qualified actuaries, who project the value of both plan assets and plan liabilities within a framework of professional standards that leave considerable flexibility for individual judgment.[19] Actuaries make their estimates based on assumptions about the future direction of both macroeconomic variables (such as inflation rates, interest rates, and the performance of equity markets) and firm-specific variables (such as projected employment levels, salary increases, and life expectancy, based on the demographics of a particular workforce).[20] In the real world, events may well deviate from assumptions. When this happens, pension funds end up holding less money (a deficit) or more money (a surplus) than they need in order to meet pension liabilities.

The 2008–09 financial crisis has frequently been described as a "perfect storm" of cascading economic events that deviated from actuarial projections, depressing pension assets, increasing pension liabilities, and plunging many plans into serious deficit. In the 1980s, a "perfect storm" produced the reverse effects, generating very significant pension surpluses.[21] Corporations anxious to free up capital fashioned strategies to gain access to those surpluses for their own purposes. Employers took what became known in the pension vernacular as "contribution holidays."[22] They also drew on the pension fund to pay plan expenses previously paid out of operating funds, merged multiple pension plans so that surpluses in one fund could be used to offset deficits in another, and terminated plans in order to extract the surplus from the fund.[23] Where these strategies appeared to contravene plan documents, many employers exercised their unilateral powers of plan amendment to change those documents and regularize their conduct, either prospectively or retroactively. In view of the billions of dollars at stake, it was predictable that these employer "raids" on surpluses would trigger opposition from employee and retiree groups. This opposition frequently took the form of legal challenges, based on arguments that pension funds were trust funds and employer attempts to appropriate surpluses were breaches of trust.

Litigation over pension surpluses was complex. Regulatory statutes and protocols were often silent, or almost so, on the issue of surpluses. Where they did address surpluses, legal rules varied considerably across the country.[24] Plans and plan documents that had been drafted in an era in which surpluses had not been contemplated were frequently ambiguous. Drafting strategies often linked plan texts and funding agreements through reciprocal incorporation by reference. These intertwined documents posed problems for courts applying orthodox judicial techniques of contract interpretation. The pension plan was understood to be part of the employment contract, but funding arrangements typically involved contractual arrangements between the employer and third parties.[25]

To further complicate the interpretive task, many plan texts had been revised over the years, a problem generated at least in part by shifting tax rules. The *Blue Books* had required employers to ensure that their pension contributions were irrevocable and "vested absolutely" in plan members,[26] a requirement that plan documents addressed through clauses providing that the fund was for the exclusive benefit of the employees ("exclusive benefit clauses"), contributions to the fund were irrevocable ("irrevocability clauses"), and any surplus would be allocated to plan beneficiaries on termination rather than returned to the employer ("non-reversion clauses"). Effective 1 January 1982, however, Canadian tax authorities reversed course. In the face of accumulating fund surpluses, they became concerned that pension funds were being used as tax shelters. New tax rules capped surpluses and required that excess surplus be returned to the employer or used to improve benefits.[27] Employers with existing plans responded to these new rules by amending their plans to ensure that they had the power to extract and appropriate surplus. Courts dealing with surplus ownership issues were therefore required not only to interpret current plan documents, but also to address arguments from plan members that amendments which altered the beneficial ownership of surplus funds were unauthorized by the original plan documents.

The so-called "pension surplus wars" raised foundational questions about rights, responsibilities, liabilities, and duties arising within workplace pension plans. They challenged judges to give concrete meaning to the abstract notion that pension plans create contractual rights and pensions are deferred wages. Up to the early 1990s, Canadian courts had picked no clear winner of the surplus wars. Struggling to adapt nineteenth-century trust doctrine to the modern pension context, they came to differing resolutions, with outcomes fairly evenly divided between employers and employees.[28] Some courts took pension trusts at face value; since they were trust funds and employees were the beneficiaries, the employees were entitled to any funds left over when the plan terminated. Other courts held that surplus funds should be returned to the settlor once all pension liabilities were paid out. Courts did not always agree, however, on the identity of the settlor. Some treated the employer as the settlor, while others saw the employer and the employees as joint settlors. Cases challenging employer contribution holidays had equally indeterminate results.[29] Little guidance was to be found in the jurisprudence of other common-law jurisdictions; while courts in the UK and US typically held that employers owned pension surpluses, they did so for a variety of conflicting reasons.[30] Despite doctrinal complexities, however, trends began to emerge in surplus cases. Labour-law scholar Bernard Adell accurately summarized the law in a 1988 report to an Ontario government task force with the observation that "a judicial presumption of sorts is arising in favour of employee rights in pension plan surpluses."[31]

SCHMIDT V AIR PRODUCTS CANADA LTD

Employers continued to push hard against this "presumption," and the surplus issue eventually made its way to the Supreme Court of Canada in the case of *Schmidt v Air Products Canada Ltd.* Pension lawyers saw *Schmidt as* an opportunity for Canada's highest court to clarify how trust law applied to workplace pension plans. Instead, the decision exposed fundamental disagreements among Supreme Court justices about the nature and scope of the pension promise and the normative role played by trust principles in interpreting and applying plan documents. *Schmidt* is undoubtedly the high-water mark of trust protection for employee pension rights in Canadian jurisprudence. As we shall see, however, in practical terms employees lost more than they gained. Likewise problematic for both employers and employees was the lack of guidance on the use and abuse of surplus in plans that were ongoing; instead of providing a clear conceptual framework, the court determined that surplus ownership claims could only be assessed on a case-by-case basis.

The *Schmidt* litigation arose out of a 1988 decision by Air Products Canada Ltd to terminate its DB pension plan. Air Products applied to the courts for a declaration that it was entitled to the accumulated surplus. Its claim of ownership was clearly supported by the language of its current plan. Plan members countered with their own owner-ship claim, arguing that, although the language of the current plan gave the surplus to the employer, that language conflicted with the terms of predecessor plans, which had assigned ownership to plan members. They characterized the original plan language as a formal declaration of trust on the part of the employer in favour of employ-ees, and argued that such a trust could not lawfully be revoked.[32] Plan members also challenged a series of employer "contribution holidays," which had come to light only on the windup of the plan, arguing that the employer's practice of drawing on plan surplus instead of making regular contributions to the fund was also a breach of trust.

All judges accepted the members' argument that in order to resolve the trust issues it was necessary to examine not only the language of the current plan, but also the plan's history and the language of predecessor plan documents. The Air Products plan was the fruit of a 1983 merger of two predecessor plans, a "Catalytic plan" initiated in 1959 and a "Stearns plan" initiated in 1973.[33] The Catalytic plan had been funded in accordance with a trust agreement between the employer and the Canada Trust Company that had been explicitly incorporated into the plan.[34] The agreement spelled out that the trust fund was for the "exclusive benefit" of plan members. It expressly prohibited the employer from reducing accrued benefits and con-tained a "non-reversion clause" barring the employer from recover-ing any sums it had contributed to the fund (paras. 23, 97–111). The Stearns plan, by contrast, had been funded under a group annuity contract purchased from an insurance company (paras. 122– 9).[35] The Stearns plan contained an "exclusive benefit" clause and language protecting "accrued benefits." However, it had no "non-reversion" clause; instead, it provided that any terminal surplus could either revert to the employer or "may be used for the benefit of Participants, former Participants, beneficiaries or estates in such equitable manner as the Company may in its discretion determine" (para. 108).

Justice Peter Cory penned the majority judgment. He acknowledged that the employer's obligation to pay employee pensions was laid out in the plan text, and that funding instruments were merely subsidiary tools developed to assist the employer to pay for pension promises made in the plan (paras. 44–5, 47). Nevertheless, his ultimate decision on the surplus ownership issue turned essentially on differences between funding arrangements rather than differences in plan texts. Based on the language of the Catalytic Trust Agreement, he held that the entire Catalytic pension fund, including any surplus, had been "impressed with a trust" (paras. 97–105). The funding arrangements for the Stearns plan, however, did not create a trust. It followed, as he saw it, that plan members whose rights could be traced back to the Catalytic plan had a right to be treated as trust beneficiaries, and Air Products' elimination of their right to surplus must be tested against *trust law* principles. However, members whose rights could be traced back to the Stearns plan were not trust beneficiaries, and the elimination of their right to surplus was required only to comply with *contract law* principles.

For Justice Cory, these two sets of principles yielded very different results. In both cases, the issue focused on whether the amendment which gave Air Products ownership of surplus was authorized by the relevant powers of amendment under the Stearns and Catalytic plans.[36] With respect to the Stearns plan, Justice Cory conducted a straightforward contract analysis and determined that the amendment was valid, because it did not encroach on existing rights under the plan (para. 141–8). With respect to the Catalytic plan, however, the question was more complex, because, as Justice Cory saw it, the employer's appropriation of surplus held in the trust involved a partial revocation of that trust. The question was not simply whether the employer could lawfully amend the plan, but whether it could amend the plan *to revoke the trust*. Justice Cory held that it could not.

While Justice Cory did not go so far as to say that a settlor could *never* revoke a trust, the analysis he applied showed clear affinities with the ethical idea that trusts and trustees must conform to fundamental rules imposed by "law" and enforced by the courts. In his view, trusts have certain "fundamental characteristics" (para. 65). One of these characteristics is that a trust involves the absolute transfer of property rights from the settlor to the trust. It is "inconsistent with the fundamental concept of a trust," he insisted, for a settlor to control the trust property once a trust is constituted (para. 66).

Somewhat paradoxically, he acknowledged that this "fundamental" characteristic was not immutable; a settlor may "reserve any power to itself that it wishes" (para. 59). But settlors who intend to depart from fundamental trust norms by making their trust transfers reversible must clear drafting hurdles that would not stand in their way if they were dealing simply with contracts. They could revoke the trust only if they reserved the power to do so within the initial trust documents, using "extremely clear and explicit language" (para. 66). The argument for insisting on such clarity was even more compelling, in Justice Cory's view, in a case where the transfer of trust property was not gratuitous but had been earned, such as a pension trust. In addition, Justice Cory emphasized that employee beneficiaries are in a vulnerable position vis-à-vis the employer plan sponsor. As he put it, "The wording of the pension plan and trust instrument are usually drawn up by the employer. The employees as a rule must rely upon the good faith of the employer to ensure that the terms of the specific trust arrangement will be fair. It would, I think, be inequitable to accept the proposition that a broad amending power inserted unilaterally by the employer carries with it the right to revoke the trust" (para. 66). Since the employer had reserved no power of revocation in the initial Catalytic plan, Justice Cory held that the plan amendment appropriating ownership of the trust was null and void with respect to former Catalytic employees.

Two judges dissented on the disposition of the terminal surplus. Justices Sopinka and McLachlin agreed with Justice Cory that the plan amendment asserting employer ownership over surplus was valid as it applied to the Stearns employees. However, they took the view that it was equally valid as applied to the Catalytic employees. For them, the key issue was the intention of the employer in establishing the pension plan and its funding arrangements. As they saw it, both Catalytic and Stearns had intended only to provide their employees with retirement pensions. The fact that they had made differing choices about how to fund those pensions did not alter that basic proposition. Both dissenters accepted the relevance of trust law in analyzing the problems; indeed, it was on a recondite point of trust doctrine that their judgments diverged from each other.[37] However, both distanced themselves from Justice Cory's ethical trust perspective, adopting the more contractarian view of trust principles.

This is most evident in Justice John Sopinka's analytical approach to interpreting the general power of amendment in the Catalytic plan. He accepted Justice Cory's conclusion that the entire Catalytic pension fund was impressed with a trust. He also agreed that the provisions of the Air Products plan, which gave the employer ownership of the surplus, were only valid if they were authorized under the general power of amendment in the Catalytic plan documents. However, he rejected Justice Cory's fundamentalist approach to interpreting that power of amendment. As he saw it, the fact that a trust was involved had no special significance in interpreting the language of the documents; the intention of the settlor should govern and "the usual canons of construction" should apply (para. 165).[38] He rejected any legal presumption that a trust was irrevocable: "[t]rusts can be revocable or irrevocable. Neither is more fundamental than the other. All we are debating is the means by which we distinguish one from the other" (para. 167). As he construed the plan language, the only relevant limitation on the power of amendment in the Catalytic plan was the stricture that amendments could not encroach on accrued benefits. In his view, a right to surplus was not an accrued benefit. Accordingly, the amendment giving the employer ownership of surplus was valid (para. 162).

Justice McLachlin held that the surplus funds did not fall within the scope of the Catalytic trust, and, accordingly, the employer could claim ownership without any need to resort to the plan's power of amendment.[39] Her contractarian perspective is very evident in the reasoning which led her to that conclusion. Her focus is on the contractual "bargain" between employer and employees. She emphasized the "private law" nature of that bargain:

> The primary rule in construing an agreement or defining the terms of a trust is respect for the intention of the parties or, in the case of a trust, the intention of the settlor. The task of the court is to examine the language of the documents to ascertain what, on a fair reading, the parties intended. Unless there is a legal reason preventing it, the courts will seek to give effect to that intention. The search for an answer to the problem before us must therefore focus primarily on the documents relating to the plans and the intention of the parties, if any, with respect to a surplus arising under a defined benefits plan. (paras. 195–6)

In Justice McLachlin's view, the "parties" intended only that the pension plan would pay the promised pensions. Accordingly, "[t]o give the employees the surplus ... is to give them more than they bargained for. It is a windfall to the employees and a denial of the equitable interest which the employer holds in the surplus" (paras. 185–6). While she characterized the governing documents as a contract, she saw no relevant distinction between trust and contract principles on the important question of the scope of the employer's power to write the rules in its favour. Whether pension documents are trusts or contracts, a court's primary duty is simply to discover and give effect to their authors' intent.

Although the court divided on the disposition of the terminal surplus, it was unanimous that the contribution holidays were lawful. From the employees' perspective, the terminal-surplus issue and the contribution-holiday issue were not distinguishable; both involved employer encroachments on the surplus in the trust fund beneficially owned by the employees, and both therefore involved breach of trust. Writing this time for the whole court, Justice Cory did not agree. His judgment turned on a distinction between what he called an "actual surplus," calculated after a plan has been terminated and all its liabilities finally determined, and an "actuarial surplus," a mere accounting entry in an ongoing plan, which may or may not become an "actual surplus" when the plan terminates (para.89). As he saw it, only an "actual surplus" raises trust issues. Since contribution holidays did not involve "actual surpluses," assessing whether they were valid called for nothing more than a contractual analysis of the Air Products plan under which the employer had taken those holidays (paras. 84–5, 95, 113). That plan required the employer to make contributions in the "amounts ... necessary to provide the retirement benefits accruing to Members during the current year" (para. 114). Under standard actuarial practice, there would be no "amounts necessary" in any year in which the existing fund was already large enough to meet its obligation to pay all outstanding benefits. In Justice Cory's view, contribution holidays were mere accounting exercises, which do not "reduce the corpus of the fund," even if they reduce the amount in the surplus column of the fund's books (para. 86). Since no trust money was accessed, there could be no breach of trust. Justice Cory therefore dismissed the claim for both groups of employees.

THE *SCHMIDT* PRINCIPLES

Those who hoped the *Schmidt* decision would resolve the competing claims of contract law and trust law as governing frameworks for workplace pension plans were disappointed. Justice Cory himself had concerns about the normative consistency of the decision; as he put it, "In both [Catalytic and Stearns] appeals the pension fund was created to benefit the employees ... It seems unfair that there should be a different result for these two groups of employees based only upon a finding that a trust was created in one case but not in the other." He called on legislatures to resolve the inconsistency, recommending that they draw on "[p]rinciples of equity and fairness" to ensure that both employees and employer share in any surplus on plan termination (para. 150).

Other commentators had problems with the doctrinal consistency of the decision. Eileen Gillese criticized Justice Cory's conclusion that contribution holidays did not raise trust issues. As a matter of trust principle, she rejected his distinction between terminal surplus and surplus in an ongoing plan; as she saw it, contribution holidays unquestionably encroached on the trust fund. Gillese nevertheless defended Justice Cory's approach to the contribution-holiday issue as an appropriate reflection of the intention of the parties. She argued that, while trust law has an important role to play on plan termination, both employers and employees intend that ongoing plans will be governed by the same law that governs the employment relationship, that is, contract law.[40] She bolstered her argument for contract law with a policy concern that legal rules which prevent employers from taking contribution holidays would operate as a disincentive for them to create and maintain pension plans.[41]

A similar concern about the practical consequences of impeding pursuit of employer self-interest lurks beneath the judgments in *Schmidt* itself. Air Products had argued that employers who are prevented from taking contribution holidays will engage in systemic underfunding of their plans. Justice Cory expressed skepticism about this argument (para. 45), but his ultimate disposition of the issue gave considerable deference to employers and their actuaries on plan funding issues. Justice McLachlin's dissenting opinion explicitly acknowledged the hazards of judicial interference with the power of employers to organize their pension affairs as they see fit. She gave serious credence to the possibility that employers who are not permitted to pursue their own pension interests will put less money into their plans, switch from defined benefit to defined contribution plans, or decline to provide pensions altogether. These consequences will ultimately fall hardest on employees, she argued: "no longer assured of a specific pension and required to assume the risk of insufficient funding themselves, [employees] would be the losers" (para. 184).

Although *Schmidt* did not resolve the "trust v contract" debate, the majority judgment nevertheless established some important and unambiguous propositions about the role of trust law in workplace pension plans, and the relationship between trust law and contract law in interpreting employee pension rights. First, *Schmidt* confirmed that trust law does have a role in determining workplace pension rights. Second, it held that where a trust is created by pension plan documents (either expressly or by implication), that trust is a "classic" or "true trust" (para. 52), subject to "all applicable trust principles" (para. 92). Third, although the decision acknowledged both trust law and contract law as contributors to the legal framework within which pension rights must be determined, it established a clear hierarchy; where there is conflict between plan terms and trust terms, trust terms take precedence, and "to the extent that applicable equitable [i.e., trust] principles conflict with plan provisions, equity must prevail" (para. 92). As we shall see, however, these propositions have been severely tested in subsequent cases, as the Supreme Court has confronted the hard question of whether it is feasible to apply the trust restrictions inherent in Justice Cory's paradigm within a workplace pension system that ultimately depends for its survival on employer willingness to establish and maintain plans.

THE RETREAT FROM *SCHMIDT*

Buschau v Rogers Cablesystems: *Not All Trust Principles Are "Applicable"*

It was another decade before the next workplace pension case involving trust law issues reached the Supreme Court of Canada. *Buschau v Rogers Cablesystems Ltd*[42] involved one of the more arcane rules of trust law, the Rule in *Saunders v Vautier* ("the Rule"). Of nineteenth-century vintage, the Rule permits a trust beneficiary to obtain a court order to collapse a trust and release the trust property to the beneficiaries, even though the settlor has expressed a clear intention that the trust continue. To use the words of the Supreme Court of Canada, the Rule "allow[s] beneficiaries of a trust to depart from the settlor's original intentions provided that they are of full legal capacity and are together entitled to all the rights of beneficial ownership in the trust property."[43] Prior to *Buschau*, the Rule had been applied by Canadian courts as one of a very few truly immutable rules of trust law.[44] In *Buschau*, the question before the court was whether pension plan members could invoke the Rule to terminate their pension trust and take advantage of their right to the surplus. Since the Rule explicitly circumvents the intention of the settlor, the members' attempt to apply it to a pension trust was a direct challenge to the employer's right to control decisions about the establishment and termination of workplace pension plans. *Buschau* was therefore a particularly demanding test of Justice Cory's core holding in *Schmidt*: that pension trusts are "classic trusts" and subject to "all applicable trust law principles."

To understand the issues at stake in *Buschau*, it is necessary to understand the basic history of the litigation that brought the case before the Supreme Court of Canada. In the background was a complex series of corporate restructurings and plan consolidations. The plan in question was established in 1974 by a company called Premier Communications Ltd (PCI). Initially funded through a trust agreement, the plan included a "non-reversion" clause that explicitly provided for any terminal surplus to be distributed among plan members (para. 4). In 1980, PCI was purchased by Rogers, together with its pension plan, and by 1983, the plan had begun to accumulate a large and growing surplus. To quote a corporate memo which emerged in the course of the litigation, Rogers was determined to "get at" the surplus for its own purposes (paras. 5–6).[45] To facilitate access, Rogers commenced a series of manoeuvres. In 1984 it closed the plan, which meant that, although the plan continued to exist, it accepted no new members. In 1985, Rogers withdrew some of the surplus, and subsequently began to take contribution holidays. It "restated" (i.e., substantially amended) the plan to retroactively authorize its conduct.[46] Along the way, it replaced actuaries and institutional trustees who were not prepared to co-operate with its strategies. Ultimately, in 1992, it merged the PCI plan with other Rogers plans that were then in deficit to create a single fund in which the PCI surplus offset the deficit in the other plans. The new merged plan expressly gave Rogers ownership of surplus, as well as permission to withdraw surplus while the plan was ongoing.

Then in 1995, in the wake of the Supreme Court's *Schmidt* decision, the PCI members decided to fight back. They initiated litigation, asserting a claim to the surplus.[47] They also challenged the company's 1985 withdrawal of surplus, its contribution holidays, and its attempts to eliminate employee surplus rights by merger and plan amendment. Before the court proceedings commenced, Rogers acknowledged that its withdrawal of surplus from the ongoing plan was in breach of trust, and repaid those funds, leaving the plan-amendment and contribution-holiday issues to be litigated.[48] The contribution-holiday claim was ultimately dismissed as out of time, although it had arguably violated federal regulations (para. 36).[49] With respect to the plan-amendment claim, however, the British Columbia Court of Appeal declared that the PCI fund, including the surplus, had been "impressed with a trust" for the benefit of PCI members, and continued to be subject to that trust, despite the plan amendments and the merger. Rogers did not appeal this decision.

The plan members wanted more than a declaration, however; they wanted the surplus itself. They had previously made it clear to both Rogers and the court that, if they were successful in establishing trust rights, they would seek to terminate the trust by invoking the Rule. The Court of Appeal did not directly address the merits of the Rule-based claim. It nevertheless made the helpful observation that "the right of the members to invoke *Saunders v Vautier* ... remains unaffected by the merger" (para. 68). Encouraged by this strong hint that the courts would look favourably on an application to collapse the trust and distribute the surplus to the plan members, those members brought a *Saunders v Vautier* application, which succeeded in the British Columbia courts.

On appeal to the Supreme Court of Canada, however, the claim was dismissed. The court was unanimous that the Rule was irreconcilable with the statutory scheme requiring an employer to maintain the pension fund as long as it maintained the plan, and could therefore not be applied to a modern pension trust. This reason alone was sufficient to dispose of the case. The court nevertheless went out of its way to discuss an additional ground for dismissing the claim; it found the Rule incompatible with the employer's pension objectives. Justice Deschamps, author of the majority judgment, emphasized the centrality of the employer's interest in the continuance of the pension plan.[50] Compared to the employer's interest, she described the interest of any individual beneficiary as "ephemeral," "passive," and "limited" (para. 34). "Employers establish plans because it is in their interest to do so," she declared, and "[u]nder normal circumstances, they have the right not to have their management decisions disturbed" (para. 30). Invoking liberal contract theory, she insisted that "[t]he application of the rule in *Saunders v Vautier* would contradict the reasonable contractual expectations of the parties" because it would "permit members of a pension plan to unilaterally vary its terms without the employer's consent" (para. 92). As she saw it, trust principles like the Rule must give way in the workplace pension context, because they "allow no room for the settlor's [i.e., the employer's] interest" (para. 92). In his concurring judgment, Justice Michel Bastarache was even more deferential to employer interests.[51] He stressed the voluntary nature of the workplace pension system, and the "unique role of the employer in respect of the pension plan and the pension Trust" (para. 94). As he saw it, applying the Rule would tilt the "fair and delicate balance between employer and employee interests" so far towards employees as to threaten the survival of the system. Such a "very significant derogation from an employer's right to voluntarily choose to offer or continue a pension plan" had no place in the workplace pension context (para. 97).

All judges emphasized the policy importance of shaping legal rules in a manner that would permit employers to achieve their business objectives for workplace pension plans; failure to do so would place the system at risk, injuring employees and destabilizing national retirement-income policy. Justice Deschamps explicitly acknowledged that the "social component of private pension plans plays a crucial role in an era in which public pension programs have not yet been reformed to ensure adequate funding." In her view, this was a factor courts should take into account in resolving pension claims: "Courts do not make social policy, but the social role of pension plans might prove relevant when it comes time to decide whether the rule in *Saunders v Vautier* can be employed to terminate a pension trust" (para. 13). Her ultimate conclusion that the Rule could not apply to a pension trust was directly linked to this policy concern: "The capital of the pension trust fund cannot be distributed without defeating the social purpose of preserving the financial security of employees in their retirement by allowing them to receive periodic payments until they die" (para. 31).[52]

While *Buschau* did not expressly repudiate *Schmidt* principles, it nevertheless took a definitive step back from the pre-eminent role that *Schmidt* had assigned to trust law. Both of the court's judgments *in Buschau* highlight the central role of the pension contract in establishing the ground rules for employee pension rights. Justice Deschamps emphasized the integrated nature of the plan text and the funding documents, and the role of the plan documents in establishing the "reasonable contractual expectations of the parties." Justice

Bastarache was even more explicit in insisting that "the terms of the contract at the root of the Trust cannot be circumvented" (para. 94). The court claimed to be respecting the holding in *Schmidt* that pension trusts are "classic trusts," subject to "all applicable trust law principles" (at para. 16). However, the emphasis has now shifted from the core of Justice Cory's famous phrase to its somewhat circular qualification: not *all* trust principles are applicable to pension trusts, and courts are free to choose which ones will be applied. The ethical idea of trust law as a shelter for employee interests against employer power has now clearly receded before the pragmatic acknowledgment that the workplace pension system rests on a foundation of employer willingness to participate. Without accommodative legal rules, that willingness will evaporate.[53]

Nolan v Kerry (Canada): "Fixing" Breaches of Trust

Three years later, in *Nolan v Kerry (Canada) Ltd*,[54] the court sent an even stronger signal that it was prepared to adapt trust doctrine to employer exigencies in the interests of saving the system. The case involved a DB plan established in 1954 by the Canadian Doughnut Company Ltd. For some thirty years, the employer had made annual contributions and paid plan-related expenses out of operating funds.[55] In the mid-1980s, when the plan began to accumulate significant surplus, the employer changed course, taking a series of contribution holidays and adopting a new practice of paying expenses out of the pension fund. It amended the plan to facilitate these transactions. In 1994, the company was bought by Kerry (Canada), which continued along the same road. Then in 2000, Kerry made further significant amendments, converting the plan into a new two-tier version that included both the old DB component (now closed to new employees) and a new DC component open both to new employees and to old employees who chose to convert their DB benefits. As part of this new approach, Kerry announced that it planned not only to continue its contribution holidays with respect to the DB component, but also to draw on the surplus accumulated in the DB plan to pay its new DC contribution obligations. Current employees opposed the registration of the amended plan, challenging both the payment of expenses out of the pension fund and the use of DB surplus to pay DC contributions.[56] Under the *Schmidt* analysis, the pension fund was unquestionably "impressed with a trust" for the "exclusive benefit" of plan members. Classic trust principles appeared to dictate that the employer should not be able to dip into that fund to pay its own bills for plan expenses or for newly created D C contribution obligations.

The employees initially brought the case before the Ontario Financial Services Tribunal.[57] The tribunal disposed of the plan-expenses issue with little difficulty. Although the plan text did not expressly authorize the payment of expenses, the tribunal held that expenses reasonably incurred in the operation of the plan and the fund were authorized by implication.[58] Accordingly, a plan amendment expressly authorizing these payments was redundant, and did not need to be validated under the general power of amendment in the plan. As the tribunal saw it, the employer's long-existing practice of paying expenses from operating funds did not displace this general rule.

The tribunal had considerably more trouble reconciling the D C contribution holiday with conventional trust analysis. It was ultimately persuaded, however, that although there was a trust law impediment standing in the way of the employer's objective, as the employees had alleged, that impediment could be removed by a minor adjustment to the boundaries of the trust. In order to understand the tribunal's reasoning, it is necessary to understand the somewhat complex funding arrangements the employer had put in place for the new combined plan. The original D B plan was funded through a conventional trust fund held by a trust company. The new plan had two distinct funding arrangements: an agreement with a trust company holding the D B trust fund, and a contract with an insurance company which held the individual D C accounts. The mechanics of drawing on the trust fund to take a contribution holiday for the D C component of the plan required that monies be transferred from the trust fund to the insurer for deposit into individual employee accounts. Inevitably, the tribunal found that a transfer of this nature would constitute a breach of trust, because it would require the employer to extract money from the trust fund in order to make the D C contributions. Less inevitably, the tribunal saw this as a technical problem only, which could be cured by a retroactive amendment to the plan documents, expanding the beneficiaries of the original trust to include the members of the D C component.[59] Once those arrangements were made, the tribunal held that it would be proper to draw on the fund surplus to finance the employer's D C contributions; the money would still move from the D B fund into individual employee accounts, but that movement would now take place within the trust envelope.

The employees' appeal from the tribunal's decision on both the plan-expenses and contribution-holiday issues ultimately made its way up to the Supreme Court of Canada, where it was dismissed on all grounds. On the plan-expenses issue, the Supreme Court unanimously upheld the tribunal decision. Justice Marshall Rothstein, writing for the full court, agreed with the tribunal that employers have implied authority to pay plan expenses from the pension fund, unless expressly precluded by the plan documents. While the plan language clearly prohibited amendments that would "authorize or permit any part of the Fund to be used for, or diverted to, purposes other than for the exclusive benefit of such employees," Justice Rothstein insisted that "the term 'exclusive benefit' [cannot] be construed to mean that no one but the employees can benefit from a use of the trust funds." After all, he pointed out, employers also benefit from workplace pension plans, since they make use of these plans for "attracting and retaining employees, paying deferred compensation, settling or avoiding strikes, providing increased compensation without increasing wages, increasing employee turnover, and reducing the likelihood of lawsuits by encouraging employees who would otherwise have been laid off to depart voluntarily" (para. 53). As he saw it, since plan expenses must be paid in order for the plan to continue, an amendment which permits those expenses to be paid out of the fund is "to the exclusive benefit of the employees, within the meaning of [the plan]" (54–5).

On the DC contribution-holiday issue, the court divided. The employees had grounded their argument on the proposition that, since the trust fund was initially established to support the DB plan, it was a trust for the benefit of DB plan members. Justice Rothstein, speaking for the majority, refused to acknowledge the essential link between the fund surplus and the defined benefit component of the plan.[60] Instead, he focused formalistically on the mechanics of the fund. Like the tribunal, he took the view that the trust law problem vanished if the plan documents were amended to ensure that the DC plan members and their individual accounts were included within the scope of the trust fund (para. 84). In the absence of a prohibition in the legislation or the plan documents, he was prepared to give the employer carte blanche to designate trust beneficiaries as it saw fit (paras. 99–114).

In a vigorous dissent, Justice LeBel, joined by Justice Morris Fish, emphasized the ethical dimensions of trust law. He argued that "[t]he employer's attempt to use the D B surplus to fund its contribution obligations toward the D C plan not only breaches the 'exclusive benefit' provisions, but also violates one of the hallmarks of trust law: the prohibition against the revocation of trust assets." Trust law, as he saw it, "provides ... an added layer of protection" (para. 191) for plan beneficiaries which is not available under contract law; the purpose of the trust is "the protection of the beneficiaries, who are entitled to have the trust property administered in their best interest" (para. 186). He rejected Rothstein's conveniently capacious interpretation of "exclusive benefit"; in his view, "it is hard to see how the D C contribution holidays benefit anyone but [the employer], who is relieved of its contribution obligations to the D C plan" (para. 184). From a trust law perspective, he found no meaningful distinction between the employer's initial strategy for accessing the surplus to make contributions (which both the tribunal and the court majority agreed would be in breach of trust), and the revamped strategy that followed from the tribunal's remedy.[61] In both cases, money moved from the trust fund which supported the D B benefits to individual employee D C accounts. From a purely functional perspective, the employer's D C contribution holiday involved "an encroachment on irrevocable trust funds" (para.144), which removed trust monies from the fund for purposes unrelated to the D B benefits for which the fund was established. Redrawing the boundaries of the trust would not change this reality; as Justice LeBel put it, "[i]t would make a mockery of the significant protections afforded to trust funds" if the D C members could be made beneficiaries of the D B trust "by the mere stroke of a pen" (para. 179). However, this view did not prevail.

STRIPPING OFF THE "ADDED LAYER OF PROTECTION"

The Supreme Court has never formally repudiated the *Schmidt* principle that pension trusts are "true" or "classic" trusts and subject to "all applicable trust rules." The court's decisions in *Buschau* and *Kerry (Canada)* nevertheless significantly reduce the role of trust law in the construction of employee pension rights, and strip it of much of its normative content. The majority in *Schmidt* had seen trust law as a curb – a somewhat feeble curb, to be sure, but nonetheless a meaningful one – on the power of employers to use their control over pension plans to the detriment of their employees' interests. As Justice

LeBel put it in *Kerry (Canada)*, trust law was intended to function as "an added layer of protection" (para. 191) for plan members against exercises of employer power that harm the interests of plan members. By the time it decided *Buschau*, however, the court was not prepared to brave the consequences of placing curbs on the power of employers. In a reversal of the spirit if not the letter of *Schmidt*, the court held that the trust rule at issue in that case was "inapplicable" *because* (among other reasons) it threatened employer control, which in turn threatened the future of the workplace pension system. The decision in *Kerry (Canada)* backtracks even further from trust primacy by allowing employers to cure breaches of trust on a retroactive basis. This approach effectively strips the ethical content from the concept of breach of trust, turning trust compliance into a technical exercise in which employers not only write their own trust rules, but can now *rewrite* them retroactively if they have failed to achieve their goals. After *Kerry (Canada)*, *Schmidt*'s high-minded pronouncements – that trust principles take precedence over contract principles and equity will prevail when its dictates clash with the terms of the pension contract – are clearly no longer good law in the pension context.

7

Fiduciary Principles and Employer Conflict of Interest

INTRODUCTION

The Supreme Court's more contractarian perspective has limited the utility of trust law as a fetter on how employers use pension trust funds, at least in ongoing plans. An additional limitation, as *Schmidt* made clear, and subsequent cases have made clearer, is that trust law applies to workplace pension plans only where the funds which support those plans were constituted directly or by implication as formal trusts. It plays no role in plans that used other forms of funding from the outset, and has no application to the wide range of functions performed by employers in the course of designing and establishing pension plans, amending plans to change benefit formulae or benefit type, terminating or restructuring plans, or making day-to-day decisions about member entitlements, except as those functions have impact on a formal trust. It follows that, even in its most ethical guise, trust law offers no recourse to employees in most situations in which an employer's pursuit of its own interests may come into conflict with the best interests of employees. Plan members in search of legal rules to restrain employer conflict of interest more generally have been forced to look outside the straitjacket of formal trust law.

One plausible place to look is to the body of law which concerns fiduciary obligations. Fiduciary law has close affinities with trust law, since the trustee/beneficiary relationship is itself a fiduciary relationship.[1] But fiduciary law has fewer technical constraints and much broader reach than trust law. It does not require a trust fund or a declaration of trust, and does not focus on property interests. Instead, its focus is on regulating abuses of power within legal relationships.

Once a fiduciary relationship is identified, "the fiduciary [must] act with absolute loyalty toward another party, the beneficiary ... in managing the latter's affairs."[2] Some relationships are acknowledged by the courts as fiduciary per se – for example, lawyer/client and parent/child relationships.[3] Others are ad hoc fiduciary relationships, identified through the application of judge-made tests that look for structural imbalances of power that enable the stronger party within the relationship to damage the interests of the weaker party.

The workplace pension relationship is an obvious candidate for fiduciary regulation. However, imposing a duty of "absolute loyalty" on employers in connection with their pension plans would be radically inconsistent with the self-interested foundation on which the workplace pension system rests. Courts considering fiduciary questions in the pension context confront a classic regulatory dilemma. Legal rules that require employers to place employee pension interests ahead of their own would offer better protection for pension rights than the rules of contract law. But such rules would inevitably reduce employer incentives to establish and maintain pension plans. Courts and tribunals are very conscious of this dilemma, as we have already seen in the trust-law context. In the context of fiduciary law as well, courts have struggled to reach an equilibrium in which legal principles can control egregious abuses of employer discretion without seriously challenging employer autonomy to frame and manage their plans as they see fit. We shall see in this chapter that their efforts to find that balance have led them to adopt a contractarian version of fiduciary law which functions much like contractarian trust law, imposing only those fiduciary obligations which employers have voluntarily agreed to assume.

THE RISE OF THE "TWO HATS" DOCTRINE

As we have seen, in their role as initiators or sponsors of pension plans, employers control decisions about whether to establish a plan, what kind of plan it will be, and what kind of benefits it will provide. They typically maintain continuing control by drafting plans in which they retain a broad range of powers and duties in their own hands, and embedding in the plan text discretionary power to change, amend, and terminate the plan. In addition, employers often assume an ongoing role as plan administrators. Under the terms of the plan itself, a plan administrator may make numerous discretionary decisions in

connection with the ongoing operation of the plan. Plan administrators also have statutory duties and responsibilities that go well
beyond the routine functions we normally regard as "administrative."[4] Plan administrators may instruct actuaries, within the param-
eters of accepted actuarial practice, about whether a plan will adopt
conservative or aggressive actuarial assumptions; these assumptions
will in turn affect plan funding levels. They may develop and implement fund investment strategies that have direct impact on the level
of risk to which member benefits are exposed. They may have direct
decision-making authority over the contribution levels of both
employers and employees.[5] They may negotiate plan-merger and
asset-transfer agreements that affect both benefit entitlements and
distribution of surplus. They may instruct legal counsel on a wide
variety of issues that affect employee benefit outcome, and make
important discretionary judgments about individual pension claims.

Regulatory statutes impose standards on plan administrators that
either replicate or closely resemble fiduciary standards, requiring
them to place the interests of plan beneficiaries ahead of their own.[6]
Many of the functions of plan administrators clearly conflict with the
interests of employers. The duty of plan administrators to ensure that
employer contributions are remitted as they come due and the duty
to report to the regulator if the employer is delinquent in making
timely remittances are only the most obvious examples.[7] Despite the
inevitability of conflicts of interest, however, most jurisdictions permit employers to take on the role of plan administrator. Few place
any statutory restrictions on employers if they do so, or acknowledge
in any way the enhanced potential for conflicts inherent in the dual
role of employer/administrator.[8]

For many years, courts and tribunals believed they had found the
key to balancing employer self-interest and fiduciary obligation in
what is now known as the "two hats" doctrine. The "two hats" doctrine acknowledges that employers play a range of conflicting roles in
the pension system, and attaches fiduciary responsibility to some but
not all of those roles. It allows employers who find themselves in conflict of interest to defend their conduct by demonstrating that, when
pursuing a course of action which runs contrary to the interests of
plan members, they were acting in a capacity to which no fiduciary
duties attach. In general, courts and tribunals that have applied "two
hats" analysis have concluded that employers bear no fiduciary

obligations when acting as "employers" and/or "plan sponsors"; they are fiduciaries only when they are acting as plan administrators.

The roots of the "two hats" doctrine are found in *Imperial Oil v Superintendent of Pensions*, a decision of the Pension Commission of Ontario (P C O).[9] In this case, the P C O was faced with an allegation that the employer had violated its fiduciary obligations in the exercise of its powers of plan amendment. Imperial Oil was the plan administrator under the statute, and the employees challenging the amendment relied primarily on the statutory duty imposed by s.22(4) of the *Pension Benefits Act, 1987*, which requires that "[a]n administrator … shall not knowingly permit the administrator's interest to conflict with the administrator's duties and powers in respect of the pension fund." The amendment challenged in this case made it more difficult for employees to qualify for early retirement pensions and thus clearly favoured the employer. If the employer had a fiduciary duty to act in the best interests of the members in exercising its powers of amendment, it had almost certainly violated that duty.

The P C O's decision focused on whether s.22(4) applied to the employer's powers of amendment under the plan. The P C O found that it did not. It held that, in amending the plan, Imperial Oil had not been acting in its capacity as plan administrator; it had been acting in its capacity as employer. As the P C O pointed out: "The Act recognizes that an employer may wear 'two hats' in respect of pension plans. Indeed, s. 8 specifically states that an employer may be an administrator. In that way, it acknowledges that an employer may play two roles" (para. 30). As the decision bluntly acknowledged, "it is self evident that the two roles may come into conflict from time to time." In the P C O's view, however, the *P B A* did not regulate *employer* conflict of interest, even when the employer was also plan administrator. In its role as *employer* – a role the P C O found to include decisions "to create a pension plan, to amend it and to wind it up" (para. 33) – the employer was unburdened by fiduciary obligations and entitled to favour its own interests. The P C O reasoned that, since a rule which prohibits employer conflict of interest would mean that "[a]n employer could never use the power to amend the plan in a way that was to its benefit, as opposed to the benefit of the employees" (para. 33), the legislature could not have intended such a rule. Unarticulated but clearly implied is the assumption that, if employers cannot use their powers of amendment to advance their own interests, they will not establish and maintain plans. Accordingly, the PCO held that s.22(4) of the statute did not prevent employers from placing their own interests ahead of plan members' interests when amending their plans.[10]

Imperial Oil was essentially an exercise in statutory interpretation. Canadian courts considering fiduciary obligations as a matter of common law could certainly have reached a different conclusion about how those obligations meshed with an employer's broader roles within the pension system. Until recently, however, courts too generally embraced the "two hats" approach, and agreed with the PCO that employers are fiduciaries only when they are wearing a plan administrator "hat."[11] When they are wearing a sponsor/ employer "hat," they are free to pursue their own interests in preference to those of plan beneficiaries. Courts in a variety of Canadian jurisdictions have applied the "two hats" doctrine to endorse employer initiatives which might well have been unlawful if fiduciary standards applied. In Sutherland v Hudson's Bay Co.,[12] an Ontario court applied the doctrine to a Buschau-like scenario, in which an employer re-opened a closed pension plan for the purpose of accessing the surplus, and amended the plan to authorize itself to draw on surplus to take contribution holidays and pay plan expenses. The court held that, in amending the plan, the employer was acting as employer/plan sponsor rather than administrator, and was free to pursue its own interests at the expense of plan beneficiaries. In Lieberman v Business Development Bank of Canada,[13] a British Columbia court applied the doctrine in a case in which the employer had allowed active employees to take a contribution holiday without providing any compensating benefit to non-active employees. The court rejected a challenge from the retired and deferred members, who argued that the employer was bound by a fiduciary duty to treat all plan members with an even hand (para. 3).[14] The judge reasoned that, since pension benefits were an integral part of the employee compensation package, a decision to improve the pension component of employee compensation by giving employees a contribution holiday engaged the employer's capacity as employer, and not as plan administrator (para. 85). Accordingly, no fiduciary obligations were involved (paras. 78–80). The Quebec Court of Appeal came to a similar conclusion in Association provinciale des retraités d'Hydro-Québec v Hydro-Québec, applying the "two hats" doctrine to dismiss a claim by retired employees that a plan administrator who

drew on plan surplus to enhance benefits for active employees violated the fiduciary duty of even-handedness.[15] The benefit enhance-
ments had been obtained in collective bargaining. The court observed
that "the respondent wears a number of different hats and changes
them to suit the circumstances. Accordingly, when sitting around the
negotiating table with the unions representing 95% of its employees,
[the employer] acts in its capacity as employer, not as trustee of the
fund" (para. 88).

Notwithstanding its ubiquity, the "two hats" approach has some
serious deficiencies. It depends for its logic and coherence not only on
the proposition that an employer owes no fiduciary duties outside its
administrator role, but also on the questionable assumption that a
clear functional line can be drawn between the role of employer/
sponsor and the role of plan administrator. In fact, the duties of plan
administrators are often either ill-defined or very broadly defined in
statutes, making the distinction much less precise than the case law
implies.[16] At common law, the line is even more fluid, dependent on
the content of plan documents and often quite circular. Very few "two
hats" decisions engage in careful functional analysis to determine
whether particular exercises of employer power are ones in which an
employer/sponsor *should* be required to submerge its own interests
in those of the employees; courts all too frequently take a question-
begging approach, labelling function first, and then concluding on the
basis of that label that fiduciary duties do or do not apply.

One exception that demonstrates both the necessity and the difficulty of functional analysis is the Ontario case of *OMERS Sponsors
Corporation v OMERS Administrative Corporation.*[17] The Ontario
Municipal Employees' Pension Plan (OMERS) is a multi-employer
plan established by the *Ontario Municipal Employees Retirement
System Act, 2006*[18] to provide workplace pension benefits for municipal and other employees in the broader public sector. The plan is
jointly sponsored by municipal employers and a group of unions representing municipal employees.[19] The parties to the litigation were
the two corporations created by the statute to carry out the governance and administrative responsibilities for OMERS. The Administrative Corporation is formally designated as the plan administrator
under the statute, and it also plays the role of plan administrator
under the *Pension Benefits Act, 1987*. The Sponsors Corporation is
the body through which union and employer co-sponsors jointly
make their "management" decisions in connection with the plan. Its

core responsibilities include making "decisions about the design of benefits to be provided by, and contributions to be made to, the OMERS Pension Plans" [s.25(2) (a)], and determining "the terms and conditions of the OMERS Pension Plans, subject to the restrictions set out in the statute [s.16(1)]." In carrying out these responsibilities, it has the power to amend the plan (ss.18, 25).

The case did not directly involve the issue of fiduciary functions. It was a "friendly" application seeking the court's approval of an agreement between these two corporations concerning what expenses of the Sponsors' Corporation could properly be paid out of the pension fund. That question required the court to address the distinction between "administrator" and "plan sponsor" functions, because it essentially turned on the principle implicit in the Supreme Court of Canada's decision in *Kerry (Canada)*: that expenses necessary to the administration of the plan could be paid out of the pension fund (unless the plan documents stood in the way), but that expenses incurred in the interests of the plan sponsor could not (para. 44).[20] If labels were the sole criterion, the expenses of a body called the Sponsors Corporation would all be regarded as incurred in the interests of the plan sponsor, and *Kerry (Canada)* would have been an impediment to their payment from the plan. However, both parties argued for a functional analysis, which recognized that, within the unique statutory context of the OMERS plan, the Sponsors Corporation played a less self-interested role than the more typical employer/plan sponsor.

The OMERS court observed that, in a traditional single-employer plan, an employer functioning as plan sponsor "decides whether to establish a plan and on its funding design ... In deciding whether to establish or terminate a plan, in defining the categories of employees who are eligible for membership, and in determining what benefits will be offered, the sponsor may act in its own interests and may prefer the company's interests over those of the employees" (para. 39). By contrast, an employer functioning as plan administrator deals with such issues as the enrolment of members, the calculation and payment of benefits under the plan, and the investment of the assets of the plan (para. 40). The court was persuaded that within the context of the OMERS statute the responsibilities assigned to the Sponsors Corporation were concerned with administration and "good governance," and the Sponsors Corporation would be expected to carry out those functions "in the best interests of the Plan as a whole" (para. 56–7). It therefore concluded that, with the exception of some minor items related to sorting out separate stakeholder interests among the plan sponsors, all the Sponsors Corporation's expenses could properly be paid for out of the fund.

"CONTRACTARIAN" FIDUCIARY LAW ECLIPSES THE "TWO HATS" DOCTRINE

As the OMERS decision illustrates, the "two hats" doctrine is not self-applying either at common law or under statute, since it lacks a mechanism for making the clear distinctions between administrative and other functions which are essential to its integrity as a tool for managing employer conflict of interest. In the abstract, it may be possible for employers to carry out some functions guided by a "duty of absolute loyalty" to employees, while simultaneously giving self-interest free reign in connection with others, but in the concrete, such compartmentalization is not realistic either to implement or to monitor. It is therefore not surprising that when the Supreme Court of Canada was squarely confronted with the doctrine, it rejected it as a tool for determining whether, when, and how fiduciary principles should be applied to employer pension conduct. However, in rejecting the "two hats" doctrine, the Supreme Court did not reject the policy behind the doctrine. As we saw in Chapter 6, the court is keenly aware of the incentive effects of legal rules on employers considering pension decisions. With the exception of *Schmidt*, its trust decisions have been driven by a desire to maintain a legal climate flexible enough to permit employers to reap the business benefits of their pension plans. In place of the "two hats" doctrine, the court sought an approach that allowed employers to take on fiduciary duties where and when they chose to do so, but did not impose them in areas where they preferred to remain free to act in their own interest.

The court found that approach in a concept of "contractarian" fiduciary law mirroring the "contractarian" trust law we examined in the previous chapter. "Contractarian" fiduciary law had already been evolving for some time in Canada before the Supreme Court brought it to bear on employer pension conduct.[21] As we have seen, contractarian trust law permits employer/settlors to craft the content of their duties as trustees in their plan documents, leaving courts simply to enforce their "intentions," unburdened by any overriding normative considerations. For many years, fiduciary law appeared more resistant to contractarianism, because ad hoc fiduciary relationships and the duties that went with them were largely created (or at least "identified") by the courts rather than by private parties. In classifying ad hoc fiduciary relationships, Canadian courts used a purposive approach based on structural imbalances of power which gave this body of law its ethical core. This approach solidified into a test known as the *Frame v Smith* test, which looked for three characteristics in an ad hoc fiduciary relationship: (1) the more powerful party "has scope for the exercise of some discretion or power"; (2) the more powerful party "can unilaterally exercise that power or discretion so as to affect the beneficiary's legal or practical interests"; and (3) the less powerful party "is peculiarly vulnerable to or at the mercy of the fiduciary holding the discretion or power."[22] If these three characteristics were present, the relationship was deemed fiduciary, and the more powerful party – the fiduciary – bore a full range of fiduciary duties to the less powerful party – the beneficiary. Above all, the fiduciary was required to place the interests of the beneficiary ahead of its own interests.

In recent years, however, the Supreme Court of Canada has backed away from this purposive conception of a fiduciary relationship. In a series of cases outside the pension context, the court held that ad hoc fiduciary obligations will not be imposed on a party *who has not voluntarily undertaken such obligations.*[23] The new test for identifying ad hoc fiduciary relationships adds a fourth prong to the *Frame v Smith* test; in addition to an imbalance of power, discretionary authority on the part of the stronger party, and vulnerability to that authority on the part of the weaker party, there must now be "an *undertaking* by the alleged fiduciary to act in the best interests of the alleged beneficiary or beneficiaries."[24] Under this four-pronged test, a more powerful party may escape identification as a fiduciary and exercise its discretion in ways that are damaging to the interests of a less-powerful party, unless it has agreed to bind itself not to do so. The new approach has important implications for the development of fiduciary law in the context of workplace pensions.

Burke v Hudson's Bay Co.: A Transitional Decision

This new contractarian approach to fiduciary obligations lurked not far below the surface of the Supreme Court's 2010 decision in *Burke v Hudson's Bay Co.*[25] *Burke* involved a surplus claim by a group of former employees of the Northern Stores Division of the Hudson's Bay Company (HBC), a division whose long and unique history was reflected in its continuing label as the "fur trade division."[26] This group, along with other HBC employees, had been members of a DB plan established by the company in 1961. In 1987, after a severe downturn in the retail industry, HBC sold the Northern Stores Division. The pension liabilities of the active employees were included in the sale. As required by the purchase agreement, HBC transferred pension assets sufficient to meet these liabilities to a new plan established by the purchaser,[27] but did not transfer any portion of the old plan's surplus.[28] The affected employees challenged this decision, arguing that they had a *Schmidt*-based trust claim to the surplus. They also argued that, irrespective of who owned the surplus, the employer had an overriding fiduciary obligation to treat all plan beneficiaries with an "even hand," an obligation which required it to transfer a pro-rata share of the surplus to the new plan for the benefit of employees relocating to the new employer, instead of retaining it all in the old plan, where it could no longer benefit the transferees.

By the time the case reached the Supreme Court of Canada, the formal trust-law issues had been effectively decided against the employees by the Supreme Court's judgments in *Buschau* and *Kerry (Canada)*; the application of fiduciary law was now the novel issue at the heart of the appeal.[29] Relying on the "two hats" doctrine, HBC argued that its decision not to transfer a portion of the surplus was not made in a fiduciary capacity.[30] The Supreme Court disagreed. The court applied the *Frame v Smith* test and concluded that the employer as plan administrator was a fiduciary:

> Subject to the text of the plan, the terms of the trust agreement, and relevant statutes, there is no doubt that HBC had wide discretion with respect to the pension plan, which it could exercise unilaterally and which could affect the interests of the employees, and to which exercise of discretion the employees were vulnerable. Therefore ... in these circumstances HBC, as plan administrator, was a fiduciary and ... a fiduciary relationship existed between HBC as administrator and the employees/beneficiaries under the pension plan (para. 41).

HBC's decision not to transfer surplus therefore attracted fiduciary analysis.

However, the court unanimously exonerated the employer of any fiduciary breach. As the court saw it, fiduciary law did not generate an obligation to treat plan members with an even hand in connection with plan administration in general; the duty of even-handedness attached only to the *rights* of the employees under the plan. These rights could be determined only by construing the plan documents. As the court put it, "[t]he duty of even-handedness must be anchored in the terms of the pension plan documentation" (para.85). Since the plan documents were careful to spell out that employee rights were limited to the retirement benefits provided by the plan, none of the employees had any *right* to surplus under the HBC plan. The employer's decision concerning surplus was therefore unfettered by the duty of even-handedness (paras. 51–63).

Burke is a transitional case. The court applied the *Frame v Smith* test in determining that HBC was a fiduciary, without directly alluding to the "two hats" doctrine. Its conclusion that the employer's decision with respect to surplus transfer was subject to fiduciary scrutiny was arguably a victory for employees, since it appeared to broaden the range of pension functions that fall into the fiduciary category. However, the court seriously watered down the normative content of fiduciary duties by its insistence that they attach only to concrete legal rights created by plan documents, requiring nothing more than that the employer administer the plan according to its terms. In the result, despite the fact that HBC made its decision while acting in a fiduciary role, the court held that the decision not to transfer any part of the surplus was a "legitimate commercial transaction" (para. 91), which did not engage its fiduciary duty. *Burke*'s refusal to apply fiduciary duty outside the strict boundaries of the legal rights created by the plan prefigures the contractarian shift which emerged explicitly in subsequent cases, clearing the way for employers to set their own limits on the scope and content of their fiduciary duties, even in the role of plan administrator.

There is an additional reason to classify *Burke* as essentially contractarian. The court's treatment of the relationship between plan text and trust documents completes the reversal of the hierarchy established in *Schmidt*. Recall that, in *Schmidt*, the court held that, where there is conflict between plan terms and trust terms, trust terms take precedence, and "to the extent that applicable equitable [i.e., trust] principles conflict with plan provisions, equity must prevail."[31] The court had already taken some steps back from trust pre-eminence in *Buschau* and *Kerry (Canada)* by emphasizing the integrated nature of plan texts and funding documents, and the centrality of employer intent. In *Burke*, the court retreated completely, according primacy to the pension plan over the trust agreement on the ground that the plan itself – the contract – established the plan as the dominant document.[32]

The PIPS Case:
Government Employers Are Not Pension Fiduciaries

In deciding *Burke*, the Supreme Court still used the old *Frame v Smith* test for identifying an ad hoc fiduciary relationship, although it applied contractarian logic to defining the scope of obligations within that relationship. Two years later, in *Professional Institute of the Public Service of Canada v Canada (PIPS)*,[33] the Supreme Court directly embraced the newer four-pronged test for application within the pension context. The PIPS case dealt with the federal government's decision to reduce a surplus that had been accumulating on the books of its three workplace pension plans – the public-service plan, the RCMP plan, and the armed-forces plan – for a number of years. These plans had been established by statute. The decision to reduce the surplus was part of a legislative package that altered the basis on which the plans were funded and changed the way employer and employee contributions to the plan would be determined. After the surplus had dropped by some $28 billion dollars, plan members brought a court challenge, arguing that they had an equitable entitlement to the surplus, and therefore the government's conduct was in breach of trust and in violation of its fiduciary duties as plan administrator.

The court held that, prior to the changes, the pension fund, including its apparent surplus, was merely an accounting entry on the government's books. Since there was no "real" fund, there was no property to which a trust could attach, and therefore no basis for a formal trust claim (paras. 108–12). It also rejected the notion that the government was a fiduciary to its employees in its role as pension plan administrator. In making that determination, the court expressly relied on the new fourth prong supplementing the *Frame v Smith* test, holding that before fiduciary obligations could be found there must be "an undertaking by the alleged fiduciary to act in the best interests of the alleged beneficiary or beneficiaries" (paras. 121–4). Indeed, the court reinforced and expanded upon this fourth prong by demanding not only that there be an undertaking to take on fiduciary obligations, but that the undertaking be exclusive and specifically linked to the employee "interest" at issue in the case. As the court put it, "It is now definitely a requirement of an *ad hoc* fiduciary relationship that the alleged fiduciary undertake, either expressly or impliedly, to act in accordance with a duty of loyalty. It is critical that the purported beneficiary be able to identify a forsaking of the interests of all others on the part of the fiduciary, in favour of the beneficiary, in relation to the specific interest at issue" (para. 124).

On the facts before it, the court found no undertaking on the part of the government to "forsake the interests of all others (including taxpayers) in favour of the Plan members with respect to the actuarial surplus – the specific interest at issue here" (para. 125).[34] The decision emphasized that by their very nature governments have multiple conflicting obligations, and courts will not cast them in the role of fiduciaries simply because they carry out functions (such as pension plan administration) which might give rise to fiduciary obligations if they involved private employers (paras. 115–20). In the absence of a trust or fiduciary obligation, the court found the government's unilateral decision to reduce plan surplus without allocating any share to the employees entirely lawful.

Sun Indalex v United Steelworkers: "Fixing" Fiduciary Breaches

Although *PIPS* was a public sector case, the decision signalled that the court was ready to apply its revamped four-pronged fiduciary test to private sector employer/plan administrators on the next convenient occasion. That occasion arose shortly afterwards in *Sun Indalex Finance LLC v United Steelworkers*,[35] an insolvency case pitting employee pension claims against the claims of secured creditors. Indalex Ltd, the Canadian operating arm of a US-based corporate conglomerate, was the administrator of two pension plans for its employees, one for unionized workers and one for salaried executives. The company ran into serious financial difficulties and applied for insolvency protection under the *Companies' Creditors Arrangement Act (CCAA)*.[36] Ultimately the business was sold for considerably less than its outstanding liabilities, which meant that it could not meet the claims of all creditors. As is now routine in restructuring cases, the initial court order placing the company under *CCAA* protection gave the highest priority ("super-priority") to a set of creditors known in the insolvency world as "DIP lenders."[37] Members of the pension plans nevertheless claimed priority over the DIP lenders for some $4.8 million, the amount necessary to make up deficiencies in the pension funds. In part, their argument was a statute-based claim that the Ontario *Pension Benefits Act, 1987* created a "deemed trust" for funding deficiencies that had statutory priority over secured claims.[38] More fundamentally for purposes of this discussion, it was also a claim that the company had violated its fiduciary obligations by preferring its own corporate interests over the interests of pension plan members throughout the restructuring proceedings. For lay observers, including pension plan members, the fiduciary argument drew additional credibility from the byzantine corporate relationships among debtors and creditors, US companies and Canadian companies, and the fact that, by the time the claims were litigated, the DIP lenders had already been repaid by the US parent company under intersecting guarantees.[39]

The Ontario Court of Appeal upheld the employees' fiduciary claim. The parties supporting the DIP lender's priority had relied heavily on the "two hats" doctrine, arguing that in its management of the *CCAA* proceedings Indalex was wearing its "corporate hat" rather than its "plan administrator hat," and was entitled to consider only the interests of the corporation. Justice Gillese, author of the Court of Appeal decision, rejected that argument. She accepted the "two hats" metaphor she had crafted in *Imperial Oil* while chairing the PCO, and agreed that Indalex could properly claim to be wearing only its "corporate hat" when making its decision to apply for *CCAA* protection, since that decision did not necessarily conflict with the interests of plan members. However, she was persuaded that Indalex wore both "hats" simultaneously throughout much of the subsequent proceedings, and was therefore accountable under fiduciary principles for resolving the ensuing conflicts of interest.[40] In her view, Indalex had mismanaged those conflicts and breached its fiduciary obligations under both statute and common law by bringing the initial application without notice to the members, seeking priority for the DIP lenders in full knowledge that the pension plans were underfunded, selling the company without making provision for ensuring the pension shortfalls would be covered, and attempting to file for bankruptcy protection in order to defeat the members' deemed trust claims under the provincial statute.[41] As a remedy for these fiduciary breaches, she imposed a "constructive trust" over the remaining corporate assets for the benefit of the pension fund,[42] with the result that the pension plans now took priority over the DIP lenders. In doing so, she took account of the fact that Indalex's parent company, as guarantor of the DIP loans, had benefited from the super-priority. While she did not suggest anything improper about the loan guarantee arrangements, she found the balance of equities in favour of the pensioners: "This is not a case in which the secured creditor is an arm's length third party taken by surprise by the claims of the Plans' beneficiaries."[43]

The majority of the Supreme Court of Canada reversed this decision, restoring the priority of the DIP loan. The court unanimously agreed with the Court of Appeal that Indalex was in a fiduciary relationship with plan members in its capacity as plan administrator, both by statute and at common law. It was also unanimous that Indalex had breached fiduciary obligations arising out of that relationship in the course of the CCAA proceedings. The court divided, however, on the nature and seriousness of the breaches, and on the appropriate remedy.[44] In two separate decisions, a majority of the judges let the company off lightly, but not on the basis of the "two hats" doctrine, which none of the judges found useful as a tool for resolving the conflict-of-interest dilemmas confronting employer/plan administrators. Indeed, Justice Deschamps expressly rejected the doctrine, which in her view ran the risk of giving employers illegitimate carte blanche to ignore employee interests: "The solution is not to determine whether a given decision can be classified as being related either to the management of the corporation or the administration of the pension. The employer may well take a sound management decision and yet harm the interests of the plan members. An employer acting as a plan administrator is not permitted to disregard its fiduciary obligations to plan members and favour the competing interests of the corporation on the basis that it is wearing a 'corporate hat'" (paras. 63–5). As she saw it, employers who assume the role of plan administrator take on the fiduciary obligations that burden administrators, and cannot shirk the task of addressing the ensuing conflicts if their corporate interests create competing obligations on specific issues (paras. 63–6). When conflicts arise, they must be resolved.

Justice Deschamps found that Indalex was in conflict of interest as soon as it became aware of the funding deficit in the pension plans, which triggered the possibility of a legal contest over whether that deficit gave rise to a trust claim (para. 66). At that point, she held, Indalex had a duty to resolve the conflict. She suggested some options. Indalex might simply have given plan members proper notice of its motion to seek approval of DIP financing on terms that would trump a claim by the pension plans for priority under the deemed trust provisions of the provincial statute. Alternatively, it might have withdrawn as plan administrator and made other arrangements for member interests to be represented in the CCAA proceedings (paras. 66–73). Its failure to take either of these steps was a breach of its fiduciary duty. However, unlike Justice Gillese, Justice Deschamps took the view that the outcome for plan members would have been the same even if the employer had complied with its fiduciary duties (para. 74). In other words, the breach of fiduciary duty did not cause the damage of which the members complained; that damage was caused by the shortfall in the pension fund. Accordingly, a constructive trust remedy making up that shortfall was not warranted.

In a concurring judgment, Justice Thomas Cromwell came to the same conclusion.[45] Like Justice Deschamps, he saw the potential for conflict of interest whenever the employer takes on the role of plan administrator: "[T]he broader business interests of the employer corporation and the interests of pension beneficiaries in getting the promised benefits are almost always at least potentially in conflict. Every important business decision has the potential to put at risk the solvency of the corporation and therefore its ability to live up to its pension obligations. The employer, within the limits set out in the plan documents and the legislation generally, has the authority to amend the plan unilaterally and even to terminate it. These steps may well not serve the best interests of plan beneficiaries" (para. 198). However, as he saw it, conflict in embryo does not per se trigger fiduciary obligations, as suggested by the Court of Appeal (para. 201). Such obligations arise only "when there is a substantial risk that the employer-administrator's representation of the plan beneficiaries would be materially and adversely affected by the employer-administrator's duties to the corporation" (para. 200), and only within the narrow compass of administrator responsibilities assigned by the plan documents and legislation.[46] Furthermore, liability does not follow merely because fiduciary duties have been triggered; it follows only if the employer does not manage its conflicts appropriately. Under this flexible standard, Justice Cromwell faulted Indalex for a single breach only: failing to bring its conflict of interest to the attention of the CCAA judge, in order to seek guidance on how the interests of plan beneficiaries should be represented in the proceedings (paras. 217–21). Like Justice Deschamps, he saw no causal link between the breach and the employees' losses, and no basis for imposing a constructive trust.

Only in the dissenting opinion of Justice LeBel do we find any trace of the notion that there is an ethical core to fiduciary responsibilities. Justice LeBel emphasized that fiduciary relationships have their basis in an imbalance of power; analysis of these relationships "ought not [to] stop at the level of a theoretical and detached approach that fails to address how, very concretely, this relationship works or can be twisted, perverted or abused, as was the situation in this case." He highlighted the vulnerability of elderly retirees in the face of employer business decisions that place their retirement benefits at risk:

These losses of benefits are, in all probability, permanent in the case of the beneficiaries who have already retired or who are close to retirement. They deeply affect their lives and expectations. For most of them, what is lost is lost for good. No arrangement will allow them to get a start on a new life. We should not view the situation of the beneficiaries as regrettable but unavoidable collateral damage arising out of the ebbs and tides of the economy. In my view, the law should give the members some protection, as the Court of Appeal intended when it imposed a constructive trust (paras. 266–7).[47]

Justice LeBel was dismissive of a "two hats" approach that would permit fiduciaries to slough off their responsibilities when faced with a conflict of interest resulting from multiple incompatible roles. He emphasized that employers have a choice about whether to become plan administrators; while the statute permits employers to play this role, it does not require it. There is therefore no statutory warrant for holding employers to a *lower* fiduciary standard than other administrators (paras. 268–70). Indeed, he implied that a *higher* standard might be appropriate. As he saw it, these employees had increased vulnerability with their employer as administrator, because "they did not enjoy the protection that the existence of an independent administrator might have given them" (para. 268). Justice LeBel found Indalex in conflict "from the moment it started to contemplate putting itself under the protection of the CCAA and proposing an arrangement with its creditors" (para 269). As soon as that conflict became apparent, Indalex should have immediately relinquished its role as plan administrator and ensured a transition to an independent administrator who could then protect the interests of the plan members (para 271). Indalex's failure to take this step was then compounded by conduct that was actively inimical to member interests (para. 266). In his view, these breaches of the employer's fiduciary duty were both serious and causally linked to the employees' losses, warranting the robust remedy of constructive trust.

From a purely doctrinal perspective, *Sun Indalex* was not a complete loss for employees. The court's decision probably rings the death knell of the "two hats" doctrine as a strategy for employer/administrators seeking to evade conflict-of-interest allegations while continuing to play both roles. It affirms that employer/administrators cannot ignore their fiduciary obligations to plan members; conflicts must be confronted and resolved. However, the court's prescription for resolution does not provide much real protection for employees. The decisions that make up the majority explicitly allow employers to prefer their corporate interests over their fiduciary obligations, inviting them to resolve conflicts simply by giving notice to employees and/or stepping out of their roles as plan administrators while continuing to pursue conduct damaging to employee interests. Even the dissenters do not insist that employer/administrators have a duty to *avoid* conflict of interest. Their threshold of tolerance for conflicts is lower than that of the majority, and the penalties they would impose for violation more stringent, but they too would permit employers to continue to pursue objectives that damage the interest of plan members, as long as they make a timely exit from their administrative roles and arrange for the substitution of a new fiduciary.

A DUTY OF GOOD FAITH?

Like the contractarian approach overtaking trust law, the contractarian approach to fiduciary law reflected in *Burke*, PIPS, and *Sun Indalex* gives fiduciaries the power to write the rules for their own conduct as plan administrators. They are fiduciaries only if they agree to be fiduciaries. They take on only the fiduciary obligations they agree to take on. In addition, they can avoid liability for substantive violation of those obligations simply by giving notice of the conflict and passing the buck to a court or withdrawing from the role of plan

administrator. This view of formal trust law and fiduciary law gives
employers very broad licence to pursue their own interests in relation
to workplace pension plans. It has forced employees challenging
employer conduct to fall back on arguments based on a duty of "good
faith," which Canadian courts have hinted may impose some lesser
but still meaningful limitation on employer pursuit of self-interest in
the pension context.[48] Explicit references to such a duty of good faith
have begun to appear in pension cases in recent years. Courts have
done little to elaborate on its substantive content, however, and it has
yet to change outcomes for employees in concrete cases.

The duty of good faith received some attention in *Buschau* in the
context of the unsuccessful attempt by employees to apply the Rule
in *Saunders v Vautier* to collapse their pension trust.[49] It will be
recalled that *Buschau* arose out of a decade-long campaign by the
employer, Rogers Communications Inc., to appropriate a plan surplus that the British Columbia courts had found to belong to the
employees. The employees argued that the Rule applied to their pension trust, because the plan associated with the trust had been closed
by Rogers and would therefore have no new beneficiaries. Rogers
countered by arguing that its powers of plan amendment were broad
enough to reopen the plan and create new beneficiaries. The British
Columbia Court of Appeal did not accept this argument. Relying
both on the language of the federal pension statute,[50] and on British
common-law authority,[51] it held that "[t]he powers of amendment
and termination given to the employer ... must be exercised in good
faith," even though they are not fiduciary powers. In light of the history of Rogers's prior manoeuvres to gain access to the surplus, it
would be "impossible," as the court saw it, for Rogers to reopen the
plan in good faith, and any attempt to do so would be set aside.[52]

As we have seen, however, the Supreme Court of Canada reversed
the Court of Appeal decision on the ground that the Rule in *Saunders
v Vautier* did not apply to the modern pension trust. The majority
decision did not directly comment on the "good faith" issue.[53] In his
concurring judgment, Justice Bastarache was dubious that there was
any factual foundation for the Court of Appeal's conclusion that
reopening the plan would constitute bad faith. He was clearly sympathetic to Rogers's position that its conduct throughout had been
driven by rational business objectives. In addition, he cast doubt on
the existence of any "duty of good faith" separate and apart from the

obligations imposed on the employer by the plan and the regulatory statute: "Any termination of the Plan and amendments to it must be examined on the basis of its terms and conditions, in consideration of the applicable provisions of the *PBSA*. What would constitute an abuse of the employer's power or would otherwise offend community standards of reasonableness in the contemplated use of the [plan] assets for the benefit of present and future employees of [Rogers] must be determined on that basis alone" (paras. 102–4).

In the wake of *Buschau*, courts considering an employer duty of good faith have hesitated to give the doctrine independent scope. In *Lloyd v Imperial Oil*,[54] the Alberta court considered whether the Imperial Oil plan amendment that had given birth to the "two hats doctrine" – an amendment increasing the qualifications for an early retirement pension – violated common-law as well as statutory fiduciary standards. As we have seen, the court dismissed the fiduciary claim on the basis that the "two hats" doctrine also applied at common law. The plaintiff argued that even if the amendment did not violate fiduciary principles, it should still be found void, because it had been passed in bad faith for the purpose of avoiding the payment of early retirement benefits to a specific group of employees who were about to be laid off. The court expressed skepticism about whether an employer duty of good faith existed, describing the employee claim as "a somewhat idiosyncratic cause of action in the pension context" (para. 62). It found it unnecessary to rule on the legal point, however, because it found no factual basis for a finding of bad faith. In the court's view, the plan amendment was motivated by the company's desire to create certainty in the administration of the pending layoffs, and to "correct" for recent changes in the applicable pension legislation, which deprived employers of discretion in approving early retirement benefits (paras. 100, 113). The court expressed the view that bad faith would require proof of conduct "in an underhanded manner or for some collateral purpose." It was confident that an employer "acting in its capacity as employer and exercising its right to amend in accordance with the terms of the Pension Plan and the applicable legislation" was not guilty of bad faith simply because it preferred its "financial self-interest" over the pension interests of its employees (para. 114).

An Ontario court took a similar approach to defining bad faith in *Sutherland v Hudson's Bay Co*.[55] Unlike the Alberta court, the

Ontario court readily accepted that employers have a duty of good faith which governs the exercise of their powers of plan amendment. The court equated this good-faith obligation with "an implied duty not to act with a view to furthering an improper purpose" (para. 321). While the court did not expressly identify the duty of good faith as a contractual duty, its subsequent analysis makes it clear that the boundaries of the duty are no broader than the employer's contractual obligations; an employer has complied with the duty if it has exercised its plan amendment powers "for a valid purpose, being a purpose which is consistent with the expectations regarding the scope and nature of the Plan at the time of its creation" (para. 320). Since those expectations are defined by the terms of the plan documents, employer conduct that complies with those documents would by definition be consistent with those expectations. As the court interpreted the plan at issue, employees could expect only the payment of promised retirement benefits. Accordingly, amendments which reopened a closed plan were bona fide, even though they were passed to permit the employer to access a surplus that would otherwise have belonged to the plan members (paras. 327–54). The court dismissed the argument that the employer's motives were relevant to the issue of good faith; good faith required only compliance with the plan and the statute (paras. 325, 350–4).

PRIVATE LAW FETTERS ON EMPLOYER DISCRETION: THE END OF THE ROAD

As the cases discussed in this chapter and the previous chapter have made clear, trust law and fiduciary law have become little more than frameworks within which employers may write their own rules of conduct through their power to draft and amend the terms of pension plans. Now that the courts have largely abandoned any role for judge-made rules controlling abuses of power and conflicts of interest in the pension context, trust and fiduciary law have become virtually indistinguishable from the contract law they were intended to supplement and ameliorate. Employers may choose whether or not to be bound by trust and fiduciary norms. Those who do not choose formal trust funding for their pension plans are not required to comply with the strictures of trust law in managing either their funds or their plans. Those who do not take on a formal role as plan administrators are not seen by the courts as pension fiduciaries, regardless of their continuing discretionary power over important pension interests of vulnerable plan members. While employers who do take on an administrative role can no longer rely on the "two hats" doctrine as a per se defence, courts will allow them to extricate themselves, by well-timed withdrawals from that role, from liability for preferring corporate goals over the pension interests of plan members. Any "duty of good faith" the courts may impose is tethered so firmly to the terms of plan documents that it adds nothing to the protection already accorded to employee pension rights under contract and statute law.

As the jurisprudence has evolved, contract law, trust law, and fiduciary law have now converged on a set of legal rules for workplace pension plans in which, for all practical purposes, the terms of the plan documents are the sole source of the governing norms to be found in private law. Since employers control those terms in most employer-sponsored plans, this means that *private* law has been relegated solely to the function of holding employers to their pension promises. The task of assessing whether employers have behaved reasonably or fairly or honourably in exercising their power over employee pension rights now belongs exclusively to *public* law, found primarily in pension statutes. In *Buschau*, the Supreme Court "passed the buck" to the regulator to deal with the request of the employee group to wind up the plan as a remedy for employer misconduct. Subsequent courts have followed this same course, emphasizing the voluntary nature of workplace pension plans, and the importance of maintaining legal rules that do not impede the ability of employers to manage their pension plans to meet their business needs.[56] It is true that courts have not entirely opted out of pension regulation. In *Burke*, the Supreme Court rejected the argument that regulatory statutes are now "complete codes," pointing out that statutes set minimum standards only. Where employers establish plans that exceed those standards, common law and equitable principles may still have a role to play.[57] As we have seen, however, that role is now limited to determining what commitments employers have agreed to take on, and holding them to those commitments. Courts are no longer prepared to impose normative standards on employer conduct derived from trust or fiduciary principles. For employees in the private sector, this means that they must look directly to the state rather than to the courts for legal rules which will hold their employers accountable for pension promises and improve the likelihood of achieving adequate, predictable, and secure pensions.

For employees in the public sector, of course, the line between the state and the employer is blurred. Public sector employers have historically done much better than private sector employers in providing pension coverage and good pension benefits for their employees. The next chapter offers a brief history of public sector plans in Canada, exploring the legal context in which those plans have flourished and the legal tools public sector employers have used to enhance their success.

8

Workplace Pension Plans
in the Public Sector

INTRODUCTION

Canadian governments at both the federal and provincial levels were early adopters of workplace pension plans, both for their own employees and for employees in what we now call the para-public or broader public sector, where government funding is a major factor in the delivery of services. As employers, governments were attracted to these plans for the same reasons as private sector employers; they saw pension plans as efficient management tools for recruiting and retaining competent and committed employees, for controlling employee behaviour in the workplace, and for facilitating mandatory retirement. However, governments are not just employers; they are also policy-makers and law-makers. Throughout much of the period we have explored in this book, governments were grappling with policy questions about retirement income provision, constructing the three-pillar retirement-income system of which workplace pension plans are an integral part, and drafting the laws they viewed as essential to the proper functioning of these plans. In structuring and operating their own plans, therefore, they had both enterprise-based management goals as employers, and the desire to demonstrate to the private sector that employment-based plans could be useful and effective vehicles for pension provision.

In meeting these more complex pension objectives, governments had a significant advantage over private sector employers. In the private sector, employers used the market power that comes with employer status to shape their pension plans to achieve their management goals. As employers, governments had that same market power.

But they also had state power, which they used to craft pension regimes to fit the unique and varied conditions of different types of public employment, and to control pension costs. Through the use of state power, they could mould regulatory and collective bargaining regimes to suit both managerial and political objectives. State power also allowed them to alter pension regimes over time in response to changing labour markets and changing economic and social conditions. Overall, state power enabled governments to craft a legal framework for public sector workplace pensions in which the benefits for them and also for their employees continue to outweigh the costs.

The result is that, amidst the general decline of the workplace pension system in Canada, the public sector is a significant exception. While private sector coverage has fallen sharply over the past three decades, public sector coverage has been rising. In 2012, nearly 88 per cent of public sector employees belonged to workplace pension plans, compared to less than 24 per cent of private sector employees.[1] More than half of all pension plan members in Canada now hold public sector jobs, and most public sector plans still offer defined benefits.[2] This chapter examines some of the unique features of the legal environment within which public sector plans have developed, and identifies factors that may account for the success of the public sector pension model in the midst of a system in overall decline. It focuses on pension provision for four significant public employee groups: the civil service (now known as the public service), municipal government employees, teachers in public education, and employees in publicly funded health care.[3]

PENSION PROVISION FOR KEY GROUPS OF PUBLIC SECTOR EMPLOYEES

Civil (Public) Service Pension Plans

In 1870, the federal government established a pension plan for its civil service as part of the business of the first parliament after Confederation, thus anticipating the Grand Trunk plan, the first private sector plan in North America, by some four years.[4] The plan was fully fleshed out in an act of parliament, revealingly entitled *An Act for better ensuring the efficiency of the Civil Service of Canada, by providing for the Superannuation of persons employed therein, in certain cases.* The government was blunt about the business objectives driving the legislation. Sir Francis Hincks, then minister of finance, advised the House of Commons that the new law "was not for the benefit of employees, but for the protection and benefit of the public and to enable the Government to get rid of persons who had arrived at a time of life when they could no longer perform their work efficiently."[5] The Preamble to the statute made this even clearer: "[F]or better ensuring efficiency and economy in the Civil Service of Canada, it is expedient to provide for the retirement therefrom, on equitable terms, of persons who, from age or infirmity, cannot properly perform the duties assigned to them."[6]

The plan itself was a simple one. The Act authorized the payment of a regular pension of up to 70 per cent of salary (s.1) to eligible "officers, clerks and other persons" (s.9) who had "served in an established capacity" in the civil service, had reached the age of sixty years, and had a minimum of ten years' service. Early-retirement pensions could be paid to those with sufficient qualifying service who were "incapacitated by bodily infirmity from properly performing [their] duties" (s.9), or had lost their jobs because of what we would now call restructuring (s.7).[7] The plan was contributory and participation was mandatory; contributions were deducted from salary for all employees subject to the legislation (s.3).[8] There was no provision for a return of contributions for employees who died or left the civil service prior to retirement.

The Act highlighted the discretionary nature of the plan: "[N]or shall any person be considered as having any absolute right to such allowance, but it shall be granted only in consideration of good and faithful service during the time upon which it is calculated, and nothing herein contained shall be understood as impairing or affecting the right of the Governor in Council to dismiss or remove any person from the Civil Service" (s.5).[9] While the Act did not specify a mandatory retirement age, it explicitly linked pensions with mandatory retirement by providing that "[r]etirement shall be compulsory on any person to whom the superannuation allowance hereinbefore mentioned shall be offered" (s.3). By legislative fiat, no stigma could be attached to being "pensioned off."[10]

In 1924 the federal government overhauled the plan.[11] The new version contained a number of key changes. It was no longer comprehensive; the plan now applied explicitly only to full-time employees with a minimum salary of $600 per annum [s.2(b)]. It established age sixty-five as the age of "regular" retirement, with a mandatory retirement age of seventy, which applied to all contributors to the plan, regardless of whether or not they were granted a pension on retirement [s.10(2)].[12] Plan contributors who left the civil service without a pension now had a right to a refund of contributions (without interest), always provided that misconduct was not the reason for their departure [s.5(a)(iii)].

However, there was still no *right* to a retirement pension. The new version of the plan was as discretionary as the old, providing that "[n]o allowance shall be granted to a contributor under this Act unless the Treasury Board reports that he is eligible within the meaning of this Act, and no superannuation or retiring allowance shall be granted unless the Treasury Board, on the advice of the Civil Service Commission, reports in addition that the granting of such allowance will be in the public interest" [s.9(1)].[13] The amount of the benefit under the 1924 Act was 2 per cent of salary per year of service, with salary averaged over the last ten years of employment, and service capped at thirty-five years [s.6(1)].[14] The formula explicitly contemplated that additional service credit could be granted to late entrants into the government's employ, a feature no doubt designed to make government jobs attractive not just to "career" civil servants but also to those who had already had successful careers in the private sector.

The 1924 Act also provided a new survivor's allowance for widows [s.5(b)] and dependent children.[15] For the widow's allowance, conditions of eligibility were established to prevent "designing women" from marrying civil servants simply to get access to their pensions. If the marriage took place after the pensioner reached the age of sixty or after retirement, or if the contributor died less than a year after the marriage, the widow did not qualify for an allowance. In the latter case, however, an allowance might still be payable if "the Treasury Board was satisfied that [the contributor] was in good health at the time of the marriage and that there [were] no other objections to the granting of the allowance" [s.9(2)]. In addition, the Act was explicit that no survivor allowance would be paid "if the person to whom it was proposed to grant the allowance is, in the opinion of the Treasury Board, unworthy of it" [s.9(2)]. Widows automatically lost their pension allowance on remarriage.

Canadian provinces eventually put similar plans in place for their own civil servants. Quebec established a statutory plan in 1876. Other provinces moved much more slowly, but Ontario's 1920 initiative set the pattern for other English-speaking provinces, and by mid-century all provinces had such plans.[16] While these plans were initially confined strictly to civil servants, most subsequently opened up to employees of Crown agencies and other public service enterprises tied directly to government. In 1973, Quebec supplemented its venerable civil service plan with a Government and Public Employees Retirement Plan covering a very broad spectrum of employees in government-service agencies, education, health care, and social services. Like the civil service plan, participation in this plan was compulsory.[17]

The general contours of most civil service plans were similar. They were compulsory contributory defined benefit plans. They typically required a contribution from employees that varied with age and/or salary level. Governments contributed an equivalent amount, or more typically credited the fund with an equivalent amount (which meant that they made no actual cash outlay for prefunding).[18] The benefit formula was based on "average salary x years of service," and paid approximately 2 per cent per year of service up to a maximum pension of 60 to 70 per cent of salary.[19] Exceptionally, British Columbia initially opted for a defined contribution plan, which was compulsory for civil servants, but available on a voluntary basis to municipalities, school boards (for non-teaching employees), and also employers in the private sector. It was not until 1958 that this plan began to offer a standard defined benefit.[20] In other provinces, there have been changes in eligibility rules and benefit structure over the years, tracking changes in government human-resource policy, regulatory standards, and social mores. In general, however, the public service model was remarkably durable until the "great policy shift" discussed below, in which many provinces converted to jointly sponsored plans.[21]

Pension Plans for Teachers

In addition to providing pensions for their own employees, governments in Canada also involved themselves early in providing pensions for teachers. Before the end of the Second World War, all provinces had enacted legislation establishing a pension plan for qualified teachers employed in public education;[22] in several provinces, teachers' pension legislation predated civil service pension legislation. This early government involvement is particularly remarkable, because teachers were employed by individual school boards, and not by the province.[23] Nevertheless, provincial governments chose to play the role of plan sponsor for all practical purposes. Plan terms were statutory, and it was the government rather than the school boards that paid (or credited) the employers' contribution and assumed responsibility for payment of the pensions.

An important feature that distinguishes teachers' plans from most other pension plans of that era is the degree to which teachers themselves had been active in promoting the establishment of the plans. As we have seen, most workplace pension plans were instigated by employers. By contrast, teachers were directly involved in the genesis of their plans from the outset. As far back as the middle of the nineteenth century, there is evidence of relatively organized teacher lobbying for pensions in several provinces.[24] The active engagement of provincial teachers' organizations is reflected in the fact that many early statutes gave teachers minority representation on the boards and commissions established to administer the plans.

Although establishing these plans was at least in part a response to pressure from teachers, the reasons publicly articulated by government for enacting teachers' pension legislation closely paralleled the motivations of private employers adopting pension plans. In a speech to the legislature at the close of the 1917 legislative session, Ontario's lieutenant-governor, Sir John Hendrie, singled out *The Teachers' and Inspectors' Superannuation Act* for special mention. While he made passing reference to the plan as "an act of justice to a very useful portion of the public service," his emphasis was on the public interest: "[T]his measure is calculated to contribute to the permanence and attractiveness of the teaching profession, and in that way to improve the efficiency of our educational institutions."[25] The 1929 debate in the Saskatchewan legislature over teachers' pensions was succinctly summarized in the *Labour Gazette* in the following terms:

A teachers' superannuation scheme, it was considered, would stabilize and unify the teaching profession; keep the profession clear of "deadwood" by retiring those rendered ineffective; by assuring every teacher of a maintenance in old age, leaving him free to devote himself to his work; attract the right kind of people to the teaching profession, and keep them there; maintain the flow of promotion that would assure that young and progressive men and women would be in charge of important positions; retain in the province the best of the profession who would otherwise go where they would find more favourable conditions.[26]

When they lobbied for the legislation, teachers themselves empha-sized such efficiency arguments.[27]

The structure of teachers' plans differed substantially from the standard employer-sponsored plan. Instead of one plan per school board, a single plan covered every teacher in the province. These plans were not multi-employer plans in the modern sense, since they were sponsored by a single entity, the provincial government, rather than by groups of employing school boards. However, they shared an important feature with modern multi-employer plans; benefits were fully portable, in the sense that individual teachers accumulated credit towards a pension regardless of which school board they worked for, as long as they continued to be employed as qualified teachers in public education in the province.[28]

Teachers' plans shared many common features. The 1917 Ontario plan was typical.[29] Membership was compulsory for qualified teach-ers employed in public education. Teachers contributed 2½ per cent of annual salary, and an equivalent amount was credited to the fund as the government's contribution.[30] The plan paid a defined benefit based on 1/60th of salary (averaged over the last ten years of ser-vice) for each year of service. A full pension was available only after forty years of service, although teachers could apply for an actuari-ally reduced pension after thirty years.[31] Teachers who left the pro-fession without qualifying for a pension were entitled to a refund of their own contributions, but had no vested right to the government's contributions. There was no survivor pension, although the estate of a deceased teacher was entitled to a refund of any teacher contri-butions that had not already been paid out in retirement benefits.[32] Again, British Columbia was an exception. As with its first plan for civil servants, its first teachers' plan took the form of a defined con-tribution plan, with a pension based on twice the individual teach-er's contributions, plus interest. By 1938, however, British Columbia had fallen into line with other provinces and paid a defined benefit for teachers.[33]

Despite the importance of the policy objective of ridding the teach-ing profession of "dead wood," most teachers' pension plans did not contain a mandatory retirement age, leaving that issue to be dealt with directly by employing school boards. There were some excep-tions. Newfoundland dealt with retirement in its general *Education Act* with a broad-brush approach, creating a presumption that any teacher who reached the age of sixty with at least fifteen years of service was incapacitated, and placing the onus on a teacher who did not wish to retire to demonstrate continued fitness to teach.[34] British Columbia gave the provincial pension board that administered the plan the task of determining on a case-by-case basis whether a teacher should be ordered to retire. The board could initiate an inquiry on its own motion, or at the request of a school board or a teacher. Grounds for ordering retirement included incapacity or reaching the age of sixty-five (sixty for women).[35]

Pension Plans for Municipal Government Employees

Provincial governments did not take on the same degree of responsibility for municipal pensions as for teachers' pensions. From the mid-nineteenth century, provinces gave municipalities the statutory authority to establish pension plans for the more dangerous occupations of policing and firefighting, either through special legislation or under city charters. Gradually, municipal statutes in most provinces were amended to give municipalities the power to establish plans for staff more generally.[36] This power was permissive in most jurisdictions,[37] however, and municipalities were slow to exercise it. A 1924 article in the *Labour Gazette* reported that municipal pension practices were "in a state of transition"; larger cities, including Montreal and Toronto, had the matter of pension plans for their general staff "under present consideration" but still had no plans providing broad coverage.[38] More than two decades later, a 1946 study of the municipal pension landscape conducted by the Institute of Local Government at Queen's University found only thirty-nine municipalities with formal pension plans among some four thousand Canadian municipalities overall.[39]

A key objective of the institute's study was to persuade municipalities to switch from ad hoc pension provision to structured and funded plans. The study marshalled the familiar business justifications, and argued that a structured approach to pensions made even more sense in the public than in the private sector because of political pressures on government: "Private employers in large numbers have established pension funds. Such private businesses are not charitable institutions. They have adopted pension plans because they return to them more in reduced costs for older employees and improved morale than such plans cost in dollars and cents. If it is good business for private business, it would seem even better business for public bodies, where the reluctance to drop older and less-efficient employees is

even greater than in the private sector" (4). To the "pension envy"–
inspired argument that municipal governments should not offer benefits to their employees which local taxpayers did not enjoy, the
study's authors responded: "It is no more unreasonable to ask the
non-pensioned taxpayer to contribute towards pensions for his own
civic employees than to expect him to contribute in the price of the
articles he buys towards the pensions of the private producer of those
goods" (4). The study identified "the elimination of over-age employees from the service" as the "main purpose of a pension plan" (61). It
emphasized both the cost to the taxpayers of carrying non-productive
employees on active municipal payrolls and the utility of pensions for
opening up avenues of advancement for "ambitious and energetic"
younger employees (3). More than half the municipal plans it examined provided for mandatory retirement (44–5).

By the mid-twentieth century, many provincial governments were
moving beyond mere facilitation, and were taking a more active role
in municipal pension provision. In 1938, British Columbia legislated
to take municipalities out of its civil service plan, substituting a separate Municipal Superannuation Plan. This new plan was open to
municipalities, school boards (for their non-teaching employees),
and hospitals. Participation was voluntary. Like the old civil service
plan, the municipal plan began as a DC plan. In 1958, a new *Municipal Superannuation Act* converted the plan to a DB plan and imposed
compulsory membership on municipalities. (The plan continued to
be voluntary for school boards and other "local boards.")[40] Mean-
while, Saskatchewan legislated in 1951 to establish a common
Municipal Employees Superannuation Plan (MESP) for "every vil-
lage, town and city in Saskatchewan,"[41] with compulsory membership of all employees, including the non-teaching employees of school
boards. Coincident with a general movement towards municipal
consolidation, Ontario established the Ontario Municipal Employee
Retirement System (OMERS) in 1962. Municipalities were not
required to participate, although they were required to use the
OMERS vehicle if they chose to provide pensions.[42] Alberta's consolidated Local Authorities Pension Plan (LAPP) was also constituted in 1962, with voluntary participation.[43] Manitoba's Municipal
Employee Pension Plan (MEPP), instituted in 1975, was compulsory
for all municipalities.[44]

Consolidation offered important benefits to both employees and
municipalities. For employees, a key benefit was portability. Like the
teachers' plans, consolidated municipal plans allowed employees to

accumulate credits towards a single pension even when they changed jobs, as long as they continued to work for an employer who participated in the plan. For employers, benefits included lower costs and simplified administrative burdens. However, not all provinces took the consolidated approach. Quebec, for example, chose to leave municipalities out of its 1973 Government and Public Employees Retirement Plan; municipalities in that province continue to offer their own individual plans.[45]

Consolidated municipal plans took a variety of approaches to the mandatory retirement issue. Several took the same approach as the teachers' plans, leaving the issue to be dealt with by individual employers. Others contained pension-eligibility rules that assumed mandatory retirement policies were in place. B C's 1938 *Municipal Superannuation Act* is the clearest example of this approach. Its eligibility rules assumed both minimum and maximum retirement ages that also varied by gender (women between fifty-five and sixty, men between sixty and sixty-five) and occupation (firefighters and police between fifty and fifty-five), and contemplated that employers could postpone an employee's retirement by up to five years.[46] The 1958 revisions took the same approach.[47]

Pension Plans for Employees in Public Health Care

While health care is now one of the most significant components of government budgets, government responsibility for the costs of health care is a relatively recent phenomenon. Unlike education and municipal services, health care was not publicly funded in the important formative years of the workplace pension system, and even where it is publicly funded, much of it is still delivered by private enterprise. Provincial governments typically did not get involved in establishing statutory pension plans for health-care workers. Public or quasi-public institutions, such as hospitals, public-health authorities, and community-care centres, were eligible to participate in some consolidated municipal plans. British Columbia's 1938 *Municipal Superannuation Act* gave hospitals the right to participate [s.3(i)].[48] Quebec's 1973 Government and Public Employees Retirement Plan provided mandatory coverage for employees in the many hospitals and health centres listed in its schedules.[49] In Prince Edward Island, health-care workers in hospitals and other "health authorities" participate in the civil service superannuation plan.[50] In other provinces, where hospitals (and sometimes other types of health-care facilities) fell under the definition of "local boards" for municipal pension purposes, hospital workers (and now considerably more types of health-care workers) could participate in municipal plans on a voluntary basis.[51]

Where they did not participate in public/municipal plans of this type, employers in the health-care sector typically made their own pension arrangements on a single-employer or multi-employer basis. These arrangements were regulated like private sector plans. The most prominent plan of this type is HOOPP, now one of the largest pension plans in Canada.[52] Formerly the Hospitals of Ontario Pension Plan, it is now known as the Healthcare of Ontario Pension Plan, reflecting a more diversified membership.

HOOPP was an initiative of the Ontario Hospital Association (OHA), a voluntary association of hospital employers, which established the plan in 1960 as a convenient umbrella for its members to provide pension benefits for their employees. It is now jointly governed by health care unions and the OHA, a result that came about through litigation rather than through collective bargaining or legislation. Although HOOPP was designed and controlled by the OHA, for many years the OHA permitted the major health-care unions to appoint representatives to a committee that administered the plan. In 1988, however, it proposed to amend the plan text to designate itself as sole administrator. The unions challenged this move, arguing that, while HOOPP had traditionally been controlled by the OHA and run like a conventional employer-sponsored plan, it was in fact a multi-employer plan and was therefore required by Ontario law to be either jointly governed or governed entirely by the employees.[53] The unions insisted that their members had a right to at least equal representation with OHA members on HOOPP's governing body. The Pension Commission of Ontario agreed, and the Divisional Court subsequently upheld that decision.[54]

While HOOPP still limits participation to employers who are members of the OHA, the OHA itself has expanded and is now open to both for-profit and non-profit enterprises operating in the health-care field. Participation is voluntary, and not all OHA members participate; some continue to provide their own employer-sponsored plans.[55] In addition, there are competing and more recently established multi-employer plans set up on the initiative of health-care unions, which target lower-paid sub-sectors of health-care employment, such as long-term-care facilities.[56] Because all these plans are non-statutory, they can and do include employers outside provincial boundaries. In several other provinces with no special statutory provision for pensions in the health-care sector, plans that also began as employer-sponsored plans in health-care institutions have now, like HOOPP, converted to jointly governed plans in which employers' organizations and health-care unions have equal representation.[57]

REGULATORY RULES AND PUBLIC SECTOR WORKPLACE PENSION PLANS

Although jurisdictions in Canada took relatively uniform approaches to the establishment of workplace pension plans in the public sector, their approaches varied on the important question of whether public sector plans should be regulated in the same way as private sector plans. These approaches fall into three general categories: those that exempt some or all public sector plans from the provisions of general regulatory statutes; those that apply general regulatory statutes to public sector plans; and those that take a hybrid approach, exempting some or all public sector plans from certain specific pension standards, usually in connection with funding obligations.[58]

In the first category is the federal jurisdiction, where the plan for public servants and other Crown employees is completely exempt from general regulatory statutes.[59] Nova Scotia takes the same approach for both its public service and its teachers' plans.[60] Alberta's *Public Sector Pension Plans Act* exempts key public sector plans from general pension legislation, but has enacted separate regulations under that Act which supplement the constituting statutes of individual plans.[61] Quebec generally follows the exemption model, although its picture is more complex. Many of its public sector plans are administered by the Commission administrative des régimes de retraite et d'assurances (CARRA).[62] CARRA-administered plans and others established by statute are not subject to the *Supplemental Pension Plans Act*.[63] However, municipal and university plans are treated like private sector plans for purposes of regulation.[64]

In the second category, only one province, New Brunswick,[65] applies its general pension regulatory statute to all plans equally, with no full or partial exemptions for public sector plans. That statute permits regulations providing partial exemptions, but currently no such regulations have been enacted. The majority of provinces fall somewhere in the broad third category. Ontario generally requires its public sector plans to conform to private sector rules, a policy choice designed to set an example of good practice both to the private sector and to other provinces whose legislation was modelled on Ontario's *PBA 1965*.[66] Ontario has not always found this principle easy to adhere to. Even in 1965, the regulations made one minor exception for public sector plans: plans administered by government were permitted to forgo special payments to resolve initial unfunded liabilities.[67] From time to time, the government has been able to keep faith with the uniformity principle only by amending the general regulatory statute to bring it into line with changes to public sector plans.[68] It now appears to have abandoned the principle; recent amendments to the *Pension Benefits Act* explicitly permit regulations that make different rules for public and private sector plans,[69] and the government has used this power to provide special exemptions from listed regulations for the teachers' and public service plans.[70] Saskatchewan generally applies its private sector rules to public sector plans, with the exception that it exempts certain public sector plans from making solvency-deficiency payments.[71] Three provinces, Manitoba,[72] Newfoundland and Labrador,[73] and British Columbia,[74] give public sector plans numerous exemptions from specific standards, most of them relating to funding.

PUBLIC SECTOR PENSION PLANS AND COLLECTIVE BARGAINING

Collective bargaining played a relatively minor role in establishing pension plans in both the public service and the broader public sector across Canada. In most provinces, collective bargaining rights for public servants did not begin to make their way into the statute books until the late 1960s and early 1970s.[75] By that time, public service pension plans had been firmly in place for many decades. When collective bargaining did belatedly come to the public service, bargaining rights were typically more limited than those enjoyed by employees and unions in the private sector. A common limitation was a restriction on the scope of bargaining, and pensions were frequently on the list of issues on which bargaining was not permitted.[76] Unions representing public servants consulted with government on pension issues, but had little formal involvement with pension plans. Fetters on pension bargaining have been gradually removed in most provinces,[77] but pensions continue to be off limits at the federal public service bargaining table.[78]

Formal collective bargaining often came later for teachers than for other public employees, and had no influence on the establishment of statutory teachers' pensions. Ontario is an instructive example. A statutory pension plan for teachers has been in place since 1917. The Ontario Teachers' Federation (OTF), an umbrella organization established in 1944, consulted regularly with government on teacher-related issues, including pensions,[79] but teachers did not acquire formal collective bargaining rights until 1974. The teachers' collective bargaining statute established full-scope bargaining, and, in theory, teachers' unions in Ontario could likely have placed pension issues on the bargaining table. However, the structure of collective bargaining was very different than the structure of the pension plan. For collective bargaining purposes, teachers were divided among five separate bargaining agents negotiating directly with local school boards, while the pension plan applied province-wide, with the government rather than the school boards as the sponsoring party.[80] Conventional collective bargaining was therefore not a practical mechanism for addressing pension issues.[81] While bargaining structures varied across the country, similar structural mismatches impeded collective bargaining over pensions in other provinces.[82]

Municipalities have historically been treated like private sector employers for collective-bargaining purposes, with full-scope bargaining and a right to strike to resolve collective-bargaining disputes for most of their employees.[83] Certain exceptional categories of municipal employees – generally police and firefighters – have been treated as essential-service workers and denied the right to strike in most Canadian jurisdictions. This means that bargaining disputes that cannot be resolved at the table go to interest arbitration, where arbitrators frequently operate under statutory constraints.[84] Courts have come to inconsistent conclusions on questions such as whether pension-related rights of retirees or spousal and dependent benefits can be addressed at interest arbitration for these workers.[85] Police and firefighter pensions are now commonly provided under consolidated municipal pension plans like OMERS.

With respect to employment in health care, there are typically no limitations on the scope of pension bargaining, even though there are restrictions on the right to strike for many health-care workers. However, in situations in which pensions are provided through multi-employer plans, conventional collective bargaining has played little role in establishing or changing the terms of plans.[86] As already noted, HOOPP, the dominant health-care pension plan in Ontario, did not emerge through collective bargaining. Once HOOPP was firmly entrenched as a province-wide plan whose boundaries encompassed multiple employers, multiple bargaining units, and non-union employees, bargaining for pensions on a unit-by-unit basis with HOOPP employers was impractical. The Royal Commission on the Status of Pensions put it this way: "HOOPP would appear to be theoretically bargainable. However, the various unions in the health sector do not have representation in all member hospitals. Even if they did, they could not realistically negotiate the provisions of the plan unless they were to bargain jointly."[87]

THE GREAT POLICY SHIFT:
JOINT GOVERNANCE AND RISK-SHARING

Despite their long history of excluding unions from involvement in public sector pension plans, governments in many Canadian jurisdictions have decided over the last few decades that it is now in their interests to shift to pension models that are jointly sponsored and jointly governed. Within many of these new arrangements, both plan terms and plan costs are determined jointly by unions and employers. This change is a dramatic about-face from past practice, in which governments controlled plans by enshrining plan texts in statute and immunizing them by law from collective bargaining and inconvenient regulation where they saw fit. This Great Policy Shift requires some explanation.

The Ontario government began its move towards joint pensions in the 1980s, largely because of cost pressures. Ontario's second-generation regulatory statute imposed new rules that would increase pension costs for employers through improved vesting standards, portability (transfer) rights, the "50-per-cent rule," and survivor benefits, among other changes.[88] As already noted, Ontario had made an earlier political decision to subject itself in its capacity as employer to the discipline of general pension legislation, and would therefore have to bear these increased costs along with private sector employers. The impact of the legislation was perceived as particularly burdensome to government, because of certain features unique to some of the largest public sector plans. Both the public service and the teachers' plans provided generous inflation protection (indexation), but did so on a non-funded (pay-as-you-go) basis.[89] The new portability rules under the *Pension Benefits Act, 1987* would require plans to transfer the full commuted value of pension benefits, including the value of indexation, out of the fund at the request of departing employees who were not eligible for immediate pension. Since the indexation benefit was not funded, the commuted value of indexation would be a significant drain on the fund. In addition, statutory public sector plans were required by law to invest fund assets in non-marketable government debentures, a practice which had cut them off from the generous investment returns that other plans enjoyed throughout much of the 1980s.[90]

The Royal Commission on the Status of Pensions considered whether public sector plans should be exempt from some of the more-costly changes contemplated for second-generation pension statutes, but did not recommend change to the uniformity principle. It did recommend, however, that the government abandon its pay-as-you-go approach to inflation protection, begin to invest in marketable securities, and search for co-operative strategies that would reduce public sector pension costs in general.[91] In response, the government embarked on a series of public sector pension consultations, which yielded several important studies, summarized in an omnibus report called *A Fresh Start*.[92] This report, which focused on the teachers' and public service plans, suggested a radical solution to the government's funding problems: the government and its unions should negotiate towards a pension model of full partnership, joint trusteeship, and "a fully-shared, self-sustaining risk/reward pension program."[93] The government embraced this collaborative approach, seeing an opportunity to secure union buy-in for plan changes that would allow it to off-load a share of its financial exposure and control future costs. Negotiations for jointly sponsored pension plans commenced under a Liberal government. When the New Democratic Party defeated the Liberals in 1990, the new government was confronted with a world-wide recession and a provincial credit rating in some jeopardy, and was happy to continue cost-saving negotiations. The government's goals for the new jointly sponsored plans were long-term, but as a bonus it sought short-term financial relief in the midst of an acute fiscal crisis.[94]

The first target for conversion to a jointly sponsored plan was the venerable teachers' plan. Preliminary negotiations with the teachers resulted in the *Teachers' Pension Plan Act*, passed by the Liberal government in 1989, which contemplated the negotiation of a joint sponsorship model for a new Ontario Teachers' Pension Plan between the Ministry of Education and the OTF.[95] That process culminated in a sponsorship agreement, effective 1 January 1992, which gave the government and the OTF – the "pension partners" – an equal role as plan sponsors in the establishment of plan terms and contribution levels, subject to a dispute resolution mechanism to sort out disagreements. Government and plan members were given equal representation on a board of trustees, which managed the plan and made investment decisions. Shortly thereafter, a similar model was negotiated for the public service plan, in which the old plan split into two plans – one for unionized employees and one for non-unionized employees – and a partnership agreement was reached for the unionized plan which came into effect in June 1994.[96] (The plan for non-unionized employees remains solely sponsored by the government.) The process of converting statutory plans to jointly sponsored plans culminated in 2006 with a new partnership structure for OMERS.[97] Although HOOPP is not a statutory plan, it has also adopted a jointly sponsored model.

Jointly sponsored pension plans (JSPPs) clearly have some downsides for plan members. Under the old public sector models, employees had classic defined benefits backstopped by government guarantees. The new JSPP model, now enshrined in Ontario in the *Pension Benefits Act*,[98] requires employees to take on a form of co-liability for their pensions. The Ontario model does not adopt "target benefits" in their conventional form;[99] defined benefits continue to be guaranteed under these plans, except in the improbable event that the plan winds up with a funding deficit. However, unions who are joint sponsors now have joint responsibility with the government for maintaining equilibrium between contributions and benefits. In addition, if JSPPs fail to meet statutory funding standards, employees are jointly liable with government to make special payments to "top up" the fund.

Unions had complex motives for agreeing to take this on, and, like the government, they had both short- and long-term goals. In the short term, unions negotiating in the early 1990s had a "gun to their heads" in the form of threatened public sector wage controls, which ultimately culminated in the *Social Contract Act, 1993*.[100] This statute imposed cost-cutting targets on the public sector, and demanded wage-related savings, which could be applied towards those targets. The opportunity to credit pension concessions to social-contract targets offered a significant incentive for unions to accept plan restructuring. In the longer term, unions judged the trade-off worthwhile to place at least some fetters on the sovereign powers of government to impose its will through legislation.[101]

Any such fetters are fragile, of course, as the Ontario Public Service Employees Union (OPSEU) discovered when it took the government to court in 1995 over violation of a commitment made in partnership negotiations. The sponsorship agreement, which provided the basis for the plan, included a list of specific exemptions from the *Pension Benefits Act* and an express promise, subsequently reflected in s.21(2) of the special legislation implementing the new plan, that "a regulation in respect of the OPSEU Plan may be made only with the concurrence of the Crown and OPSEU."[102] After the legislation was passed, the government enacted a regulation exempting the plan from s.69 of the *Pension Benefits Act,* which gives the Superintendent of Pensions the right to declare a full or partial windup of a plan. This exemption was not on the agreed-upon list, and OPSEU was successful in obtaining a court declaration that the regulation was void, because it contravened s.21(2) of the special legislation.[103] The government's response to the court's decision was to amend the plan statute to provide for the exemption.[104] The message was clear: although the new plan was a partnership, the government was ultimately not prepared to permit any serious encroachment on its sovereign powers.

Following Ontario's example, joint-sponsorship models have now spread to other provinces, where governments have recognized the advantages of distributing the risks of sponsorship more widely. Between 1999 and 2002, British Columbia implemented joint sponsorship for its four largest public sector plans, under the auspices of the *Public Sector Pension Plans Act.*[105] An Auditor General's report on the British Columbia conversion process stressed the importance to government of reducing both its overall pension costs and its exposure to future cost risks, with a minimum of conflict with employees.[106] In describing the trade-offs the government was forced to make to achieve these objectives, the report touches only lightly on loss of control over the plan. It notes that "the employer would have to give up half its claim on any future surpluses generated by a pension plan, and unilateral control of management of the plan." But the report did not view this as a serious loss, since "this theoretical discretion was already fettered by the realities of public sector collective bargaining (although pensions were not formally negotiated) and had become a growing source of friction with employees."[107]

While other provinces have also been attracted to risk-reduction strategies that assign more responsibility to members for their own pension benefits, they have shown reservations about moving as directly as Ontario and British Columbia to full joint governance. Nova Scotia's 2012 *Public Service Superannuation Act* put in place a trusteed public service plan, with representation on the board of trustees from public sector unions, as well as from non-unionized members and retired members. Union representation is not equal, however, and the trustee body has no direct control over the terms of the plan, which continues to be statutory.[108] Some provinces that have attempted to implement risk-sharing reforms without the direct involvement of public sector unions have triggered significant backlash. In 2014, Alberta proposed to replace its defined benefit public sector plans with a "target benefit"-type model. The draft legislation contemplated future negotiations with unions towards joint sponsorship agreements, but unlike Ontario and British Columbia, made it clear that the government intended to implement benefit reforms unilaterally prior to entering into joint sponsorship. Alberta public sector unions put up so much resistance that the proposed reforms were put on hold.[109] Likewise, Quebec's unilateral effort to reform plans in the municipal sector by imposing fifty-fifty cost sharing and a form of target benefits in place of defined benefits likewise hit political turbulence. The new law came into effect in December 2014, but not without significant amendments that delayed the reforms and left more room for collective bargaining.[110]

New Brunswick's 2012 "shared risk" model attracted more labour support, although it too does not provide any statutory guarantees of power-sharing with plan members or their unions. This model is a remarkable departure from Canadian public sector pension norms, since it applies a full-fledged target-benefit concept, which contemplates the possibility of reductions to benefits already accrued (including pensions in pay) if assets in the fund drop sufficiently below liabilities.[111] The amendments to New Brunswick's *Pension Benefits Act* that facilitate the new "shared risk" model apply equally to the private and the public sector. The model is designed to be "self-adjusting," minimizing the need for substantive governance decisions. Solvency funding standards have been replaced by annual "stress testing," calibrated to maintain a constant balance between assets and liabilities. If assets fall below liabilities, there are automatic adjustments in contributions, benefits, and asset allocation, based on predetermined protocols. The employer is no longer the plan administrator; shared-risk plans must be governed by arm's-length trustees. Where decisions are necessary, they are made by the trustees, with third-party dispute resolution available in the absence of agreement. There is no statutory requirement for employee (or union) consent either to the establishment of a shared-risk plan, or to the conversion of an existing defined benefit plan to a shared-risk plan. In practice, however, conversions which have taken place in New Brunswick's statutory public service and teachers' plan have been implemented in accordance with agreements which give unions an equal right with government to appoint trustees.[112] Now that these new shared-risk models are in place, the old specialized pension statutes have been repealed, although, in the teachers' case, the old Act has been replaced by a new *Teachers' Pension Plan Act*, underlining the reality that the government retains continued control over the fate of the new model.[113]

THE LESSON FROM PUBLIC SECTOR PENSION MODELS

Although public sector employers established pension plans for their employees for essentially the same reasons as private sector employers, public sector pension models have been considerably more durable and more successful than private sector models. Public sector plans continue to provide impressive coverage, and most continue to deliver adequate, predictable, and (relatively) secure benefits, while many private sector plans are closing or being converted from defined benefit to defined contribution plans. The reasons why public sector models have succeeded are complex, and cut across the boundaries of economics, politics, and law. It is clear, however, that public sector models differ from private sector models in significant ways, which depend for their efficacy at least in part on state action and on the use of legal tools that only governments have at their disposal.

Two features lie at the core of the public sector model: very broad scale and mandatory membership across the boundaries of individual workplaces. Although governments had the natural advantage of being very large employers at the provincial and federal level, most quickly saw the benefits of expanding the boundaries of their plans beyond their own employee group, using their legislative power to sweep in Crown agencies and other related bodies. Size gave these plans both economies of scale in administrative and investment costs and the broader, more diversified, risk pools that are necessary to nurture financially sound defined benefit plans. The model was applied to teachers, providing mandatory coverage for very large groups of employees, reducing administrative burdens on local school boards, and offering plan members the significant benefit of pension credits that were portable within the teaching profession. Approaches have been more varied for municipal employees, but most provinces have taken a co-operative, broad-based approach, designing multi-employer plans in which costs to the public purse were controlled by economies of scale and employees had portable benefits. None of this could happen within a voluntary, employer-controlled private system; it took legislative power to build these structures and apply them to sufficiently large groups of employers and employees.

Legislative power was also the key tool for effecting the Great Policy Shift – the recent restructuring of large public sector plans across the country from employer-sponsored "pure" defined benefit plans to jointly sponsored plans with various forms of risk-shared benefits. These restructurings have been publicly packaged as co-operative efforts between employers and employees, and there is no doubt that governments have been greatly assisted in making change by the fact that their workforces were largely represented by unions who could speak for plan members and were institutionally capable of taking on the joint responsibility these new structures demand. But union and employee agreement to these new structures came more readily because of the background threat that, without agreement, there would be legislative "fixes" that would be far less palatable to unions and plan members. Furthermore, the new structures themselves could only be facilitated (or imposed, where agreement was not sought or not obtained) through changes to existing legislation.

The crucial point is that, while public sector plans are workplace pension plans, they are not generated within the confines of standard labour and employment law. They are enabled by the tools of the state. Accordingly, they cannot be replicated in the private sector within Canada's current voluntary system. As a model, they lead not towards, but away from, the employment relationship as a platform for delivery of adequate, predictable, and secure pensions.

9

Lessons from History and the Road Ahead

THE PARADOX OF THE VOLUNTARY SYSTEM

Throughout the period surveyed in this book, we have seen the transformation of workplace pensions from discretionary gifts to regulated rights. In twenty-first-century Canada, pension promises are enforceable, and plans must be managed according to modern fiduciary and solvency standards. Yet fewer and fewer workers have good pensions. This is not a coincidence. On the contrary, it is the foreseeable consequence of a voluntary, employment-based system. The legal transformation of pension rights has also transformed the employer cost-benefit equation, the practical driver of the system. The creation and strengthening of pension rights has made pensions more expensive and less useful for employers, making it much less likely that employers will voluntarily establish and maintain good plans.

This is *not* an argument that over-regulation is killing an otherwise functional system. Prior to the transformation of workplace pensions from gifts to rights, pension promises were empty promises even for members of workplace pension plans. The creation and strengthening of employee pension rights and pension funding rules was not a policy error; it was a necessary step to giving pension promises substantive content. But while regulation was a necessary step, it was not a sufficient step. The policy error was assuming that regulation would be effective even though pension promises remained embedded within a voluntary system resting on the platform of the employment relationship. Within that relationship, employers make pension decisions in their own business interests. Neither employment law nor pension law gives workers effective tools to challenge those decisions when they do not meet employee needs. In consequence, pension promises do not translate into promises of adequate, predictable, and secure retirement income. For most Canadian workers, pension promises remain empty promises.

A voluntary employment-based system works only if employers decide to create plans that yield good pensions for their employees. Some employers made that decision, and in the 1960s law-makers believed – or hoped – that more would follow. Even then, governments knew there were problems with the pension plans that employers created. But they believed – or hoped – that those problems could be fixed through regulation, and that employers would continue to provide pensions on the new regulated pension model, even though they were not compelled to do so. The basis for those hopes and beliefs was never articulated. While the trend towards pension provision still had momentum in the 1960s, it was predictable that regulatory interventions enhancing employee pension rights would increase employer pension costs. It was equally predictable that, as pension costs increased, employers would recalculate the ratio of costs to benefits, and respond either by reducing pension quality or abandoning pension provision altogether. This is the central contradiction of the voluntary workplace pension system – the legal rules that make pensions a valuable benefit for employees also make them a benefit that employers are less and less willing to provide.

While workplace pension plans are responsive to the legal environment, they also respond to broader socio-economic conditions – demographics, conditions on capital markets, the structure of workplaces, and the organization of work. Factors like these were initially favourable to workplace pensions, encouraging employers to establish and maintain plans. They might have continued to evolve in ways that offset the higher cost of rights-based pensions, at least for a time. Unfortunately, the opposite has occurred. Increasing longevity means that workplace pension plans must pay out pensions longer. The volatility of global capital markets in recent years has caused the value of pension assets to fluctuate severely and unpredictably, requiring employers to top up their pension funds based on factors unrelated either to firm profitability or worker productivity.[1] Unionized jobs in large firms that provide full-time work and long-term permanent status – the kinds of jobs historically associated with good pension coverage – are disappearing from the modern workplace.[2]

A voluntary system might nonetheless have flourished if employees had enough bargaining power to force employers to shift their focus away from their own interests. As we have seen, however, the common law gave employees little assistance in this regard. In general, Canadian courts took the view that employers were free to use their economic power to hedge their pension promises with "boiler-plate" discretionary clauses that left them in continuing control of decisions crucial to the adequacy, predictability, and security of benefits. Collective-bargaining laws were expected to change that, and in the 1960s there was still some prospect that collective bargaining could be used to persuade employers to establish pension plans and design benefits to better address employee needs. But collective bargaining did not work out that way. Despite the fact that pensions fall within the scope of bargaining, employers who did not want to cede control over their pension plans encountered few legal impediments, and arbitrators have generally taken the view that, even in unionized workplaces, pensions remain under employer control unless employers have specifically agreed otherwise.

Outside unionized workplaces, collective bargaining has little influence on pension provision or pension quality. Where unions hold bargaining rights, unions have had some impact on extending pension coverage and improving benefits in existing plans. But bargaining structures do not align well with pension structures, a factor that has constrained the ability of unions to use their bargaining power to confront employer control of pension provision. The mismatch between pension-plan boundaries and bargaining-unit boundaries is likely to create even greater problems in future, as it becomes increasingly clear that successful pension plans require economies of scale and innovative governance structures that will not be generated within conventional private sector collective bargaining relationships.[3]

In this concluding chapter, I return to some of the key labour-market factors that motivated employers to establish workplace pension plans in the first place, and examine how legal, social, and economic change have affected those factors, limiting both the ability and the incentives of employers to use pension plans to promote mandatory retirement and control employee behaviour and job tenure. I take a summary look at the current round of pension reform discussions, in which governments are seeking once again to patch up a system that has been declining for decades, and is now in what may well be its terminal phase. I conclude that, on the basis of the evidence revealed in this history, workplace pension plans should be declared a failure. With the sole exception of the public sector, such plans will not develop into vehicles for adequate, predictable, and secure retirement income for Canadians as long as they remain voluntary and anchored to the employment relationship. However, there are lessons to be learned from their history which will be useful in shaping and evaluating options for their replacement.

THE END OF MANDATORY RETIREMENT

As we have seen, a crucial – perhaps the *most* crucial – motivator for employers in establishing pension plans was the facilitation of orderly retirement through the mechanism of mandatory retirement policies. For many years, such policies were supported by law in Canada through human rights codes that protected workers from age discrimination only up to age sixty-five. In the last decades of the twentieth century, however, the Canadian legal environment governing mandatory retirement has been almost completely transformed. Human-rights activists mounted persistent challenges to the practice, arguing that the equality-rights provisions of the *Canadian Charter of Rights and Freedoms* required broader protection against age discrimination. In a 1990 decision in *McKinney v University of Guelph*,[4] the Supreme Court of Canada concluded that mandatory retirement was prima facie age discrimination, but was justifiable as a "reasonable limit" on equality rights under s.1 of the *Charter*. A key factor in the justification analysis was the court's concern that mandatory retirement policies were so intimately tied to workplace pension plans that their elimination would threaten workplace pension provision.[5] The Canadian Labour Congress justified its intervention against the plaintiffs in the *McKinney* case based on the same concern: that if mandatory retirement policies disappeared, workplace pension plans might well disappear along with them.[6]

While the *McKinney* plaintiffs and others like them[7] lost the battle in the Supreme Court, they won the war in Canadian legislatures, which have now turned decisively against mandatory retirement. Even prior to *McKinney*, some jurisdictions had reduced or eliminated the legal protection previously afforded to mandatory retirement policies. In 2006, the Ontario government, which had vigorously defended mandatory retirement in *McKinney* sixteen years earlier on the basis that is was part of a "complex web" of social and economic policies that could not be disentangled without courting catastrophe, amended its own human rights code to prohibit the practice. Mandatory retirement is still acceptable in the few occupations where it can be justified as a bona fide occupational requirement, and some provinces still permit it where it can be demonstrated that it is necessary to the workings of a bona fide pension plan.[8] But as of 2011, mandatory retirement is no longer lawful in Canada as a feature of general human-resource-management policy.[9] This new public policy is motivated only in part by human rights concerns; a serious practical concern is that, with increased longevity, policies that promote retirement put severe pressures on both public and private pension systems.

Economists continue to debate what impact the elimination of mandatory retirement will have on workplace pension provision, and the evidence from recent legislative changes is not yet in. Some contrarians argue that the elimination of mandatory retirement may have a *positive* impact on workplace pension plans, since benefits can be structured to provide incentives for timely retirement as a lawful substitute for mandatory retirement.[10] But when the loss of mandatory retirement is compounded by other pressures on pension plans discussed in the next sections, a more plausible prediction is that employers will respond to the elimination of mandatory retirement exactly as the Supreme Court and the CLC feared – by disengaging from their involvement in pension provision.

CHANGING LABOUR MARKETS IN A GLOBALIZED ECONOMY

As we have seen, an important market factor in the growth of workplace pension plans was the spread of new, more-structured management methods in the large, stable bureaucracies and manufacturing enterprises which had become widespread in Canada in the period after the Second World War. The policy thinking that shaped Canada's retirement-income system in the mid-twentieth century was based on the assumption that workplaces like these would continue to dominate the economy. That has not been the case. Such workplaces are changing rapidly, if not vanishing altogether.[11] Both the kinds of workplaces that fostered the growth of pension plans and the kinds of jobs that generated the best pension benefits are on the decline in Canada. Since the 1980s, the larger domestic business enterprises that were formerly the engines of job creation are being replaced by smaller, nimbler, more globally competitive firms offering less-secure forms of employment. Work patterns are changing along with business models. The "standard employment contract" – characterized by full-time, continuous, and often unionized employment with a single employer – is disappearing in favour of increasingly contingent work arrangements: part-time work, short-term contract work, relatively transient attachments to any single employer, and "own account" self-employment. Unionization is also declining, particularly sharply in the private sector.[12] The new non-standard work arrangements are often labelled "precarious work," defined by Canadian sociologist Leah Vosko as "forms of work involving limited social benefits and statutory entitlements, job insecurity, low wages and high risks of ill health."[13] Precarious work is rarely accompanied by pension entitlements.[14]

Not all non-standard work conforms to Vosko's definition of "precarious work." Non-standard work may also be challenging, highly skilled, and well-compensated work that enhances workers' autonomy and capacity for self-actualization and frees them from the "bonds of subordination"[15] that define the standard contract of employment.[16] Those fortunate enough to turn non-standard work to their advantage may well be able to make their own provision for retirement income. Few would disagree, however, that trends away from the standard employment contract generally run counter to the acknowledged determinants of workplace pension coverage and good workplace pensions. Writing in the late 1990s, government researchers saw direct links between trends in the labour market and the downward trajectory of workplace pension plan coverage.[17] While the 2007 *Arthurs Report* was prepared to draw only "guarded conclusions" on the causes of loss of pension coverage, the report identifies both "decreasing employment in sectors where DB pensions were historically most common" and the secular decline in union density as key factors in the decline of workplace pensions.[18] It is clear that labour-market trends do not favour the future growth and health of workplace pension plans.

THE COST OF PENSION RIGHTS

As we have seen, both the facilitation of orderly retirement and the types of structured benefits that induced loyalty and deterred turnover in the new Fordist workplaces and bureaucratic businesses of the twentieth century were linked to the mechanics of defined benefit plans. Such plans were inexpensive for employers in pre-regulatory Canada, since prefunding was not required and most employees never collected benefits. The shift from gift theory to contract theory that made pension promises enforceable did not, on its own, add significantly to the cost of defined benefits or greatly impede the ability of employers to structure their D B plans as they saw fit, since they were still free to draft plans which provided no meaningful benefits. Trust and fiduciary doctrines had the potential to limit the ability of employers to use drafting and plan-administration strategies to undermine pension adequacy and security. As courts became increasingly aware of the paradox built into the voluntary system, however, they reshaped these legal doctrines to leave employers in substantial control. For a time, the *Schmidt* principles placed potentially expensive impediments in the way of employer access to plan surpluses. But employers could avoid the impact of these principles in new plans by ensuring that trusts were not created, and courts soon removed barriers to contribution holidays, plan conversion, and expense payments, allowing employers with old plans to use surpluses for their own purposes, even if they could not extract them without risk of being found in breach of trust.

The legal change with the most profound long-term impact – the change that added exponentially to the cost of pensions – was statutory regulation, which changed the essential nature of the defined benefit. Pre-retirement vesting rules introduced in first-generation regulatory statutes created concrete pension liabilities for employers at relatively early stages of employee careers. Prior to statutory regulation, employers could take their chances on whether they would have the funds to honour their pension promises when they came due; under the new rules, employers were required to prefund their liabilities to statutory standards. As vesting standards improved under second-generation statutes, pension liabilities accelerated.[19] Other new rights created by second-generation statutes imposed even more new costs. Some of these costs, such as grow-in rights, were triggered by plan windups. This meant that employer restructuring decisions that might formerly have produced pension savings now created significant additional liabilities. Court decisions determined that under at least some pension statutes employers were required to distribute surplus to members affected by partial as well

as full plan windups,[20] placing additional cost pressures on employers who had intended to use surplus for contribution holidays and
plan expenses. The new portability and transfer rights created the
potential for significant and unpredictable cash draws on pension
funds. Tighter funding standards required higher annual contributions and increased the likelihood that employers would have to
come up with periodic "special payments" to "top up" funding deficiencies. Where volatility in investment returns created unanticipated
fund deficits, the solvency-funding requirements imposed by second-
generation statutes imposed substantial new costs in the current climate of atypically low interest rates.[21]

These regulatory costs have never been globally quantified. They
have crept up incrementally, and declining pension coverage cannot
be mapped directly onto either first- or second-round regulatory
reform.[22] The *Arthurs Report* concluded that other factors – in particular, declines in union density and in manufacturing jobs – have
likely made more significant contributions to declining plan coverage
than the features of the regulatory system of which plan sponsors
complained most vigorously.[23] However, the costs imposed by regulation have been enormous and significant. In light of the almost
complete absence from the pension landscape of new defined benefit
plans in recent decades,[24] it is hard to avoid the conclusion that
employers no longer feel that the expense of such plans is justified
from a business perspective.[25]

The growing and unpredictable cost of DB plans is unquestionably
a primary cause of the clear shift away from DB plans to plans which
provide more contingent forms of benefits. There are many variations on the contingent-benefit model. These include the classic DC
plan, commonplace now in the private sector, in which the employer's pension promise is limited to a fixed annual contribution into a
fund – typically an individual account – which is then used by an
individual employee to buy a retirement annuity or otherwise generate a retirement income stream.[26] As we saw in Chapter 8, the preferred alternative to DB plans now making its way into public sector
plans is a "target benefit" model, in which employers and employees
share responsibility for maintaining equilibrium between contributions and benefits.[27] In addition, some plans offer what are known as
"hybrid benefits," usually a combination of conventional DB and DC
benefits.[28] Although the trend away from classic DB is apparent in
both the private and the public sector, that trend is particularly strong

in the private sector, where only about half of plan members belonged to DB plans in 2012, down from 90 per cent in 1980. The other half belong either to classic DC plans (29 per cent, up from 8 per cent) or plans like the Kerry (Canada) plan, which retain a DB element, but impose DC membership on new entrants.[29]

The common thread in all these alternatives to the DB benefit is that they relieve employers of some of the risks to employee retirement income that have traditionally been borne by the employer in classic DB plans. In these plans, employers guarantee the benefits. They therefore absorb three of the most significant retirement-income risks: longevity risk (risk that individual employees will outlive their retirement savings), investment risk (risk that plan investments will not produce a sufficiently large amount of capital), and interest-rate risk (risk that market interest rates at the time of retirement will not be high enough to generate sufficient annuity income). In DC plans, employers bear none of these risks, since their only obligation is to make a fixed contribution. In target-benefit plans, employers share the risks with plan members to a greater or lesser degree, depending on the specific model chosen. The risks are constant, however; they do not go away, and those not borne by employers are simply shifted to employees, with the result that employee pensions become less adequate, predictable, and secure.[30]

Reduced predictability and security are inherent in the DC model, since neither the size of the lump sum available on retirement or the amount of retirement income that lump sum will generate can be predicted with any certainty.[31] Reduced pension adequacy is not built into the model, but it is likely to follow. Under current conditions, Canadian DC plans certainly produce lower pensions.[32] This is explained in part by factors associated with the typical DC investment model: the high fee structure that comes with individual investment accounts, the investing errors chronically made by individual investors, and the difficulty in achieving appropriate diversification in small pools of capital.[33] One very important factor, however, is simply that employers are not prepared to contribute as much as they have historically contributed to DB plans. Recent data suggests that per-employee contributions to DC plans may be less than half of comparable contributions to DB plans, and significantly less than will be required to generate adequate retirement incomes for plan members.[34]

THIRD-ROUND PENSION REFORM

The first major round of Canadian pension reform in the 1960s entrenched voluntary workplace pensions within Canada's retirement-income system. They survived the second reform round – the Great Pension Debate of the 1980s – because governments, under pressure from business and the financial-services industry, were not prepared to move away from employer-driven solutions and fully embrace a public pension solution. Even then it was apparent that workplace pensions were in difficulties so serious that federal and provincial legislative committees studying the problem essentially put them on probation. Ontario's Select Committee on Pensions rejected the mandatory workplace system which had been recommended by its royal commission, and prescribed another dose of regulatory fixes. It observed, however, that "[i]f the private system fails to respond quickly and effectively [to second-generation regulation] it may then become necessary to reconsider."[35] The federal Parliamentary Task Force on Pension Reform likewise decided "to give the private sector a further opportunity to demonstrate that coverage of adequate scope and depth can be achieved without recourse to a universal public plan." It warned, however, that "if our recommendations do not lead to early evidence of dramatic improvement in the coverage problems we have identified, then either significant expansion of the C / QPP or mandatory expansion of private plans is likely to be irresistible."[36] Now, decades later, the voluntary workplace pension system still limps along in worse shape than ever, delivering increasingly inferior pensions to fewer and fewer Canadians.

Canada has now embarked on a protracted third round of pension reform, with the "public versus private" choice inevitably back on the policy table.[37] In its January 2010 paper, *Options for Increasing Pension Coverage Among Private Sector Workers in Canada*, a Steering Committee of Provincial/Territorial Ministers on Pension Coverage and Retirement Income Adequacy observed that "the appropriate role for governments in providing solutions is controversial. While some support a stronger role for governments in both setting the legislative framework and ensuring the ongoing sustainability of the policy solution, others favour a private sector solution that could be developed with governments only acting to provide an appropriate regulatory framework. This difference of opinion appears to be a

fundamental driver for what type of solution is preferred."[38] Strong
voices in both government and the private sector continue to oppose
calls for broader public engagement with pensions, arguing, as they
did in the previous two rounds of pension reform, that government
expansion of the public system is unaffordable, that mandatory systems are inflexible and paternalistic, and that the market can always
provide instruments capable of meeting the diverse retirement-income
needs of Canadians.[39] There continue to be demands for "moderniza-
tion" of the regulatory environment to make it more flexible and less
hostile to financial innovation, including calls for loosening funding
standards for workplace pension plans.[40]

These thinly veiled calls for pension deregulation received considerable attention from the various task forces and expert commissions
appointed by government to study the workplace pension systems in
this third round of reform.[41] Unlike similar bodies who reported during the Great Pension Debate, the primary mandate of these experts
was not to find ways to expand the workplace system or improve the
quality of its benefits; the focus was simply on stemming the tide of
decline. The reports convey acute awareness that the voluntary system
has become increasingly fragile. They characterize third-generation
pension reform as a complex balancing act between "the potentially
contradictory goals of improved benefit security and higher participation,"[42] with an inevitable trade-off between pension standards and
pension coverage. All heard arguments that a major contributor to
the systemic problems facing workplace pension plans has been "regulatory burden." Although the *Arthurs Report* is generally skeptical,
the others accept some version of these arguments. The recommended
remedy is to leave more flexibility within the regulatory framework
for "the parties" – employers and employees – to make their own
"pension deals," less hedged in by minimum benefit standards and
funding rules.[43] These reports ignore the fact – very evident in the
history reviewed in this book – that, in most Canadian workplaces,
the "parties" to the pension contract are a legal fiction. The party that
will dictate the content of the "deal" will be the employer, and any
"salvage operation" for workplace pension plans which depends on
the dilution of regulatory standards will inevitably require employees
to accept poorer, less-secure pensions.

An option that has received considerable support in third-round
debates, as it did in second-round debates, is expansion of the CPP.
A number of scholars, policy analysts, and the Canadian Labour

Congress have made specific expansion proposals, which have been discussed in detail elsewhere.[44] They include proposals that would improve the income-replacement ratio up to average salary levels, as well as proposals that would focus on replacing higher levels of income. To date, all would preserve the current contributory principle on which the CPP is grounded, which means that higher benefits would require higher contribution rates for both employers and employees. They also preserve the mandatory and universal nature of the CPP, although there is some interest in adding a second tier to the plan, to which voluntary contributions could be made.

However, Canada's polarized political climate has impeded federal-provincial consensus to date about future directions in pension reform. Stephen Harper's Conservative federal government initially supported some measure of CPP expansion, but subsequently rejected that option,[45] and instead promoted a new private instrument called a Pooled Retirement Pension Plan (PRPP), which closely resembles a group RRSP.[46] PRPPs are voluntary. Employers who establish them are not required to make contributions, and they provide no guaranteed payout.[47] Some provinces have adopted the federal PRPP prototype for use within their own boundaries, while others have not.[48] Ontario initially ruled out PRPPs and pushed hard for CPP expansion. It has now legislated to facilitate PRPPs,[49] but has also decided, in the absence of federal cooperation and in an eerie echo of 1963, to go it alone with a new pension vehicle, the Ontario Retirement Pension Plan ("ORPP").[50] Like the CPP, the ORPP will be compulsory (but only for employers that do not have "equivalent" workplace plans). Since the Trudeau Liberal government, elected in October 2015, is more open than its predecessor to considering CPP expansion, some analysts predict that, in another echo of 1963, the ORPP may be overtaken by national pension reform. However, Ontario's 2016 Budget continues to promise full implementation by 2020, although initial collection of premiums, originally slated to commence in 2017, has now been delayed by one year.[51]

THE ROAD AHEAD:
SOME FINAL THOUGHTS ON PENSION REFORM

This book has explored the problems and contradictions which flow from building retirement-income vehicles on the foundation of the employment relationship. It explains how market forces have worked within the dynamics of the employment relationship to produce pension plans that meet the needs of employers rather than employees, and why the law has been ineffective in correcting for those problems and contradictions within a voluntary system. The conclusion to be drawn from this history is that workplace pension plans have had their day. The employment relationship was feasible as a platform for generating good pensions only as long as employers saw business benefit in bearing the costs and risks associated with pension provision. Since most employers no longer do so, a voluntary employment-based pension system can no longer be counted on to play an important role within Canada's national retirement income system.

Now that we know workplace pension plans will not do the job for us, the next step is to develop alternatives. While it was never the purpose of this book to perform that task, it offers some useful lessons for those engaged in the policy process. The first is that leaving the job to the market dynamics of the employment relationship is not workable, for all the reasons discussed at length here. Indeed, now that employers no longer have a compelling business interest in employment-based pensions and are no longer willing to take on the risks and costs of supplying retirement income as an employment benefit, the efficiency arguments for leaving pension provision under employer control are no longer salient. We must search outside the employment relationship for workable alternatives.

The second important lesson is most evident in our examination of the one continuing success story in the workplace pension system: public sector pension plans. These plans deliver good pensions in part because their size and scale allow them to keep administrative and investment costs down, distribute pension risks widely, and provide highly portable benefits. But more fundamentally, they work because they are shaped by employer-governments motivated not simply by business interests, but also by broader concerns of social and economic policy. These employer-governments have access to policy tools – most fundamentally, the power to make laws – which allow them to adapt pension structures to changing social and economic conditions, so that they will continue to produce adequate, predictable, and secure pensions. They are in essence state plans.

If national pension policy can break free – as it must – from its dependence on the employment relationship as a key platform for retirement-income delivery, the success of public sector pension models provides strong support for state action in shaping future pension vehicles. Initiatives like Ontario's ORPP are positive steps in the direction of providing broader pension coverage and higher income-replacement levels. However, they are not the solution, because they remain tethered to the employment relationship. The ORPP is applicable only to workers whose work arrangements are formally structured as "employment." As currently configured, it applies only to employees whose current employers do not have "equivalent" plans. Inevitably, there are sharp differences of opinion about "equivalence."[52] Regardless of how those differences are ultimately resolved, linking coverage to whether there is an equivalent plan in the workplace means that the pension rights of individual workers will continue to revolve around unilateral decisions made by their employers about workplace pension provision. This flaw will almost certainly affect pension adequacy, reliability, and security.

Much more promising for retired Canadian workers is an expanded version of the CPP, in which pensions depend on the paid work and income of workers, but are independent of particular workplaces, and of the pension objectives of particular employers. Vehicles like the CPP are likely to be the most efficient, cost-effective, and reliable option for Canadians as a whole. CPP expansion means more state action, not less state action, and this option will therefore be displeasing to those who argue that the state should stay out of pension provision. But as economist Nicholas Barr has pointed out, it is a myth that "private pensions get governments out of the pension business."[53] Modern political, social, and economic life cannot be so neatly divided into distinct and coherent public and private spheres.[54] As we have seen, the state is deeply implicated in the network of laws that have nurtured the workplace pension plan system, including tax law;[55] employment and labour law; contract, trust, and fiduciary law; pension regulatory law; and the other many manifestations of common and statute law which have converged to shape "pension law" in the course of this history. In the context of pension provision, the public-private debate is not a battle over *whether* the state will be involved. It is a battle over *how* the state will be involved.

This fact is well understood by politicians and business leaders who argue against state options. As legal realist Morris Cohen observed in 1933 in the midst of the Great Depression, "those who talk about 'keeping the government out of business' are the last to desire that the government shall not help or protect, by proper rules, the business in which they are involved. The differences which divide men [*sic*] in this respect concern the question of what interests should be protected and who should control the government."⁵⁶ The quest for a new pension framework inevitably engages the role of the state in setting clear goals, in identifying what social risks must be addressed collectively rather than individually, in establishing distributive (or redistributive) objectives that are most consistent with national values, and in enacting laws that will effectively implement public policy decisions. The state action that brought us the workplace pension system has not yielded great benefits for most Canadians. We now have a chance to make better use of the tools of the state to produce adequate, predictable, and secure pensions. In this third round of pension reform, we need to make sure our politicians use those tools, including law, for that purpose.

Notes

CHAPTER ONE

1 Dominion Bureau of Statistics, *Survey of Pension Plan Coverage, 1965*, 8 (Table B); Tamagno, *Occupational Pension Plans in Canada*, 5 (Figure 2).

2 Statistics Canada, "Percentage of Labour Force and Employees Covered by a Registered Pension Plan (RPP)," online: http://www.statcan.gc.ca/tables-tableaux/sum-som/lo1/csto1/labor26a-eng.htm. The survey indicates that "[e]mployees refer to employees in the public and private sector and include self-employed workers in incorporated business (with and without paid help)." All figures include both full- and part-time workers.

3 Baldwin, *The Long-Term Capacity of Workplace Pension Plans*, Table 4 (14).

4 More than 80 per cent of pension wealth is held by one-quarter of Canadian households: see Baldwin, *The Long-Term Capacity of Workplace Pension Plans*, 16; Morissette and Zhang, "Revisiting Wealth Inequality." Men hold considerably more pension wealth than women: see Denton and Boos, *Gender Inequality in the Wealth of Older Canadians*.

5 Lipsett and Reesor, *Employer-Sponsored Pension Plans: Who Benefits?*, 3. The data in this study included group RRSPs. See also *Arthurs Report*, 38–40.

6 See Morissette, "Pensions: Immigrants and Visible Minorities," 16; Marier and Skinner, "The Impact of Gender and Immigration." See also Block, *Ontario's Growing Gap*; Townson, *Women's Poverty and the Recession*, 33; Townson, "The Impact of Precarious Employment," 367–9.

7 Statistics Canada, "Percentage of Labour Force and Employees Covered by a Registered Pension Plan (RPP)," shows that 33.8 per cent of female workers belonged to plans in 2013, compared to 30.7 per cent of male workers.

8 See Gunderson, *Incentive Effects*, 46, Table 2. See also Baldwin and
   Laliberté, "Incomes of Older Canadians," 45, reporting a decline from
   68.8 cents on the dollar in 1981 to 57 cents in 1996; Tamagno,
   Occupational Pension Plans in Canada, 11. For a more detailed examina-
   tion of how women fare within the workplace pension system, see Shilton,
   "Gender Risk."

9 In 1980, 94 per cent of Canadian pension-plan members belonged to
   DB plans, but by 2012 that figure had dropped to 73 per cent: Baldwin,
   "Economic Impact," Table 1. See also Gougeon, "Shifting Pensions," 18.
   For a discussion of even more rapid drops in DB coverage in the US and
   the UK, see Munnell, "Employer-Sponsored Plans."

10 See *Arthurs Report*, 179–83. See also Baldwin, "The Shift from DB to
   DC Coverage." Changes in public sector benefits are discussed in more
   detail in Chapter 8.

11 Dramatic plan failures in recent years in Canada include Gay Lea
   Foods (discussed in *Gay Lea Foods Co-operative Limited v Ontario
   (Superintendent Financial Services)*, 2010 ONFST 10), Indalex
   (discussed in *Sun Indalex Finance LLC v United Steelworkers*, 2013
   SCC 6), and Nortel Networks (extensively litigated in both the US
   and Canada).

12 Numerous company-specific regulations have been enacted under pension
   statutes in various Canadian jurisdictions, extending statutory timelines
   for meeting obligations to resolve pension-fund deficits.

13 Canada ranked fourth among OECD countries in 2009 in reliance on
   voluntary workplace pension plans, after the UK, the US, and Ireland:
   OECD, *Pensions at a Glance: Retirement-Income Systems in OECD
   Countries*, 30, Figure 1.2, and 60. See also Casey and Yamada, "The
   Public-Private Mix of Retirement Income," 397–9.

14 Canada has a version of the "three-pillar" approach promoted by the
   World Bank in *Averting the Old Age Crisis*. The "three-pillar" (or "three-
   tier") approach was subsequently embraced by the OECD as well: OECD,
   Maintaining Prosperity in an Aging Society and *Reforms for an Aging
   Society*. The "three pillar" metaphor has now become widespread in the
   language of comparative social-welfare policy. In World Bank/OECD
   typologies, Pillar 1 instruments address poverty relief, Pillar 2 instruments
   are directed to basic income (or consumption) "smoothing" across the life
   course, and Pillar 3 instruments depend on individual savings, which defer
   immediate consumption during a working life in order to obtain a higher
   standard of living in retirement.

15 Quebec has its own second-pillar pension plan, the Quebec Pension Plan (QPP), for reasons discussed in Chapter 4. The QPP largely mirrors the CPP, and references to the CPP in this book apply generally to both the CPP and the QPP.

16 Comparative international data from the 1960s can be found in Appendix A of the submission of the Canadian Labour Congress to the federal government committee considering the CPP: see Special Joint Committee *Minutes*, 1648–54. Data from the 1980s shows that Canadian Pillar 1 and 2 pensions combined replaced about 57 per cent of average income for one-earner couples, compared to Sweden at 80 per cent and France at 77 per cent: see *Lazar Report*, Vol. I, 30–1. Canada's public pension system remains ungenerous by international standards for middle- and higher-income earners: see Steering Committee of Provincial/Territorial Ministers on Pension Coverage and Retirement Income Adequacy, *Options for Increasing Pension Coverage*, 6–7.

17 Although the appropriate income-replacement target is contested, the 70 per cent estimate continues to be a useful benchmark: see Myles, *Old Age in the Welfare State*, 55; LaRochelle-Coté, Myles, and Picott, *Income Security During Retirement*, 6; Baldwin, "Economic Impact," 2–6. The Canadian income-tax system is designed to support an income-replacement level of 70 per cent of preretirement income, up to a maximum of approximately twice average earnings ($100,000 in 2007 figures) (Li, *Tax Expenditure Analysis*, 17). Those with lower preretirement incomes will need to meet higher replacement targets in order to maintain a decent standard of living in retirement.

18 In 2012, several countries, including Denmark, the Netherlands, Italy, and Austria readily met the 70 per cent target from mandatory pension sources (i.e., state-provided or state-mandated pensions) for employees at average wage levels: OECD, *Pensions at a Glance 2013*, 137, Table 4.4. Canada compares at 39.2 per cent.

19 Industrial Relations Section. School of Commerce and Administration, *Industrial Retirement Plans in Canada*, Bulletin No. 1 [*Queen's Study*], 8–19. The *Queen's Study* was based on a 1937 Canadian National Employment Commission Survey of private occupational pension plans in Canada, the first in Canada. The data sources used in the study are not comparable to modern data sources, making comparisons with modern coverage rates unreliable.

20 Ibid., 38–59.

21 Ibid., 108.

22 Committee on Portable Pensions, *Second Report*, 65–9. The *Second Report* is the background paper to the earlier *Summary Report*.

23 Ibid., 69. The fate of this recommendation is discussed in Chapter 4.

24 Key studies include the *Lazar Report*; Royal Commission on the Status of Pensions in Ontario, *Report*, 10 vols [Royal Commission, *Report*]; *COFIRENTES +*; Special Senate Committee, *Retirement Without Tears*; Economic Council of Canada, *One in Three*; Department of Finance, *Green Paper*; Department of Finance, *White Paper*; House of Commons, *Report of the Parliamentary Task Force on Pension Reform*; Select Committee on Pensions, *Final Report*. For a discussion and comparison of the key reports, see Ascah, "Recent Pension Reports."

25 Myles and Teichroew, "The Politics of Dualism," 93. Official government reports supporting expansion of the CPP include the *Lazar Report*; Special Senate Committee, *Retirement Without Tears*; and *COFIRENTES +*.

26 This solution was recommended by the Royal Commission on the Status of Pensions in Ontario.

27 The key exceptions to the call for mandatory state intervention were the committees of elected politicians appointed to review the expert reports: the federal *Parliamentary Task Force on Pension Reform* (69–72) and Ontario's Select Committee on Pensions (31–2). The dissenting members of the Select Committee, New Democrats Bob Mackenzie and Ross McClellan, recommended the expansion of the CPP: 153–62.

28 Bryden, *Old Age Pensions*; Myles, *Old Age in the Welfare State*; Orloff, *The Politics of Pensions*; Snell, *The Citizens' Wage*.

29 *Monsanto Canada Inc. v Ontario (Superintendent of Financial Services)* at para. 1 per Justice Deschamps.

30 Kaplan and Frazer, *Pension Law*, 83.

31 See Association of Canadian Pension Management, *Back from the Brink*, 8.

32 Fourteen per cent of Canadian plan members belong to union-sponsored plans: Carmichael and Quarter, *Money on the Line*, 16.

CHAPTER TWO

1 There were earlier public sector plans: see Chapter 8.

2 See M.W. Latimer, *Industrial Pension Systems*, 20–56; *Queen's Study*, 8–21. These two studies contain much early data on workplace pension plans in both the US and Canada. Latimer's work includes valuable statistical data, assembled by him and his team of researchers, as well as a

detailed analysis of the terms of all 397 formal industrial pension plans that fell within the purview of his study, which was limited to formal plans in the private sector. The *Queen's Study* drew on Latimer's data, supplemented by the 1937 National Employment Commission (NEC) survey, which excluded workplaces employing fewer than fifteen workers.

3 See H.D. Clark, "The Development of the Retirement Income System in Canada," 1–11.

4 The NEC survey included both formal and informal plans, but did not include public sector plans (9).

5 This fact is confirmed by numerous studies from a variety of academic disciplines and political perspectives: for example, Sass, *The Promise of Private Pensions*; Graebner. *History of Retirement*; Munnell, *The Economics of Private Pensions*; Stevens, *Complementing the Welfare State*; Hannah, *Inventing Retirement*; Quadagno, *The Transformation of Old Age Security*; Deaton, *The Political Economy of Pensions*; Ghilarducci, *Labor's Capital*; Ippolito, *Pension Plans and Employee Performance*; Klein, *For All These Rights*.

6 For a discussion of welfare capitalism in Ontario in the first part of the twentieth century, see McCallum, "Corporate Welfarism in Canada, 1919–1939"; Tudiver, "Forestalling the Welfare State." For a US perspective, see Brandes, *American Welfare Capitalism: 1880–1940*.

7 Emory R. Johnson, "Railway Departments," 66–7.

8 The plan text is in the archives of the Canadian Pacific Railway. Its provisions are summarized in "The Superannuation and Pension Fund of the Canadian Pacific Railway Company," *Labour Gazette* (1903): 552: 552–4.

9 M.W. Latimer, *Industrial Pension Systems*, 18.

10 Ibid., 18, 894.

11 *Queen's Study*, 5–6. The *Queen's Study* drew heavily on Latimer's earlier work.

12 The picture was similar in the US: see Sass, *The Promise of Private Pensions*, 38–55. Sass divides US enterprises with workplace pension plans into three distinct types: "rationalizing industries," such as governments, banks, and insurance companies that used their pension plans to attract and maintain a "loyal, experienced and permanent administrative staff"; enterprises operating in the welfare-capitalist tradition, including many railways, which used welfare schemes such as pension plans both to keep a firm hold on a trained and experienced blue-collar workforce and to rid themselves of workers "injured or worn out in the service" of the company; and complex modern, managerial enterprises that required a highly

specialized and differentiated labour force, and depended on internal labour markets. While these categories are useful in understanding employer pension objectives, there is overlap among them, and Canadian pension plans cannot be so neatly pigeon-holed. For the picture in the UK, see Hannah, *Inventing Retirement*.

13 To greatly oversimplify, internal labour markets are job-progression systems, in which higher-paid jobs require training and skills acquired in lower-paid jobs, and there is an expectation of promotion up the job hierarchy: see Stone, *From Widgets to Digits*, 53–63.

14 M.W. Latimer, *Industrial Pension* Systems, 54; *Queen's Study*, 18–21.

15 For background on the history of pensions in the railways, see Seargeant, "Superannuation of Railway Employés [*sic*]," 173 (Seargeant was general manager of the Grand Trunk Railway of Canada, as well as president of the Chicago & Grand Trunk Railway Company). See also Johnson, "Railway Departments"; Riebenack, *Railway Provident Institutions*, a 444-page compendium described as "a consolidation of Reports submitted to the Permanent International Commission of the International Railway Congress at Brussels, Belgium, Europe, under date of July 1st and October 22d, 1904, respectively"; Hannah, *Inventing Retirement*, 10–11; and Sass, *The Promise of Private Pensions*, 18–37.

16 Sass, *The Promise of Private Pensions*, 19. A year later, American Express (then a goods-transportation company) established the first such plan in the US (ibid., at 23).

17 M.W. Latimer, *Industrial Pension Systems*, 28–30; the comparable figures in the US were 39.8 per cent and 82.4 per cent.

18 *An Act to Consolidate the Mortgages and other Preferential Charges of the Grand Trunk Railway Company of Canada, and for raising further Capital, and for establishing a Superannuation and Provident Fund Association, and for other purposes*, SC 1874, c 65 [*Grand Trunk 1874 Act*]. Seargeant discusses the establishment of this plan: "Superannuation of Railway Employés [*sic*]," 173.

19 Grand Trunk Railway of Canada Superannuation and Provident Fund Association. *Rules of the Grand Trunk Railway of Canada Superannuation and Provident Fund Association 1874*, Library and Archives Canada, AMICUS No. 14056072.

20 *Grand Trunk 1874 Act*, ss 11–12.

21 Striking a modern note, the 1874 statute required the company to at least match employee contributions. It also spelled out that the company's contributions "shall for all purposes of priority be considered as a payment of wages due to the servants of the Company." *Grand Trunk 1874 Act*, s 13.

22 *An Act respecting the Grand Trunk Railway Company*, SC 1878, C 25, ss 2–4.

23 See Grand Trunk Railway Insurance and Provident Society, *Rules and By-laws of the Grand Trunk Railway Insurance and Provident Society, 1896*, Library and Archives Canada, AMICUS No. 34882325 [*IPS Rules and IPS By-laws*]. The Archives also holds an earlier version of the governing documents for the society, which was founded in 1884 (AMICUS No. 34882320). I refer to the 1896 version, because it was in effect at the time of the litigation discussed in this section.

24 *IPS By-laws*, s 15: "In consideration of the subscription of the Grand Trunk Railway Company to the funds of the Society no member thereof or his representatives shall have any claim against the Company for compensation on account of injury or death from accident."

25 *IPS Rules*, s 65.

26 See *Ferguson v Grand Trunk Railway Co.*, 1901 CarswellQue (WLCan) 155 (CSR); *Holden v Grand Trunk R.W. Co.*, [1903] OLR 301 (CA). Other railways, including the Intercontinental, owned by the federal government, had successfully relied on similar waiver-of-liability arrangements: see *R v Grenier* (1899), 6 Ex. CR 276; rev'd 30 SCR 42, leave to appeal refused (1900) AC 467, ultimately overruled by the Privy Council in *Miller v Grand Trunk Railway Company of Canada*, [1906] AC 187 (PC).

27 *An Act to Amend the Railway Act, 1903*, SC 1904, C 31, S 1.

28 *Grand Trunk Railway Company of Canada v AG Canada*, [1907] AC 65 (PC); aff'ing *In Re Railway Act Amendment, 1904* [1905] 36 SCC 136. The Grand Trunk Railway contested the validity of the legislation, arguing that it concerned employment and was therefore a provincial matter. The railway insurance-waiver cases were extensively reported in the *Labour Gazette*: see "Employees' Provident Societies," *Labour Gazette* (1901): 315–16; "Railway Employees and Provident Societies," *Labour Gazette* (1901): 365–6; "Railway Employees and Provident Societies," *Labour Gazette* (1902): 482–3; "Grand Trunk Railway Provident Society Case," *Labour Gazette* (1903): 713; "Provident Society Regulation," *Labour Gazette* (1904): 824–5; "Right of Railway Companies to Contract Themselves out of Liability for Injuries Sustained by Employees," *Labour Gazette* (1906): 694–5; "Right of Action against a Railway Company for Damages for Death of Employee," *Labour Gazette* (1906): 1054–6.

29 The 1907 Grand Trunk Plan is reprinted in "Pension Department of the Grand Trunk Railway Company of Canada," *Labour Gazette* (1908): 995–6.

30 See Peitchinis, *Labour-Management Relations in the Railway Industry*,
   61–97.
31 Emory Johnson lists the deterrence of strikes as one reason why railway
   companies established welfare plans: see "Railway Departments." Pension
   historians have expressed differing views about the general importance
   and effectiveness of anti-union motivations in the evolution of pension
   plans: see Ghilarducci, *Labor's Capital*, 14; M.W. Latimer, *Industrial
   Pension Systems*, 894, 936; *Queen's Study*, 6–7. The Grand Trunk eliminated the pension rights of participants in a strike against the company in
   1910; they were restored in 1923 when the Grand Trunk was absorbed
   into the government-owned Canadian National Railway: see Morton and
   McCallum, "Superannuation to Indexation," 8. Mary MacKinnon's
   detailed analysis of the occupational characteristics associated with receipt
   of a CPR pension concludes that "[g]oing on strike was the only occupational characteristic to have a clear [negative] effect on the probability of
   receiving a pension." MacKinnon, "Providing for Faithful Servants," 75.
   Well into the twentieth century, strike participation could have a detrimen-
   tal impact on pension entitlement. During a legal strike in 1961, the CPR
   sent letters to strikers, advising that, if they did not return to work, they
   would lose both their jobs and their pensions: see *Hotel and Club
   Employees Union, Local 299 v Canadian Pacific Railway* [1961] OJ
   No. 392; 61 CLLC; aff'd [1962] SCJ No. 43 (*sub nom Canadian Pacific
   Railway Co. v Zambri*). The court ultimately found that workers continued to be employees during a legal strike and were protected by the
   Labour Relations Act from being penalized for exercising their right
   to strike.
32 Jill Quadagno documents a US example in which pensioners were sum-
   moned back to work to assist their former employer to break the strike
   and lost pension as a penalty for their refusal: see *The Transformation of
   Old Age Security*, 83–5.
33 The 1917 Bell plan is summarized in "Pension and Benefit Plan of the Bell
   Telephone Company," *Labour Gazette* (1917): 314–15. A copy of the plan
   is part of the court record from *Williamson v Ontario (Treasurer)*, [1941]
   OJ No. 206 (HC), [1942] 3 DLR 736, a case discussed at length in
   Chapter 3. That record can be found in the Archives of Ontario, Supreme
   Court Central Office Series, Reference code RG 22–5800, File 960A, Box
   Barcode B131540.
34 This point was further underlined in s 12§1, which provided that
   "[p]ensions or benefits may be suspended or terminated in the discretion

of the Committee, in cases of misconduct or conduct prejudicial to the interests of the Company."

35 This death benefit resembles a modern life-insurance benefit more than a pension death benefit.

36 See Risk, "This Nuisance of Litigation."

37 In a show of goodwill, the plan recited the company's intention "to include all such employees re-entering the service of the Company ... regard being had to Government pensions."

38 Bylaw 16 of the Bell Telephone Company, passed 22 February 1917. A copy of this bylaw is in the court file in *Williamson v Ontario (Treasurer)*, note 33 above.

39 1939 Bell plan. A copy of this plan is in the court file in *Williamson v Ontario (Treasurer)*, note 33 above.

40 While a specific mandatory retirement age was removed from the 1939 plan, retirement could be imposed on any employee eligible for pension, regardless of age.

41 The plan recites that the pension trust fund came into effect in 1928. Although the plan also covered disability pensions and sickness-and-accident benefits, these benefits were treated as operating expenses and were not charged against the trust fund, which was dedicated solely to what the company called "service pensions": see Board Minutes, 28 February 1928 (Ontario Archives file in *Williamson v Ontario (Treasurer)*, note 33 above.

42 M.W. Latimer, *Industrial Pension Systems*.

43 For example, Conant, *A Critical Analysis of Industrial Pension Plans*; Cloud, *Pensions in Modern Industry*; O'Neill, *Modern Pension Plans*.

44 See Stone, *From Widgets to Digits*, 27–63. Stone describes "Fordism" as characterized by "deskilling tasks, defining jobs narrowly and encouraging long-term attachment between the worker and the firm" (46). See also Supiot, *Beyond Employment: Changes in Work and the Future of Labour Law in Europe*, 1. Jacoby, *Employing Bureaucracy*, uses the term "bureaucratization" to describe the adoption of structured management strategies, and identifies World War I and the Great Depression as key periods in the bureaucratization of work: 99–123, 14–178. Both Stone and Jacoby emphasize the importance of "internal labour markets" and employment benefits that tied workers to their jobs for the long term. In "Forestalling the Welfare State," Neil Tudiver brings a Canadian perspective to analyzing the relationship between corporate welfare programs like pension plans, and changes in management philosophy and personnel policy from the late nineteenth century to the mid-twentieth century.

45 "The Problem of Old Age Pensions in Industry: Results of Study by
   Pennsylvania Old Age Pension Commission," *Labour Gazette* (1927):
   1051.

46 MacKinnon's study covers a sample of workers hired prior to 1945. It
   shows that the percentage of employees retiring with pensions increased
   over time; the 7 per cent figure applies to the entire period of her study.
   She notes that "[n]ew workers typically stayed with the company for less
   than a year": MacKinnon, "Providing for Faithful Servants," 69. She
   found that turnover rates had decreased by the 1920s, but doubted that
   the pension regime could be credited with reducing turnover (70).

47 Klein, *For All These Rights*, 62–3. Klein's conclusion refers to the US, but
   is likely true of Canada as well.

48 See discussion in Chapter 8.

49 *Queen's Study*, 20.

50 See W. Latimer, "Pension Plans and Income Tax."

51 See Hannah, *Inventing Retirement*, 27, 43, and Chap. 2, note 51 (162).
   Statutory provisions prohibiting unauthorized wage deductions were rem-
   nants of the English "truck acts"; they include provisions like s 13 of the
   Ontario *Employment Standards Act, 2000*, SO 2000, c 41. Many US states
   had similar provisions: see Ransom, Sutch, and Williamson, "Inventing
   Pensions," 14.

52 David McCarthy outlines and critiques this classical economic perspective
   in "Occupational Pension Scheme Design."

53 Any such expectations would have found little support in the courts of
   that era. Latimer's study found judges unwilling to construe pension plans
   as providing legal entitlements, regardless of whether they were contributory or non-contributory: see M.W. Latimer, *Industrial Pension Systems*,
   706, and discussion in Chapter 3. However, Latimer's survey also found
   that contributory plans were somewhat more likely to spell out some level
   of entitlement within the plan text: some 70 per cent of contributory plans
   provided some financial guarantee to employees, as opposed to only
   55 per cent of non-contributory plans: ibid., 725–8. Contributory plans
   were also more likely to use insurance as a funding instrument. The *Queen's
   Study* found a similar correlation among insurance funding, contributory
   plans, and acknowledgment of employee pension rights (11–21).

54 M.W. Latimer, *Industrial Pension Systems*, 44.

55 See Dominion Bureau of Statistics, *Survey of Pension Plan Coverage, 1965*,
   9, Table D, and Statistics Canada, CANSIM Table 280-0008, "Registered
   pension plan (RPP) members, by area of workplace, sector, type of plan,
   and contributory status, 2009–2013."

56 See for example, O'Neill, *Modern Pension Plans*, 6–7; *Labour Gazette*, "Vesting Provisions" (1955): 36.

57 The law of wrongful dismissal in Canada in the early part of the twentieth century was still very much in flux. Although common-law notice obligations existed for employment of indefinite duration, they were not onerous: see Mummé, "'That Indispensable Figment of the Legal Mind,'" 166–75. Mummé observes that wrongful dismissal was rarely litigated, and when it was, damage awards rarely exceeded six months' salary. Any risk of termination costs could be avoided entirely simply by giving sufficient notice. In the US, where the mandatory retirement pension model first became widespread, the "employment at will" doctrine was well established as early as the 1880s (see Stone, *From Widgets to Digits*, 24), which meant that employers did not have to give any notice of termination. Stone's discussion of the importance of employee morale to the proper functioning of the modern industrial enterprises helps us to understand the business benefit to employers of maintaining employee goodwill, even in the absence of a legal obligation (41–3, 56–8, 87–92).

58 Graebner, *History of Retirement*, 149. Graebner argues that unions collaborated with companies in permitting this "sloughing off."

59 *An Act to empower the employees of incorporated companies to establish Pension Fund Societies*, SC 1887, c 21 [*Pension Fund Societies Act*]. A *Pension Fund Societies Act* is still on the federal statute books (RSC 1985, c P-8), very little changed from its original form. General legislation enabling pension fund societies was predated by special legislation establishing pension societies for specific corporations: see, for example, *An Act to Incorporate the Annuity and Guarantee Funds Society of the Bank of Montreal*, SC 1860, c.17; and *An Act to Incorporate the Pension Fund Society of the Bank of Montreal*, SC 1885, c 13.

60 For a discussion of the corporate capacity issue in the US issue, see O'Neal, "Stockholder Attacks on Corporate Pension Systems."

61 See: *An Act respecting Benevolent, Provident and other Societies*, RSO 1877, c 172. This statute replaced an earlier one, *An Act for Incorporating Charitable, Philanthropic, and Provident Associations*, passed in 1850: S Prov C 1850 (22 Vict), c 71.

62 *The Insurance Corporations Act, 1892*, SO 1892, c 39.

63 An important purpose of the statute was to regularize the activities of friendly societies, most of which did not deal with pensions, but with more conventional types of insurance: see Hunter, *The Insurance Corporations Act, 1892*.

64 For example, friendly societies were required to provide copies of the rules relating to insurance contracts and management of funds to any members upon demand, at a price of twenty-five cents [s 32(1)].

65 *The Government Annuities Act*, SC 1908, c 5.

66 The first insured group pension plan in Canada was underwritten by Sun Life in 1923: see E.S. Jackson, "Insurance Companies in the Pension Market."

67 The structure of the government group-annuity contract is discussed in *Porter v Canada*, [1956] 1 ExCR 200, in which the Exchequer Court dismissed a constitutional challenge to the federal government's power to provide these annuities.

68 See Bryden, *Old Age Pensions*, 51–9; Morton and McCallum, "Superannuation to Indexation," 8–16. A *Government Annuities Act* is still on the statute books (RSC 1970, c G-6), but pursuant to the *Government Annuities Improvement Act*, SC 1974-75-76, c 83, ss 13–14, no new annuities may be sold.

69 *Grand Trunk 1874 Act*, s 13.

70 The 1919 *Labour Gazette* reported that, in 1918, the Bell pension fund paid out $147,265.26 in benefits. At that rate, the fund would have been depleted in less than three years. It was contemplated, however, that the fund would be "topped up" by the company on an as-needed basis [*Labour Gazette* (1917): 314].

71 See Ghilarducci, *Labor's Capital*, 8–110. Many of the practices Ghilarducci documents are unlawful in Canada under the current regulatory regime, but would have been lawful at least prior to the 1960s.

72 R.M. Clark, *Economic Security for the Aged*, 73; McBride, "The Growth and Coverage of Insured and Trusteed Pension Plans." The same competition between insurance vehicles and trust funding vehicles took place in the US and the UK: see Sass, *The Promise of Private Pensions*, 56–87; Hannah, *Inventing Retirement*, 31–45; M.W. Latimer, *Industrial Pension Systems*, 51.

73 The history of Canadian income-tax treatment of pension contributions and pension funding vehicles is discussed in R. M. Clark, *Economic Security for the Aged*, 45–55. For a more detailed treatment up to the mid-1960s, see Edwards, "Canadian Private Pension Plans," 281–300.

74 R.M. Clark, *Economic Security for the Aged*, 73. Clark observes that the number of trusteed plans was relatively small compared to the overall number of plans, but since they were the plans of large employers, more than half of plan members belonged to trusteed plans.

75 By 1957, 17.8 per cent of plans were funded by insurance; 24.1 per cent by trusts administered by professional trust companies; 23.5 per cent by trusts that were privately trusteed; and 8.8 per cent by federal government annuities. The rest (25.8 per cent) were public service pensions, armed-forces pensions, or teacher/professor plans, which were either unfunded or not funded by the employer: see R.M. Clark, ibid., Tables, 99–100, and Committee on Portable Pensions, *Second Report*, 12–13. The same competition between the insured and the trusteed model of pension funding was evident in both the UK and the US over the same period: see Hannah, *Inventing Retirement*, 18–29; Sass, *The Promise of Private Pensions*, 61–79; 145–68.

CHAPTER THREE

1 M.W. Latimer, *Industrial Pension Systems*, 9–10.
2 Blackstone's *Commentaries* were originally published by the Clarendon Press between 1765 and 1769. The discussion of "annuities" is found in Chapter 3, "Of Incorporeal Hereditaments," Vol. 2, 40. "Incorporeal hereditaments" were not just property; they were "real property" (as opposed to "personal property"). Rents and tithes also belonged in this category. For a discussion of Blackstone's categories and their influence on American legal thought, see Vandenvelde, "The New Property of the Nineteenth Century"; Kennedy, "The Structure of Blackstone's Commentaries."
3 Blackstone's *Commentaries*, Vol. 2, 20.
4 Courts in both the UK and Canada were divided on whether testamentary trusts established to pay pensions for employees were valid charitable trusts: see *Re Gosling* (1900), 48 WR 300; *Re Massey*, [1959] OJ 697; [1959] OR 608 (Ont. HCJ); *Re Cox*, [1951] OJ No. 548; [1951] OR 205 (CA); [1952] SCJ No. 53; [1955] JCJ No. 4; *Re Allanson*, [1971] OJ No. 1620; [1971] 3 OR 209 (CA); *Jones v T. Eaton Co.*, [1973] SCJ No. 65.
5 *Balderson v The Queen* (1898), 28 SCR 261, 25 Hals. 89 (per Taschereau J), aff'ing (1897) 6 Ex. CR 8.
6 Per Justice Taschereau. *The Civil Service Superannuation Act* under which Balderson made his claim is discussed in detail in Chapter 8.
7 Ibid.
8 *In the Matter of the Petition of Right of Lucien C.G.T. Bacon, Suppliant and His Majesty the King, Respondent* (1921), 21 Ex. CR 25 at 28.
9 See also *Kidd v Canada*, [1924] Ex. CR 29.

10 See Mummé, "That Indispensable Figment of the Legal Mind," 74–81.
    For discussion of the struggles of common-law judges in the UK to apply
    emerging contract theory to the employment relationship, see Deakin, *The*
    Contract of Employment. More generally on nineteenth-century contract
    doctrine at common law, see Horwitz, "The Historical Foundations of
    Modern Contract Law."

11 The problems of "past consideration" and pension credit for past service
    are discussed at length in O'Neal, "Stockholder Attacks on Corporate
    Pension Systems," 359–66, reviewing both UK and US case law.

12 See, for example, Ackerman, "The Legal Aspects of Amendments to a
    Pension Plan"; Comment, "Consideration for the Employer's Promise";
    Isaacson, "Employee Welfare and Pension Plans"; Lauritzen, "Perpetuities
    and Pension Trusts"; Note, "Legal Problems of Private Pension Plans";
    O'Neal, "Stockholder Attacks on Corporate Pension Systems"; Somers
    and Schwartz, "Pension and Welfare Plans."

13 See Hepple, "Intention to Create Legal Relations."

14 *Wright (The Rev. Joel Tombleson) v the Incorporated Synod of the*
    Diocese of Huron, [1881] OJ No. 217, 29 Gr 348 (Ontario Court of
    Chancery), rev'd *sub nom Wright v Huron*, 9 OAR 411 [*Wright* CA], aff'd
    [1885] SCJ No. 11 [*Wright* SCC].

15 The clergy reserves were lands originally set aside by the Crown in 1791
    for the maintenance of Protestant clergy. Claims by the Church of England
    to exclusive control of these lands and their revenue were a serious politi-
    cal pressure point in pre-Confederation Upper Canada. The reserves were
    eventually "secularized" in 1854 (see *An Act to make better provision for*
    the appropriation of Moneys arising from the Lands therefore known as
    the Clergy Reserves, by rendering them available for municipal purposes,
    S Prov C 1854 (18 Vict), c 2), and compensation paid to the church,
    resulting in the creation of the fund at issue in this case.

16 *Wright* CA.

17 *Wright* SCC.

18 *Dionne v Québec* (1895), 24 SCR 451.

19 The only Canadian case identified by LexisNexis as citing *Dionne* is
    Sneddon v British Columbia (Hydro and Power Authority), 2004 BCCA
    292, decided more than a century later, in which the decision is distin-
    guished on the facts and the statutory context. *Wright* does not appear
    to have been cited anywhere.

20 *Armstrong v Toronto Police Benefit Fund*, [1902] OJ No. 669, 1 OWR
    829 (CA). The Toronto Police Benefit Fund is described in the case report

as a friendly society established in 1881 "to insure against death and to grant life-time benefits" (ibid., para. 1): see discussion in Chapter 2 on the role of friendly societies in early pension provision.

21 *Pension Fund Society of La Banque Nationale, Trudel v Lemoine et al,* [1925] 4 DLR. 97 [*Trudel SCC*], aff'd [1926] 3 DLR 988 (PC) (sub nom *Pension Fund Society of La Banque Nationale, Audet v Trudel*). The fund had been established under the provisions of the 1906 *Pension Fund Societies Act*: see discussion of pension fund societies in Chapter 2.

22 *Trudel SCC* at 97.

23 The decision cites a definition from Rolland de Villargues *Repertoire, verbo Droit* [*sic*]: a *droit acquis* is "a right which has become definitely vested in a man's estate, and which cannot be divested without the consent of the holder."

24 To qualify for a pension, an employee had to be at least sixty and have twenty-five years of service. There were also disability pensions and pensions for those with twenty-five years' service who were not yet sixty, but had lost their jobs as a result of lack of employment (or in modern parlance, were laid off). A related issue in the case was whether the shutdown of the bank triggered this situation for all employees; the court decided that it did not.

25 The decision of the Supreme Court of Canada was formally issued only in French, and was subsequently reported in English in the *Dominion Law Reports*, with an editor's note to the following effect: "'Droits acquis' has been translated 'acquired rights' throughout the case though 'vested rights' is the more English form. As both phrases are somewhat technical it has been thought better not to confuse them."

26 M.W. Latimer, *Industrial Pension Systems*, 681–706.

27 *McNevin v Solvay Process Company*, 32 App. Div. (New York, 1898). Harbrecht, *Pension Funds and Economic Power*, identifies an earlier case, *Pennie v Reis*, 132 US 464 (1889) as the first US case involving pension rights. In *Pennie v Reis*, the court denied a pension claim by a police officer, despite the fact that he had contributed to the plan, apparently on the basis, as explained by Harbrecht, that although his contributions had been described as part of his compensation, the money had been deducted at source and, accordingly, he had never actually received or controlled it.

28 M.W. Latimer, *Industrial Pension Systems*, 682–5.

29 Ibid., 706.

30 Ibid., 705.

31 The US case law to the mid-twentieth century is summarized in detail in
Comment, "Consideration for the Employer's Promise of a Voluntary
Pension Plan"; and Note, "Legal Problems of Private Pension Plans."

32 See, for example, *Schofield v Zion's Co-operative Mercantile Institution*,
85 Utah 281, 39 P (2d) 342 (1934); *Wilson v Rudolph Wurlitzer Co.*,
48 Ohio App 450, 194 NE 441 (1934); *Nemser v Aviation Corp*, 47 F
Supp 515 (DDel 1942).

33 The "unilateral contract" theory as applied to pension plans is developed
in Comment, "Consideration for the Employer's Promise of a Voluntary
Pension Plan," 102–3, 108–10. The *locus classicus* of unilateral contract
theory is *Carlill v Carbolic Smoke Ball Co.*, [1892] 2 QB 484, in which a
company's promotional promise to pay £100 to anybody who contracted
influenza despite having used its patent remedy was found to be contractually binding in the case of a user who did catch the flu (see Waddams,
The Law of Contracts, Chapter 4, "Unilateral Contracts," 158–66).

34 National Industrial Conference Board, Inc., *Industrial Pensions in the
United States*, 51.

35 M.W. Latimer, *Industrial Pension Systems*, 684.

36 See, for example, *Gummerson v Toronto Police Benefit Fund* [1905]
No. 399, 5 OWR 581 (HC), aff'd on other grounds, [1905] OJ No. 29,
11 OLR 194.

37 American courts took a similar approach, applying doctrines of estoppel,
good faith, and procedural fairness from time to time to award pensions
to employees, even in the absence of contractual obligations: see M.W.
Latimer, *Industrial Pension Systems*, 697; Benjamin Aaron, *Legal Status of
Employee Benefit Rights*, 8–9.

38 *Lapointe v Montreal Police Benefit Society*, [1906] CRAC 379, on appeal
from the Supreme Court of Canada. (The 1904 SCC decision and the
decision of the Privy Council are combined in the same case report.)
The Supreme Court had quashed the plaintiff's appeal, holding that the
value of the pension arrears at issue fell below the appeal threshold. The
Privy Council then heard the appeal from the lower court judgment by
special leave.

39 The benefit society appears to have been established under Quebec
legislation, although the report does not cite the specific statute involved.
Literally translated, *audi alteram partem* means "hear the other side"; it is
a legal rule which requires adjudicators to hear both sides of the case
before they make decisions.

40 "The action in substance, though not in form, is an action to administer
the trusts of the pension fund, and to compel the trustees – that is, the

board of directors – to administer those trusts in Lapointe's favour in a proper and legal manner": *Lapointe v Montreal Police Benefit Society* at 386.

41 Deviations from proper procedure included appointing a subcommittee to conduct a unilateral investigation of Lapointe's entire work history with the police force, failing to advise him of the allegations against him, and putting the ultimate decision to a vote of the whole membership, instead of making a decision itself on the basis of the evidence. The Privy Council admonished the directors that they "must bear in mind that they are judges, not inquisitors": ibid. at 386.

42 The Privy Council did in fact refer to *Russell v Russell* (1880), 14 CHD 471, a leading UK case applying the *audi alteram partem* rule to the proceedings of a private club.

43 See also *Welsh v Toronto Police Benefit Fund*, [1915] OJ No. 715; 9 OWN 2 (HC), in which the Ontario Supreme Court reached a similar result without reference to authority drawn from administrative law.

44 *Tawny v City of Winnipeg*, [1936] MJ No. 9, [1936] 2 WWR 123 (Man. KB) [*Tawny*]. See also *Reid v International Union of Mine, Mill and Smelter Workers, Local 598*, [1960] OJ No. 39 (Ont. HC).

45 *Mantha v Montreal (City)*, [1939] SCR 458 [*Mantha*].

46 The court's holding in *Mantha* that in the absence of a proper determination by a pension plan's internal decision-making bodies a court was free to make its own findings was applied by the Saskatchewan Court of Appeal in *Douglas v Saskatoon*, [1947] SJ 80 to a firefighter's claim for an occupational disability pension from the city. *Mantha* has been cited only rarely since by Canadian courts.

47 *Williamson v Ontario (Treasurer)*, [1942] 3 DLR 736, [1941] OJ No. 206 (HC) [*Williamson*].

48 *Succession Duty Act*, 1939, SO, c 1940, s 10(b). The government also relied on s 10(e), which included in the estate "any property of which the person dying was at the time of his death competent to dispose, and a person shall be deemed competent to dispose of property if he has such an estate or interest therein or such general power as would, if he were *sui juris*, enable him to dispose of the property as he thinks fit, whether the power is exercisable by instrument *inter vivos* or by will or both" (e). The court concluded that the death benefit was not "property" over which the deceased had any power of disposition (para. 16).

9 This type of amendment/termination language is still relatively standard in pension plans. Under modern pension statutes it is interpreted as protecting benefits accrued by active employees as well pensioners, up to the

time the language changes or the plan is terminated: see, for example,
Dinney v Great-West Life Assurance Co., [2005] MJ No. 69, 252 DLR
(4th) 660 (CA); *McGrath v Superintendent of Financial Services, OMERS Administration Corporation and OMERS Sponsors Corporation*, 2010
ONFST 5.

50 *McDougall v MNR*, [1949] Ex. CR 314 [*McDougall*].
51 *Succession Duty Act*, SC 1940–41, c 14.
52 *McDougall*. The booklet, in Q & A form, included the following:
   Question: What important amendments have been made to the Plan?
   Answer: a. The Plan, when first established in 1917, contained a
   stipulation that the Plan was tentative only. This stipulation has been
   removed from the revised Plan.
   b. The Plan previously stipulated that there was no contract or
   contractual relation or obligation between the Company and any
   employee or the legal representatives or the dependents of any
   employee. This stipulation has been removed from the revised Plan and
   the payment of pensions and benefits subject to the provisions of the
   Plan, is now an obligation of the Company.
   c. The Plan previously contained the provision that pensions or benefits
   could be suspended or terminated, in the discretion of the Employees'
   Benefit Committee, in cases of misconduct or conduct prejudicial to the
   interests of the Company. This provision has been removed from the
   revised Plan.
53 These latter words were added in 1942, almost certainly intended to
   counteract the result in *Williamson*.
54 The court's reference to collective bargaining is interesting. There was no
   statutory framework governing collective bargaining at the federal level in
   1939 when the plan was established, but by 1949, when *McDougall* was
   decided, formal collective bargaining legislation was in place. There had
   been collective bargaining at Bell since 1944 (see Weiss and Bedard,
   Contextual Negotiations, 5), but the pension plan was unconnected to
   the collective agreement. See Chapter 5 generally for a discussion of the
   impact of collective bargaining on workplace pension plans.
55 The court was also influenced by language in the plan designed to ensure
   that benefits under the plan were for "personal use" and did not confer
   "any right or interest capable of being assigned or otherwise alienated, or
   of being seized, attached, garnisheed, or otherwise made subject to any
   process of proceeding in law of [*sic*] equity." The court interpreted this
   language (almost certainly wrongly) as barring legal action by third
   parties, such as surviving spouses (or perhaps even by pensioners); this

language, still relatively common in plans, is intended simply to protect pensions from claims by creditors.

56 *McDougall* is one of the few Canadian cases to touch on the issue of whether companies have the corporate capacity to establish pension/ benefit plans, an issue that was a matter of serious debate in the US courts: see O'Neal, "Stockholder Attacks on Corporate Pension Systems."

57 See also *Heirs of N.T. Cronk, represented by Barclays Trust Co. of Canada v MNR*, [1949] 49 DTC 612 (Ex Ct) (dealing with the pension plan of Northern Electric Limited, a Bell subsidiary). In a slightly later decision dealing with the CPR plan, *Flintoft Estate v Canada (Minister of National Revenue)* [1951] Ex. CR 211, the Exchequer Court found a new loophole to dismiss the government's claim for succession duty, holding that, because the CPR had paid the death benefit out of operating funds, it was not payable out of a "superannuation or pension fund" and was therefore not taxable.

58 The strict constructionist approach to the interpretation of taxing statutes is implicit in most of these cases and explicit in *Flintoft Estate v Canada (Minister of National Revenue)* [1951] Ex. CR 211.

CHAPTER FOUR

1 See Banting, *The Welfare State and Canadian Federalism*; Bryden, *Old Age Pensions*; Deaton, *The Political Economy of Pensions*; Simeon, *Federal Provincial Diplomacy*; Guest, *The Emergence of Social Security in Canada*; Myles, *Old Age in the Welfare State*; Myles and Teichroew, "The Politics of Dualism"; Orloff, *The Politics of Pensions*; Snell, *The Citizens' Wage*.

2 Dominion Bureau of Statistics, *Survey of Industrial Pension Welfare Plans, 1947*.

3 "Pension and Welfare Plans in Canadian Industry," *Labour Gazette* (1949): 694; "Types of Pension and Retirement Plans in Canadian Industry," *Labour Gazette* (1950): 191; "Pension Plans in Canadian Industry," *Labour Gazette* (1950): 443; "Contribution, Benefit Formulas in Canadian Industrial Pension Plans," *Labour Gazette* (1954): 519 ["Contribution, Benefit Formulas"]; "Types of Retirement Policy in Canadian Industrial Pension Plans," *Labour Gazette* (1954): 1238 ["Types of Retirement Policy"]; "Vesting Provisions in Canadian Industrial Pension Plans," *Labour Gazette* (1955): 30 ["Vesting Provisions"]; "Number of Workers Covered by Pension Plans in Canada," *Labour Gazette* (1955): 784.

4 Over the years, survey methodologies and terminology have varied considerably. The unreliability of statistical data on Canadian pensions is an issue that has troubled pension researchers for more than a century: see *Arthurs Report*, 28.

5 "Pension and Welfare Plans in Canadian Industry," 695.

6 Ibid., 696. See also Table 3, 698.

7 Ibid.

8 Ibid., 695 (author's calculation).

9 "Pension Plans in Canadian Industry," 42; see also Dominion Bureau of Statistics, *Pension Plans: Non-financial Statistics, 1960*, 23–34.

10 "Vesting Provisions," 31–3. Larger workplaces were those with five hundred or more employees.

11 "Contribution, Benefit Formulas," 519–21. The study found that, in larger Canadian companies, more than 80 per cent of plans were contributory. Where plans were contributory, employees were normally required to contribute between 4 and 5 per cent of earnings.

12 See discussion in Chapter 2.

13 "Vesting Provisions," 36.

14 Ibid., 35. As late as 1965, a government survey reported that less than 3 per cent of departing employees left behind them an entitlement to a deferred pension, while the "vast majority" took a return of contributions: Dominion Bureau of Statistics, *Survey of Pension Plan Coverage, 1965* [*1965 Survey*], 11.

15 "Contribution, Benefit Formulas," 521.

16 Ibid., 523.

17 Ibid., 524. The study did not define "negotiated plans," and many of these plans would have been established prior to formal collective bargaining laws.

18 From 1938, Canadian tax laws permitted employers to deduct contributions for the past service credit: see Edwards, "Canadian Private Pension Plans," 281–2.

19 "Vesting Provisions," 36.

20 "Types of Retirement Policy," 1238–9.

21 Ibid., 1239–40. This five-year age difference was ubiquitous but never well explained.

22 "Vesting Provisions," 36.

23 "Pension Plans in Canadian Industry," 444–5.

24 See Edwards, "Canadian Private Pension Plans," 56–60. Pension and benefit plans were found by the Canadian National War Labour Board to

fall within the definition of wages, and were therefore subject to wage controls: see "Wartime Wage Control in Canada," *Labour Gazette* (1942): 282; "Decisions of the National War Labour Board," *Labour Gazette* (1944): 39 and 466. The board was lenient, however, in allowing employers to establish new plans, especially if they were contributory, since they were "not inconsistent with the prime purpose of [the Wage Control Order], namely the stabilization of wages," *Labour Gazette,* (1944): 466. Similar wartime wage controls fostered growth in workplace pension plans in the US: see Klein, *For All These Rights,* 163–83.

25 The 1946 version of the *Blue Book, Statement of Principles and Rules respecting Pension Plans for the Purposes of the Income War Tax Act: Tax Ruling No. 2 (1946 47)* [*1946 Blue Book*] was subsequently revised and reissued in 1950 as *Statement of Principles and Rules respecting Pension Plans for the Purposes of the Income Tax Act* [*1950 Blue Book*].

26 The role of the *Blue Books* is discussed in R.M. Clark, *Economic Security for the Aged,* 45–55. See also William Latimer, "Pension Plans and Income Tax," 103–8.

27 By 1950, this rule had been relaxed to permit inclusion of directors and officers: see *1950 Blue Book,* s 2.

28 The rules do not spell out how significant a contribution the employer must make to qualify.

29 Pensions could not exceed 70 per cent of average salary for the employee's last five years of service.

30 The *1950 Blue Book* prohibited the exclusion of female employees, although plans could continue to impose different minimum age or service requirements on both men and women.

31 The employee's estate also had a right to a return of the employee's contributions if the employee died before retirement. There was no right to interest on returned contributions (s 11).

32 R.M. Clark, *Economic Security for the Aged,* 50–1. It is not clear how the ministry defined a "collectively bargained" plan.

33 See William Latimer," Pension Plans and Income Tax," 103–6; R.M. Clark, *Economic Security for the Aged,* 46–51. The *Blue Books* were replaced by Information Bulletin No. 14, a much less directive document, which had itself been withdrawn by 1961.

34 Bryden, *Old Age Pensions,* 51–9.

35 RSC 1927, c 156.

36 See Bryden, *Old Age Pensions,* 61–101; Guest, *The Emergence of Social Security in Canada,* 74–8.

37 Orloff, *The Politics of Pensions*, 294–8. The *Social Security Act of 1935* combined a means-tested flat-rate old age benefit, with a mandatory, earnings-based, and contributory public pension.

38 Bryden, *Old Age Pensions*, 106, 123; Orloff, *The Politics of Pensions*, 19.

39 *Reference Re: Workplace and Social Insurance Act (Canada)* [1936] SCR 427 (PC), 6.

40 Bryden explains that the term "social insurance" was widely used at the time in a variety of different senses, ranging from "benefits which were directly related to ('purchased by') premiums" to "a guarantee to the entire population of a basic income in (insurance against) adversity": *Old Age Pensions*, 110.

41 *Old Age Security Act*, SC 1951, c 18 and *Old Age Assistance Act*, SC 1951, c 55. See Bryden, *Old Age Pensions*, 104–6.

42 Guest, *The Emergence of Social Security in Canada*, 137; Bryden, *Old Age Pensions*, 142.

43 There was a belated and unsuccessful constitutional challenge: see *Porter v Canada*, [1956] 1 Ex. CR 200 (Exchequer Court of Canada).

44 See Bryden, *Old Age Pensions*, 61–3.

45 The version of Section 94A of the *British North America Act* enacted in 1951 read: "The Parliament of Canada may from time to time make laws in relation to old age pensions in Canada, but no law made by the Parliament of Canada in relation to old age pensions shall affect the operation of any law present or future of the Provincial Legislature in relation to old age pensions."

46 The constitutional amendment eventually enacted in 1964 provided that the federal government could "make laws in relation to old age pensions and supplementary pensions, including survivor and disability benefits irrespective of age," but continued to acknowledge provincial paramountcy.

47 Bryden, *Old Age Pensions*, 166–73.

48 Committee on Portable Pensions, *Second Report*, 22–5, 64–71.

49 Ibid., 20. The study labelled this phenomenon "wastage."

50 In the debates surrounding the repeal of the 1962–63 legislation in preparation for the enactment of the *PBA, 1965*, Premier Robarts offered the following definition of portability: "By portability, we mean that the employee has a right to pension benefits from his employer's contributions, as well as his own, and further that these benefits cannot be surrendered or commuted for a cash refund except to a very limited extent as set out in the Act." Legislative Assembly, *Official Report of Debates (Hansard)*, No. 79 (28 April 1964) at 2504 (Hon. John Robarts). In contemporary pension parlance, the term "portability" usually refers not

simply to vested rights, but to the ability to transfer those vested rights out of the plan to some other retirement-income vehicle, such as another pension plan or other locked-in instrument.

51 *The Pension Benefits Act, 1962–63*, SO 1962–63, c 103. For an account of the background to this statute and a defence of its approach from a member of the Committee on Portable Pensions, see R.M. Clark, "The Pension Benefits Act of Ontario," 27.

52 Robarts, "The Ontario Approach to Pensions," 1–3.

53 Robarts, "The Ontario Approach to Pensions," 3, 5. Judy LaMarsh, the federal Liberal cabinet minister responsible for the implementation of the C / QPP, saw Ontario's role in the federal-provincial negotiations as little more than capitulation to the insurance-industry lobby. She described the role of the insurance companies in opposing the CPP as "a shameful chapter in the history of Canadian business." LaMarsh, *Memoirs of a Bird in a Gilded Cage*, 88. For a more detailed discussion of the role of the insurance industry in the debates surrounding the introduction of the CPP, see Murphy, "Corporate Capital and the Welfare State," 31–9, 63–76.

54 Bryden, *Old Age Pensions*, 155–6.

55 Canada. Department of National Health and Welfare, *The Canada Pension Plan*, August 1964, 21–6.

56 Ibid.

57 See Legislative Assembly, *Official Report of Debates (Hansard)*, No. 104 (21 May 1965), at 3195 (Hon. John Robarts). Ontario's prototype statute contemplated a network of provincial and federal pension authorities that would work together to minimize duplication and inconsistency: see s 10(2) of the *Pension Benefits Act, 1965*, SO 1965, authorizing the Pension Commission of Ontario to enter into reciprocal agreements with federal and other provincial pension authorities "for the reciprocal registration, audit and inspection of pensions plans," and for the delegation of Pension Commission functions, powers, and duties to other pension commissions, or to a joint Canada-wide association of pension commissions.

58 *Pension Benefits Act, 1965*, SO 1965, c 96.

59 Quebec also passed its first regulatory statute in 1965. Alberta and the federal government followed suit in 1966. Not all provinces moved so quickly; British Columbia did not legislate to regulate pensions until 1993, and as late as February 2016, Prince Edward Island still had no operative *Pension Benefits Act*.

60 Legislative Assembly, *Official Report of Debates (Hansard)*, No. 104 (21 May 1965), at 3194 (Hon. John Robarts). While the legislation acknowledged the existence of defined contribution plans [see s 1(h)(ii):

definition of "pension plan"], their unique needs went largely unaddressed by the legislation. Likewise, multi-employer plans and statute-based public and para-public plans got scant recognition, although they were governed by the *PBA 1965*.

61 The Pension Commission of Ontario administered the Act, monitored the registration system, and conducted statistical and other pension research [s 10(1)], but its duties did not include direct intervention with employers to enforce member rights. It was a summary-conviction offence to contravene the statute [s 26(1)]; an employer convicted of an offence would be required to pay into the pension fund any sums it had been convicted of wrongfully withholding [s 26(2)].

62 The Act did not mandate death benefits, although both survivor benefits and death benefits were expressly permitted [s 21(5)].

63 There were two limited exceptions. The statute permitted pension plans to provide for the lump-sum cash withdrawal of very small pensions [s 21(3)(b)], and up to 25 per cent of the value of any pension [s 21(4)].

64 The concept of inalienability was further reinforced by s 21(2), which spelled out that pension benefits and deferred life annuities could not be commuted into cash during the lifetime of the employee.

65 Governments (including municipal governments) were exempt from this requirement.

66 The accompanying regulation (O Reg 103/66) gave legal force to such actuarial concepts as current service costs, initial unfunded liabilities, and experience deficiencies, and set out very specific timetables for employers to make good on any funding deficits.

67 O Reg 103/66, s 14(2). There were some exceptions to the federal rules written into the regulation.

68 O Reg 103/66, s 14(7).

69 Coxe, "A Look at the Pension Iceberg," 92–4; Little, *Fixing the Future*, 51–2.

70 The role played by the labour movement in workplace pension plans is discussed in detail in Chapter 5.

71 Myles and Teichroew, "The Politics of Dualism," 93.

72 See Battle, "The New Old Age Pension"; Pierson, "The Politics of Pension Reform."

73 Canada, Department of Finance, *Better Pensions for Canadians* [*Green Paper*]. In Canadian government parlance, a Green Paper is a consultation document; a White Paper sets out the government's subsequent policy positions.

74 There is conflicting information on what year pension coverage peaked in Canada, and at exactly what level. Tamagno, *Occupational Pension Plans in Canada*, 5 (Figure 2) suggests a peak of 46.2 per cent in 1977; the *Green Paper* claims a higher figure of 47.9 per cent in 1978, although it does not identify its source (19).

75 The gendered language of the 1964 *White Paper* (Department of National Health and Welfare, *The Canada Pension Plan*) reflects its conceptualization of a worker as "a man." The key CPP policy initiative for women was the survivor benefit.

76 See Fortin and Huberman, "Occupational Segregation and Women's Wages," S11, noting that female labour-force participation in Canada rose from less than 30 per cent in 1961 to more than 75 per cent in 1996. The paper identifies 1961 as the "beginning of the surge in female labour force participation that characterizes the second half of the twentieth century" (S16).

77 *Frith Report*, 74. For more information about the gendered impact of both workplace and public pension plans, see House of Commons, Standing Committee on the Status of Women, *Pension Security for Women*; Woodman, "The Fiscal Equality of Women"; Young, "Pensions, Privatization, and Poverty"; Kodar, "Pensions and Unpaid Work"; Hansen and Turnbull, "Disability and Care"; Shilton, "Gender Risk."

78 *Lazar Report*, 337.

79 For a discussion of the debate, both inside and outside the women's movement, over gendered pension issues, see Dulude, *Pension Reform with Women in Mind*; Ascah, "Recent Pension Reports," 421–2; Kodar, "Pensions and Unpaid Work," 187–99.

80 Myles, *Old Age in the Welfare State*, 112–14. See also Myles and Teichroew, "The Politics of Dualism," 93–4.

81 This analysis is amply supported by Barbara Murphy's research in "Corporate Capital and the Welfare State." Murphy explains that shifts in corporate positions on pensions over the twentieth century reflect "changes in the function which pensions and pension policy have performed for business in pursuit of profits and capital accumulation" (8). She argues that, by the 1980s, corporate Canada was focused primarily on the importance of workplace pensions as a source of private investment capital, although there was continued interest in pensions as wage instruments and as profitable business opportunities for financial-services business and pension consultants (57–90). Writing in 1982, when the Great Pension Debate was still unresolved, Murphy was prescient in predicting

that "the resolution of the current debate is likely to leave intact the private pension system and its important capital formation role" (97).

82　See discussion in Chapter 1.

83　Department of Finance, *Action Plan for Pension Reform: Building Better Pensions for Canadians* [*White Paper*].

84　*Pension Benefits Standards Act, 1985*, RSC 1985, c 32 (2nd Supp).

85　*Pension Benefits Act, 1987*, SO 1987, c 35 (now RSO 1990, c P.8). Ontario made some interim fixes in 1980 in *The Pension Benefits Amendment Act, 1980*, SO 1980, c 80, including the establishment of the Pension Benefits Guarantee Fund, the protection of pension contributions as "deemed trusts," and "grow-in rights." These reforms became part of the PBA, *1987*, and I have treated them for purposes of this discussion as part of the second generation of regulatory reforms.

86　See also *General*, RRO 1990, O. Reg 909, s 54.

87　In 1997, the Pension Commission was replaced by the Financial Services Commission of Ontario as regulator, and the Financial Service Tribunal as adjudicator: *Financial Services Commission of Ontario Act, 1997*, SO 1997, c 28.

88　There are exemptions from this requirement for some multi-employer and collectively bargained plans.

89　Not all part-time employees were included; the right was restricted to those who earned at least 35 per cent of Yearly Minimum Pensionable Earnings (YMPE) in the two years prior to applying for plan membership. The employer could meet its obligation either by including part-timers in the main plan or setting up a "reasonably equivalent" plan (s 35).

90　See, for example, CAW-*Canada Local 2007 v Superintendent of Financial Services and Woodbine Entertainment Group*, FST Decision Number P0345-2009-1, 2010 ONFST 1, aff'd Div Ct, 11 March 2011, unreported.

91　Section 52(2) spelled out options for administrators to produce sex-neutral outcomes for employees, including the use of "annuity factors that do not differentiate as to sex" and employer contributions that vary on the basis of sex in order to generate equal benefits. For a fuller discussion of how these sections work, see Shilton, "Insuring Inequality," 417–21. The problem of excluding women from plan membership had been previously addressed by human rights codes and employment standards legislation; it was also addressed in the *PBA 1987*, s 53(1)(c).

92　While the "joint and survivor" pension was the default option, it could be waived by agreement of both spouses [s.45(2)], unlike the CPP spousal benefit, which is not waivable. The cost of survivor benefits could be charged to the individual plan member, resulting in a reduction in the member's monthly payment, whereas, under the CPP, the cost of survivor benefits is born by the plan as a whole.

93 See *PBA, 1987*, s 1(1), definition of "spouse." The definition was amended in 2005 to include same-sex relationships: see *Spousal Relationships Statute Law Amendment Act, 1985*, SO 1985, c 5, s 56.

94 In 1987, the Ontario government appointed a task force chaired by Martin Friedland to explore inflation protection for employee pension plans: see Ontario, Task Force on Inflation Protection for Workplace Pension Plans, *Research Studies*. The task force reported in 1988, recommending an inflation-adjustment formula linked to the consumer price index, but no action was ever taken on this recommendation.

95 A "going concern" valuation assigns values to assets and liabilities, "using methods and actuarial assumptions that are consistent with accepted actuarial practice for the valuation of a continuing pension plan": *General*, RRO 1990, O. Reg 909, s 1. By contrast, a solvency valuation requires assumptions that would be relevant if the plan were to be wound up on the valuation date. These valuations may be quite different.

96 Employer-sponsored pension funds were required to contribute annually to the Pension Benefits Guarantee Fund.

97 While the statutory conditions were stringent, they were far from clear, and the surplus issue has remained contentious: see Chapters 6 and 7.

98 In practice, this was a four-year vesting rule, since employers could impose a two-year waiting period before new employees could join the plan.

99 The act defines "commuted value" as "the value calculated in the prescribed manner and as of a fixed date of a pension, a deferred pension, a pension benefit, or an ancillary benefit" (s 1). The calculation is performed by an actuary.

100 This death benefit could be offset by an amount payable under employer-funded group life insurance: see s 49 (11). First-generation statutes had given surviving dependents a right to sue if death benefits provided by the plan were not paid, but did not require that such benefits be provided.

101 This problem was identified by the Committee on Portable Pensions, *Second Report*, 29. The report concluded that the employer's contribution began to equal (and then to exceed) the employee's own contribution only at some point between ages forty-five to fifty.

102 The mechanics of DB funding and its distributive effects on younger, more junior, employees are discussed in Gunderson and Pesando, "Does Pension Wealth Peak at the Age of Early Retirement?"

103 For an explanation of the mechanics of the grow-in right, see Kaplan and Frazer, *Pension Law*, 530–2, and *Firestone Canada Inc. v Ontario (Pension Commission)*, [1990] OJ No. 2316 (CA).

104 Advisory committees were entitled to more information than plan members about the plan and fund, although the statutory standards are vague. Most second-generation statutes provided no role for plan members in governance; the exception is Quebec, which required all registered plans to be administered by a "pension committee," with some member representation: see *Supplemental Pension Plans Act*, SQ 1989, c 38, s 147. The Ontario statute recognized a role for employees in plan governance only in multi-employer plans established by collective agreement or trust agreement: *PBA, 1987*, s 8(1)(e).

CHAPTER FIVE

1 US studies show that union attitudes to both public and private pensions were complex and varied over time: see Quadagno, *The Transformation of Old Age Security*, 51–75, 116–23, 153–77; Skocpol, *Protecting Mothers and Soldiers*, 212–47; Klein, *For All These Rights*, 204–57; Ghilarducci, *Labor's Capital*, 25–51. For a Canadian perspective, see Morton and McCallum, "Superannuation to Indexation," 3; Bryden, *Old Age Pensions*, 48, 111–19; Milling, "Labour's Interest in Pension Planning"; Pilkey, "Public vs. Private Pensions."

2 Brandeis, "Our New Peonage."

3 Ross, "Do We Have a New Industrial Feudalism?"

4 M.W. Latimer, *Trade Union Pension Systems*; Ghilarducci, "Organized Labor and Pensions," 389; Quadagno, *The Transformation of Old Age Security*, 54–60.

5 Ghilarducci, *Labor's Capital*, 29–41. Notable US strikes included a 147-day United Mine Workers of America strike in the bituminous coal industry in 1947, a major strike in the steel industry in 1949 led by the United Steelworkers of America, and a 104-day United Auto Workers strike at Chrysler in 1952.

6 Steven Sass describes single-employer plans in unionized workplaces as "largely standardized affairs. They were funded, non-contributory, defined benefit plans paying modest benefits and granting full credit for past service": see "Pension Bargains," 104. See also Sass, *The Promise of Private Pensions*, 121–44; Slichter, Healy, and Livernash, *The Impact of Collective Bargaining on Management*, 396–8; Ghilarducci, *Labor's Capital*, 41;

Klein, *For All These Rights*, 246; Harbrecht, *Pension Funds and Economic Power*, 93–4, 96.

7 Ghilarducci, *Labor's Capital*, 26–7, 39.

8 Fudge and Tucker, *Labour Before the Law*, 295.

9 The 1947 survey discussed in "Pension and Welfare Plans in Canadian Industry," *Labour Gazette* 49 (1949) found about 3 per cent of pension plans associated with collective agreements (see 697–8), but does not iden-tify where these plans were to be found or what relationship they had to collective agreements.

10 "Pension and Welfare Plans in Canadian Industry," 697.

11 "The Report of the Conciliation Board appointed in connection with the UAW-Ford negotiations," reprinted in *Labour Gazette* (1950): 454.

12 The feature section was called "Acquisition of Pension Benefits through Collective Bargaining" from 1955 to 1965, when it was renamed "Acquisition of Pension Benefits through Strike/Lock-out." The feature ran until 1978.

13 "Second Constitutional Convention of the Canadian Labour Congress," *Labour Gazette* (1958): 604. These standards resembled those in the AFL-CIO's *Pension Plans Under Collective Bargaining: A Reference Guide for Trade Unions*.

14 For historical pension coverage data, see Deaton, *The Political Economy of Pensions*, Appendix C–1.

15 For Ontario data, see Shillington, *Occupational Pension Plan Coverage in Ontario*.

16 See discussion of public sector collective bargaining in Chapter 8.

17 Peitchinis, *Labour-Management Relations in the Railway Industry*, 61–97.

18 See Special Joint Committee, *Minutes*, 1465–95.

19 For historical union-density data, see Statistics Canada, "Union Membership in Canada, 1911–1975"; Morissette, Schellenberg, and Johnson, "Diverging Trends in Unionization"; Mainville and Olineck, "Unionization in Canada."

20 *1965 Survey*, 8, Table B.

21 Milling, "Labour's Interest in Pension Planning," 185.

22 Royal Commission, *Report*, Vol. I, 37–8, 63. The rules governing pension bargaining in the public sector are discussed in Chapter 8.

23 Dominion Bureau of Statistics, *Pension Plans: Non-financial Statistics, 1960*, described as "the first compilation of its kind in Canada"; the *1965 Survey* updated the 1960 data.

24 "Vesting Provisions in Canadian Industrial Pension Plans," 30–1, Table 1.

25 *1965 Survey*, 24, Table 23. The table shows that 22 per cent of plan members still had no vesting whatsoever.

26 See "Vesting Provisions in Canadian Industrial Pension Plans." Similar discrepancies in vesting standards between unionized and non-unionized workplaces were evident in the US: see Freeman and Medoff, *What Do Unions Do?*, 194; Slichter, Healy, and Livernash, *The Impact of Collective Bargaining on Management*, 188.

27 "Vesting Provisions in Canadian Industrial Pension Plans," 9. Defined benefit plans were preferred by larger employers. While money purchase plans covered only 6.5 per cent of members (down from 13 per cent in 1960), they greatly outnumbered defined benefit plans. The most popular benefit formula continued to be a "unit benefit" formula, in which years of service leveraged a percentage of earnings (14).

28 Ibid. at 12 (See Tables 35, 31).

29 Slichter, Healy, and Livernash, *The Impact of Collective Bargaining on Management*, 387. Later studies found measurable union effects on fringe benefits, including pensions: see Allen and Clark, "Unions, Pension Wealth, and Age-Compensation Profiles"; Freeman and Medoff, *What Do Unions Do?* Some of these effects were more evident in smaller than in larger unionized workplaces.

30 *Supplemental Pensions Act*, SQ 1965, c 25, s 12. The Quebec statute was also unique in ensuring that pension plans subject to collective bargaining did not expire along with collective agreements, providing that "[t]he provisions respecting a supplemental plan contained in a collective labour agreement shall constitute a contract having an existence separate from that of the collective labour agreement and shall remain in force notwithstanding its expiry or cancellation": ibid., s 3.

31 Canadian Labour Congress, *The CLC Proposal for Pension Reform*.

32 This silence was puzzling in light of the fact that second-generation statutes explicitly recognized multi-employer plans, many of which had been established exclusively by trade unions, or jointly by trade unions and employer groups. The *PBA 1987* acknowledged a member interest in the governance of these plans, but no union interest; MEPPs established under collective agreements or trust agreements were required to be administered by boards of trustees that included at least equal representation from plan members, s 8(1)(e), but the relationship between plan members and their unions was not addressed by pension statutes.

33 Recent amendments to s 24 of the *PBA, 1987*, not yet proclaimed, give unions a broader representative role in the establishment of advisory committees, but do not expand the role of the advisory committee.

34 Ghilarducci, *Labor's Capital*, 36–41.
35 This part of the legislative history of the NLRA is referred to in *Inland Steel Company and Local Union Nos. 1010 and 64, United Steelworkers of America, (CIO)*, 77 NLRB No. 1 (1948) [*Inland Steel NLRB*] at 7–9, 11–13; see also Jensen, "Pensions and Retirement Plans," 234.
36 *Inland Steel NLRB*, aff'd 170 F, 2d 247 (US Court of Appeals, Seventh Circuit) *sub nom Inland Steel Co. v National Labor Relations Board* [*Inland Steel CA*], cert. denied 336 US 960 (1949).
37 The pension plan was originally implemented in 1936, prior to the 1941 certification of the union as bargaining agent. The company had suspended the operation of the mandatory retirement policy because of wartime labour shortages, but reinstated it effective 31 December 1945: *Inland Steel NLRB*, 15–16.
38 *Inland Steel CA* at 250. The company also relied on the management rights clause in the collective agreement, an argument that the board dismissed as irrelevant in view of the expiry of the collective agreement and the company's fixed position that it would not bargain over pension issues under any circumstances: *Inland Steel NLRB*, 3, 13–15. The argument based on the management-rights clause was not pursued on appeal.
39 *Inland Steel NLRB* at 3–7; *Inland Steel CA* at 249.
40 *Inland Steel CA* at 253. This argument is not discussed in the NLRB decision.
41 *Inland Steel NLRB Decision* at 4–5.
42 *Inland Steel CA* at 251–3.
43 Ibid. at 253.
44 Ibid. at 249–50.
45 The issue of whether pensions fell within the scope of bargaining eventually reached the Supreme Court of Canada in 1978 in *British Columbia Hydro and Power Authority et al. v British Columbia Labour Relations Board*, [1978] 1 SCR 1015. The Supreme Court upheld the decision of the BC Labour Relations Board requiring BC Hydro to bargain over pension issues, even though the plan at issue was a statutory plan in which the employer had only limited legal authority to make plan amendments. As late as 1982, however, the CLC was obviously still uneasy about the legal status of pension bargaining: see discussion above.
46 Canadian labour law requires good-faith bargaining on all lawful issues, whereas the US makes a distinction between mandatory and permissive issues, and allows employers to refuse to bargain about permissive issues: *Dayco (Canada) Ltd v National Automobile, Aerospace, and Agricultural Implement Workers Union of Canada (CAW-Canada)* [*Dayco*], [1993]

2 SCR 230 at para. 63 (per La Forest J). See also Langille, "Equal Partnership in Canadian Labour Law," 503–5.

47 *Pulp and Paper Industrial Relations Bureau v Canadian Paperworkers Union*, [1977] BCLRBD No. 7 [*Pulp and Paper*].

48 Ibid. In the US, retiree pensions are considered a permissive subject of bargaining, which means that employers are not required to bargain about this issue, it cannot become a strike issue, and employers can make unilateral changes during the life of the collective agreement: see discussion in Stone, "The Post-War Paradigm," 1547–8 and note 210.

49 *Pulp and Paper*, [1977] BCLRBD No. 7 at 6.

50 For a critical discussion of the contradictions inherent in this approach to good-faith bargaining, see Langille and Macklem, "Beyond Belief."

51 Parts of this section and the following section in this chapter have been previously published as Shilton, "Enforcing Workplace Pension Rights for Unionized Employees: Is There a 'Weber Gap'?"

52 For discussion of this debate, see Stone, "The Post-War Paradigm," 1544–59; Langille, "Equal Partnership in Canadian Labour Law," 532–6; Beatty and Langille, "Bora Laskin and Labour Law," 698–700; Weiler, *Reconcilable Differences*, 89–118.

53 *International Chemical Workers Union, Local 279 v Rexall Drug Co. Ltd* (1953), 4 LAC1468 (Laskin) [*Rexall*]. *Rexall* is the first reported arbitration decision to deal with a workplace pension issue.

54 Ibid. at 1468.

55 Ibid. at 1469.

56 This contextual approach was typical of how Laskin approached the role of the arbitrator: see Beatty and Langille, 692–711. Laskin's role in the "reserved rights" debate is discussed at 699–711. *Rexall* is discussed at 708–9.

57 *Re Canadian Union of Public Employees, Local 1000 and Hydro-Electric Power Commission of Ontario* (1966), 17 LAC 244 (Thomas) [*Hydro-Electric*]. The nature of the grievance is mentioned only in the headnote; it is not discussed in the body of the reported decision. Ironically, the decision purports to rely on *Rexall* for its conclusion that an arbitration board had no jurisdiction to deal with the issue. Almost certainly Laskin would have reached the opposite conclusion.

58 While the reported decision provides no details of the form this integration took, integration typically involved cutting benefits provided by the employer's workplace plan in order to stabilize its overall pension costs.

59 *Hydro-Electric*, emphasis added. Not all arbitrators allowed employers to impose integration unilaterally: see, for example, *International Assn of*

Machinists and Aerospace Workers, Flin Flon Lodge No. 1948 v Hudson Bay Mining and Smelting Co., [1968] SCR 113.

60 *Canadian Car & Foundry Company Limited v Dinham and Brotherhood of Railway Carmen of America*, [1960] SCR 3; *Bell Canada v Office and Professional Employees' International Union, Local 131*, [1974] SCR 335.

61 *Re Palm Dairies Ltd and Retail, Wholesale & Department Store Union, Local 580* (1980), 26 LAC (2d) 414 (Hope).

62 For example, *Re Sudbury Mine, Mill & Smelter Workers' Union & Falconbridge Nickel Mines Ltd* (1958), 9 LAC 105 (Little); *Re University College of Cape Breton and Nova Scotia Government Employees Union*, [1997] NSLAA No. 14 (Wright)

63 For example, *United Mine Workers of America, District No. 26 v Cape Breton Development Corp.*, [1987] NSJ No. 425 (TD), [1988] NSJ No. 158 (CA).

64 Brown and Beatty, *Canadian Labour Arbitration*, 4: 1400, "*Pension, Insurance and Welfare Plans.*"

65 Ibid., 4: 1440.

66 See *Du Pont Canada Inc. v Kingston Independent Nylon Workers Union* (1987), 30 LAC 376 (Solomantenko); *St Mary's Cement v United Steelworkers* (2010), 195 LAC (4th) 72 (Hunter); *Royal Ontario Museum v Service Employees International Union (Brewery, General & Professional Workers' Union), Local 2 (Policy Grievance)*, [2011] OLAA No. 292 (Raymond); *Royal Ontario Museum v OPSEU*, 18 January 2013, unreported (Saltman).

67 *Rexall* at 1470

68 See *Re Steinberg Inc., Miracle Food Mart Division and Teamsters Union, Local 419*, [1982] OLAA No. 105; 7 LAC (3d) 289, in which an arbitration board chaired by George Adams observed that "there can be no term or condition of workplace, by contract or otherwise, existing outside the collective agreement to which the union has not agreed" (para. 45). See also *Re Gray Forging & Stampings Ltd and International Union of Electrical, Radio & Machine Workers Union, Local 557* (1978), 20 LAC (2d) 278 (Gorsky); *Re Consolidated-Bathurst Packaging Ltd (Hamilton Plant) and Int'l Woodworkers of America, Local 6-29* (1980), 28 LAC (2d) 230 (Brunner).

69 *McGavin Toastmaster Ltd v Ainscough et al.*, [1976] 1 SCR 718.

70 In *Canadian Assn of Industrial, Mechanical and Allied Workers, Local 14 v Paccar of Canada Ltd*, [1989] 2 SCR 983, the court held that, under collective bargaining statutes, individual contracts of employment and

common-law contract principles have no relevance, even in a residual sense, as long as the union continues to have bargaining rights. In *Isidore Garon Ltée v Tremblay*, [2006] 1 SCR 27 [*Isidore Garon*], the court held that "[t]he individual contract does not cease to exist, but is simply suspended" (para. 27).

71 *Isidore Garon* at para. 27. For a more recent application of this principle, see *Baker v Navistar*, [2013] OJ No. 2974.

72 *Isidore Garon* at para 25. The issue was whether the "notice of termination" provisions in the Quebec Civil Code applied to employees covered . by a collective agreement. The majority held that these provisions were incompatible with the collective bargaining framework. Justice LeBel, speaking for the dissenters, agreed with the majority that individual freedom of contract for employees is completely abrogated under a collective bargaining regime (paras. 135, 139), but found statutory notice-of-termination rules compatible with that regime. See Drouin and Trudeau, "What Does *Isidore Garon* Mean for Arbitral Jurisprudence in Quebec?"

73 See, for example, *Jones et al. v Shipping Federation of British Columbia et al.*, [1963] BCJ No. 118, 37 DLR (2d) 273; *Jameson v Dominion Steel and Coal Corporation Ltd* (1970), 19 DLR (3d) 203 (NSSC, CA), rev'ing [1970] NSJ No. 87 (NSSC, TD); *Jean v Canada (Treasury Board)*, [1974] 2 FC 725 (TD); *Canadian Union of Public Employees-C.L.C. et al. and Ontario Hydro* (1987), 59 OR (2d) 31 (Div Ct), rev'd *Canadian Union of Public Employees-C.L.C., Ontario Hydro Employees Union, Local 1000 v Ontario Hydro (1989)*, 68 OR (2d) 620 (CA), leave to appeal refused 7 December 1989; *National Automobile Aerospace and Agricultural Implement Workers Union of Canada et al. and White Farm Manufacturing Canada Ltd et al.* (1988), 66 OR (2d) 535 (HC), aff'd [1990] OJ No. 1988 (CA); *Ontario Teachers' Pension Plan Board v York University*, [1990] OJ No. 1376; 74 OR (2d) 714 (HC); *McKinney v University of Guelph*, [1990] 3 SCR 229; *Saskatchewan Government Employees Association v Saskatchewan*, [1991] SJ No. 660 (QB); *Otis Canada Inc. v Ontario (Superintendent of Pensions)*, [1991] OJ No. 251; 2 OR (3d) 737 (Gen Div), at para. 44 [*Otis*]; *Bathgate v National Hockey League Pension Society* (1992), 11 OR (3d) 449 (Gen Div) [*Bathgate*], aff'd [1994] OJ No. 265 (CA), leave to appeal refused [1994] SCCA No. 170.

74 In Ontario, pension claims were dismissed by courts primarily on the basis of s 3(3) of the *Rights of Labour Act*, RSO 1990, c R-33, which provides that "[a] collective bargaining agreement shall not be the subject of any action in any court unless it may be the subject of such action irrespective

of this Act or of the *Labour Relations Act.*" See *Cummings v Hydro-Electric Power Commission of Ontario,* [1966] 1 OR 605; *Drohan v Sangamo* (1976), 11 OR (2d) 65 (HCJ). In *Drohan,* the court dismissed the matter with obvious reluctance, since it had been before the courts for several years prior to the employer raising this jurisdictional objection.

5 *Weber v Ontario Hydro,* [1995] 2 SCR 929.

6 In Ontario, the statutory basis for the jurisdiction of an arbitrator is found in s 48(1) of the *Labour Relations Act, 1995,* SO 1995, c 1, Sched. A: "Every collective agreement shall provide for the final and binding settlement by arbitration, without stoppage of work, of all differences between the parties arising from the interpretation, application, administration or alleged violation of the agreement, including any question as to whether a matter is arbitrable." Since 1993, this jurisdiction has been supplemented by s 48(12)(j), which gives arbitrators the power "(j) to interpret and apply human rights and other workplace-related statutes, despite any conflict between those statutes and the terms of the collective agreement."

7 McLachlin J. was writing for the whole court on this issue, although the court was not unanimous on the disposition of the constitutional claim (three judges dissented, holding that a labour arbitrator was not a "court of competent jurisdiction" to deal with such claims).

8 McLachlin J. linked the tort and *Charter* claims to the fact that the surveillance was related to employer concerns about fraud in the receipt of collectively bargained sick benefits, and also to broad language in the agreement permitting grievances (but not arbitration) over "unfair treatment": *Weber* at paras. 72–3.

9 *New Brunswick v O'Leary,* [1995] 2 SCR 967 at paras. 7–10. The court linked the employer's tort claim to the management rights clause and to the health and safety provisions of the collective agreement.

10 *Progistix-Solutions Inc. v Communications, Energy and Paperworkers Union of Canada (Connolly Grievance),* [2002] CLAD No. 188 (Keller); *Beachville Lime Ltd v Communications, Energy, and Paper Workers Union, Local 3264 (Wenzel Grievance),* [2002] OLAA No. 512 (Williamson); *National Steel Car v United Steelworkers of America, Local 713 (Pedron Grievance),* [2006] OLAA No. 126 (Herman).

11 *Nexen Inc. v Communications, Energy and Paperworkers Union of Canada, Local 697,* [2003] BCCAAA (Munroe).

12 *Teamsters, Local 132 v Unilever Canada (Pension Calculation Grievance),* [2005] OLAA No. 115 (Howe).

13 *Re City of Etobicoke and* CUPE, *Local 185,* [1996] OLAA No. 84, 54 LAC (4th) 229 (Springate).

84 *Kenora Assn for Community Living v Ontario Public Service Employees Union, Local 702* (Harasemchuk Grievance), [2003] OLAA No 295 (Roberts).

85 *Ontario Public Service Employees Union v Ontario (Ministry of Community, Family and Childrens' Services) (Ashley Grievance)*, [2003] OGSBA No. 128 (Abramsky). The Divisional Court had previously described this plan as incorporated by reference into the collective agreement (see *OPSEU, Local 439 and Royal Ottawa Health Care Group*, [2001] OJ No. 446).

86 *Grain Services Union v Dawn Foods Canada* (2002), 108 LAC (4th) 51 (Hood), aff'd [2003] SJ No. 61 (QB) (*sub nom Grain Services Union, Local 3000 v Saskatchewan Wheat Pool*).

87 *Bisaillon v Concordia University*, [2006] 1 SCR 666.

88 *Atlas Copco Exploration Products v International Assn of Machinists and Aerospace Workers, Local 2412 (Pension Plan Grievance)*, [2008] OLAA No. 672 (R. Brown) at para. 20. Arbitrator Brown acknowledged that *Bisaillon* was "ambiguous" on the issue of whether the language in the plans at issue gave arbitrators jurisdiction to enforce the plans themselves, but dismissed the court's discussion of this issue as *obiter dicta* (para. 20).

89 *Telus Communications Inc. v Telecommunications Union (Kellie Grievance)*, [2008] CLAD No. 106 (Sims) at para. 4.

90 Ibid. at para. 73. This was a disability insurance case, not a pension case.

91 *Bell Canada v Communications, Energy and Paperworkers Union of Canada, Local 27 (Chawda Grievance)*, [2010] CLAD No. 70 (Burkett) at para. 36, aff'd [2010] OJ No. 2681, 2011 ONSC 2517 (*sub nom Communications, Energy and Paperworkers Union of Canada, Local 27 v Bell Canada*). This case too involved a disability claim.

92 The Divisional Court did not distance itself from Arbitrator Burkett's interpretation of *Bisaillon* as calling for a "one-stop shopping" model of arbitral jurisdiction.

93 *National Automobile, Aerospace and Agricultural Implements Workers Union of Canada, Local 1015 v Scotsburn Dairy Group (Pension Funds Grievance)*, [2008] NSLAA 1 (Christie).

94 In *Atlas Copco*, Brown mistakenly includes Christie in his list of arbitrators who saw *Bisaillon* as supporting the four-category test; Christie expressed considerable skepticism about both the pre- and post-*Bisaillon* utility of that test, and refused to apply it in the case before him.

95 See paras. 339–41. He dismissed claims regarding employer contributions because of excessive delay (para. 122). See also *City of Vancouver and CUPE Local 15* (2006) 153 LAC (4th) 97 (Munroe).

96 In addition to the cases discussed here, post-*Bisaillon* decisions applying versions of the four-category test include *West Parry Sound Centre v Ontario Nurses Assn (Pension Plan Contribution Grievance)*, [2008] OLAA No. 705 (Parmar); *Grand River Hospital Corp. v Ontario Nurses' Association (Collective Agreement Grievance)* (2010), 200 LAC (4th) 363 (Howe); *United Way of Lower Mainland* (2013), 239 LAC (4th) 428 (Dorsey); *Rouge Valley Health System v Ontario Nurses Association*, 2013 CANLII 8001 (ON LA) (Stout).

97 See *Atlas Copco* at paras. 21–6.

98 *Glacier Ventures International Corp. (Prince George Citizen) v Communications, Energy and Paperworkers Union of Canada, Local 2000 (Alexander Grievance)*, [2012] BCCAAA No. 38 (Burke) at paras. 41–56.

99 For example, *Sault Area Hospital v Ontario Nurses' Assn (Seisel Grievance)*, [2012] OLAA No. 229 (Steinberg).

100 For example, *Bell Canada v Communications, Energy and Paperworkers Union of Canada, Local 27 (Chawda Grievance)*; *Rouge Valley*; *Shepherd's Care Foundation v Alberta Union of Provincial Employees*, 2011 ABQB 281; *Independent Electricity System Operator v Power Workers Union*, 2013 ONSC 2131.

101 For example, *Bell c Sobeys Inc.*, [2006] JQ No. 7738, CS, aff'd [2008] JQ No. 1390 (CA) *sub nom Bell c Régime de retraite pour les employées et employés de Sobeys Inc.*; leave to appeal refused [2008] SCCA No. 175; *Hamilton v ICI Canada Inc.*, [2001] OJ No. 3916; *Seborro v Pidvalny*, 2004 CarswellOnt 6075 (WLCan); *Duke v Toronto District School Board*, [2006] OJ No. 1983; *Frances v BC2 Claims and Barrymore Furniture*, 2011 ONSC 198; *Dzehverovic v Great-West Life Assurance Co.*, 2010 ONSC 2387; *Waterson v Canadian Broadcasting Corp*, [2010] OJ No. 4534; *Syndicat des communications de Radio-Canada v Canadian Broadcasting Corporation*, 2011 QCCA 768, leave to appeal refused [2011] SCCA No. 241; *Calgary (City) v International Assn of Fire Fighters (Local 255)*, 2012 ABQB 90.

102 Langille, "Equal Partnership," 534–5.

103 Sass, "Pension Bargains," 103; Ghilarducci, *Labor's Capital*, 25–51.

104 Van der Heiden-Aantjes, "The Quality of the Dutch Pension System," 123–4, 128–35; Van Riel, Hemerijck, and Visser, "Is There a Dutch Way to Pension Reform."

105 For differences between Canadian and European models of collective bargaining, see Adams, *Industrial Relations under Liberal Democracy*, Chapter 4.

106 See McPhillips, "The Appropriate Bargaining Unit."

107 See Fudge, "The Gendered Dimension of Labour Law," 233–8; Forrest, "Bargaining Units and Bargaining Power."

108 See Baldwin, *Determinants of the Evolution of Workplace Pension Plans in Canada*. Baldwin reports that, in 2004, 48.1 per cent of plans (covering 72.0 per cent of plan members) were all-employee plans. Only 6.4 per cent of plans (covering 14.4 per cent of plan members) were confined only to bargaining-unit members. Baldwin noted that the data reported has "changed very little over the period since the mid 1970s" (4).

109 In *Cominco Pensioners Union, sub-local of the United Steelworkers of America, Local 651 v Cominco*, [1979] BCLRBD No. 49, the British Columbia Labour Relations Board refused to certify a union to represent a group of retirees, holding that they were not "employees."

110 *Pulp and Paper*, [1977] BCLRBD No. 7 at 11–16.

111 *Dayco* at para. 88; *Association provincial des retraités d'Hydro-Québec v Hydro-Québec*, [2005] QJ No. 1644 (CA) at paras. 50–3, 57–9 (leave to appeal refused [2005] CSCR No. 215). For a discussion of the role of unions in negotiating retiree benefits, see Davis, "Security of Retirement Benefits in Canada."

112 *Dayco*.

113 See, for example, *Bohemier v Centra Gas Manitoba* (1999), 170 DLR (4th) 310 (Man CA), in which the Court of Appeal reversed a decision of the lower court dismissing a retiree challenge to a surplus-sharing agreement on the ground that the dispute was governed by the collective agreement. The court held that retirees were not parties to the collective agreement and did not have any practical avenue for pursuing a remedy through the grievance procedure. See also *Bennett v British Columbia*, [2007] BCJ No. 4 (CA), leave to appeal refused 21 June 2007, in which the court allowed both contract and fiduciary claims of unionized retirees to proceed by way of class action together with those of non-unionized retirees; *Ormrod et al. v Etobicoke (Hydro-Electric Commission)* (2001), 53 OR (3d) 285 (SCJ); *Kranjcec v Ontario*, [2004] OJ No. 19. But see *Alberta Teachers Assn v Calgary School District No. 19 (Board of Trustees)*, [2006] AJ No. 1315, in which the Alberta Court of Queen's Bench struck out a statement of claim filed by seven trade unions claiming a share of demutualization proceeds, holding that the issues fell within the exclusive jurisdiction of a labour arbitrator, despite the fact that part of the claim included employees no longer in the bargaining unit. According to the court, "any question about employee entitlements to the surpluses and refunds arise[s] out of the fact of the collective agreement and can be said to have crystallized upon retirement" (para. 31).

114 The argument was based on *Supplemental Pension Plans Act*, RSQ,

c R–17, s 6, which explicitly provides that "[a] pension plan is a contract under which retirement benefits are provided to the member."
5 *Association provincial des retraités d'Hydro-Québec v Hydro-Québec*, [2005] QJ No. 1644 (CA) at paras. 48–50.

CHAPTER SIX

1 *Schmidt v Air Products Canada Ltd* (1990), 66 DLR (4th) 230 (Alta QB), aff'd (1992), 89 DLR 4th 762 (Alta CA) [*Schmidt*], aff'd in part, [1994] 2 SCR 611.
2 Gillese, "Pension Plans and the Law of Trusts," 224, 250. Gillese was then Dean of Law at the University of Western Ontario and Chair of the Pension Commission of Ontario. She later became a justice of the Ontario Court of Appeal and author of many of that court's pension decisions. Her more current views on the relationship between trust and contract law are reflected in Gillese, "Two Decades after Schmidt: Where Has Pension Law Been and Where Is It Going?"
3 *Bardal v Globe & Mail*, [1960] OJ No. 149 at 28. The case was decided by Chief Justice McRuer. There is no express finding that the pension claim had a contractual basis, but it is clearly implied, since the Chief Justice rejected similar claims related to the inclusion of a Christmas bonus and a profit-sharing plan on the ground that they had no "contractual basis." *Bardal* is still the leading case in Canada on the issue of the factors relevant to the calculation of wrongful dismissal damages: see *Honda Canada v Keays*, 2008 SCC 39 at paras. 25–32.
4 For example, *Drohan v Sangamo* (1976), 11OR (2d) 65 (HCJ); *Pulp and Paper*, [1977] BCLRBD No. 7; *Cominco Pensioners Union, sub-local of the United Steelworkers of America, Local 651 v Cominco*, [1979] BCLRBD No. 49.
5 For example, *Bradley v Saskatchewan Wheat Pool*, [1984] SJ No. 234 (QB) (discussing US case law accepting the "deferred wages" theory); *Baxter v Abbey*, [1986] BCJ No. 1214 (CA).
6 *Otis Canada Inc. v Ontario (Superintendent of Pensions)*, [1991] OJ No. 251; 2 OR (3d) 737 (Gen Div) [*Otis*] at para. 44. Justice Marie Corbett was a pioneering pension-law practitioner prior to her judicial appointment. See also *Bathgate v National Hockey League Pension Society* (1992) 11OR (3d) 449 (Gen Div), in which Justice George Adams, a former chair of the Ontario Labour Relations Board, held that players' pension entitlements were "irrevocably earned upon the expenditure of their efforts" and the employer pension contributions could be "reasonably characterized as deferred wages" (49). Both these cases involved

employees represented by unions, although neither judge grounds the contractual nature of the obligation within the framework of collective bargaining.

7 For example, *IBM Canada Limited v Waterman* 2013 SCC 70 at paras. 85–91 (per Justice Cromwell) and paras. 136–48 (per Justice Rothstein, diss.).

8 Waddams, *The Law of Contracts*, ¶66–7; ¶442–556; Swan, *Canadian Contract Law*, 737–863.

9 For example, *Châteauneuf c TSCO of Canada Ltd [Cie Singer du Canada]*, [1995] JQ N 86, [1995] RJQ 637. For a general discussion of the theoretical problems related to contracts of this nature, see Kessler, "Contracts of Adhesion."

10 *Otis* at para. 27.

11 The origin of the English Chancery Court lies in the prerogative of the sovereign to dispense a form of justice, often called equity, which mitigated the technical rigours of the common law. As explained by Gary Watt in his text *Trusts and Equity*, "[t]he function of the common law is to lay down rules for society, generally – to regulate society one might say – whereas the function of equity is to regulate the common law" (15). Courts of law and courts of equity were merged in most jurisdictions (including in Canada) in the latter part of the nineteenth century.

12 The term "settlor" may describe either the donor of the trust property or the person who has established the terms of the trust. In family trusts, these are almost always the same person. In workplace pension plans, however, they may not be, because the property transferred to the trust, whether by the employer or through employee contributions, is part of employee compensation.

13 In order to qualify as a trust, an arrangement must involve what are frequently described as the "three certainties": certainty of intention to create a trust, certainty of subject matter sufficient to identify the trust property, and certainty of objects/beneficiaries: Gillese and Milczynski, *The Law of Trusts*, 38–45. While most trusts are created by relatively formal written documents, they may also be created by implication.

14 In addition to the basic duty to put the interests of the beneficiaries ahead of their own interest, trustees also have duties frequently described as a duty to act reasonably, and a duty to treat beneficiaries equally: Nobles, *Pensions, Workplace and the Law*, 11; Gillese and Milczynski, *The Law of Trusts*, 142–56.

15 For example, *Pension Benefits Standards Act, 1985*, RSC 1985, c 32, 2d Supp, s 8(3). See Chapter 7, note 6, for a list of current provisions in

regulatory statutes across Canada imposing trust or trust-like obligations on plan administrators and managers of pension funds.

6 Langbein, "The Contractarian Basis of the Law of Trusts." See also Alexander, "The Transformation of Trusts" (Alexander uses the terms "regulative" and "facilitative" to describe the two views of trust law (344); Duggan, "Fiduciary Obligations in the Supreme Court of Canada."

7 This tension and its implications for Canadian pension jurisprudence is also discussed in Shilton, "Employee Pension Rights and the False Promise of Trust Law."

8 The federal *Pension Benefits Standards Act* defines a pension "surplus" as "the amount, determined in the prescribed manner, by which the assets of a pension plan exceed its liabilities": *Pension Benefits Standards Act, 1985*, RSC, 1985, c 32, 2d Suppl., s 2(1), P-7.01. Surpluses can only be generated within defined benefit plans; by definition, assets and liabilities are always in equilibrium in defined contribution plans.

9 Ontario law requires that plan valuations be prepared in a manner "consistent with accepted actuarial practice and with the requirements of the Act and this Regulation": *General*, RRO 1990, O. Reg 909, s 16. Other Canadian regulatory statutes contain similar provisions.

10 The range of factors taken into account by actuaries is discussed in *Schmidt* per Justice Cory at para. 5; per Justice McLachlin (diss.) at para. 178.

11 See Nachshen, "Access to Pension Fund Surpluses."

12 "An employer takes a 'contribution holiday' when it does not make a remittance into the pension fund in a given year to meet its normal cost-funding obligations and, instead, applies the notional surplus in the pension fund towards that obligation": Kaplan and Frazer, *Pension Law*, 399. See also Gillese, "Contribution Holidays."

13 Gillese, "Contribution Holidays," 61.

14 The regulatory law on pension surpluses across Canada in the mid-1980s is summarized by Nachshen, "Access to Pension Fund Surpluses," 67–70 and 81–5. See also Adell, *Pension Plan Surpluses*, 219–22.

15 The *Blue Books* and the subsequent *Information Bulletin No. 14* required that pension plans and trusts "must together form the plan": see *Information Bulletin No. 14* (Department of Revenue, *circa* 1959) at s 15(a).

16 To qualify for beneficial tax treatment, plans were required to provide that, if they were discontinued, "all monies paid under the plan must vest absolutely in the employees concerned and any surplus not apportioned must be distributed by an equitable formula to provide increased benefits

for those employees then covered": *1946 Blue Book*, s 14. *Blue Book* rules are discussed in detail in Chapter 4.

27 Revenue Canada, *Information Circular No. 72-13R7* (31 December 1981), ss 13.1, 39, now *Information Circular No. 72–13R8* (16 December 1988). Current rules provide that "Plans may state that surplus will be paid to employees or employers or both": The Canada Revenue Agency, Technical Manual for registered pension plans, 8.3 8502(d) – "Permissible Distributions," online: http://www.cra-arc.gc.ca/tx/rgstrd/mnnl/tch-o8-eng.html#prmssblc.

28 The Canadian case law on surplus up to 1988 is discussed in Nachshen, "Access to Pension Fund Surpluses," and Adell, *Pension Plan Surpluses.* The case law on contribution holidays is discussed in Gillese, "Contribution Holidays." Kaplan and Frazer provide a Table of Surplus Ownership Cases updated to 2012: *Pension Law*, 601–4. The table shows thirty-eight victories going to employers and thirty-one to employees. The list does not include contribution-holiday cases.

29 See *CUPE Local 1000 v Ontario Hydro* (1989), 58 DLR (4th) 552 (Ont CA); *Askin v Ontario Hospital Association* (1991), 2 OR (3d) 641 (CA).

30 UK courts often applied resulting trust doctrine, while US courts reached the same result by giving a broad interpretation to employer amendment clauses. See *Schmidt* (per Justice McLachlin at paras. 188–9). See also Nachshen, "Access to Pension Fund Surpluses," 74. In the UK, workplace pension plans (typically called "occupational pension schemes") are constructed entirely as trusts. See Nobles, *Pensions, Workplace and the Law*, 1–11.

31 Adell, *Pension Plan Surpluses*, 218.

32 The relevant provisions of the plan documents are set out in full in Appendix A to Justice Cory's decision.

33 Catalytic Enterprises Ltd and Stearns-Rogers Canada Ltd were the corporate predecessors of Air Products Canada Ltd: *Schmidt* at para. 9.

34 Section V of Catalytic Plan, Appendix A to the decision of Justice Cory.

35 There had been an earlier Stearns DC plan, but the court found that it had been validly terminated, which made the 1970 plan the starting point for its analysis of the pension history for the former Stearns employees.

36 In the Stearns case, the power of amendment was located in the plan, and generally permitted amendments, subject to the proviso that "[n]o amendment shall have the effect of diverting any part of the Fund to purposes other than for the exclusive benefit of the Participants" (*Schmidt* at para. 122). In the Catalytic case, there were two powers of amendment, one in the trust agreement, which generally permitted amendments "provided ...

that without the approval of the Minister of National Revenue no such amendment shall authorize or permit any part of the fund to be used for or diverted to purposes other than for the exclusive benefit of such persons and their estates as from time to time may be designated in or pursuant to the plan as amended from time to time" (Article V of the Trust Agreement, *Schmidt*, Appendix to the decision of Justice Cory), and one in the 1959 plan itself that permitted amendments as long as they did not reduce accrued benefits (Section XXII at para. 161).

7 Justice McLachlin held that the surplus did not fall within the boundaries of the trust, and should therefore be dealt with by applying the doctrine of "resulting trust," under which trust funds revert to their original owner. Justice Sopinka held that, as a matter of construction, the surplus *did* fall within the trust, but that trust principles permitted the employer to amend the trust documents to claim ownership of surplus.

8 Justice Sopinka did not identify the "settlor." Elsewhere he referred to the "intention of the parties" (presumably the employer and the employees: paras. 167–8). Justice McLachlin used the phrases "intention of the settlor" and "intention of the parties" almost interchangeably; presumably the first is relevant to the trust deed and the second to the pension plan, but the distinction is not always clear.

9 She concluded that the surplus was not impressed with a trust, because it was never intended to be used for the exclusive benefit of the employees. The initial plan documents were therefore "silent" on the issue of surplus ownership, and the employer could have successfully claimed ownership of the surplus, even in the absence of plan amendments: *Schmidt* at para. 220–1.

0 Gillese, "Contribution Holidays," 145–7, 162–7. See also Gillese, "Pension Plans and the Law of Trusts," 235–6.

1 Gillese, "Contribution Holidays," ibid. at 166–7. Gillese, now Justice Gillese, has since tempered her criticism of the Supreme Court's decision in *Schmidt*; see "Two Decades after *Schmidt*: Where Has Pension Law Been and Where Is It Going?," in which she argues that Justice Cory can be absolved of the charge of inconsistency if his decision on the contribution holiday issue is understood as an application of contract law rather trust law (12).

2 *Buschau v Rogers Cablesystems Ltd*, [2006] 1 SCR 973 [*Buschau SCC*], on appeal from two decisions of the British Columbia Court of Appeal, reported as 2004 BCCA 80 [*Buschau* No. 2] and 2004 BCCA 282 [*Buschau* No. 3]. These decisions build on a prior decision of the British Columbia Court of Appeal reported as [2001] BCJ No. 50 (CA) [*Buschau*

No. 1]. Related *Buschau* litigation subsequent to the release of the 2006 Supreme Court of Canada decision is reported as *Buschau v Canada (Attorney General) (appeal by Rogers Communications Inc.)*, [2009] FCJ No. 1119 (CA) [*Buschau No. 4*], leave to appeal refused [2009] SCCA No. 457.

43 *Buschau SCC* at para. 21 (per Justice Deschamps).

44 See Waters, Gillen, and Smith, *Waters' Law of Trusts in Canada*, 1175–94. The Rule is controversial, and has been abolished by statute in a number of Canadian jurisdictions: see Law Reform Commission of Saskatchewan, *The Rule in Saunders v Vautier and the Variation of Trusts*, 4. In the US, it has been substantially modified by the common law. See Alexander, "The Dead Hand and the Law of Trust," 1200–4. Despite the controversy, it had nevertheless been applied previously in Ontario in the pension context: see Gillese, "Pension Plans and the Law of Trusts," 242–3.

45 The company strategy is described more fully in *Buschau No. 2* at para. 85.

46 Rogers had already made piecemeal changes to the plan language to this effect, going back as far as 1981: *Buschau No. 1* at para. 7.

47 By 2002 the plan had only 112 members, and a surplus which had started out in 1980 at approximately $800,000 had grown to $11 million: *Buschau SCC* at paras. 1–2, 5.

48 *Buschau No. 1* at paras. 23–4, 37.

49 Unlike the companies involved in *Schmidt*, Rogers was a federally regulated company.

50 Justices LeBel, Fish, and Abella joined in this judgment.

51 Chief Justice McLachlin and Justice Charron joined in this judgment.

52 See also *Buschau SCC* at para. 96, per Justice Bastarache.

53 The *Buschau* case had a happy ending for Rogers, but not for the plan members. The Supreme Court "passed the buck" to the regulator, the federal Office of the Superintendent of Financial Institutions, on the issue of whether the plan should be wound up and the surplus in the fund distributed to the employees (*Buschau SCC* at paras. 34–59). When the members applied to the superintendent for an order to wind up the plan, Rogers countered with a parallel application, seeking the superintendent's approval to dissolve the 1992 merger with other Rogers plans and re-open the plan as a free-standing plan, which would allow the company to access the surplus to fund new member benefits. The superintendent sided with Rogers and dismissed the members' application for windup, on the basis that continuation of the plan was a "worthy goal" consistent with the overall purpose of the statute. Absent statutory violations, she saw no role

for the regulator in supervising the employer's conduct. The Federal Court upheld this decision as reasonable: *Buschau* No. 4. The superintendent's decisions are issued by letter to the parties and are unpublished. Key passages from the decision are quoted in *Buschau* No. 4. The Supreme Court of Canada refused leave to appeal.

4 *Nolan v Kerry (Canada) Ltd*, 2009 SCC 39 ["*Kerry (Canada)* SCC"], aff'ing *Nolan v Ontario (Superintendent of Financial Services)*, [2007] OJ No. 2176 (CA) [*Kerry (Canada) ca*], rev'ing [2006] OJ No. 960 (Div Ct) [*Kerry (Canada) Div. Ct.*)], rev'ing [2004] OFSCD No. 192 [*Kerry (Canada)* OFST No. 1] and [2004] OFSCD No. 193 [*Kerry (Canada)* OFST No. 2].

5 *Kerry (Canada)* SCC at paras. 3–6.

6 The employees also challenged the DB contribution holidays, but this claim was dismissed at all levels on the basis of *Schmidt*. The Supreme Court decision also addressed additional issues which are not discussed here, including whether costs could be awarded out of the pension trust fund.

7 *Kerry (Canada)* OFST No. 1 and *Kerry (Canada)* OFST No. 2.

8 *Kerry (Canada)* OFST No. 1 at paras. 24–8. Most of the challenged expenses were found to be authorized.

9 *Kerry (Canada)* OFST No. 2 at paras. 32–4, 41.

10 In *Schmidt*, Justice Cory made the obvious point that "[p]ension surpluses can only arise in 'defined benefit' pension plans" (para. 3).

11 As Justice LeBel explained it, "DB plans and DC plans are not cut from the same cloth"; they "carry a different set of risks and rewards": ibid at para. 159.

CHAPTER SEVEN

1 Gillese and Milcynski, *The Law of Trusts*, 10–11; Watt, *Trust and Equity*, 328–56; Rotman, *Fiduciary Law*, 241–3.

2 *Alberta v Elder Advocates of Alberta Society*, [2011] 2 SCR 261, 2011 SCC 24 at para. 22. Rotman extrapolates on the duty of "absolute loyalty," explaining that a fiduciary is expected to "act selflessly, with honesty, integrity, fidelity and the utmost good faith in the interest of the beneficiary": *Fiduciary Law*, 244, 303.

3 See *Alberta v Elder Advocates of Alberta Society* at para. 31 for a list of relationships classified in Canadian law as fiduciary per se.

4 Employer/plan administrators frequently contract out the more routine administrative functions to financial services or other pension

professionals, retaining for themselves the compliance, governance, and management functions that are likely to have the most significant impact on employee pension rights.

5 The Ontario Court of Appeal has held that decision-making by a plan administrator about contribution levels is a fiduciary duty, and "fulfillment of that duty would have led to maximizing the contributions that [the company] would make to the Plans as that would best protect the Plan members' pensions": *Morneau Sobeco Limited Partnership v Aon Consulting*, 2008 ONCA 196 at para. 34, leave to appeal refused [2008] SCCA No. 230 (*sub nom Rogers v Morneau Sobeco Limited Partnership*).

6 There is some variation across the country in the language of the statutory standards imposed on administrators. Some jurisdictions specifically designate administrators as "fiduciaries": e.g., *Pension Benefits Standards Act*, RSBC 1996, c 352, s 8 (5)–(6); *Employment Pension Plans Act*, RSA 2000, c E–8, s 13(5); *The Pension Benefits Act*, SS 1992, c P-6.001, s 11(1); *The Pension Benefits Act, 1992*, SS 1992, c P-6.001, s 11(2). Some do not use the term "fiduciary," but impose obligations such as a duty of care and/or a duty to avoid conflict of interest that replicate the common-law duties of fiduciaries: e.g., *Pension Benefits Act*, RSO 1990, c P–8, s 22; *Pension Benefits Act*, SNB 1987 c P–51, s 17; *Pension Benefits Act*, RSNS 1989, c 340, s 29; *The Pension Benefits Act*, RSM 1987, c P32, CCSM c P32, s 28.1. Some expressly designate administrators as trustees for "the employer, the members of the pension plan, former members, and any other persons entitled to pension benefits under the plan": e.g., *Pension Benefits Standards Act, 1985*, RSC 1985, c 32 (2d Supp), s 8(3)–(6); or simply as "trustees": *Supplemental Pension Plans Act*, RSQ, c R–15.1, s 150; *Pension Benefits Act 1997*, SNL 1996, c P–4.01, s 14(1).

7 For example, *Pension Benefits Act*, RSO 1990, c P–8, s 56(1)–(2).

8 Quebec does not permit employers to administer pension plans; they must be administered by a pension committee, except in the early stages prior to registration: *Supplemental Pension Plans Act*, RSQ c R–15.1, ss 147, 149. However, the employer has considerable power in appointing the pension committee. Manitoba does not permit employers to administer plans with more than fifty members: *The Pension Benefits Act*, RSM 1987, c P32, CCSM c P32, s 26.1(1)(d), *Pension Benefits Regulation*, Man Reg 39/2010, s 3.4. Newfoundland and Labrador requires that "[w]here the employer is the administrator of a pension plan under paragraph 12(1)(a), if there is a conflict of interest between the employer's role as administrator and the employer's role in any other capacity, the employer shall: (a) within 30 days after becoming aware of the conflict, declare the conflict to the

pension committee or to the members of the plan; and (b) act in the best interests of the members of the plan": *Pension Benefits Act, 1997*, SNL 1996, C P-4.01, S 17(3). Similar language appears in the federal statute: *Pension Benefits Standards Act, 1985*, RSC 1985, C 32 (2d Supp), S 8(10).

ꜟ *Imperial Oil v Ontario (Superintendent of Pensions)* (1995), 18 CCPB 198. The PCO, chaired at the time by Eileen Gillese, was the predecessor of the current Financial Services Tribunal.

ꜜ The PCO also observed that, on its face, s 22(4) prohibited conflict of interest only with respect to the fund, and not the plan. Accordingly, even if it had applied, the PCO would not have found a statutory violation, since the amendment related to the plan and not the fund (para. 36).

ꜛ In *Lloyd v Imperial Oil*, [2008] AJ No. 695 (QB), the plaintiffs attempted to challenge the validity of the same set of plan amendments considered by the PCO in *Imperial Oil v Superintendent of Pensions*, this time under the common-law fiduciary test. The Alberta court found that the plaintiffs were barred by the doctrine of issue estoppel from relitigating the issue of fiduciary breach, but also addressed the issue on the merits, concluding that the employer had not been acting as plan administrator when it amended the plan to limit eligibility for early retirement benefits and was therefore not acting in a fiduciary capacity (para. 58).

ꜞ *Sutherland v Hudson's Bay Co.*, [2007] OJ No. 2979 at paras. 310–16.

ꜟ *Lieberman v Business Development Bank of Canada*, [2009] BCJ 1938 at paras. 75–90.

ꜝ The court also rejected trust-based claims addressing the ownership of plan surplus and the payment of pay plan expenses out of the trust. *Association provinciale des retraités d'Hydro-Québec v Hydro-Québec*, [2005] QJ No 1644 at paras. 87–9. As discussed in Chapter 6, the court also rejected the claim of retired members that the plan could not be amended without their consent.

ꜞ A typical example is s 19(1) of Ontario's *PBA, 1987*: "The administrator of a pension plan shall ensure that the pension plan and the pension fund are administered in accordance with this Act and the regulations."

ꜟ *OMERS Sponsors Corporation v OMERS Administrative Corporation*, [2008] OJ No 425.

ꜝ *Ontario Municipal Employees Retirement System Act, 2006*, SO 2006, C 2.

ꜝ See Chapter 8 for a discussion of jointly sponsored pension plans in the public sector in Ontario.

ꜝ Strictly speaking, the Supreme Court's decision addresses only the question of whether the expenses of administration can properly be paid out of the pension fund; it does not discuss the payment of sponsor expenses.

However, that question is addressed in the Tribunal and Court of Appeal decisions the Supreme Court upheld. Both rejected the payment of a consulting expense that properly belonged to the employer alone, since it was determined not to be for the "exclusive benefit" of plan members.

21 For a discussion of the Supreme Court's shifting views over the past two decades on the role of fiduciary obligations in contractual relationships, see Duggan, "Fiduciary Obligations in the Supreme Court of Canada." Duggan observes, "There are two competing views on the relationship between contract and fiduciary law. The first, the 'contractarian position,' is that fiduciary obligations are consensual, and so they must take second place to the parties' own preferences as expressed or implied in the contract. The opposing view, the 'anti-contractarian' position, is that fiduciary obligations are imposed, and a court may use them to over-ride the parties' contract for public interest reasons or to enforce some form of higher morality" (455).

22 *Frame v Smith*, [1987] 2 SCR 99 at 136 (per Wilson J., diss.), subsequently adopted by the court in *Lac Minerals Ltd v International Corona Resources Ltd*, [1989] 2 SCR 574 at para. 32. See also *Hodgkinson v Simms*, [1994] 3 SCR 377 at 408.

23 *Galambos v Perez*, 2009 SCC 48; *Ermineskin Indian Band and Nation v Canada*, 2009 SCC 9; *Alberta v Elder Advocates of Alberta Society*, [2011] 2 SCR 261, 2011 SCC 24.

24 Ibid. at para. 36 (emphasis added).

25 *Burke v Hudson's Bay Co.* 2005 CANLII 47086 (ON SC) [*Burke ONSC*], 2008 ONCA 394 (CA) [*Burke CA*]; aff'd 2010 SCR 34 [*Burke SCC*].

26 *Burke ONSC*, ibid. at para. 30.

27 The plan was registered in Ontario, where this type of transaction is governed by ss 80–1 of the *Pension Benefits Act, 1987*. At that time, the statute was silent on the issue of surplus transfers in successorship situations of this type.

28 The parties to the sale transaction were aware that the decision not to transfer surplus might be controversial; the agreement of purchase and sale provided for a price adjustment if HBC were at any time ordered to make a surplus transfer: see *Burke ONSC* at para. 130.

29 The trust-law issues included a challenge to HBC's contribution holidays, dismissed at trial and not appealed. The employees also challenged the payment of plan expenses. This issue was disposed of by the Supreme Court of Canada on the same basis as in *Kerry (Canada)* and is not discussed here.

30 See *Burke SCC* (Factum of the Respondent filed with the SCC at para. 109 and footnote 123): http://www.scc-csc.gc.ca/WebDocuments-DocumentsWeb/

32789/FM020_Respondent_Governor-and-Company-of-Adventurers-of-England-Trading-into-Hudson's-Bay.pdf.

31 *Schmidt* at para. 92.

32 *Burke* SCC at para. 79. The court's analysis began with a pro forma obeisance to *Schmidt*, acknowledging that, if the pension plan is a trust, it must be analyzed in accordance with trust principles (para 48). In the balance of the decision, however, there is no doubt that the court gives the plan terms primacy.

33 *Professional Institute of the Public Service of Canada v Canada*, 2012 SCC 71 [*PIPS*].

34 The court held that the claim failed on other aspects of the fiduciary test as well; in view of its finding that there was no "real" surplus, it found that the claimants had not proved vulnerability to the exercise of government discretion in relation to the surplus, or a legal or practical interest at stake: paras. 137, 141–2.

35 *Sun Indalex Finance*, LLC *v United Steelworkers*, [2013] 1 SCR 271, 2013 SCC 6 [*Sun Indalex*], rev'ing in part 2011 ONCA 265 (*sub nom Re Indalex Limited*) [*Indalex CA*]. The employer of the plan members was Indalex Limited; the corporate group was known as the Indalex Group. Sun Indalex Finance LLC, which gave its name to the case, participated in the litigation as the principal secured creditor of the parent company. Its corporate relationship to members of the Indalex Group is not discussed in the decision.

36 *Companies' Creditors Arrangement Act*, RSC 1985, c C–36.

37 "DIP" stands for "debtor-in-possession"; a DIP lender is a lender willing to advance new money to an insolvent company to support its restructuring efforts: see Janis Sarra, *Rescue!*

38 The Court of Appeal upheld the statutory "deemed trust" claim for the unionized employees' plan, which was in the process of winding up prior to the company's CCAA application, but not for the executive plan, which had not yet reached the windup stage. The Supreme Court of Canada dismissed the statutory claim for both groups; while a majority found a deemed trust established under provincial legislation for the unionized employees, it also found that, under the doctrine of federal paramountcy, the priority established for the DIP lenders under the federal CCAA order trumped the provincial deemed trust.

39 *Indalex CA* at paras. 198, 204; *Sun Indalex* at paras. 94, 236. Under these intersecting arrangements, Sun Indalex "inherited" the right to pursue the legal claim of the original DIP lenders.

40 *Indalex CA*, at paras. 129–37, 143.

41 Ibid. at paras. 139–40.

42 Waters explains the concept of constructive trust as follows: "A constructive trust comes into existence, regardless of any party's intent, when the law imposes upon a party an obligation to hold specific property for the benefit of another": Waters, Gillen, and Smith, *Waters' Law of Trusts in Canada*, 478.

43 *Indalex* CA at para. 185.

44 Justice Cromwell wrote the plurality decision, joined by Chief Justice McLachlin and Justice Rothstein. Justice Deschamps, writing for herself and Justice Moldaver, concurred in the result. Justice LeBel dissented on behalf of himself and Justice Abella on the issue of the remedy; he would have upheld the constructive trust.

45 The principal difference between Justice Deschamps's judgment and that of Justice Cromwell relates to the issue of whether the PBA created a deemed trust for the unionized employees; she held that it did, whereas he held that it did not.

46 He found two specific statutory obligations relevant to Indalex's fiduciary responsibility in this case: ss 56 and 59 of the *Pension Benefits Act, 1987*, which require an administrator to monitor and report delinquent payments from the employer and take court action to collect.

47 Recall that Justice LeBel also dissented in *Kerry (Canada)*, where he argued that trust law should provide an "extra layer of protection" for vulnerable plan members: see discussion in Chapter 6.

48 Academic and judicial debate continues over what role a duty of "good faith" in contract performance has in Canadian common law. In *Bhasin v Hrynew*, 2014 SCC 71, the Supreme Court accepted a duty of good faith as an "organizing principle" within the common law of contract, but went no further than adopting a duty of honesty in contract performance: para. 33. The court made it clear, however, that any broader duty of good faith would not be a fiduciary duty, and would not carry with it a duty of loyalty or a requirement to put the interests of the other party first: para. 65. See also O'Byrne, "Good Faith in Contractual Performance"; McCamus, "Abuse of Discretion"; Banks, "Progress and Paradox."

49 See Chapter 6.

50 *Pension Benefits Standards Act, 1985*, RSC, 1985, c 32, 2d Suppl, s 2(1), P–7.01, s 8(10)(b) (requiring the employer as plan administrator to act in the best interests of plan members where there is material conflict of interest).

51 *Buschau No. 2* at para. 60. The court cited *Imperial Group Pension Trust Ltd v Imperial Tobacco Ltd*, [1991] 1 WLR. 589 (Chancery Div).

52 *Buschau No. 2* at paras. 60–1; see also para. 11.

53 Justice Deschamps determined that issues related to Rogers's past conduct were more properly dealt with by the regulator (para. 53).

54 *Lloyd v Imperial Oil*, 2008 ABQB 379.

55 *Sutherland v Hudson's Bay Co.*, [2007] OJ No 2979.

56 For example, *Lacroix v Canada Mortgage and Housing Corporation*, 2012 ONCA 243, application for leave to appeal refused 2012 CANLII 59 (SCC) at para. 78; *Lomas v Rio Algom Ltd*, 2010 ONCA 175 at para 61.

57 *Burke SCC* at paras. 42–7.

CHAPTER EIGHT

1 In 1980, about 80 per cent of public sector employees belonged to workplace pension plans, compared to 33 per cent in the private sector. Pension-plan participation (coverage) rates were custom-calculated by Bob Baldwin based on data from Statistics Canada CANSIM 280–0016 and CANSIM 282–0012. For pension purposes, Statistics Canada defines a public sector organization as the "[t]ype of organization that includes municipal, provincial and federal governments and enterprises, crown corporations, government boards, commissions and agencies, and public educational and health institutions. Terminology and the scope of statutory coverage varies from province to province, and it is important to consult statutory definitions to determine precisely what types of workplaces and employees are covered by particular statutes at particular times." A private sector organization is the "[t]ype of organization that includes incorporated and unincorporated businesses, religious, charitable and other non-profit organizations, co-operatives, trade or employee associations, and private educational and health institutions": Statistics Canada, *Definitions, Data Sources, and Methods*.

2 See Statistics Canada, *The Daily*, 19 December 2013. See also Pozzebon, "The Outlook for Canada's Public Sector Employee Pensions," 144–7.

3 These are the largest groups of public employees, although many plans in the public sector cover public employees outside these groups. A recent study in Ontario identified more than one hundred public sector pension plans in Ontario alone: Ministry of Finance. *Facilitating Pooled Asset Management for Ontario's Public-Sector Institutions: Report from the Pension Investment Advisor to the Deputy Premier and Minister of Finance*, 8.

4 In taking this step, the Canadian government was following recent UK precedent. For the history of UK civil service pensions, see Raphael, *Pensions and Public Servants*, 123–62. Raphael dates the modern civil

service pension system in the UK to the 1850s, although statutory
precursors can be found as far back as 1810: see 124, 149.

5 Canada, *House of Commons Debates*, 16 April 1870, 1054.

6 *An Act for better ensuring the efficiency of the Civil Service of Canada, by
providing for the Superannuation of persons employed therein, in certain
cases*, SC 1870, c 4.

7 Employees who took early retirement as a result of restructuring were
subject to recall to a comparable position (s 8).

8 The contribution rate varied with the employee's salary level; those paid in
excess of $600 per annum contributed 4 per cent of salary, while those
paid less contributed 2½ per cent. Contributions were required for the
first thirty-five years of service.

9 In dismissing employee pension claims under this statute, courts emphasized the discretionary nature of the benefit: see *Balderson v The Queen*
(1898) 28 SCR 261, discussed in Chapter 3.

10 The Act provided that the offer of a pension "shall not be considered as
implying any censure upon the person to whom it is made" (s 3).

11 *The Civil Service Superannuation Act, 1924*, SC 1924, c 69. There had
been some changes in the intervening years: see Dawson, *The Civil Service
of Canada*, 186–91.

12 The employer could still force those between sixty-five and seventy to
retire by offering them a pension: s 10(1). There was also a procedure for
permitting employees to remain past the age of seventy to a maximum of
age seventy-five, at the employer's option.

13 See also ss 10(1) and (3).

14 Under the 1870 Act, salary was averaged over the last three years (s 1).

15 There was no comparable allowance for widowers. Quebec civil service
pensions provided survivor benefits as far back as 1877. The right of a
widow to survivor benefits under the Quebec civil service plan was at the
heart of Edmeé Dionne's claim to standing in *Dionne v Québec* (1895),
24 SCR 451: see discussion in Chapter 3.

16 Listed in chronological order, the following statutes established initial
civil service plans in each province: Quebec, *An Act to Establish a
Superannuation and Aid Fund in Favor of Certain Public Employees
and their Families*, SQ 1876, c 10; Ontario, *The Ontario Public Service
Superannuation Act, 1920*, SO 1920, c 4; British Columbia, *Superannuation
Act*, SBC 1921, c 60; Alberta, *The Superannuation Act*, SA 1922, c 11;
Nova Scotia, *The Public Service Superannuation Act*, SNS 1923, c 5
(not in force until 1934); Saskatchewan, *Civil Service Superannuation*

Act, 1927, ss 1927, c 2; New Brunswick, *The Public Service Superannuation Act*, snb 1931, c 17; Manitoba, *Manitoba Civil Service Superannuation Act*, sm 1939, c 65; Prince Edward Island, *The Public Service Superannuation Act*, spei 1945, c 31; Newfoundland and Labrador, *The Civil Service Act*, rsnl 1952, c 22, s 21.

17 *An Act Respecting the Government and Public Employees Retirement Plan*, rsq c r–10. Covered employees are listed in Schedules I and II. Employers who participate in the plans are required to match employee contributions. Universities and municipalities are not covered by this plan.

18 For example, *The Ontario Public Service Superannuation Act, 1920*, so 1920, c 4, ss 11–12.

19 The definition of "salary" ranged from Quebec's "career average" to Ontario's "average over the last three years." For a description of provincial civil service plans in place by the first quarter of the twentieth century, see "Employees Superannuation in Canada: Existing Public and Private Schemes for Retirement Insurance," *Labour Gazette* (1924): 127.

20 *Superannuation Civil Service (Amendment) Act*, sbc 1958, c 4, s 11. By the time this change was made, coverage for employees other than the government's own workforce was no longer available. Since 1977, Saskatchewan's public service plan has been a dc plan for new employees.

21 For a detailed review of the changes in the Ontario civil service plan from its inception in 1920 to the late 1970s, see Jamieson, "Legislative History of Major Public Sector Pension Plans," 177–87.

22 Listed in chronological order, the following statutes established initial teachers' plans in each province: Quebec, *An Act concerning a Pension and Benevolent Fund in Favor of Officers of Primary Instruction*, sq 1880, c 22; Ontario, *An Act Respecting Superannuation for Certain Teachers and Inspectors*, so 1917, c 58, s 11(1)(d) [*1917 Ontario Teachers Superannuation Act*]; Manitoba, *An Act to Establish a Teachers' Retirement Fund*, sm 1925, c 60; Nova Scotia, *An Act to Provide Pension for Public School Teachers*, sns 1928, c 6; British Columbia, *An Act Respecting Teachers' Pensions*, sbc 1929, c 62; Newfoundland, *Education Act*, snl 1927, c 14, Part 10 (not yet part of Canada at the time); Saskatchewan, *An Act Respecting Superannuation for Teachers*, ss 1930, c 93; Prince Edward Island, *An Act to Provide Superannuation Allowances for School Teachers*, spei 1931, c 8; Alberta, *An Act to Establish a Teachers' Retirement Fund*, sa 1939, c 21; New Brunswick, *An Act to Provide for the Payment of Pensions to Teachers and School Officials*, snb 1944, c 17. Members included classroom teachers, principals and

vice-principals, inspectors, and other local education administrators, as well as employees in faculties of education and provincial department of education officials who held teaching qualifications.

23 School boards had their own taxing authority, and in most provinces money for education was raised locally from the municipal rather than the provincial tax base. For an historical perspective on the mix between provincial and local education funding in Ontario, see *Ontario English Catholic Teachers' Assn v Ontario (Attorney General)*, [2001] 1 SCR 470, 2001 SCC 15, particularly at para. 48. That mix varied from province to province and over time.

24 See Joannette, "Worn Out," 360–1; McNay, "The Teachers of British Columbia and Superannuation," 40–4; Heap and Prentice, "The Outlook for Old Age Is Not Hopeful," 76–94.

25 *Journals of the Legislative Assembly of the Province of Ontario*, 14th Leg, 3d Sess, Vol LI (12 April 1917), 275.

26 "Benefits of Teacher Superannuation Schemes," *Labour Gazette* (1929): 121. The bill under discussion was not passed until 1930.

27 McNay, "The Teachers of British Columbia and Superannuation," 36–9.

28 The term "teacher" included educational administrators like principals, vice-principals, and more senior administrators.

29 A detailed description of the evolution of the Ontario plan can be found in Jamieson, "Legislative History of Major Public Sector Pension Plans," 187–99.

30 Manitoba initially established its plan in 1925 without any employer contribution. Five years later, the province became a matching contributor. For additional information on the history of the Manitoba plan, see "TRAF: Together, through 75 Years of Growth" (2000), 14, on the Teachers' Retirement Allowance Fund website, online: http:// www.traf.mb.ca/images/stories/Publications/75th_anniversary_book.pdf.

31 A disability pension was also available with fifteen years of service.

32 The Quebec plan paid a survivor benefit. This benefit had a discriminatory impact on women teachers; although women as a group contributed four times as much to the pension fund as men teachers, women teachers drew out only one-quarter of the amount paid to male teachers and their widows. In 1914–15, the average pension of a retired female teacher was $111.09 annually, as compared to $343.25 for an average male teacher and $200.67 for the average widow of a male teacher. See Heap and Prentice, "The Outlook for Old Age Is Not Hopeful," 82.

33 SBC 1940, c 52, s 12.

34 *Education Act*, SNL 1927, c 14, s 75(j).

35 *An Act Respecting Teachers' Pensions*, SBC 1929, c 62, s 25.
36 For a detailed historical summary of the statutory authority of municipali-
    ties to establish pension plans, see Institute of Local Government,
    Canadian Municipal Pension Plans, 9–14.
37 Again, the exception was British Columbia, which amended its statute in
    1927 to provide that municipalities must enrol their employees if 75 per
    cent of them petitioned to join the plan: SBC 1926–27, c 68, s 2. This pro-
    vision was repealed in 1938: see Institute of Local Government, *Canadian
    Municipal Pension Plans*, 13.
38 "Employees Superannuation in Canada: Provision for Retirement of
    Municipal Employees," *Labour Gazette* (1924): 390. Toronto's "consider-
    ation" apparently lasted for another nineteen years; its city plan was not
    established until 1943.
39 Institute of Local Government, *Canadian Municipal Pension Plans*, 17.
40 *Municipal Superannuation Act*, SBC 1958, c 55.
41 *The Urban Employee Superannuation Act, 1951*, SS 1951 c 52, s 2(5)(a).
    Thirteen named cities and towns were excepted; they have subsequently
    been admitted.
42 *Ontario Municipal Employees Retirement System Act*, SO 1961–62, c 97.
    This requirement also applied to "local boards," a broad category
    which included school boards (for their non-teaching employees).
    For additional information on the history of OMERS, see Jamieson,
    "Legislative History of Major Public Sector Pension Plans," 200–6; and
    Task Force on the Investment of Public Sector Pension Funds, *In Whose
    Interest?* 187–96.
43 *The Local Authorities Pension Act*, SA 1962, c 47.
44 *Municipal Act*, SM 1975, c 19, subdivision XIX.
45 The municipal sector currently accounts for some 20 per cent of all plans
    registered in Quebec: see Comité des experts sur l'avenir du système de
    retraite québécois, *Rapport – Innover pour pérenniser le système de
    retraite* ["*D'Amours Report*"], 93.
46 *Municipal Superannuation Act*, SBC 1938, c 55, s13.
47 *Municipal Superannuation Act*, SBC 1958, c 55, s 3.
48 For hospitals, a majority of the employees had to agree before an
    employer could participate, although other groups that participated on a
    voluntary basis could do so on the request of the employer alone (based
    on a two-thirds majority of the governing body). The 1958 act removed
    the requirement for the consent of the employees [s 3.(1)(d)].
49 *An Act Respecting the Government and Public Employees Retirement
    Plan*, RSQ c R–10. Schedules I and II.

50 The *Participating Employer Regulations*, PEI Reg EC414/0, s 1(2)(j.1)
    under the *Civil Service Superannuation Act*, RSPEI 1988, c C–9, s 2, (J1)
    lists Health PEI as a participating employer.

51 Alberta is an example; see *Local Authorities Pension Act*, SA 1962, c 47,
    s 2(b)(iii).

52 See Sadakova, "2014 Top 100 Pension Funds Report."

53 Section 8(1)(e) of the *Pension Benefits Act* requires that "if the pension
    plan is a multi-employer pension plan established pursuant to a collective
    agreement or a trust agreement" it must be administered by "a board of
    trustees appointed pursuant to the pension plan or a trust agreement
    establishing the pension plan of whom at least one-half are representatives
    of members of the multi-employer pension plan."

54 *Canadian Union of Public Employees (CUPE) v Ontario Hospital
    Association* (Pension Commission of Ontario, 26 June 1991, unreported),
    aff'd (1992) 91 DLR (4th) 436 (Ont Div Ct). The PCO found that HOOPP
    had been established pursuant to a trust agreement. The unions involved
    were the Canadian Union of Public Employees, the Ontario Public Service
    Employees Union, the Service Employees International Union, and the
    Ontario Nurses' Association; together, they represented 60 per cent of
    HOOPP members.

55 For example, the Hospital for Sick Children and St Michael's Hospital in
    Toronto maintain their own plans, although they have reciprocal agree-
    ments with HOOPP for transferring credits between plans.

56 For example, the Nursing Homes and Related Industries Pension Plan is
    union-sponsored and governed by trustees appointed by the Service
    Employees International Union, the Canadian Union of Public Employees,
    Unifor, and the Ontario Nurses' Association. It provides pensions for
    employees of nursing homes, retirement homes, and employees in related
    industries.

57 The Nova Scotia Health Employees' Pension Plan was established in 1961.
    The Saskatchewan Healthcare Employees' Pension Plan was established in
    1962. Manitoba's Hospital Employee Pension Plan was established in
    1997 as a merger of earlier plans. The background to this plan is described
    in *Manitoba Health Organizations Inc. v Healthcare Employees Pension
    Plan – Manitoba (Trustees of)*, [1998] MJ No. 170 (QB). New Brunswick
    now has two plans that cover hospital workers, divided on the basis of
    union representation.

58 Prince Edward Island cannot yet be categorized, since its general pension
    standards legislation (*Pension Benefits Act*, Bill 41, 2012) has not yet been
    proclaimed. The bill does not bind the Crown.

59 *Pension Benefits Standards Act, 1985*, RSC 1985, c 32 (2d Supp),
    ss 4(5)–(6) and *Pension Benefits Standards Regulations, 1985*, SOR/87-19,
    s 4 and Schedule 1, the combined effect of which is to exclude employees
    covered by the *Public Service Superannuation Act*, RSC 1985, C P–36.
    Schedule I of the act contains a lengthy list of federal agencies, boards,
    and commissions that are considered part of the public service for
    pension purposes.

60 *Pension Benefits Regulations Made under Section 105 of the Pension
    Benefits Act*, NS Reg 164/2002, s 49(2). Nova Scotia also exempts certain
    public sector plans, such as those for municipal workers, school boards,
    and the police association, from the application of specific provisions of
    the statute relating to solvency deficiencies: ibid., Part 2, s 5(1A).

61 *Public Sector Pension Plans (legislative provisions) Regulation*, Alta Reg
    365/93; *Local Authorities Pension Plan*, Alta Reg 366/93; *Public Service
    Pension Plan*, Alta Reg 368/93; *Management Employees Pension Plan*,
    Alta Reg 367/93; *Special Forces Pension Plan*, Alta Reg 369/93.

62 *An Act Respecting the Commission Administrative des Régimes de
    Retraite et d'Assurances*, CQLR c C–32.1.2.

63 *Supplemental Pension Plans Act*, CQLR c R–15.1, s 2(4).

64 *D'Amours Report*, 28.

65 *Pension Benefits Act*, SNB 1987, c P–5.1, ss 2–3.

66 Ontario. *Report to the Treasurer of Ontario.*

67 O Reg 103/66, s 2(12). "Government" was defined to include the provin-
    cial government, Crown agencies, municipalities, and local boards [s 1(e)].
    Governments were also permitted to administer their own pension funds,
    rather than assigning that job to trustees or financial institutions [s 18(1)].

68 The most obvious example is the 1974 change in legislation that permitted
    plans to provide inflation protection without prefunding the benefit. This
    was done to permit the government to provide guaranteed inflation index-
    ing in the public service and teachers' plans (and anomalously, the
    Ryerson Superannuation Plan) without incurring the considerable addi-
    tional contribution expense that prefunding would have required: see
    Ontario, *Report to the Treasurer of Ontario*, I-1-I-4.

69 The definition of "public sector plan" covers a broad range of plans,
    including those applicable to employees of the Crown, Crown agencies,
    boards and commissions, school boards, local health-service providers,
    colleges and universities, municipalities, and children's-aid societies: see
    s 1(5). Some differences between public and private sector plans have been
    built into the statute itself: see, for example, s 55.2(2), dealing with the use
    of letters of credit.

70 *Pension Benefits Act,* s 115(5.1); *General,* RRO 1990, O Reg 909, ss 47.1, 47.2, and 47.3. Most of these special rules apply to funding and plan-conversion issues.

71 *The Pension Benefits Act, 1992,* SS 1992, c P–6.001; *Pension Benefits Regulations,* 1993, RRS c P-6.001 Reg 1, s 36.7(1) and Part II, Table 1.

72 Part 4, Division 2, s 4.5(2)(b) and (c) of the *Pension Benefits Regulation,* Man Reg 39/2010 exempts *The Civil Service Superannuation Act* and *Teachers' Pension Act* from s 26(1)(a) of the Act (funding and solvency of plans). See also the *Solvency Exemption for Public Sector Pension Plans Regulation,* Man Reg 81/2010, which permits public sector pension plans to opt out of certain solvency provisions and transfer deficiency provisions.

73 Part IX, s 41(1) of the *Pension Benefits Act Regulations,* NLR 114/96 emphasizes the general application of the statute to all public sector pension plans (NLR 114/96), but goes on in subsections (2) to (5) to list various specific exemptions for the Teachers' Pension Plan, Public Service Pension Plan, Memorial University Pension Plan, and Provincial Court Judges Pension Plan respectively.

74 *Pension Benefits Standards Act,* RSBC 1996, c 352, s 1(8)(a). For this purpose, public sector pension plans are those to which the *Public Sector Pension Plans Act,* SBC 1999, c 44 applies. For exemptions, see *Pension Benefits Standards Regulation,* BC Reg 433/93. See also s 42, governing the identity and conduct of administrators, which is not applicable to public sector plans. British Columbia also exempts public sector plans from the application of the "fifty-per-cent rule" [s 32(8)].

75 In all Canadian jurisdictions except Saskatchewan, Crown employees were excluded from general collective bargaining statutes enacted in the late 1940s and 1950s: see Fudge and Tucker, *Labour Before the Law,* 311.

76 Fryer, "Provincial Public Sector Labour Relations," 341–5.

77 In 1993, Ontario enacted a new *Crown Employees Collective Bargaining Act, 1993,* SO 1993, c 38, which restructured labour relations in the public service and some Crown agencies, and removed restrictions on the scope of bargaining.

78 Swimmer, "Collective Bargaining in the Federal Public Service of Canada," 371, 389–90; *Public Service Labour Relations Act,* SC 2003, c 22, s 2, §113.

79 *The Teaching Profession Act, 1944,* SO 1944, c 64, s 8. The current version of this statute specifies that the OTF represents all members of the teachers' pension plan in the administration and management of the plan: see *Teaching Profession Act,* RSO, c T2, s 3(f).

80 See Shilton, "Collective Bargaining for Teachers in Ontario," 230–2. See also Rose, "The Evolution of Teacher Bargaining in Ontario," 199.

81 In presentations in the late 1970s to Ontario's Royal Commission on the Status of Pensions, the OTF did not support the general call by public sector unions for collective bargaining on pensions, expressing itself satisfied with current representative arrangements and concerned about the potential fragmentation that would likely result from placing pensions on the regular bargaining table: see Royal Commission, *Report*, Vol. 6 at 195.

82 See Slinn and Schucher, "Cross-Currents." This summary article highlights similarities and differences among the provinces in teacher collective bargaining structures.

83 Graham, "Collective Bargaining in the Municipal Sector."

84 See Jackson, "Police and Firefighter Labour Relations in Canada," Table 1, 322–3, which sets out in comparative format the bargaining regimes governing police and firefighters across the country.

85 See *Town of Dryden and Dryden Police Association*, [1973] 1 OR 619 (HCJ) (statutory language permitting bargaining over pensions for "members of the police force" does not permit bargaining over pension benefits for widowed spouses and orphans of police officers); *Metropolitan Toronto Police Association and Board of Commissioners of Police for Metropolitan Toronto* (1980), 111 DLR (3d) 658 (Ont Div Ct) (bargaining over pensions for widowed spouses and orphans is permissible, but bargaining over inflation protection for retired officers is not).

86 Haiven, "Industrial Relations in Health Care." There are recent exceptions; for example, the Nursing Homes and Related Industries Pension Plan referred to in note 56 above.

87 Royal Commission, *Report*, Vol. 6, 193.

88 See Ontario, Public Sector Pension Consultation, *The Pension Benefits Act, 1987*, and Chapter 4.

89 See *Superannuation Adjustment Benefits Act*, RSO 1980, c 490 (repealed in 1994). The government expressly amended the *Pension Benefits Act* to facilitate this departure from solvency funding standards for public and private sector plans alike, but private plans did not typically offer anything more than ad hoc inflation protection. This issue is discussed in Ontario, *Report to the Treasurer of Ontario*, Part 1.

90 Ontario, *Report to the Treasurer of Ontario*, Part 4.

91 Royal Commission, *Report*, Vol. 10 (Summary). The relevant recommendations are Numbers 108, 116, and 121.

92 Public Sector Pension Consultations. *A Fresh Start*. This undated report was issued in 1988. It builds in particular on two earlier reports generated

by the consultations, Ontario, *Report to the Treasurer of Ontario*, and Ontario, Task Force on the Investment of Public Sector Pension Funds, *In Whose Interest?*

93 Public Sector Pension Consultations, *A Fresh Start*, 90. The report laid out an agenda for these negotiations at 71–2.

94 The government was successful in negotiating a $400-million three-year contribution deferral in the newly formed Ontario Public Service Employees' Pension Plan: see *OPSEU v Ontario (Attorney General)* (1995), 131 DLR (4th) 572.

95 *Teachers' Pension Plan Act, 1989*, SO 1989, c 92, now RSO 1990, c T.1.

96 *Ontario Public Service Employees' Union Pension Plan Act, 1994*, SO 1994, c 17, Sch.

97 See *Ontario Municipal Employees Retirement System Act, 2006*, SO 2006, c 2.

98 JSPPs have some unique regulatory requirements in terms of both structure and funding: see *PBA*, s 1(2); *General*, RRO 1990, Reg 909, s 3.1. There is no statutory requirement that members of JSPPs be represented by trade unions.

99 The *Arthurs Report* explains "target benefit" plans as follows:

> In a target benefit plan, contributions are fixed, and on the basis of a best estimate of what the funding will provide, benefits are promised. However, if it is later determined that the "target" benefit cannot be achieved with the available resources – contributions and the return on investment – both accrued and future benefits can be adjusted downward and, for that matter, upward, if and when the plan's fortunes recover. Thus, from the viewpoint of the member, the plan may be perceived as a DB plan. Indeed, the benefit is defined and has all the characteristics of a DB plan except one: it is contingent on the plan's success. However, from the viewpoint of the plan sponsor or sponsors, the plan functions like a DC plan. Contributions are fixed or defined: once those contributions have been made, the sponsor has no obligation to make good any notional deficiency, because the benefits will be adjusted rather than paid in full (*Arthurs Report*, 182).

100 *Social Contract Act, 1993*, SO 1993, c 5.

101 They would have had Saskatchewan in mind. In 1977, the Saskatchewan government replaced its old DB plan with a DC plan for new employees, and moved again in 1979 to convert its DB teachers' plan into a DC plan. In order to retain as much of the DB model as possible, the Saskatchewan Teachers' Federation took over sole sponsorship of the plan in 1990–91:

see *Saskatchewan Teachers' Retirement Plan Overview*, online: https://www.stf.sk.ca/benefits/pdf/strp/strp_overview.pdf.

102 *Ontario Public Service Employees' Union Pension Act, 1994*, SO 1994, c 17, s 143 Sched., s 21(2).

103 *OPSEU v Ontario (Attorney General)* (1995), 131 DLR (4th), 572.

104 See *Ontario Public Service Employees' Union Pension Act, 1994*, SO 1994, c 17, s 14.1, passed in 1996.

105 *Public Sector Pension Plans Act, 1999*, SBC 1999, c 44. The plans affected are those covering colleges, the public service, teachers, and the municipalities and other publicly funded agencies participating in the municipal plan.

106 British Columbia, Auditor General, *A Review of Government Oversight*, 2–3, 25–7.

107 Ibid., 27.

108 *Public Service Superannuation Act*, SNS 2012, c 4, Sch B.

109 Bill 9, the *Public Sector Pension Plans Amendment Act, 2014*. For the union perspective, see Labour Coalition on Pensions Response: Government of Alberta, "Charting a New Course: A Vision for Public Sector Pension Reform," December 2013, online: http://rdc.ab.ca/sites/default/files/uploads/documents/52634/lapp-brief-v11-dec-2013.pdf.

110 See *An Act to Foster the Financial Health and Sustainability of Municipal Defined Benefit Pension Plans*, SQ 2014, c 15.

111 *Pension Benefits Act*, SNB 1987, c P-5, Part 2, ss 100.2–100.9; *Shared Risk Plans Regulation – Pension Benefits Act*, NB Reg 2012–75, s 7.1.

112 The innovative process by which these agreements were reached is described in Leech and McNish, *The Third Rail*, 33–68. See also Munnell and Sass, "New Brunswick's New Shared Risk Pension Plan."

113 See *Teachers' Pension Plan Act*, SNB 2014, c 61. The old *Public Service Superannuation Act*, RSNB 1973, c P-26 has been repealed (SNB 2013, c 44), and was not replaced with a new statute. As of February 2016, there remains an outstanding constitutional challenge to the potential for benefit reductions created by the new model, filed on behalf of pensioners.

CHAPTER NINE

1 OECD, *Pensions at a Glance: Retirement-Income Systems in OECD Countries*, 25–53; *D'Amours Report*, 81–91; *Arthurs Report*, 56–7.

2 Lipsett and Reesor, 37–8. See also Vosko, "Precarious Employment," 3 and 11; Stone, *From Widgets to Digits*, 67–116.

3 A report to the Ontario government placed the cut-off for efficient, cost-effective pension funds at $50 billion: Ministry of Finance, *Facilitating Pooled Asset Management*, 16. No single-employer private sector plan in Canada comes close to that level.

4 *McKinney v University of Guelph*, [1990] SCJ No. 122. *McKinney* involved a challenge to the mandatory retirement policies of four Ontario universities, and likewise to the Ontario *Human Rights Code*'s definition of "age," which excluded those over sixty-five. It was heard together with three cases from British Columbia: *Harrison v University of British Columbia*, [1990] 3 SCR 451; *Stoffman v Vancouver General Hospital*, [1990] 3 SCR 483; and *Douglas/Kwantlen Faculty Assn v Douglas College*, [1990] 3 SCR 570.

5 *McKinney v University of Guelph* at paras. 83–96, 101, 111, 114–15 (per Justice La Forest).

6 See Klassen and Forgione, "Forced Retirement."

7 See also *Dickason v University of Alberta*, [1992] 2 SCR 1103; *Large v Stratford (City)*, [1995] 3 SCR 733.

8 The New Brunswick statute provides a broader defence: see *New Brunswick (Human Rights Commission) v Potash Corporation of Saskatchewan Inc.*, [2008] 2 SCR 604, 2008 SCC 45.

9 Current laws governing mandatory retirement in Canada and elsewhere are reviewed in detail in Alon-Schenker, "Ending Mandatory Retirement," 28–32. Several Canadian jurisdictions, including Ontario, continue to permit discrimination in disability and other benefit plans against those age sixty-five and over.

10 Much of this debate is summarized in Morley Gunderson's literature review on this issue in *Incentive Effects of Occupational Pension Plans*, 26–8.

11 This process is not unique to Canada, and has been going on for some time: see Stone, *From Widgets to Digits*, 67–116.

12 See Anderson, Beaton, and Laxer, "The Union Dimension," 302–6; Riddell and Riddell, "Changing Patterns in Unionisation," 155–62.

13 Vosko, "Precarious Employment," 3 and 11. For discussion of the challenges of applying labour/employment law norms and minimum standards to precarious work, see Bernstein, Lippel, Tucker, and Vosko, "Precarious Employment and the Law's Flaws"; Rittich, "Feminization and Contingency"; Stone and Arthurs, "The Transformation of Employment Regimes: A Worldwide Challenge."

14 This fact has been constant over the period of this study. The mismatch between the employment patterns of workers who do not hold long-term, full-time jobs, and the mechanisms that generate good pensions within the

standard workplace pension plan were noted in Latimer's 1932 study, in the 1938 *Queen's Study*, and in Ontario's Committee on Portable Pension's *Second Report* in the early 1960s, as well as in many later studies.

15 The phrase comes from Supiot, *Beyond Employment*, 1.

16 See Gomez and Gunderson, "Non-standard and Vulnerable Workers: A Case of Mistaken Identity," 190.

17 Lipsett and Reesor, 37–8.

18 *Arthurs Report* at 51.

19 Several Canadian jurisdictions now require immediate vesting; this means that employers begin to incur liabilities as soon as an employee becomes a plan member: for example, *Pension Benefits Act*, RSO 1990, c P–8, s 37.

20 See *Monsanto Canada Inc. v Ontario (Superintendent of Financial Services)*, [2004] 3 SCR 152, 2004 SCC 54. The *Monsanto* rule does not apply in all jurisdictions in Canada: see *Cousins v Canada (Attorney General)*, [2008] FCJ No. 1011 (CA), leave to appeal refused 2008 SCCA Nos. 400, 428–31.

21 See *D'Amours Report*, 81–91; *Arthurs Report*, 56–7.

22 Gunderson, *Incentive Effects*, 2, fn 1, notes that there is very little data on employer pension costs over time. In one study undertaken in 2004, Canadian labour economists concluded that certain types of regulation – expanded membership eligibility rules and, surprisingly, earlier vesting – may have had a *positive* effect on pension coverage in the private sector: Luchak, Fang, and Gunderson, "How Has Public Policy Shaped Defined-Benefit Pension Coverage?" 477–8, 481.

23 *Arthurs Report*, 47. The particular regulatory costs about which sponsors complained to Arthurs included:

> funding rules that that force sponsors to make large, unpredictable and unsustainable contributions to maintain plan solvency without the prospect of swiftly recovering occasional surpluses as an offset; regulatory constraints on innovation in investments, plan design and administration; the need to comply with different regulatory requirements across the country; the imposition of professional standards such as "mark-to-market" accounting rules, which expose plans to additional pressures; and the application of trust law doctrines, which impose on sponsors, trustees and service providers tighter restrictions and greater responsibilities than were anticipated when plans were first established (47).

24 In a report to the Nova Scotia government, an expert panel concluded that it "could find no instance of a truly new private sector pension plan being

implemented on a Defined Benefit basis in the last ten years": Nova Scotia. Pension Review Panel, *Promises to Keep*, 9.

25 The impact of some of these regulatory costs on employer pension decision-making is discussed in Litner and Marin, "Private-Sector Pension Plans."

26 While the DC model assumes fixed contributions into a pension fund, how that lump sum is treated once it is contributed depends on the particular mechanics of the plan. While some DC plans pool funds for investment purposes and allocate portions of the fund to individuals simply as a bookkeeping transaction, many operate on the basis of individual investment accounts.

27 See discussion in Chapter 8. Until recently, target benefits were not permitted in single-employer plans in most jurisdictions, although they were permitted in multi-employer plans established under collective agreements. That is now changing: e.g., *Pension Benefits Act*, RSO 1990, c P.8, s 39.2 (not yet in force as of February 2016)

28 For an explanation of hybrid benefits, see Albrecht, Coche, Maurer, and Rogalla, "Understanding and Allocating Risks in a Hybrid Pension Plan." While the possibilities for combining benefit types are limited only by the tax laws, a common option is a guaranteed DB base pension, which can be expanded either by supplementary individual DC accounts, or on a more collective basis by reference to the investment performance of the general pension fund. Hybrid benefits may also be offered on a "best of" basis, in which employees are guaranteed a DB benefit, but may get a larger pension if their DC account has a better-than-expected investment performance.

29 See Baldwin, "Economic Impact," 11, Table 1. See also Gougeon, "Shifting Pensions."

30 This is part of a broader trend since the late 1970s towards shifting workplace and social risks from employers to employees: see Stone, "Rethinking Labour Law"; Stone, *From Widgets to Digits*, 289–90.

31 Baldwin, "Economic Impact," at 26–8.

32 Modelling the impact of the shift from DB to DC for participants in registered pension plans with birth years from 1925 to 1950, Bob Baldwin and Kevin Moore concluded that, if all workplace plans had been DC plans, before-tax retirement income from workplace pension plans would have been about 75 per cent of what was actually produced by DB plans. (After tax, it would have been 93 per cent.) They point out that while income tax rules cushion the negative impact of DC on individuals, this comes at the cost of depressing public revenues and increasing public expenditures:

Baldwin and Moore, "The Shift in Workplace Pension Plans from D B to D C."

33 These issues are discussed by Jack Mintz in Canada, Research Working Group on Retirement Income Adequacy of Federal-Provincial-Territorial Ministers of Finance, *Summary Report on Retirement Income Adequacy Research*, 18–22. See also Baldwin, "Economic Impact," 17–23.

34 Baldwin, "Economic Impact," 14–17. Even more damaging to the quality of pensions is the trend toward such Pillar 3 instruments as group Registered Retirement Savings Plans ("R R S P s") and the new Pooled Retirement Pension Plans (P R P P s), which are given favourable income-tax treatment, but otherwise have none of the risk-pooling characteristics of workplace pension plans and do not require an employer contribution. More than half of the employers who offer group R R S P s make no contribution to these plans (Baldwin, "Economic Impact," 11–18).

35 Ontario, Select Committee on Pensions, *Final Report 1982*, 32.

36 *Frith Report*, 69–72.

37 Kesselman, "Expanding Canada Pension Plan Retirement Benefits."

38 Steering Committee of Provincial/Territorial Ministers on Pension Coverage and Retirement Income Adequacy, *Options for Increasing Pension Coverage*.

39 The Honourable Ted Morton, then Alberta Minister of Finance, proposed that, before acting on C P P expansion, the private sector should be given another ten years to explore new retirement-income options: see Janet McFarland, "Slow Approach Urged on Pension Reform," *Globe & Mail*, 13 April 2010.

40 Some proposals for reform are summarized in Steering Committee of Provincial/Territorial Ministers on Pension Coverage and Retirement Income Adequacy, *Options for Increasing Pension Coverage*, 12 and 24–7; Baldwin and Fitzgerald, *Seeking Certainty in Uncertain Times*; and Kesselman, "Expanding Canada Pension Plan Retirement Benefits," 25–8.

41 *Arthurs Report*; British Columbia and Alberta, Joint Expert Panel on Pension Standards, *Getting Our Acts Together*; Nova Scotia, Pension Review Panel, *Promises to Keep*; *D'Amours Report*. The first three of these reports are summarized in Baldwin and Fitzgerald, *Seeking Certainty in Uncertain Times*.

42 British Columbia and Alberta, Joint Expert Panel on Pension Standards, *Getting Our Acts Together*, i.

43 The British Columbia/Alberta report makes particularly generous use of the term "deals," but all reports favour increased flexibility for employers and employees to make their own pension arrangements. The reports

proceed from the implicit assumption that employees have a voice in pension arrangements. Only Arthurs insists on regulatory changes that would ensure a meaningful role for plan members in the new target benefit plans he proposes: *Arthurs Report*, 176.

44 See for example, Kesselman, "Expanding Canada Pension Plan Retirement Benefits," 6–8.

45 In May 2015, on the eve of a federal election campaign, the government announced that it was willing to reopen consultations with the provinces about options for expanding the CPP on a voluntary basis.

46 See *Pooled Registered Pension Plans Act*, SC 2012, c 16.

47 PRPPs are criticized in Shilton, "Gender Risk," 133–9. They are given more positive treatment in Litner and Marin, "Private-Sector Pension Plans," 172–180.

48 As of February 2016, there is no PRPP legislation in Manitoba, New Brunswick, Prince Edward Island, and Newfoundland and Labrador.

49 *Pooled Registered Pension Plans Act, 2015*, SO 2015, c 9 (not yet in force as of February 2016).

50 *Ontario Retirement Pension Plan Act, 2015*, SO 2015, c 5.

51 Ontario, *2016 Budget: Jobs for Today and Tomorrow*, Chapter 1, Section F.

52 See Hugh Mackenzie, "Two Cheers for the Details of the Ontario Retirement Pension Plan," 11 August 2015, online: http://behindthe numbers.ca/2015/08/11/two-cheers-for-the-details-of-the-ontario-retirement-pension-plan/.

53 Barr, *Reforming Pensions*. See also Barr, *The Welfare State as Piggy Bank*.

54 The elusive (and illusory) nature of the public/private divide, first discussed in the context of law by the Legal Realists of the early twentieth century, has continued to be a central theme in critical legal studies and in much feminist legal analysis: e.g., Klare, "The Public/Private Distinction in Labor Law"; Morton Horwitz, "The History of the Public Private Distinction"; Boyd, *Challenging the Public/Private Divide: Feminism, Law and Social Policy*.

55 The value of the tax subsidy to private pension plans is massive. A recent research report estimates that it costs the Canadian income-tax system some $20 billion a year, 70 per cent as much as the cost of the entire OAS Pillar 1 benefit: Li, "Tax Expenditure Analysis of Employer-Sponsored Registered Pension Plans," 35, Table J. See also Li, "Impact of Tax Policy on Coverage and Funding of Occupational Pension Plans."

56 Cohen, "The Basis of Contract," 565.

Bibliography

Aaron, Benjamin. *Legal Status of Employee Benefit Rights Under Private Pension Plans.* Homewood, Ill., Irwin, 1961.

Ackerman, Harmon. "The Legal Aspects of Amendments to a Pension Plan." *Labor Law Journal* 1 (1950): 929–34.

Adams, Roy. *Industrial Relations under Liberal Democracy: North America in Comparative Perspective.* Columbia, SC: University of South Carolina Press, 1995.

Adell, Bernard. *Pension Plan Surpluses and the Law: Finding a Path for Reform.* Reprint Series No. 75. Kingston: Queen's Industrial Relations Centre, 1988.

AFL-CIO. *Pension Plans Under Collective Bargaining: A Reference Guide for Trade Unions* (AFL-CIO Publication No. 132) (Revision by Richard E. Shoemaker [no date], originally prepared by Lane Kirkland in 1952 and revised in 1954).

Albrecht, Peter, Joachim Coche, Raimond Maurer, and Ralph Rogalla. "Understanding and Allocating Risks in a Hybrid Pension Plan." In *Restructuring Retirement Risks,* edited by David Blitzstein, Olive S. Mitchell, and Stephen P. Utkus, 204–25. Oxford: Oxford University Press, 2006.

Alexander, Gregory S. "The Dead Hand and the Law of Trust." *Stanford Law Review* 37 (1984–85): 1189–1266.

– "The Transformation of Trusts as a Legal Category, 1800–1914." *Law and History Review* 5 (1987): 303–50.

Allen, Steven G., and Robert B. Clark. "Unions, Pension Wealth and Age-Compensation Profiles." *Industrial and Labor Relations Review* 39 (1986): 502–17.

Alon-Schenker, Pnina. "Ending Mandatory Retirement: Re-Assessment."
    Windsor Review of Legal and Social Issues 35 (2014): 22–53.
Anderson, John, James Beaton, and Kate Laxer. "The Union Dimension:
    Mitigating Precarious Employment." In *Precarious Employment:
    Understanding Labour Market Insecurity in Canada*, edited by Leah F.
    Vosko, 301–17. Montreal and Kingston: McGill-Queen's University
    Press, 2006.
Arthurs Report. See Ontario. Expert Commission on Pensions. *A Fine
    Balance.*
Ascah, Louis. "Recent Pension Reports in Canada: A Survey." *Canadian
    Public Policy* 10 (1984): 415–28.
Association of Canadian Pension Management. *Back from the Brink:
    Securing the Future of Defined Benefit Pension Plans* (August 2005),
    online: http://acpm.com/ACPM/media/media/resources/7/pdf/
    ACFD2B.pdf.
Baldwin, Bob. *Determinants of the Evolution of Workplace Pension Plans
    in Canada.* Caledon Institute of Social Policy, March 2007.
– *The Long-Term Capacity of Workplace Pension Plans to Deliver
    Retirement Income: A Review of Key Issues.* Caledon Institute of Social
    Policy, March 2007.
– "The Shift from DB to DC Coverage: A Reflection on the Issues."
    Canadian Public Policy 34 (2008): 29–37.
– "The Economic Impact on Plan Members of the Shift from DB to DC
    in Workplace Pension Plans." *Canadian Labour and Employment Law
    Journal* 19 (2015): 23–68.
Baldwin, Bob, and Brian Fitzgerald. *Seeking Certainty in Uncertain Times:
    A Review of Recent Government Sponsored Studies on the Regulation
    of Canadian Pension Plans.* Toronto: C.D. Howe Institute Pension
    Papers, 2010.
Baldwin, Bob, and Pierre Laliberté. *Incomes of Older Canadians: Amounts
    and Sources, 1973–1996.* Canadian Labour Congress Research Paper
    #15, December 1999.
Baldwin, Bob, and Kevin Moore. "The Shift in Workplace Pension Plans
    from DB to DC: Measuring the Impact Using LifePaths." *Canadian
    Labour and Employment Law Journal* 19 (2015): 69–104.
Banks, Kevin. "Progress and Paradox: The Remarkable Yet Limited
    Advance of Employer Good Faith Duties in Canadian Common Law."
    Comparative Labor Law and Policy Journal 32 (2010–2011): 547–91.
Banting, Keith. *The Welfare State and Canadian Federalism.* Montreal and
    Kingston: McGill-Queen's University Press, 1982.

Barr, Nicholas. *Reforming Pensions: Myths, Truths, and Policy Choices.*
IIMF Working Paper WP/00/139, International Monetary Fund,
August 2000.
– *The Welfare State as Piggy Bank: Information, Risk, Uncertainty, and
the Role of the State.* Oxford: Oxford University Press, 2001.
Battle, Kenneth. "The New Old Age Pension." In *Reform of Retirement
Income Policy: International and Canadian Perspectives,* edited by Keith
G. Banting and Robin Boadway, 135–90. Kingston: Queen's University
School of Policy Studies, 1997.
Beatty, David, and Brian Langille. "Bora Laskin and Labour Law: From
Vision to Legacy." *University of Toronto Law Journal* 35 (1985):
672–727.
Bernstein, Stephanie, Katherine Lippel, Eric Tucker, and Leah Vosko.
"Precarious Employment and the Law's Flaws: Identifying Regulatory
Failure and Securing Effective Protection for Workers." In *Precarious
Employment: Understanding Labour Market Insecurity in Canada,*
edited by Leah F. Vosko, 203–220. Montreal and Kingston: McGill-
Queen's University Press, 2006.
Blackstone, William. *Commentaries on the Laws of England.* 4 vols.
Oxford: Clarendon Press, 1765–69, reprinted as a facsimile of the first
edition, Chicago, University of Chicago Press, 1979.
Block, Sheila. *Ontario's Growing Gap: The Role of Race and Gender.*
Ottawa: Canadian Centre for Policy Alternatives, 2010.
Blue Books. See Ministry of National Revenue, Taxation Division.
*Statement of Principles and Rules Respecting Pension Plans for the
Purposes of the Income War Tax Act* ["*1946 Blue Book*"]; *Statement
of Principles and Rules Respecting Pension Plans for the Purposes of
the Income Tax Act* ["*1950 Blue Book*"].
Boyd, Susan B., ed. *Challenging the Public/Private Divide: Feminism,
Law, and Social Policy.* Toronto: University of Toronto Press, 1997.
Brandeis, Louis D. "Our New Peonage: Discretionary Pensions." *The
Independent* 73 (1912): 187–91.
Brandes, Stuart D. *American Welfare Capitalism: 1880–1940.* Chicago:
University of Chicago Press, 1970.
Brown, Donald J.M., and David M. Beatty. *Canadian Labour Arbitration,*
4th ed. Aurora, ON: Canada Law Book, 2006.
Bryden, Kenneth. *Old Age Pensions and Policy-Making in Canada.*
Montreal and Kingston: McGill-Queen's University Press, 1974.
Canadian Labour Congress. *The CLC Proposal for Pension Reform.*
Canadian Labour Congress, 1982.

Carmichael, Isla, and Jack Quarter. *Money on the Line: Workers' Capital in Canada*. Toronto: Canadian Centre for Policy Alternatives, 2003.

Casey, Bernard H., and Atsuhuro Yamada. "The Public-Private Mix of Retirement Income in Nine OECD Countries: Some Evidence from Micro Data and an Exploration of Its Implications." In *Rethinking the Welfare State: The Political Economy of Pension Reform*, edited by Martin Rein and Winfried Schmahl, 395–411. Cheltenham, UK: Edward Elgar, 2004.

Clark, Hart D. "The Development of the Retirement Income System in Canada." In Task Force on Retirement Income Policy (Harvey Lazar, Chairman). *The Retirement Income System in Canada: Problems and Alternative Policies for Reform*. Vol. 2., Appendix 1, 1-1–1-14. Ottawa: Ministry of Supply and Services, 1980.

Clark, Robert M. *Economic Security for the Aged in the United States and Canada: A Report Prepared for the Government of Canada*. Vol. 2. Ottawa: Queen's Printer, 1960.

– "The Pension Benefits Act of Ontario and Its Relation to the Federal Pension Proposals." In *Pensions in Canada: A Compendium of Fact and Opinion*, edited by Laurence E. Coward, 27–44. Don Mills: CCH Canadian Ltd, 1964.

Cloud, Arthur David. *Pensions in Modern Industry: The Legal, Actuarial, and Economic Principles of the Problems of the Aged*. Chicago: Hawkins and Loomis, 1929.

COFIRENTES+. See Comité d'étude sur le financement du régime de rentes et sur les régimes supplementaires des rentes. *La sécurité financière des personnnes âgées au Québec*.

Cohen, Morris. "The Basis of Contract." *Harvard Law Review* 56 (1933): 553–92.

Conant, Luther, Jr. *A Critical Analysis of Industrial Pension Plans*. New York: MacMillan, 1922.

Comment. "Consideration for the Employer's Promise of a Voluntary Pension Plan." *University of Chicago Law Review* 23 (1955–56): 96–110.

Coxe, Donald. "A Look at the Pension Iceberg." In *Pensions Today and Tomorrow: Background Studies*, edited by David W. Conklin, Jalynn H. Bennett, and Thomas J. Courchene, 439–44. Toronto: Ontario Economic Council, 1984.

D'Amours Report. See Quebec. Comité des experts sur l'avenir du système de retraite québécois. *Rapport: Innover pour pérenniser le système de retraite*.

Davis, Ronald B. "Security of Retirement Benefits in Canada: You Bet
Your Life?" *Canadian Labour and Employment Law Journal* 17 (2013):
65–100.

Dawson, Robert MacGregor. *The Civil Service of Canada*. London:
Oxford University Press, 1929.

Deakin, S. *The Contract of Employment: A Study in Legal Evolution*.
ESRC Centre for Business Research, University of Cambridge, Working
Paper No. 203, June 2001.

Deaton, Richard Lee. *The Political Economy of Pensions: Power, Politics,
and Social Change in Canada, Britain, and the United States*.
Vancouver: University of British Columbia Press, 1989.

Denton, Margaret, and Linda Boos. *Gender Inequality in the Wealth
of Older Canadians*. McMaster University Research Institute for
Quantitative Studies in Economics and Population, QSEP Research
Report No. 413, 2007.

Drouin, Renée-Claude, and Gilles Trudeau. "What Does *Isidore Garon*
Mean for Arbitral Jurisprudence in Quebec?" *Canadian Labour and
Employment Law Journal* 13 (2006–07): 347–73.

Duggan, Anthony. "Fiduciary Obligations in the Supreme Court of Canada:
A Retrospective." *Canadian Business Law Journal* 50 (2011): 453–73.

Dulude, Louise. *Pension Reform with Women in Mind*. Ottawa: Canadian
Advisory Council on the Status of Women, 1981.

Economic Council of Canada. *One in Three: Pensions for Canadians in
2030*. Economic Council of Canada, 1979.

Edwards, Adrian Charles. "Canadian Private Pension Plans: A Study of
their History, Trends, Taxation, and Investments." PhD dissertation,
Ohio State University, 1967.

Forrest, Anne. "Bargaining Units and Bargaining Power." *Relations
Industrielles/Industrial Relations* 41 (1986): 840–50.

Fortin, Nicole M., and Michael Huberman. "Occupational Segregation
and Women's Wages in Canada: An Historical Perspective." *Canadian
Public Policy* 28S (2002): S11–39.

Freeman, Richard B., and James L. Medoff. *What Do Unions Do?*
New York: Basic Books, 1984.

Frith Report. See Canada. House of Commons. *Report of the
Parliamentary Task Force on Pension Reform*.

Fryer, John L. "Provincial Public Sector Labour Relations." In *Public
Sector Collective Bargaining in Canada: Beginning of the End or End of
the Beginning*, edited by Gene Swimmer and Mark Thompson, 341–67.
Kingston, ON: Industrial Relations Centre, Queen's University, 1995.

Fudge, Judy. "The Gendered Dimension of Labour Law: Why Women
Need Inclusive Unionism and Broader-Based Bargaining." In *Women
Challenging Unions: Feminism, Democracy, and Militancy*, edited by
Linda Briskin and Pat McDermott, 231–48. Toronto: University of
Toronto Press, 1993.

Fudge, Judy, and Eric Tucker. *Labour Before the Law: The Regulation of
Workers' Collective Action in Canada, 1900–1948*. Don Mills: Oxford
University Press, 2001.

Ghilarducci, Teresa. *Labor's Capital: The Economics and Politics of
Private Pensions*. Cambridge, Mass: MIT Press, 1992.

– "Organized Labor and Pensions." In *The Oxford Handbook of Pensions
and Retirement Income*, edited by Gordon L. Clark, Alicia H. Munnell,
and J. Michael Orszag, 381–98. Oxford: Oxford University Press, 2006.

Gillese, Eileen E. "Contribution Holidays." *Estates and Trust Journal* 15
(1995–96): 136–68.

– "Pension Plans and the Law of Trusts." *Canadian Bar Review* 75
(1996): 221–50.

– "Two Decades after *Schmidt*: Where Has Pension Law Been and Where
Is It Going?" *Canadian Labour and Employment Law Journal* 19
(2005): 1–22.

Gillese, Eileen E., and Martha Milcynski. *The Law of Trusts*. 2d ed.
Toronto: Irwin Law, 2005.

Gomez, Raphael, and Morley Gunderson. "Non-standard and Vulnerable
Workers: A Case of Mistaken Identity." *Canadian Labour and
Employment Law Journal* (2005) 12: 177–203.

Gougeon, Philippe. "Shifting Pensions." *Perspectives on Labour and
Income* 10, no. 5 (2009): 16–23.

Graebner, W.A. *History of Retirement*. New Haven: Yale University Press,
1980.

Graham, Katherine A. "Collective Bargaining in the Municipal Sector." In
*Public Sector Collective Bargaining in Canada: Beginning of the End or
End of the Beginning*, edited by Gene Swimmer and Mark Thompson,
180–200. Kingston, ON: Industrial Relations Centre, Queen's
University, 1995.

Green Paper. See Canada. Department of Finance. *Better Pensions for
Canadians*.

Guest, Dennis. *The Emergence of Social Security in Canada*. 3d ed.
Vancouver: University of British Columbia Press, 1997.

Gunderson, Morley. *Incentive Effects of Occupational Pension Plans:
A Report Prepared for the Ontario Expert Commission on Pensions*.
Ontario Expert Commission on Pensions, October 2007.

Gunderson, Morley, and James Pesando. "Does Pension Wealth Peak at the Age of Early Retirement?" *Industrial Relations: A Journal of Economy and Society* 30 (1991): 79–95.

Haiven, Larry. "Industrial Relations in Health Care: Regulation, Conflict, and Transition to the 'Wellness Model.'" In *Public Sector Collective Bargaining in Canada: Beginning of the End or End of the Beginning*, edited by Gene Swimmer and Mark Thompson, 236–71. Kingston, ON: Industrial Relations Centre, Queen's University, 1995.

Hannah, Leslie. *Inventing Retirement: The Development of Occupational Pensions in Britain*. Cambridge: Cambridge University Press, 1986.

Hansen, Nancy, and Lorna Turnbull. "Disability and Care: Still Not 'Getting It.'" *Canadian Journal of Women and the Law* 23 (2013): 11.

Harbrecht, Paul P. *Pension Funds and Economic Power*. New York: Twentieth Century Fund, 1959.

Heap, Ruby, and Alison Prentice. "'The Outlook for Old Age Is Not Hopeful': The Struggle of Female Teachers over Pensions in Quebec, 1880–1914." *Social History/Histoire Sociale* 26:51 (1993): 67–94.

Hepple, B.A. "Intention to Create Legal Relations." *Cambridge Law Journal* 28 (1970): 122–37.

Horwitz, Morton. "The Historical Foundations of Modern Contract Law." *Harvard Law Review* 87 (1973–74): 917–56.

– "The History of the Public/Private Distinction." *University of Pennsylvania Law Review* 130 (1981–82): 1423–8.

Hunter, William Howard. *The Insurance Corporations Act, 1892: With Practical Notes and Appendices*. Toronto: Carswell, 1892; online: https://archive.org/details/cihm_10635.

Industrial Relations Section. School of Commerce and Administration. *Industrial Retirement Plans in Canada*. Bulletin No. 1 [*Queen's Study*]. Queen's University, Kingston, Ontario, 1938.

Institute of Local Government. *Canadian Municipal Pension Plans*. Kingston: Queen's University, 1946.

Ippolito, Richard. *Pension Plans and Employee Performance: Evidence, Analysis, and Policy*. Chicago: University of Chicago Press, 1997.

Isaacson, William J. "Employee Welfare and Pension Plans: Regulation and Protection of Employee Rights." *Columbia Law Review* 59 (1959): 96–124.

Jackson, E. Sydney. "Insurance Companies in the Pension Market." In *Pensions in Canada: A Compendium of Fact and Opinion*, edited by Laurence E. Coward, 145–54. Don Mills: CCH Canadian Ltd, 1964.

Jackson, Richard L. "Police and Firefighter Labour Relations in Canada." In *Public Sector Collective Bargaining in Canada: Beginning of the End* or *End of the Beginning*, edited by Gene Swimmer and Mark Thompson, 313–40. Kingston, ON: Industrial Relations Centre, Queen's University, 1995.

Jacoby, Sanford M. *Employing Bureaucracy: Managers, Unions, and the Transformation of Work in the 20th Century*. rev. ed. Mahwah, NJ: Lawrence Erlbaum Associations, 2004.

Jamieson, Ann. "*Legislative History of Major Public Sector Pension Plans*." In Royal Commission on the Status of Pensions in Ontario. *Report*. Vol. 7. 175–235. Government of Ontario, 1981.

Jensen, Vernon H. "Pensions and Retirement Plans as a Subject of Collective Bargaining." *Industrial and Labor Relations Review* 2:2 (1949): 227–36.

Joanette, Nelson Kim. "Worn Out: The Origins and Early Development of Pensions in Canada." PhD dissertation, University of Waterloo, 1993.

Johnson, Emory R. "Railway Departments for the Relief and Insurance of Employés [*sic*]." *Annals of the American Academy of Political and Social Science* 6 (Nov. 1895): 64.

Kaplan, Ari, and Mitch Frazer. *Pension Law*. 2d ed. Toronto: Irwin Law, 2013.

Kennedy, Duncan. "The Structure of Blackstone's Commentaries." *Buffalo Law Review* 28 (1978–79): 205–382.

Kesselman, Jonathan R. "Expanding Canada Pension Plan Retirement Benefits/Assessing Big CPP Proposals," University of Calgary School of Public Policy Research Papers, October 2010, online: http://www.policyschool.ucalgary.ca/sites/default/files/research/kesselman-cpp-online.pdf.

Kessler, Friedrich. "Contracts of Adhesion: Some Thoughts About Freedom of Contract." *Columbia Law Review* 43 (1943): 629–42.

Klare, Karl. "The Public/Private Distinction in Labor Law." *University of Pennsylvania Law Review* 130 (1981–82): 1358–422.

Klassen, Thomas R., and David Forgione. "Forced Retirement: Organized Labour's Predicament." In *Time's Up! Mandatory Retirement in Canada*, edited by C.T. Gillin, David McGregor, and Thomas R. Klassen, 74–89. Toronto: Lorimer, 2005.

Klein, Jennifer. *For All These Rights: Business, Labor, and the Shaping of American's Public-Private Welfare System*. Princeton: Princeton University Press, 2003.

Kodar, Freya. "Pensions and Unpaid Work: A Reflection on Four Decades of Feminist Debate." *Canadian Journal of Women and the Law* 24:1 (2012): 180–206.

Labour Gazette. See Government Documents. Department of Labour.
Labour Gazette.

LaMarsh, Judy. *Memoirs of a Bird in a Gilded Cage.* Toronto: McClelland and Stewart, 1968.

Langbein, John H. "The Contractarian Basis of the Law of Trusts." *Yale Law Review* 105 (1995–96): 625–75.

Langille, Brian. "Equal Partnership in Canadian Labour Law." *Osgoode Hall Law Journal* 21 (1983): 496–536.

Langille, Brian, and Patrick Macklem. "Beyond Belief: Labour Law's Duty to Bargain." *Queen's Law Journal* 13 (1988): 62–102.

LaRochelle-Côté, Sébastien, John F. Myles, and Garnett Picott. *Income Security During Retirement.* Ontario Expert Commission on Pensions, 2007.

Latimer, Murray Webb. *Industrial Pension Systems in the United States and Canada.* 2 Vols. New York: Industrial Relations Counselors, Incorporated, 1932.

– *Trade Union Pension Systems and Other Superannuation and Permanent and Total Disability Benefits in the United States and Canada.* New York: Industrial Relations Counselors, 1932.

Latimer, William. "Pension Plans and Income Tax." In *Pensions in Canada: A Compendium of Fact and Opinion,* edited by Laurence E. Coward, 103–13. Don Mills: CCH Canadian Ltd, 1964.

Lazar Report. See Task Force on Retirement Income Policy. *The Retirement Income System in Canada.*

Leech, Jim, and Jacquie McNish, *The Third Rail: Saving Canada's Pension System.* Toronto: Signal/McClelland and Stewart, 2013.

Lauritzen, Christian Marius III. "Perpetuities and Pension Trusts." *Taxes* 24 (1946): 519–32.

Li, Jinyan. *Impact of Tax Policy on Coverage and Funding of Occupational Pension Plans.* Ontario Expert Commission on Pensions, 2007.

– *Tax Expenditure Analysis of Employer-Sponsored Registered Pension Plans.* Ontario Expert Commission on Pensions, 2007.

Lipsett, Brenda, and Mark Reesor. *Employer-Sponsored Pension Plans: Who Benefits?* Human Resources Development Canada, W-97-2E, December 1997.

Litner, Paul, and Jonathan Marin. "Private-Sector Pension Plans: Have Recent Pension Reforms Addressed the Needs of Plan Sponsors?" *Canadian Labour and Employment Law Journal* 17 (2013): 143–80.

Little, Bruce. *Fixing the Future: How Canada's Usually Fractious Governments Worked Together to Rescue the Canada Pension Plan.* Toronto: University of Toronto Press, 2008.

Luchak, Andrew, T. Fang, and Morley Gunderson. "How Has Public Policy Shaped Defined-Benefit Pension Coverage?" *Journal of Labor Research* 25 (2004): 469–84.

MacKinnon, Mary. "'Providing for Faithful Servants': Pensions at the Canadian Pacific Railway." *Social Science History* 21, no. 1 (1977): 59–83.

Mainville, Dianne, and Carey Olineck. "Unionization in Canada: A Retrospective." *Perspectives on Labour and Income*, Summer 1999: S1–35.

Marier, Patrik, and Suzanne Skinner. "The Impact of Gender and Immigration on Pension Outcomes in Canada." *Canadian Public Policy* 34 (2008): S59–78. (Special Supplement: *Private Pensions and Income Security in Old Age: An Uncertain Future.*)

McBride, W. Leonard. "The Growth and Coverage of Insured and Trusteed Pension Plans in Canada." In *Pensions in Canada: A Compendium of Fact and Opinion*, edited by Laurence E. Coward, 137–44. Don Mills: CCH Canadian Ltd, 1964.

McCallum, Margaret E. "Corporate Welfarism in Canada, 1919–1939." *Canadian Historical Review* 71 (1990): 46–79.

McCamus, John D. "Abuse of Discretion, Failure to Cooperate and Evasion of Duty: Unpacking the Common Law Duty of Good Faith Contractual Performance." *Advocates Quarterly* 29 (2004–05): 72–101.

McCarthy, David. "Occupational Pension Scheme Design." In *The Oxford Handbook of Pensions and Retirement Income*, edited by Gordon L. Clark, Alicia H. Munnell, and J. Michael Orszag, 543–661. Oxford: Oxford University Press, 2006.

McNay, Diane. "The Teachers of British Columbia and Superannuation." *BC Studies* 2 (Summer 1969): 30–44.

McPhillips, D.C. "The Appropriate Bargaining Unit: The Need for Policy Consistency by Canadian Labour Boards." *Relations Industrielles / Industrial Relations* 43 (1988): 63–84.

Milling, Gordon. "Labour's Interest in Pension Planning." In *Pensions in Canada: A Compendium of Fact and Opinion*, edited by Laurence E. Coward, 185–92. Don Mills: CCH Canadian Ltd, 1964.

Morissette, René. "Pensions: Immigrants and Visible Minorities." *Perspectives on Labour and Income* 3, no. 6 (June 2002): 13–18.

Morissette, René, Grant Schellenberg, and Anick Johnson. "Diverging Trends in Unionization." *Perspectives on Labour and Income* 6 (April 2005): 5–12.

Morissette, René, Grant Schellenberg, Anick Johnson, and Xuelin Zhang. "Revisiting Wealth Inequality." *Perspectives on Labour and Income.* (December 2000): 5–16.

Morton, Desmond, and Margaret E. McCallum. "Superannuation to Indexation: Workplace Pensions in the Public and Private Sector in Canada, 1870–1970." In *Task Force on Inflation Protection for Workplace Pension Plans, Research Studies*, Vol. 1, 1–35. Toronto: Queen's Printer, 1988.

Mummé, Claire. "'That Indispensable Figment of the Legal Mind': The Contract of Workplace at Common Law in Ontario, 1890–1979." PhD dissertation, York University, 2013.

Munnell, Alicia H. *The Economics of Private Pensions*. Washington, DC: The Brookings Institute, 1982.

– "Employer-Sponsored Plans: The Shift from Defined Benefit to Defined Contribution." In *The Oxford Handbook of Pensions and Retirement Income*, edited by Gordon L. Clark, Alicia H. Munnell, and J. Michael Orszag, 359–80. Oxford: Oxford University Press, 2006.

Munnell, Alicia H., and Steven A. Sass. *New Brunswick's New Shared Risk Pension Plan*. State and Local Pensions Plans Issues in Brief, No. 33, Centre for Retirement Research, Boston College, August 2013.

Murphy, Barbara. "Corporate Capital and the Welfare State: Canadian Business and Public Pension Policy in Canada Since World War II." MA dissertation, Carleton University, 1982.

Myles, John. *Old Age in the Welfare State: The Political Economy of Pensions*. rev. ed. Lawrence, Kansas: University of Kansas Press, 1989.

Myles, John, and Les Teichroew. "The Politics of Dualism: Pension Policy in Canada." In *States, Labor Markets, and the Future of Old-Age Policy*, edited by John Myles and Jill Quadagno, 84–104. Philadelphia: Temple University Press, 1991.

Nachshen, Gary. "Access to Pension Fund Surpluses: The Great Debate." In *New Developments in Workplace Law*, Meredith Memorial Lectures, Faculty of Law, McGill University, 60–86. Yvon Blais: Cowansville, 1988.

National Industrial Conference Board, Inc., *Industrial Pensions in the United States*. New York, 1925.

Nobles, Richard. *Pensions, Workplace, and the Law*. Oxford: Clarendon Press, 1993.

Note. "Legal Problems of Private Pension Plans." *Harvard Law Review* 70 (1957): 491–509.

O'Byrne, Shannon Kathleen. "Good Faith in Contractual Performance: Recent Developments." *Canadian Bar Review* 4 (1995): 70–96.

OECD. *Maintaining Prosperity in an Aging Society*. Paris: OECD, 1998.

– *Reforms for an Aging Society*. Paris: OECD, 2000.

– *Pensions at a Glance: Retirement-Income Systems in* OECD *Countries.*
   Paris: OECD, 2009.
– *Pensions at a Glance, 2013:* OECD *and G20 Indicators.* Paris: OECD,
   2013.
O'Neal, F. Hodge. "Stockholder Attacks on Corporate Pension Systems."
   Vanderbilt Law Review 2 (1949): 351–78.
O'Neill, Hugh. *Modern Pension Plans, Principles and Practices.* New York:
   Prentice Hall, 1947.
Orloff, Ann Shola. *The Politics of Pensions: A Comparative Analysis of
   Britain, Canada, and the United States: 1880–1940.* Madison:
   University of Wisconsin Press, 1993.
Peitchinis, Stephen G. *Labour-Management Relations in the Railway
   Industry.* Task Force on Labour Relations, Study No. 20. Ottawa: Privy
   Council, 1971.
Pierson, Paul. "The Politics of Pension Reform." In *Reform of Retirement
   Income Policy: International and Canadian Perspectives,* edited by Keith
   G. Banting and Robin Boadway, 273–93. Kingston, ON: Queen's
   University School of Policy Studies, 1997.
Pilkey, Cliff. "Public vs. Private Pensions." In *Pensions Today and
   Tomorrow: Background Studies,* edited by David W. Conklin, Jalynn H.
   Bennett, and Thomas J. Courchene, 432–8. Toronto: Ontario Economic
   Council, 1984.
Pozzebon, Silvana. "The Outlook for Canada's Public Sector Employee
   Pensions." In *The Future of Public Employee Retirement Systems,* edited
   by Olivia S. Mitchell and Gary Anderson, 143–63. Oxford: Oxford
   University Press, 2009.
Quadagno, Jill. *The Transformation of Old Age Security: Class and
   Politics in the American Welfare State.* Chicago: University of Chicago
   Press, 1988.
Queen's Study. See Industrial Relations Section. School of Commerce and
   Administration, *Industrial Retirement Plans in Canada.*
Ransom, Roger L., Richard Sutch, and Samuel H. Williamson. "Inventing
   Pensions: The Origins of the Company-Provided Pension in the United
   States, 1900–1940." In *Societal Impact of Aging: Historical Perspectives,*
   edited by Warner K. Schaie and W. Andrew Achenbaum, 1–38. New
   York: Springer, 1993.
Raphael, Marios. *Pensions and Public Servants: A Study of the Origins of
   the British System.* Paris: Mouton and Co., 1964.
Riddell, Chris, and W. Craig Riddell. "Changing Patterns in Unionisa-
   tion: The North American Experience, 1984–1998." In *Unions in the*

21st Century: An International Perspective, edited by Anil Verma and Thomas A. Kochan, 146–64. New York: Palgrave Macmillan, 2004.

Riebenack, M. *Railway Provident Institutions in English-Speaking Countries*. Philadelphia: Pennsylvania Railway Company, 1905.

Risk, R.C.B. "'This Nuisance of Litigation': The Origins of Workers' Compensation in Ontario." In *Essays in the History of Canadian Law*, edited by David H. Flaherty, 418–92. Vol. 2. Toronto: Osgoode Society, 1983.

Rittich, Kerry. "Feminization and Contingency: Regulating the Stakes of Work for Women." In *Labour Law in an Era of Globalization: Transformative Practices and Possibilities*, edited by Joanne Conaghan, Richard Michael Fischl, and Karl Klare, 117–36. Oxford: Oxford University Press, 2002.

Robarts, John. "The Ontario Approach to Pensions." In *Pensions in Canada: A Compendium of Fact and Opinion*, edited by Laurence E. Coward, 1–5. Don Mills: CCH Canadian Ltd, 1964.

Rose, Joseph. "The Evolution of Teacher Bargaining in Ontario." In *Dynamic Negotiations: Teacher Labour Relations in Canadian Elementary and Secondary Education*, edited by Sara Slinn and Arthur Sweetman, 199–220. Montreal and Kingston: McGill-Queen's University Press, 2012.

Ross, Arthur M. "Do We Have a New Industrial Feudalism?" *The American Economic Review* 48, no. 5 (1958): 903–20.

Rotman, Leonard L. *Fiduciary Law*. Thomson Carswell, 2005.

Sadakova, Yaldaz. "2014 Top 100 Pension Funds Report." *Benefits Canada* (June 2014): 15–23.

Sarra, Janis. *Rescue! The Companies' Creditors Arrangement Act*. Toronto: Thomson Carswell, 2007.

Sass, Steven. *The Promise of Private Pensions: The First Hundred Years*. Cambridge: Harvard University Press, 1997.

– "Pension Bargains: The Heyday of US Collectively Bargained Pension Arrangements." In *Workers versus Pensioners: Intergenerational Justice in an Ageing World*, edited by Paul Johnson, Christoph Conrad, and David Thomson, 92–112. Manchester and New York: Manchester University Press, 1989.

Seargeant, L.J. "Superannuation of Railway Employés [*sic*]." In *Addresses Delivered before the World's Railway Commerce Congress, Held in Chicago, Ill., June 19–23, 1893*. Chicago: The Railway Age and Northwestern Railroader, 1893.

Shillington, Richard. *Occupational Pension Plan Coverage in Ontario: Statistical Report.* Ontario Expert Commission on Pensions, 2007.

Shilton, Elizabeth. "Employee Pension Rights and the False Promise of Trust Law." *Dalhousie Law Journal* 34 (2011): 82–114.

– "Collective Bargaining for Teachers in Ontario: Central Power, Local Responsibility." In *Dynamic Negotiations: Teacher Labour Relations in Canadian Elementary and Secondary Education,* edited by Sara Slinn and Arthur Sweetman, 221–46. Montreal and Kingston: McGill-Queen's University Press, 2012.

– "Insuring Inequality: Sex-Based Mortality Tables and Women's Retirement Income." *Queen's Law Journal* 37 (2012): 383–435.

– "Gender Risk and Employment Pension Plans in Canada." *Canadian Labour and Employment Law Journal* 17 (2013): 101–41.

– "Enforcing Workplace Pension Rights for Unionized Employees: Is There a 'Weber Gap'?" *Canadian Labour and Employment Law Journal* 19 (2015): 136–69.

Simeon, Richard. *Federal Provincial Diplomacy: The Making of Recent Policy in Canada.* Toronto: University of Toronto Press, 1972.

Skocpol, Theda. *Protecting Mothers and Soldiers: The Political Origins of Social Policy in the United States.* Cambridge: Harvard University Press, 1992.

Slichter, Sumner H., James J. Healy, and E. Robert Livernash. *The Impact of Collective Bargaining on Management.* Washington: The Brookings Institution, 1960.

Slinn, Sara, and Karen Schucher. "Cross-Currents: Comparative Review of Elementary and Secondary Teachers Collective Bargaining Structures in Canada." In *Dynamic Negotiations: Teacher Labour Relations in Canadian Elementary and Secondary Education,* edited by Sara Slinn and Arthur Sweetman, 13–47. Montreal and Kingston: McGill-Queen's University Press, 2012.

Snell, James. *The Citizens' Wage: The State and the Elderly in Canada, 1900–1951.* Toronto: University of Toronto Press, 1996.

Somers, A. Norman, and Louis Schwartz. "Pension and Welfare Plans: Gratuities or Compensation?" *Industrial and Labor Relations Review* 4:1 (1950): 77–88.

Stevens, Beth. *Complementing the Welfare State: The Development of Private Pensions, Health Insurance and Other Employee Benefits in the United States.* Geneva: International Labour Organization, 1986.

Stone, Katherine V.W. "The Post-War Paradigm in American Labor Law." *Yale Law Journal* 90 (1981): 1509–80.

- *From Widgets to Digits: Employment Regulation for the Changing Workplace*. Cambridge: Cambridge University Press, 2004.
- "Rethinking Labour Law: Employment Protection for Boundaryless Workers." In *Boundaries and Frontiers of Labour Law: Goals and Means in the Regulation of Work*, edited by Guy Davidov and Brian Langille, 115–80. Oxford: Hart Publishing, 2006.

Stone, Katherine V.W., and Harry Arthurs. "The Transformation of Employment Regimes: A Worldwide Challenge." In *Rethinking Workplace Regulation: Beyond the Standard Contract of Employment*, edited by Katherine V.W. Stone and Harry Arthurs, 1–20. New York: Russell Sage Foundation, 2013.

Supiot, Alain. *Beyond Employment: Changes in Work and the Future of Labour Law in Europe*. Oxford: Oxford University Press, 2001.

Swan, Angela. *Canadian Contract Law*. 2d ed. LexisNexis, 2009.

Swimmer, Gene. "Collective Bargaining in the Federal Public Service of Canada: The Last Twenty Years." In *Public Sector Collective Bargaining in Canada: Beginning of the End or End of the Beginning*, edited by Gene Swimmer and Mark Thompson, 368–407. Kingston: Industrial Relations Centre, Queen's University, 1995.

Tamagno, Edward. *Occupational Pension Plans in Canada: Trends in Coverage and the Incomes of Seniors*, Caledon Institute of Social Policy, December 2006.

Townson, Monica. "The Impact of Precarious Employment on Financial Security in Retirement." In *New Frontiers in Research on Retirement*, edited by Leroy O. Stone, 345–82. Ottawa: Statistics Canada, 2006.
- *Women's Poverty and the Recession*. Ottawa: Canadian Centre for Policy Alternatives, 2009.

Tudiver, Neil. "Forestalling the Welfare State: The Establishment of Programmes of Corporate Welfare." In *The Benevolent State: The Growth of Welfare in Canada*, edited by Allan Moscovitch and Jim Albert, 186–202. Toronto: Garamond Press, 1987.

Vandenvelde, Kenneth. "The New Property of the Nineteenth Century: The Development of the Modern Concept of Property." *Buffalo Law Review* 29 (1980): 325–67.

Van der Heiden-Aantjes, Leny H. "The Quality of the Dutch Pension System: Will It Be Sustainable in the Twenty-First Century?" In *Rethinking the Welfare State: The Political Economy of Pension Reform*, edited by Martin Rein and Winfried Schmahl, 122–49. Cheltenham, UK: Edward Elgar, 2004.

Van Riel, Bart, Anton Hemerijck, and Jelle Visser. "Is There a Dutch Way to Pension Reform." In *Pension Security in the 21st Century: Redrawing the Public-Private Debate*, edited by G.L. Clark and Noel Whiteside, 64–92. Oxford: Oxford University Press, 2003.

Vosko, Leah. "Precarious Employment: Towards an Improved Understanding of Labour Market Insecurity." In *Precarious Employment: Understanding Labour Market Insecurity in Canada*, edited by Leah F. Vosko, 3–39. Montreal and Kingston: McGill-Queen's University Press, 2006.

Waddams, S.M. *The Law of Contracts*. 5th ed. Toronto: Canada Law Book, 2005.

Waters, Donovan W.M., Mark Gillen, and Lionel Smith, eds. *Waters' Law of Trusts in Canada*. 4th ed. Toronto: Carswell, 2012.

Watt, Gary. *Trusts and Equity*. 3rd ed. Oxford: Oxford University Press, 2008.

Weiler, Paul. *Reconcilable Differences*. Toronto: Carswell, 1980.

Weiss, David S., and Stephen R. Bedard. *Contextual Negotiations*. Queen's University: Industrial Relations Press, 2000.

White Paper. See Department of Finance, *Action Plan for Pension Reform: Building Better Pensions for Canadians*.

Woodman, Faye. "The Fiscal Equality of Women: Proposed Changes to Legislation Governing Private Pension Plans in Alberta, British Columbia, Ontario, and Nova Scotia." *Canadian Journal of Women and the Law* 22 (2010): 129.

Young, Claire. "Pensions, Privatization, and Poverty: The Gendered Impact." *Canadian Journal of Women and the Law* 23 (2011): 661.

World Bank. *Averting the Old Age Crisis: Policies to Protect the Old and Promote Growth*. Oxford University Press, 1994.

GOVERNMENT DOCUMENTS

British Columbia and Alberta. Joint Expert Panel on Pension Standards. *Getting Our Acts Together: Pension Reform in Alberta and British Columbia*. Report of the Joint Expert Panel on Pension Standards, November 2008.

British Columbia. Auditor General. *A Review of Government Oversight of Multi-Employer Public Sector Pension Plans in British Columbia*. 2002/2003, Report No. 9.

Canada.

    Department of Finance. *Action Plan for Pension Reform: Building Better Pensions for Canadians*. Ottawa: Minister of Supply and Services, 1984 ["*White Paper*"].

Department of Finance. *Better Pensions for Canadians.* Ottawa:
  Minister of Supply and Services, 1982 ["*Green Paper*"].
Department of Labour. *Labour Gazette.*
"Employees' Provident Societies." *Labour Gazette* 2 (1901): 315–16.
"Railway Employees and Provident Societies." *Labour Gazette*
  2 (1901): 365–6.
"Railway Employees and Provident Societies." *Labour Gazette*
  3 (1902): 482–3.
"The Superannuation and Pension Fund of the Canadian Pacific
  Railway Company." *Labour Gazette* 3 (1903): 552–4.
"Grand Trunk Railway Provident Society Case." *Labour Gazette*
  3 (1903): 713.
"Provident Society Regulation." *Labour Gazette* 4 (1904): 824–5.
"Right of Action Against a Railway Company for Damages for Death
  of Employee." *Labour Gazette* 6 (1906): 1054–6.
"Right of Railway Companies to Contract Themselves Out of
  Liability for Injuries Sustained by Employees." *Labour Gazette*
  7 (1906): 694–5.
"Pension Department of the Grand Trunk Railway Company of
  Canada." *Labour Gazette* 8 (1908): 995–6.
"Pension and Benefit Plan of the Bell Telephone Company." *Labour
  Gazette* 17 (1917): 314–15.
"Employees Superannuation in Canada: Existing Public and Private
  Schemes for Retirement Insurance." *Labour Gazette* 24 (1924):
  127–34.
"Employees Superannuation in Canada: Provision for Retirement of
  Municipal Employees." *Labour Gazette* 24 (1924): 390–5.
"The Problem of Old Age Pensions in Industry: Results of Study by
  Pennsylvania Old Age Pension Commission." *Labour Gazette* 27
  (1927): 1051–2.
"Benefits of Teacher Superannuation Schemes." *Labour Gazette* 29
  (1929): 121.
"Wartime Wage Control in Canada." *Labour Gazette* 42 (1942): 282–3.
"Decisions of the National War Labour Board." *Labour Gazette* 44
  (1944): 38–44, 466–76.
"Pension and Welfare Plans in Canadian Industry." *Labour Gazette*
  49 (1949): 694–700.
"The Report of the Conciliation Board appointed in connection with
  the UAW-Ford negotiations." *Labour Gazette* 50 (1950): 454–9.
"Types of Pension and Retirement Plans in Canadian Industry."
  Labour Gazette 50 (1950): 191–2.

"Pension Plans in Canadian Industry." *Labour Gazette* 50 (1950): 443–53.

"Contribution, Benefit Formulas in Canadian Industrial Pension Plans." *Labour Gazette* 54 (1954): 519–25 ["Contribution, Benefit Formulas"].

"Types of Retirement Policy in Canadian Industrial Pension Plans." *Labour Gazette* 54 (1954): 1238–3 ["Types of Retirement Policy"].

"Vesting Provisions in Canadian Industrial Pension Plans." *Labour Gazette* 55 (1955): 30–7 ["Vesting Provisions"].

"Number of Workers Covered by Pension Plans in Canada." *Labour Gazette* 55 (1955): 784–7.

"Second Constitutional Convention of the Canadian Labour Congress." *Labour Gazette* 58 (1958): 586–607.

Department of National Health and Welfare. *The Canada Pension Plan.* Ottawa: Department National Health and Welfare, August 1964.

Department of Revenue. *Information Bulletin No. 14.* Department of Revenue, 1959.

Dominion Bureau of Statistics. *Pension Plans: Non-financial Statistics, 1960.* Ottawa, 1962.

Dominion Bureau of Statistics, *Survey of Industrial Pension Welfare Plans, 1947.* Ottawa, 1949.

Dominion Bureau of Statistics. *Survey of Pension Plan Coverage, 1965.* Ottawa: Queen's Printer, 1967 ["*1965 Survey*"].

House of Commons. *Debates*, 1st Parl., 3rd Sess. (16 April 1870).

House of Commons. Standing Committee on the Status of Women. *Pension Security for Women*, December 2009 (Hon. Hedy Fry, Chair).

House of Commons. *Report of the Parliamentary Task Force on Pension Reform.* Ottawa, 1982 ["*Frith Report*"].

Ministry of National Revenue, Taxation Division. *Statement of Principles and Rules Respecting Pension Plans for the Purposes of the Income War Tax Act: Tax Ruling No. 2 (1946–47).* Library and Archives Canada, AMICUS No. 9668351 ["*1946 Blue Book*"].

Ministry of National Revenue, Taxation Division. *Statement of Principles and Rules Respecting Pension Plans for the Purposes of the Income Tax Act* [1950]. Library and Archives Canada, AMICUS No. 566459 ["*1950 Blue Book*"].

Research Working Group on Retirement Income Adequacy of Federal–Provincial–Territorial Ministers of Finance. *Summary Report on*

Retirement Income Adequacy Research (Jack Mintz), 18 December
  2009, online: https://www.fin.gc.ca/activty/pubs/pension/pdf/
  riar-narr-BD-eng.pdf.
Canada Revenue Agency. Information Circular No. 72 – 3R7
  (31 December 1981) [now Information Circular No. 72-13R8
  (16 December 1988)].
Special Joint Committee of the Senate and of the House of Commons
  Appointed to consider and report on Bill C – 136. *An Act to establish
  a comprehensive program of old age pensions and supplementary
  benefits in Canada payable to and in respect of contributors* [i.e., the
  Canada Pension Plan], *Minutes of Proceedings and Evidence*, 26th
  Parl, 2nd Sess (1964–65) 2 Vols. Ottawa: Queen's Printer, 1965.
  [Special Joint Committee, *Minutes*].
Special Senate Committee on Retirement Age Policies. *Retirement
  Without Tears*. Ottawa: Supply and Services, 1979.
Statistics Canada.
  Definitions, Data Sources and Methods online: http://www23.
    statcan.gc.ca/imdb- bmdi/document/2609_D3_T9_V1-eng.htm
    (accessed 8 September 2015).
  "Pension Plans in Canada, as of January 1, 2012," *The Daily*,
    19 December 2013.
  "Registered Pension Plan (RPP) Members, by Area of Workplace,
    Sector, Type of Plan, and Contributory Status, 2009–2013."
    CANSIM (database) Table 280–0008.
  "Percentage of Labour Force and Employees Covered by a
    Registered Pension Plan (RPP)," online: http://www.statcan.gc.ca/
    tables-tableaux/sum-som/l01/cst01/labor26a-eng.htm (accessed
    8 September 2015).
  "Union Membership in Canada, 1911–1975." In *Historical Statistics
    of Canada*, Catalogue No. 11- 516 x, Section E: Wages and
    Working Conditions, Series 175 – 7, online: http://www.statcan.
    gc.ca/pub/
    11-516-x/11-516-x1983001-eng.htm.
  "Registered pension plans (RPPs), members and market value of
    assets, by type of plan, sector and contributory status, annual."
    CANSIM (database), Table 280–0016.
  "Labour force survey estimates (LFS), employment by class of
    worker, North American Industry Classification System (NAICS)
    and sex, annual (persons)." CANSIM (database), Table 282-0012.

Task Force on Retirement Income Policy. *The Retirement Income System in Canada: Problems and Alternative Policies for Reform.* Ottawa: Ministry of Supply and Services, 1980 *[Lazar Report].*
"Contribution, Benefit Formulas." See Canada. Department of Labour. *Labour Gazette.*
Nova Scotia. Pension Review Panel. *Promises to Keep.* Government of Nova Scotia, 27 January 2009.
Ontario.
  2016 Budget: Jobs for Today and Tomorrow, online: http://www.fin.gov.on.ca/en/budget/ontariobudgets/2016/ch1f.html.
  Committee on Portable Pensions. *Second Report.* Toronto: Queen's Printer, Aug. 1961.
  – *Summary Report.* Ontario, 1961.
  Expert Commission on Pensions. *A Fine Balance: Safe Pensions, Affordable Plans, Fair Rules.* Queen's Printer for Ontario, 2000 [*"Arthurs Report"*], online: http://www.fin.gov.on.ca/en/consultations/pension/report/Pensions_Report_Eng_web.pdf.
  Journals of the Legislative Assembly of the Province of Ontario. 14th Leg, 3rd Sess, Vol. 51 (12 April 1917).
  Legislative Assembly. *Official Report of Debates (Hansard).* 26 Parl, 2nd Sess, No. 79 (28 April 1964).
  Legislative Assembly. *Official Report of Debates (Hansard).* 26th Parl, 3rd Sess, No. 104 (21 May 1965).
  Legislative Assembly. Select Committee on Pensions. *Final Report.* In 32nd Parl, 2nd Sess, 31 Elizabeth II. Toronto: Ontario Legislative Assembly, 1982.
  Ministry of Finance. *Facilitating Pooled Asset Management for Ontario's Public-Sector Institutions: Report from the Pension Investment Advisor to the Deputy Premier and Minister of Finance* (William Morneau). October 2012, online: http://www.fin.gov.on.ca/en/consultations/pension/recommendations-report.pdf.
  Public Sector Pension Consultation. *The Pension Benefits Act, 1987: Implications for the Public Sector Pensions Consultations* (David W. Conklin). Report No. 5, Public Sector Pension Consultations, 1987.
  Public Sector Pension Consultations. *A Fresh Start: Report to the Treasurer of Ontario, the Chairman of Management Board of Cabinet and the Minister of Education on Teachers' and Public Servants' Pensions* (David W. Slater). Government of Ontario, 1988.
  Report to the Treasurer of Ontario on the Financing of Benefits under the Superannuation Adjustment Benefits Act and Associated

Superannuation Plans (Lawrence E. Coward). Government of
Ontario, 1987.
Task Force on Inflation Protection for Workplace Pension Plans.
Research Studies. Vol. I. Toronto: Queen's Printer, 1988.
Task Force on the Investment of Public Sector Pension Funds. *In Whose
Interest?* (Malcolm Rowan). Government of Ontario, 1987.
Quebec.
    Comité des experts sur l'avenir du système de retraite québécois.
    Rapport – Innover pour pérenniser le système de retraite.
    Bibliothèque et Archives Nationales du Québec, 2013 [*"D'Amours
    Report"*].
    Comité d'étude sur le financement du régime de rentes et sur les régimes
    supplementaires des rentes. *La sécurité financière des personnnes
    âgées au Québec.* Québec: Editeur officiel, 1977 [*"COFIRENTES
    +"*].
Royal Commission on the Status of Pensions in Ontario. *Report.* 9 Vols.
Toronto: Government of Ontario, 1981. [Royal Commission, *Report*].
Saskatchewan. Law Reform Commission of Saskatchewan. *The Rule
in Saunders v Vautier and the Variation of Trusts.* June 1994.
(Consultation on the Law of Trusts #1), online: http://
lawreformcommission.sk.ca/Saunders_v_Vautier_and_Variation_of_
Trusts_Consultation.pdf.
Steering Committee of Provincial/Territorial Ministers on Pension
Coverage and Retirement Income Adequacy. *Options for Increasing
Pension Coverage Among Private Sector Workers in Canada.* January
2010, online: http://www.fin.gov.bc.ca/pension_plan_options_paper.pdf.

Cases Cited

Alberta v Elder Advocates of Alberta Society, [2011] 2 SCR 261, 2011 SCC 24.

Alberta Teachers Assn v Calgary School District No. 19 (Board of Trustees), [2006] AJ No. 1315 (QB).

Armstrong v Toronto Police Benefit Fund, [1902] OJ No. 669, 1 OWR 829 (CA).

Askin v Ontario Hospital Association (1991), 2 OR (3d) 641 (CA).

Association provincial des retraités d'Hydro-Québec v Hydro-Québec, [2005] QJ No. 1644 (CA) [leave to appeal refused, [2005] CSCR No. 215].

Atlas Copco Exploration Products v International Assn of Machinists and Aerospace Workers, Local 2412 (Pension Plan Grievance), [2008] OLAA No. 672 (R. Brown).

Baker v Navistar, [2013] OJ No. 2974.

Balderson v The Queen (1898) 28 SCR 261, 25 Hals. 89 (per Taschereau J.), aff'ing (1897) 6 Ex. CR 8.

Bardal v Globe and Mail, [1960] OJ No. 149.

Bathgate v National Hockey League Pension Society (1992), 11 OR (3d) 449 (Gen Div), aff'd [1994] OJ No. 265 (CA); leave to appeal refused, [1994] SCCA No. 170.

Baxter v Abbey, [1986] BCJ No. 1214 (CA).

Beachville Lime Ltd v Communications, Energy, and Paper Workers Union, Local 3264 (Wenzel Grievance), [2002] OLAA No. 512 (Williamson).

Bell Canada v Communications, Energy and Paperworkers Union of Canada, Local 27 (Chawda Grievance) (Burkett), [2010] CLAD No. 70, aff'd [2010] OJ No. 2681, 2011 ONSC 2517 *(sub nom Communications, Energy and Paperworkers Union of Canada, Local 27 v Bell Canada)*.

*Bell Canada v Office and Professional Employees' International Union,
   Local 131*, [1974] SCR 335.
Bell c Sobeys Inc., [2006] JQ No. 7738 (CS), aff'd [2008] JQ No. 1390
   (CA) *sub nom Bell c Régime de retraite pour les employées et employés
   de Sobeys Inc.*, leave to appeal refused, [2008] SCCA No. 175.
Bennett v British Columbia, [2007] BCJ No. 4 (CA), leave to appeal
   refused 21 June 2007, unreported.
Bhasin v Hrynew, 2014 SCC 71.
Bisaillon v Concordia University, [2006] 1 SCR 666.
Bohemier v Centra Gas Manitoba (1999), 170 DLR (4th) 310 (Man CA).
Bradley v Saskatchewan Wheat Pool, [1984] SJ No. 234 (QB).
*British Columbia Hydro and Power Authority et al. v British Columbia
   Labour Relations Board*, [1978] 1 SCR 1015.
Burke v Hudson's Bay Co. 2005 CANLII 47086 (ON SC) [*Burke ONSC*],
   2008 ONCA 394 (CA) [*Burke CA*], aff'd 2010 SCR 34.
Buschau v Rogers Cablesystems Ltd, 2004 BCCA 80 [*Buschau No. 2*] and
   2004 BCCA 282 [*Buschau No. 3*], aff'd [2006] 1 SCR 973 [*Buschau SCC*].
Buschau v Rogers Cablesystems Ltd, [2001] BCJ No. 50 (CA) [*Buschau
   No. 1*].
*Buschau v Canada (Attorney General) (appeal by Rogers Communications
   Inc.)* [2009] FCJ No. 1119 (CA) [*Buschau No. 4*], leave to appeal
   refused, [2009] SCCA No. 457.
Calgary (City) v International Assn of Fire Fighters (Local 255), 2012
   ABQB 90.
*Canadian Assn of Industrial, Mechanical and Allied Workers, Local 14
   v Paccar of Canada Ltd* [1989] 2 SCR 983.
*Canadian Car and Foundry Company Limited v Dinham and
   Brotherhood of Railway Carmen of America*, [1960] SCR 3.
*Canadian Union of Public Employees-C.L.C., Ontario Hydro Employees
   Union, Local 1000 and Ontario Hydro (1989)*, 68 OR (2d) 620 (CA),
   leave to appeal refused, [1989] SCCA No. 287.
*Canadian Union of Public Employees (CUPE) v Ontario Hospital
   Association* (Pension Commission of Ontario, 26 June 1991, unre-
   ported), aff'd (1992) 91 DLR (4th) 436 (Ont Div Ct).
Carlill v Carbolic Smoke Ball Co., [1892] 2 QB 484.
*CAW-Canada Local 2007 v Superintendent of Financial Services and
   Woodbine Entertainment Group*, 2010 ONFST 1, aff'd Div Ct,
   unreported 11 March 2011.
Châteauneuf c TSCO of Canada Ltd [Cie Singer du Canada], [1995] JQ
   No 86, [1995] RJQ 637.

City of Vancouver and CUPE *Local 15* (2006), 153 LAC (4th) 97 (Munroe).

Cominco Pensioners Union, sub-local of the United Steelworkers of America, Local 651 v Cominco, [1979] BCLRBD No. 49.

Cousins v Canada (Attorney General), [2008] FCJ No. 1011 (CA), leave to appeal refused 2008 SCCA No. 400.

Cummings v Hydro-Electric Power Commission of Ontario, [1966] 1 OR 605.

CUPE *Local 1000 v Ontario Hydro* (1989), 58 DLR (4th) 552 (Ont CA).

Dayco (Canada) Ltd v National Automobile, Aerospace and Agricultural Implement Workers Union of Canada (CAW-Canada), [1993] 2 SCR 230.

Dickason v University of Alberta, [1992] 2 SCR 1103.

Dinney v Great-West Life Assurance Co., [2005] MJ No. 69, 252 DLR (4th) 660 (CA).

Dionne v Québec (1895), 24 SCR 451.

Douglas/Kwantlen Faculty Assn v Douglas College, [1990] 3 SCR 570.

Douglas v Saskatoon, [1947] SJ 80.

Drohan v Sangamo (1976), 11 OR (2d) 65 (HCJ).

Duke v Toronto District School Board, [2006] OJ No. 1983.

Du Pont Canada Inc. v Kingston Independent Nylon Workers Union (1987), 30 LAC 376 (Solomantenko).

Dzehverovic v Great-West Life Assurance Co., 2010 ONSC 2387.

Ermineskin Indian Band and Nation v Canada, 2009 SCC 9.

Ferguson v Grand Trunk Railway Co., 1901 CarswellQue 155 (CSR) (WLCan).

Firestone Canada Inc. v Ontario (Pension Commission), [1990] OJ No. 2316 (CA).

Flintoft Estate v Canada (Minister of National Revenue), [1951] Ex. CR 211.

Frame v Smith, [1987] 2 SCR 99.

Frances v BC2 Claims and Barrymore Furniture, 2011 ONSC 198.

Galambos v Perez, 2009 SCC 48.

Gay Lea Foods Co-operative Limited v Ontario (Superintendent of Financial Services), 2010 ONFST 10.

Glacier Ventures International Corp. (Prince George Citizen) v Communications, Energy and Paperworkers Union of Canada, Local 2000 (Alexander Grievance), [2012] BCCAAA No. 38 (Burke).

Grain Services Union v Dawn Foods Canada (2002), 108 LAC (4th) 51 (Hood), aff'd [2003] SJ No. 61 (QB), (*sub nom Grain Services Union, Local 3000 v Saskatchewan Wheat Pool).*

Grand River Hospital Corp. v Ontario Nurses' Association (Collective Agreement Grievance) (2010), 200 LAC 4th 363 (Howe).

Grand Trunk Railway Company of Canada v AG Canada, [1907] AC 65 (Privy Council), aff'ing *Re Railway Act Amendment, 1904*, [1905] 36 Supreme Court of Canada 136.

Gummerson v Toronto Police Benefit Fund [1905] No. 399; 5 OWR 581 (HC), aff'd on other grounds [1905] OJ No. 29; 11 OLR 194.

Hamilton v ICI Canada Inc., [2001] OJ No. 3916.

Harrison v University of British Columbia, [1990] 3 SCR 451.

Heirs of N.T. Cronk, represented by Barclays Trust Co. of Canada v Ministry of National Revenue, [1949] 49 DTC 612 (Ex Ct).

Hodgkinson v Simms, [1994] 3 SCR 377.

Holden v Grand Trunk R.W. Co., 1903 OLR 301 (CA).

Honda Canada v Keays, 2008 SCC 39.

Hotel and Club Employees Union, Local 299 v Canadian Pacific Railway, [1961] OJ No. 392; 61 CLLC, aff'd [1962] SCJ No. 43 (*sub nom Canadian Pacific Railway Co. v Zambri*).

Hydro-Electric. See *Re Canadian Union of Public Employees, Local 1000 and Hydro-Electric Power Commission of Ontario.*

IBM Canada Limited v Waterman, 2013 SCC 70.

Imperial Group Pension Trust Ltd v Imperial Tobacco Ltd, [1991] 1 WLR 589 (Ch D).

Imperial Oil v Ontario (Superintendent of Pensions) (1995), 18 CCPB 198.

In the Matter of the Petition of Right of Lucien C.G.T. Bacon, Suppliant and His Majesty the King, Respondent (1921), 21 Ex. CR 25.

Independent Electricity System Operator v Power Workers Union, 2013 ONSC 2131.

Inland Steel Company and Local Union Nos. 1010 and 64, United Steelworkers of America, (CIO), 77 NLRB No. 1 (1948) [*Inland Steel NLRB*], aff'd 170 F 2d 247 (1948) (US Court of Appeals, Seventh Circuit) *sub nom Inland Steel Co. v National Labor Relations Board* [*Inland Steel CA*], cert. denied 336 US 960 (1949).

International Assn of Machinists and Aerospace Workers, Flin Flon Lodge No. 1948 v Hudson Bay Mining and Smelting Co., [1968] SCR 113.

International Chemical Workers Union, Local 279 v Rexall Drug Co. Ltd (1953), 4 LAC 1468 (Laskin) [*Rexall*].

Isidore Garon Ltée v Tremblay, [2006] 1 SCR 27.

Jameson v Dominion Steel and Coal Corporation Ltd (1970), 19 DL (3d) 203 (NSSC CA), rev'ing [1970] NSJ No. 87 (NSSCTD).

Jean v Canada (Treasury Board), [1974] 2 FC 725 (TD).

Jones et al. v Shipping Federation of British Columbia et al., [1963] BCJ No. 118, 37 DLR (2d) 273.

Jones v T. Eaton Co., [1973] SCJ No. 65.

Kenora Assn for Community Living v Ontario Public Service Employees Union, Local 702 (Harasemchuk Grievance), [2003] OLAA No. 295 (Roberts).

Kidd v Canada [1924] Ex. CR 29.

Kranjcec v Ontario, [2004] OJ No. 19.

Lac Minerals Ltd v International Corona Resources Ltd, [1989] 2 SCR 574.

Lacroix v Canada Mortgage and Housing Corporation, 2012 ONCA 243.

Lapointe v Montreal Police Benefit Society, [1906] CRAC 379.

Large v Stratford (City), [1995] 3 SCR 733.

Lieberman v Business Development Bank of Canada, [2009] BCJ 1938.

Lloyd v Imperial Oil, [2008] AJ No. 695 (QB).

Lomas v Rio Algom Ltd, 2010 ONCA 175.

Manitoba Health Organizations Inc. v Healthcare Employees Pension Plan – Manitoba (Trustees of), [1998] MJ No. 170 (QB).

Mantha v Montreal (City) [1939] SCR 458.

McDougall v MNR [1949] Ex. CR 314.

McGavin Toastmaster Ltd v Ainscough et al., [1976] 1 SCR 718.

McGrath v Superintendent of Financial Services, OMERS Administration Corporation and OMERS Sponsors Corporation, 2010 ONFST 5.

McKinney v University of Guelph, [1990] 3 SCR 229.

McNevin v Solvay Process Company, 32 App. Div. (New York, 1898).

Metropolitan Toronto Police Association and Board of Commissioners of Police for Metropolitan Toronto (1980), 111 DLR (3d) 658 (Ont Div Ct).

Miller v Grand Trunk Railway Company of Canada, [1906] AC 187 (PC).

Monsanto Canada Inc. v Ontario (Superintendent of Financial Services), [2004] 3 SCR 152; 2004 SCC 54.

Morneau Sobeco Limited Partnership v Aon Consulting, 2008 ONCA 196, leave to appeal refused [2008] SCCA No. 230 (*sub nom Rogers v Morneau Sobeco Limited Partnership*).

National Automobile Aerospace and Agricultural Implement Workers Union of Canada et al. and White Farm Manufacturing Canada Ltd et al. (1988), 66 OR (2d) 535 (HC), aff'd [1990] OJ No. 1988 (CA).

National Automobile, Aerospace and Agricultural Implements Workers Union of Canada, Local 1015 v Scotsburn Dairy Group, [2008] NSLAA 1 (Christie).

National Steel Car v United Steelworkers of America, Local 713 (Pedron Grievance), [2006] OLAA No. 126 (Herman).

Nemser v Aviation Corp., 47 F. Supp. 515 (D Del 1942).

New Brunswick (Human Rights Commission) v Potash Corporation of Saskatchewan Inc., [2008] 2 SCR. 604, 2008 SCC 45.

New Brunswick v O'Leary, [1995] 2 SCR 967.

Nexen Inc. v Communications, Energy and Paperworkers Union of Canada, Local 697, [2003] BCCAAA (Munroe).

Nolan v Kerry (Canada) Ltd, 2009 SCC 39 [*Kerry (Canada) SCC*], aff'ing *Nolan v Ontario (Superintendent of Financial Services)*, [2007] OJ No. 2176 (CA) [Kerry (Canada) CA], rev'ing [2006] OJ No. 960 (Div Ct)[*Kerry (Canada) Div. Ct.*)], rev'ing [2004] OFSCD No. 192 [*Kerry (Canada) OFST No. 1*] and [2004] OFSCD No. 193 [*Kerry (Canada) OFST No. 2*].

OMERS Sponsors Corporation v OMERS Administrative Corporation, [2008] OJ No. 425.

Ontario English Catholic Teachers' Assn v Ontario (Attorney General), [2001] 1 SCR 470, 2001 SCC 15.

Ontario Public Service Employees Union v Ontario (Ministry of Community, Family and Childrens' Services) (Ashley Grievance), [2003] OGSBA No. 128 (Abramsky).

Ontario Teachers' Pension Plan Board v York University, [1990] OJ No. 1376; 74 OR (2d) 714 (HC).

OPSEU, Local 439 and Royal Ottawa Health Care Group, [2001] OJ No. 446.

OPSEU v Ontario (Attorney General) (1995), 131 DLR (4th) 572.

Ormrod et al. v Etobicoke (Hydro-Electric Commission) (2001), 53 OR (3d) 285 (SCJ).

Otis Canada Inc. v Ontario (Superintendent of Pensions), [1991] OJ No. 251; 2 OR (3d) 737 (Gen Div).

Pennie v Reis, 132 US 464 (1889).

PIPS. See Professional Institute of the Public Service of Canada v Canada.

Porter v Canada, [1956] 1 Ex. CR 200.

Progistix-Solutions Inc. v Communications, Energy and Paperworkers Union of Canada (Connolly Grievance), [2002] CLAD No. 188 (Keller).

Professional Institute of the Public Service of Canada v Canada 2012 SCC 71 [*PIPS*].

Pulp and Paper Industrial Relations Bureau v Canadian Paperworkers Union, [1977] BCLRBD No. 7.

R v Grenier (1899), 6 Ex. CR 276, rev'd XXX SCR 42, leave to appeal refused (1900) AC 467.

Re Allanson, [1971] OJ No. 1620; [1971] 3 OR 209 (CA).

Re Canadian Union of Public Employees, Local 1000 and Hydro-Electric Power Commission of Ontario (1966), 17 LAC 244 (Thomas) [*Hydro-Electric*].

Re Cox, [1951] OJ No. 548, [1951] OR 205 (CA), [1952] SCJ No. 53, [1955] JCJ No. 4.

Re City of Etobicoke and CUPE, *Local 185,* [1996] OLAA No. 84, 54 LAC (4th) 229 (Springate).

Re Consolidated-Bathurst Packaging Ltd (Hamilton Plant) and Int'l Woodworkers of America, Local 6-29 (1980), 28 LAC (2d) 230 (Brunner).

Reference Re: Workplace and Social Insurance Act (Canada), [1936] SCR 427 (P.C.).

Re Gosling (1900), 48 WR 300.

Re Gray Forging and Stampings Ltd and International Union of Electrical, Radio and Machine Workers Union, Local 557 (1978), 20 LAC (2d) 278 (Gorsky).

Reid v International Union of Mine, Mill and Smelter Workers, Local 598, [1960] OJ No. 39 (HC).

Re Massey, [1959] OJ 697; [1959] OR 608 (HCJ).

Re Palm Dairies Ltd and Retail, Wholesale and Department Store Union, Local 580 (1980), 26 LAC (2d) 414 (Hope).

Re Steinberg Inc., Miracle Food Mart Division and Teamsters Union, Local 419, [1982] OLAA No. 105; 7 LAC (3d) 289 (Adams).

Re Sudbury Mine, Mill and Smelter Workers' Union and Falconbridge Nickel Mines Ltd (1958), 9 LAC 105 (Little).

Re University College of Cape Breton and N.S.G.E.U., [1997] NSLAA No. 14 (Wright).

Rexall. See *International Chemical Workers Union, Local 279, in re Rexall Drug Co. Ltd.*

Rouge Valley Health System v Ontario Nurses Association, 2013 CANLII 8001 (ON LA) (Stout).

Royal Ontario Museum v OPSEU, 18 January 2013, Saltman.

Royal Ontario Museum v Service Employees International Union (Brewery, General & Professional Workers' Union), Local 2 (Policy Grievance), [2011] OLAA No. 292 (Raymond).

Russell v Russell (1880), 14 CHD 471.

Saskatchewan Government Employees Association v Saskatchewan, [1991] SJ No. 660 (QB).

Sault Area Hospital v Ontario Nurses' Assn (Seisel Grievance), [2012] OLAA No. 229 (Steinberg).

Schmidt v Air Products Canada Ltd, [1994] 2 SCR 611, aff'ing in part 89 DLR 4th 762 (Alta CA), aff'ing (1990), 66 DLR (4th) 230 (Alta QB).

Schofield v Zion's Co-operative Mercantile Institution (Utah 1934) 39 P (2d) 342.

Seborro v Pidvalny, 2004 CarswellOnt 6075 (WLCan).

Shepherd's Care Foundation v Alberta Union of Provincial Employees, 2011 ABQB 281.

Sneddon v British Columbia (Hydro and Power Authority), 2004 BCCA 292.

St Mary's Cement v United Steelworkers (2010), 195 LAC (4th) 72 (Hunter).

Stoffman v Vancouver General Hospital, [1990] 3 SCR 483.

Sun Indalex Finance, LLC v United Steelworkers, [2013] 1 SCR 271, 2013 SCC 6 [*Sun Indalex*], rev'ing in part 2011 ONCA 265 (*sub nom Re Indalex Limited*) [*Indalex CA*].

Sutherland v Hudson's Bay Co., [2007] OJ No. 2979.

Syndicat des communications de Radio-Canada v Canadian Broadcasting Corporation, 2011 QCCA 768, leave to appeal refused [2011] SCCA No. 241.

Tawny v City of Winnipeg, [1936] MJ No 9; [1936] 2 WWR 123 (Man KB).

Teamsters, Local 132 v Unilever Canada (Pension Calculation Grievance), [2005] OLAA No. 115 (Howe).

Telus Communications Inc. v Telecommunications Union (Kellie Grievance), [2008] CLAD Mo. 106 (Sims).

Thomas v Canada, [1926] Ex. CR 26.

Town of Dryden v Dryden Police Association, [1973] 1 OR 619 (HCJ).

Trudel v Lemoine et al., [1925] 4 DLR 97, aff'd (*sub nom Pension Fund Society of La Banque) Nationale, Audet v Trudel*, [1926] 3 DLR 988 (Privy Council).

United Mine Workers of America, District No. 26 v Cape Breton Development Corp. [1987] NSJ No. 425 (TD), [1988] NSJ No. 158 (CA).

United Way of Lower Mainland (2013), 239 LAC (4th) 428 (Dorsey).

Waterson v Canadian Broadcasting Corp., [2010] OJ No. 4534.

Weber v Ontario Hydro, [1995] 2 SCR 929.

Welsh v Toronto Police Benefit Fund, [1915] OJ No. 715; 9 OWN 2 (HC).

West Parry Sound Centre v Ontario Nurses Assn (Pension Plan Contribution Grievance), [2008] OLAA No. 705 (Parmar).

Williamson v Ontario (Treasurer), [1942] 3 DLR 736, [1941] OJ No. 206 (HC).

Wilson v Rudolph Wurlitzer Co., 48 Ohio App 450, 194 NE 441 (1934).

Wright (The Rev. Joel Tombleson) v The Incorporated Synod of the Diocese of Huron [1881] OJ No. 217, 29 Gr 348 (Ontario Court of Chancery); rev'd 9 OAR 411 [*Wright CA*] (*sub nom Wright v Huron*); aff'd [1885] SCJ No. 11 [*Wright SCC*].

Index

of workplace pensions; fund solvency (pension plans)
court jurisdiction. *See* jurisdictional boundaries, arbitrators, and courts
Cromwell, Justice Thomas: *Sun Indalex*, 141–2, 234nn44–6

Dayco (Canada) Ltd v National Automobile, Aerospace, and Agricultural Implement Workers Union of Canada (CAW-Canada) (1993), 101
death and survivor benefits, 19, 21, 23, 71, 152, 236n15; *PBA 1965* regulations, 68, 208n62; *PBA 1987* regulations, 75, 76, 210–11nn92–3, 211n100; succession duty cases, 52–5, 201n48, 202n52, 203n57. *See also* insurance and pension plans
Deaton, Richard, 10
deferred annuities, compensation, or wages: annuities, 28, 68, 76; compensation, 46–7; wages, 103, 105, 110, 223–4n6. *See also* property law in pension plans
deficits and failures of pension plans. *See* fund solvency (pension plans)
defined benefit (DB) plans: 50 per cent rule, 76–7, 163, 242n74; advantages of, 27–8, 178; civil (public) service pension plans, 153; compared to defined contribution (DC) plans, 178, 229nn60–1, 248–9n32; converted to defined contribution (DC), 121–4, 244–5n101;

definition, 6; fund solvency in, 68; in jointly sponsored pension plans, 165; pension surplus wars, 107–15 (*see also* surpluses); railway pension plans, 18, 27; in recent decades, 177, 248–9n24; statistics, 82, 186n9; statutory regulation and, 176; teachers' pension plans, 155; termination of, 111–15; unit-benefit and flat-rate, 59–60, 214n27. *See also* contribution holidays by employers; retirement income system, three pillar/tier
defined contribution (DC)/money purchase plans: civil (public) service pension plan, 153; compared to defined benefit (DB) plans, 178, 229nn60–61, 248–49n32; converted from DB plans, 121–24; definition, 6; gifts or contracts (early US cases), 45–46; imposed by employers, 90; in Ontario statute, 207–8n60; statistics, 82, 214n27; teachers' pension plans, 155; treatment of funds, 177, 248n26. *See also* investment capital, pension funds as; retirement income system, three pillar/tier
Deschamps, Justice Marie: *Buschau*, 119–20, 235n53; *Isadore Garon*, 92; *Sun Indalex*, 140–1, 234nn44–5
Dionne v Québec (1895), 41–2, 198n19, 236n15
disability benefits, 18–20, 21, 23, 48–50, 151, 193n41, 199n24; waivers of liability, 19–20

discretionary benefits: *Blue Books* (1942–57), 62–3 (see also *Blue Books*); civil (public) service plans, 151–3; contributory/non-contributory pension plans, 29, 194n53; in early plans (1874–1939), 20–1, 22, 23–4, 25–7, 151; procedural and substantive review by courts, 51, 56; vested benefits and, 59. *See also* forfeited benefits; rights, pensions as; vesting and vested rights
Douglas v Saskatoon (1947), 201n46
Drohan v Sangamo (1976), 218–19n74
droits acquis, 43–4, 199n23. *See also* vesting and vested rights
Duff, Justice Lyman: *Mantha*, 50, 51–2

early-retirement incentive plans: jurisdiction over complaints, 94
Education Act (NL), 155–6
eligibility for pension. *See* membership eligibility
employers: administrative control of plans by, 18, 22, 78, 83–4 (*see also* administration of pension plans); corporate capacity to establish plans, 203n56; cost-benefit calculus after pension reform, 77–8, 170–3 (*see also* cost of pensions); employee goodwill, 195n57; improper credits and calculations, 94; legal fiction of "parties" in pension plans, 180; liberal contract theory advantage to, 105–6; motivation for (no) pension plans, 3–5, 9, 15–16, 123, 170–3; objectives of pension plans, 16–17, 21–2, 192n31, 194n46 (*see also* human resource management; investment capital, pension funds as); objectives of pension plans for governments, 3–5, 150–1, 154–5, 157 (*see also* public sector workplace pension plans); preference for DB plans, 27–8 (*see also* defined benefit plans); right to amend plans, 54, 74, 108–9, 111–15, 118–19, 121–4, 125, 129–30, 145–6 (*see also* amendment/termination of plans); unions negotiating pensions and, 87–91, 101–2 (*see also* collective bargaining and pension plans). *See also* labour-market forces
employment-based pension plans. *See* private sector workplace pension plans; public sector workplace pension plans
English Court of Chancery, 106, 224n11
estoppel principles, 48–9, 98, 200n37, 231n11
ethical v contractarian version of fiduciary law, 142–3
ethical v contractarian version of trust law, 104, 107, 113–14, 121, 123–4, 125, 126. *See also* contract law in pension plans; trust law in pension plans
European pension plans: Canada compared to, 7, 186n13
Excess Profits Tax (1940s), 61. *See also* tax law and pension plans

197n75. *See also* cost of pensions; defined benefit (DB) plans; defined contribution (DC) plans; investment capital, pension funds as

fund solvency (pension plans): 2008–09 financial crisis, 108–9; actuarial estimates, 108, 115, 116, 128, 208n66, 211n95, 225n19; DIP lenders, 139, 233nn37–9; employer contributions' shortfall, 90; going concern standard, 75, 211n95; grow-in right, 77; plan deficits and failures, 6, 108–9, 186nn11–12; priority over DIP lenders, 138–43; statutory minimum standards for, 68–9, 75; surplus rules (*see* surpluses). *See also* funding of workplace pensions

gender issues. *See* women
Ghilarducci, Teresa, 80
gifts and charitable trusts: early common law decisions, 36–9; early US cases, 45–6; funding of plans, 197n4, 197n75; gift theory influence on cases, 103, 104–5; succession duty cases, 52–5, 56. *See also* annuities in early pension plans; discretionary benefits; trust law in pension plans
Gillese, Justice Eileen, 104, 116, 223n2, 227n41, 231n9; *Sun Indalex*, 139
globalized economy, 174–5
Government and Public Employees Retirement Plan (Quebec), 153, 158

government annuities, 33, 65, 196n68, 206n43
Government Annuities Act (1908, Canada), 196n65, 196n68
government pensions. *See* public sector workplace pension plans
Graebner, William: *History of Retirement*, 31
Grand Trunk 1874 Act, 18, 190n21
Grand Trunk Railway Company of Canada v AG Canada (1907), 191n28
Grand Trunk Railway pension plan, 14, 17–22, 25, 29, 31, 33–4, 191n24; 1907 new pension plan, 20–1; waiver of liability, 19–20, 191nn26–8
Great Depression, 30, 64, 79
Great Pension Debate, 8, 69–73, 83. *See also* retirement income system, three pillar/tier
Great Policy Shift (joint governance), 163–8, 169
Great War: veterans and Bell pension plan, 23–4
Green Paper. See *Better Pensions for Canadians* (Canada)
group registered retirement savings plans (RRSPs), 6
grow-in right, 77, 176, 212n103
Gwynne, Justice John: *Dionne*, 42

Hannah, Leslie, 10
Harper, Stephen, 181
Healthcare of Ontario Pension Plan (HOOPP), 159, 163, 165, 240nn54–5
health-care workers. *See* public health care employees' pension plans

National Labor Relations Board (NLRB, US), 85–6
Netherlands, 99
New Brunswick: public sector pension plan regulation, 160; public sector pension plans, 236–7n16, 237–8n22, 240n57; shared risk model pension plan, 167–8, 245n113
New Brunswick v O'Leary (1995), 94, 219n79
Newfoundland and Labrador: public sector pension plan regulation, 161; public sector pension plans, 236–7n16; regulation of plan administration, 230–1n8; teachers' pension plan, 155–6, 237–8n22
Nolan v Kerry (Canada) Ltd (2009), 121–4, 124–5, 132, 135, 137, 229n56
non-contributory pension plans. *See* contributory/non-contributory pension plans
non-reversion clauses, 109, 118
non-standard work, 175. *See also* part-time, temporary, or casual workers
Nova Scotia: jointly sponsored pension plans, 167; pension benefits laws, 97; public sector pension plan regulation, 160; public sector pension plans, 236–7n16, 237–8n22, 240n57, 241n60

Old Age Pensions Act (Canada), 64
Old Age Security (OAS), 7, 57, 64, 206nn45–6. *See also* retirement income system, three pillar/tier

OMERS Sponsors Corporation v OMERS Administrative Corporation (2008), 131–3
Ontario: collective bargaining impact, 81; development of provincial and national pension laws, 8, 65–9, 73–8, 181, 183, 206–7n50, 207n53, 207n57; fiduciary duties, 230n5; healthcare workers' pension plans, 159; insurance regulation, 32–3; jointly sponsored pension plans, 163–8; Pension Commission of Ontario (PCO), 68, 74, 129–30, 208n61, 210n87, 231nn9–10; plan valuations, 225n19 (*see also* fund solvency); public sector pension plan regulation, 161; public service pension plans, 152–3, 235n3, 236–7n16, 239n38; Royal Commission on the Status of Pensions, 81, 163, 164; succession duty and pension benefits, 52–3; teachers' pension plans and statutes, 154, 155, 162, 237–8n22; "two hats" doctrine, 130, 131–3, 145–6; workers' compensation legislation, 23. See also *Pension Benefits Acts* (Ontario)
Ontario Federation of Labour (OFL), 81
Ontario Financial Services Tribunal, 122
Ontario Hospital Association (OHA), 159
Ontario Municipal Employees' Pension Plan (OMERS), 131–3, 157, 162, 165, 239n42

pension reform: argument of this book, 9–13; current situation, 8–9; future and, 181–4; Great Pension Debate, 69–72 (*see also* retirement income system, three pillar/tier); statutory regulation (*see* statutory pension regulation); third round (current debate), 179–81

pension surpluses. *See* surpluses

PIPS. See *Professional Institute of the Public Service of Canada v Canada (PIPS) (1956)*

pooled retirement pension plans (PRPPS), 6, 181, 249n34

portability of pensions, 8, 65–6, 68, 164, 169; definition, 206–7n50

Porter v Canada (1956), 196n67

precarious work, 175

Premier Communications Ltd (PCI). See *Buschau v Rogers Cablesystems Ltd* (2004)

pre-retirement vesting, 25. *See also* vesting and vested rights

Prince Edward Island, 158–9, 207n59, 236–7n16, 237–8n22

private law. *See* common law role in pension plans; contract law in pension plans; property law in pension plans; trust law in pension plans

private sector workplace pension plans: collective bargaining and, 81; as compulsory, Ontario's call for, 66–7, 181; overview, 15–17; in primary labour market, 58, 61; public utilities, 22–5; railway pension plans, 17–22; retirement benefits

structure, 27–8; terminology, 235n1. *See also* cost of pensions; discretionary benefits; mandatory retirement; statutory pension regulation; workplace pension system in Canada

procedural fairness. *See* administration of pension plans

Professional Institute of the Public Service of Canada v Canada (PIPS) (1956), 137–8, 143

property law in pension plans: deferred wages concept, 103, 105, 110, 223–4n6; *droits acquis*, 44; in early pension cases, 40; language of "vesting," 42 (*see also* vesting and vested rights). *See also* trust law in pension plans

Proudfoot, Vice-Chancellor William: *Wright*, 40

provincial pension plans and laws. *See* municipal government pension plans; teachers in public education pension plans

public health care employees' pension plans, 158–60, 239n48, 240nn54–7; collective bargaining and, 162–3

public pension plan model. *See* Canada Pension Plan (CPP); pension reform; retirement income system, three pillar/tier; workplace pension system in Canada

public pension policy development: federal-provincial dynamic in, 65–7; future and pension reform, 181–4 (*see also* pension reform); jointly

sponsored pension plans (policy
shift), 163–8; overview, 11; war
years (1940s), 61–3. *See also*
retirement income system, three
pillar/tier; statutory pension
regulation
public-private divide, 183, 250n54
Public Sector Pension Plans Act
(Alberta), 160
Public Sector Pension Plans Act
(BC), 166–7
public sector workplace pension
plans: civil service, 150–3; collective bargaining and, 81–2, 161–
3, 242–3nn75–81; contributory,
28–9; coverage statistics, 150;
fiduciary responsibility of
employers, 137–8; jointly sponsored pension plans, 163–8;
lessons from, 168–9, 182–3;
managerial and political objectives of, 149–50, 154–5, 157–8,
182–3; overview, 12–13; regulatory rules, 160–1, 242n72; terminology, 235n1, 235n3, 241n67,
241n69. *See also* municipal government pension plans; public
health care employees' pension
plans; statutory pension regulation; teachers in public education
pension plans; workplace pension system in Canada
Public Service Superannuation Act
(NS), 167

Quadagno, Jill, 192n32
Quebec: collective agreements and
pension plans, 83, 160, 214n30;
first statute regulating workplace
pensions, 207n59; health-care

workers' pension plans, 158;
jointly sponsored pension plans,
167; municipal pension plans,
158; pension committees,
212n104, 230n8; public sector
pension plan regulation, 160;
public sector pension plans, 152–
3, 158, 236nn15–17, 237–8n22,
238n32, 239n45; "two hats"
doctrine, 130–1. See also *Dionne
v Québec* (1895)
Quebec Pension Plan, 65, 179,
187n15
Queen's Study (of workplace pension plans), 7–8, 16, 58,
187n19, 188–9n2, 194n53,
247–8n14

Railway Act: waivers of liability,
20, 191n28
railway pension plans, 14, 17–22,
192n31; collective bargaining
and, 81
*Re Canadian Union of Public
Employees, Local 1000, and
Hydro-Electric Power
Commission of Ontario* (1966)
[Hydro-Electric], 89–90
recognition rule, 87–91, 92, 95,
98–9. *See also* collective bargaining and pension plans
reform of pensions. *See* pension
reform
registered retirement savings plans
(RRSPs), 6, 181, 249n34
regulation of pension plans. *See*
statutory pension regulation
reserved-rights theory, 89–91,
93–4, 98–9. *See also* collective
bargaining and pension plans

vesting and vested rights: in 1947 survey results, 59; *Blue Books* (1942–57), 62–3, 68; collective bargaining and, 82; contributory/non-contributory pension plans, 59; *droits acquis* as, 43–4, 199n23, 199n25; evolving concept in pension rights, 39–45, 56, 103; government annuities, 33; immediate vesting, 63, 80, 247n19; jointly sponsored pension plans, 163–4; lack of portability and, 65–6, 68; *PBA 1987* regulations, 76, 211n98, 211n101; statistics of vesting standards, 82, 214n25; statutory minimum standards for, 68, 76. *See also* rights, pensions as
"Vesting Provisions in Canadian Industrial Pension Plans" study, 60–1
voluntary workplace pension system: central to Canadian system, 77–8; compulsory system and, 20, 66–7, 72–3; countries compared, 186n13; employers' business needs and, 147–8; failure of, 170–3, 180; in Great Pension Debate, 8, 72–3, 188n27; minimum-standards regulation and, 66; no incentive for employers, 170–3; overview of, 4–5. *See also* compulsory participation; contract law in pension plans; gifts and charitable trusts; retirement income system, three pillar/tier; statutory pension regulation
Vosko, Leah, 175

waiting periods, 59, 74, 211n98. *See also* membership eligibility

Waters, Donovan W.M., 234n42
Watt, Gary, 224n11
Weber v Ontario Hydro (1995), 93–4, 95, 98
white-collar workers: bargaining units, 100; plans geared to, 17; in railway pension plans, 19
White Paper. See Action Plan for Pension Reform (White Paper, Canada)
Williamson v Ontario (Treasurer) (1942), 52–5, 103, 104
Winnipeg (city), 48–9
women: eligibility for pension plan membership, 59, 62, 74–5, 210–11nn91–3; employee turnover, 28; gender issues in reform of CPP, 71–2, 73, 209nn75–6; mandatory retirement ages, 60, 156, 158; pension statistics compared, 5–6, 185n7; qualifying age for pensions, 22; same-sex benefits, 94; in teachers' pension plans, 238n32; widows, 152, 236n15. *See also* spousal pension claims
workers' compensation, 23
workplace pension system in Canada: definition and scope of book, 13–14; future and pension reform, 181–4; gender issues and, 71–2; at mid-century (1900s), 58–61; overview of, 5–6; in retirement income system, 7–8, 57–8, 186–7nn13–17 (*see also* retirement income system, three pillar/tier); statistics, 5–6; studies of, 188n24. *See also* private sector workplace pension plans; public sector workplace pension plans; voluntary workplace pension system